Stitched

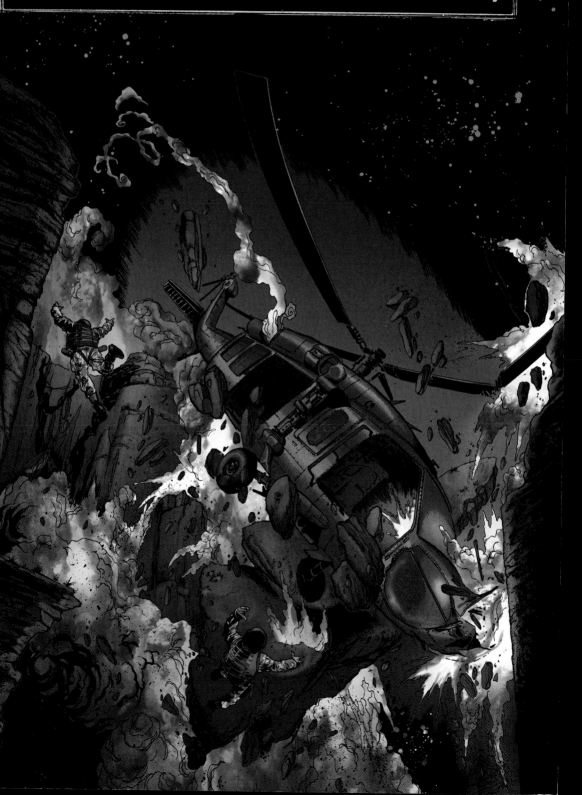

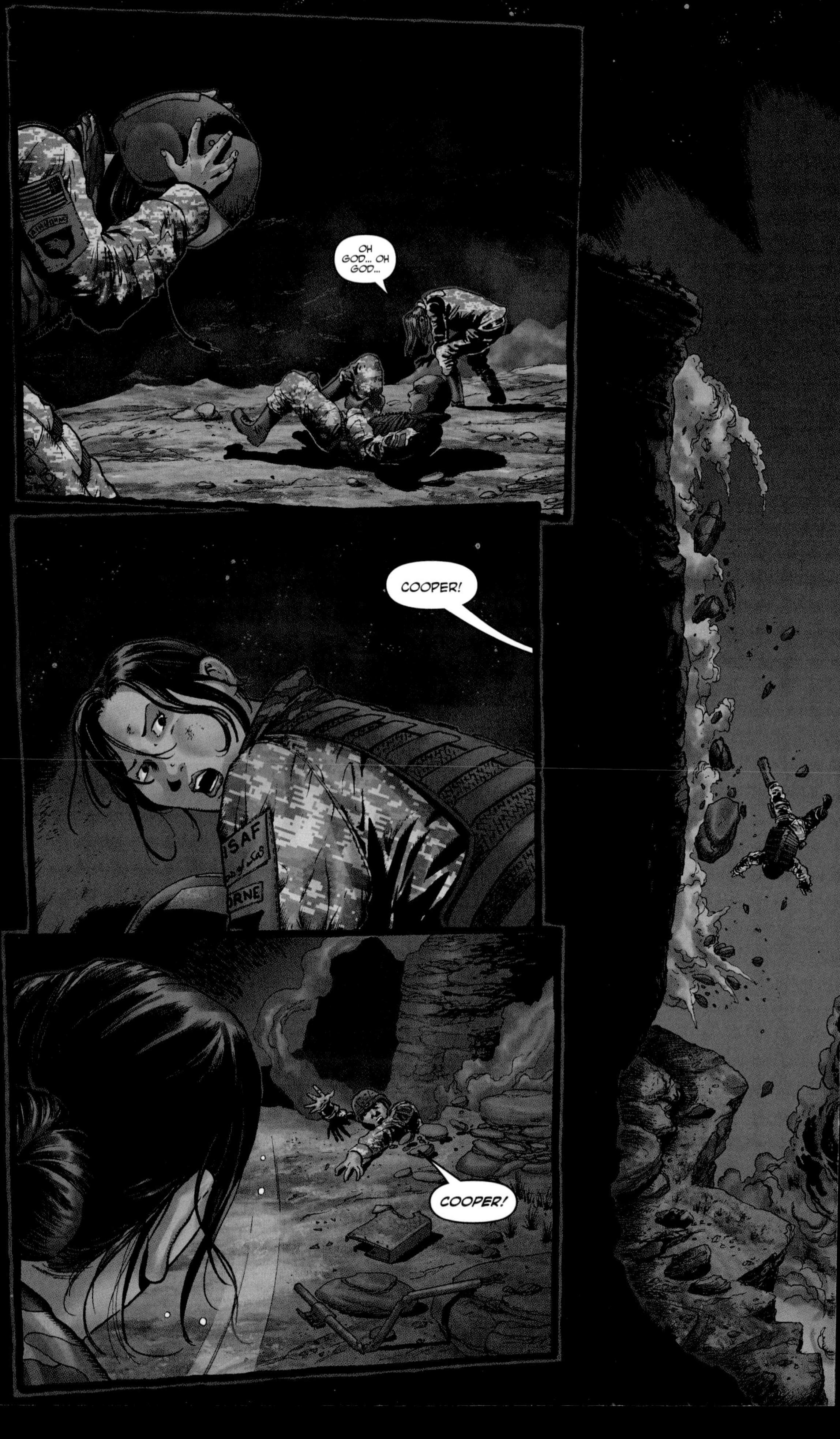
OH GOD... OH GOD...
COOPER!
ISAF
COOPER!

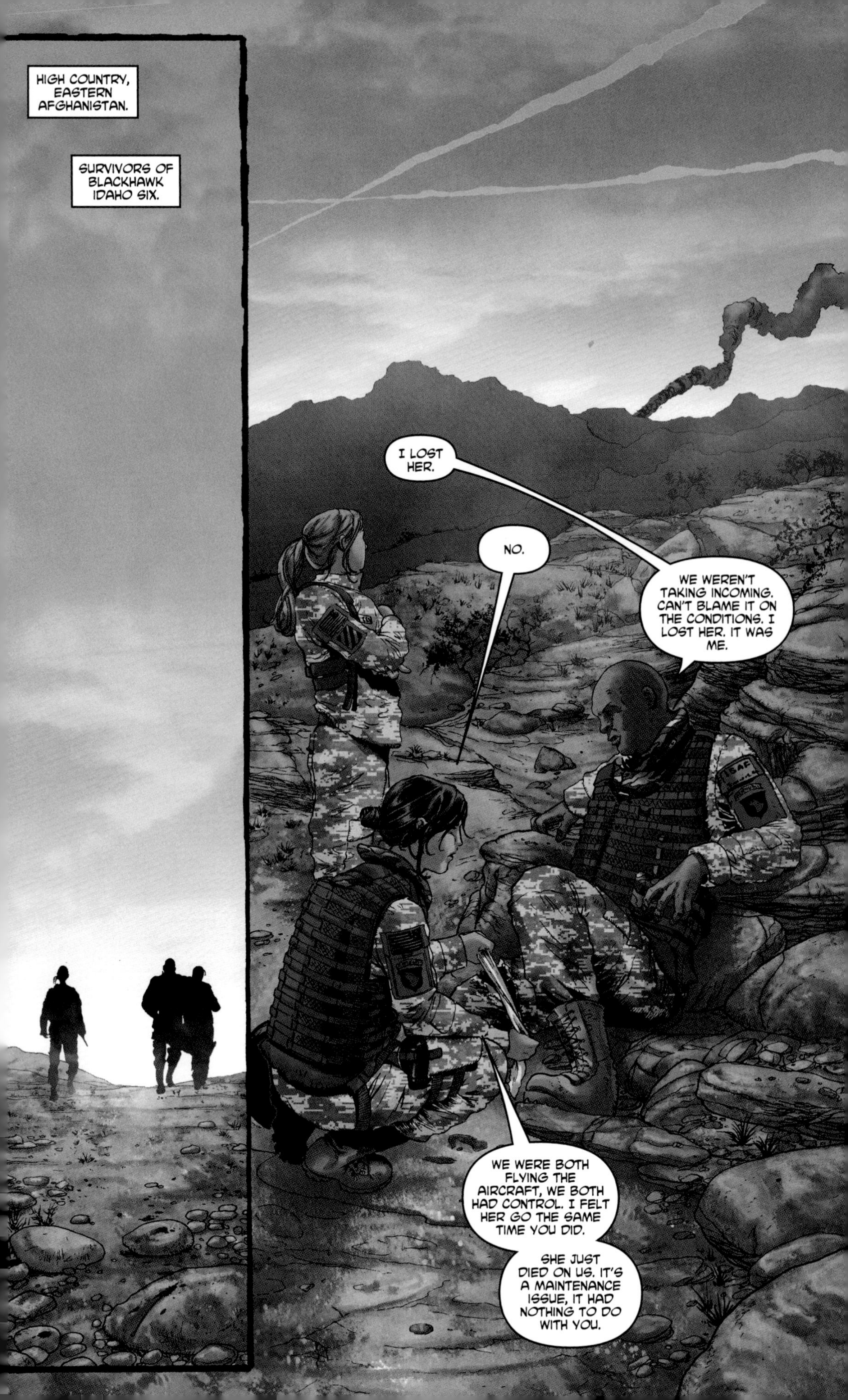
HIGH COUNTRY, EASTERN AFGHANISTAN.
SURVIVORS OF BLACKHAWK IDAHO SIX.
I LOST HER.
NO.
WE WEREN'T TAKING INCOMING. CAN'T BLAME IT ON THE CONDITIONS. I LOST HER. IT WAS ME.
WE WERE BOTH FLYING THE AIRCRAFT, WE BOTH HAD CONTROL. I FELT HER GO THE SAME TIME YOU DID.
SHE JUST DIED ON US. IT'S A MAINTENANCE ISSUE, IT HAD NOTHING TO DO WITH YOU.

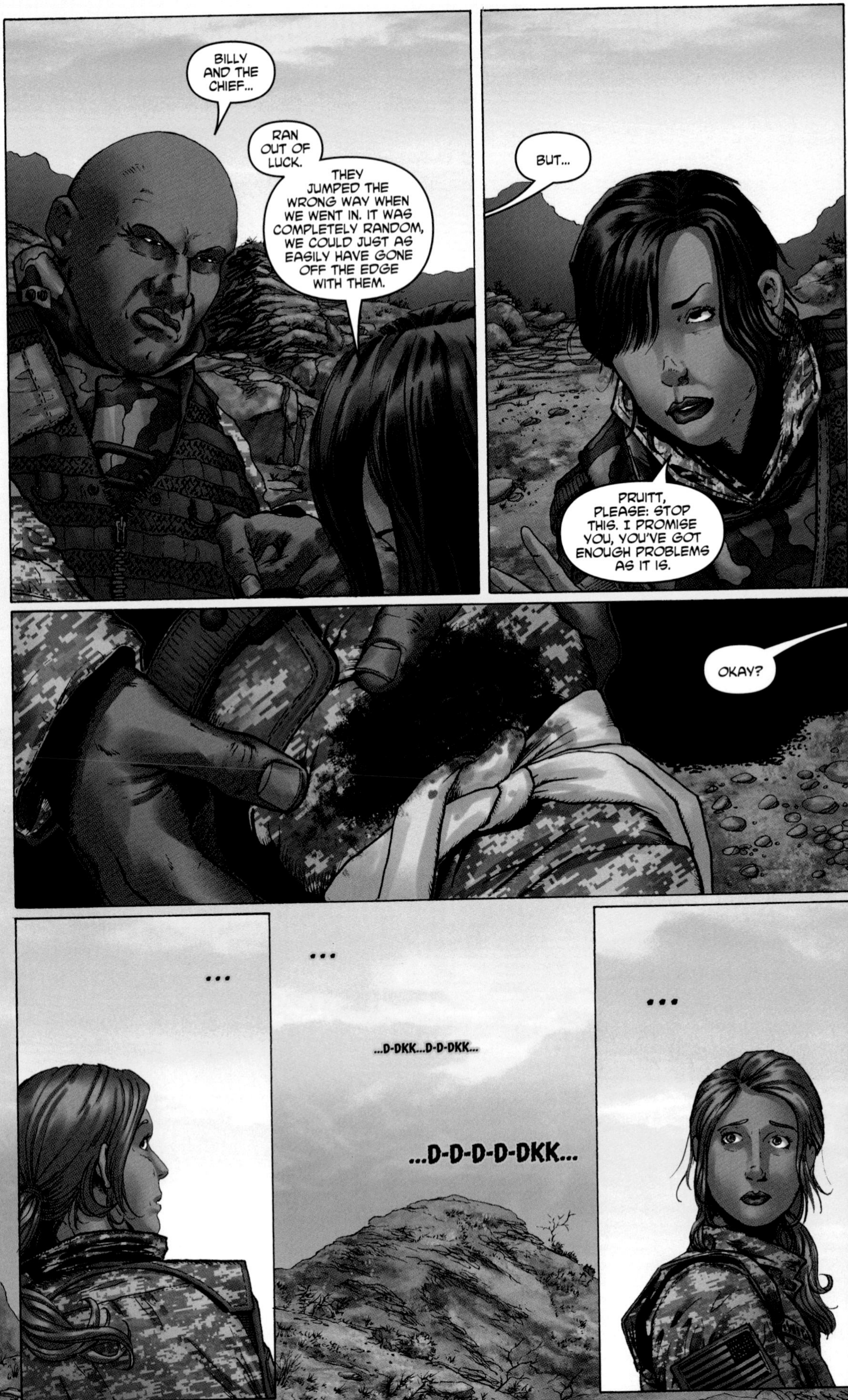
BILLY AND THE CHIEF...
RAN OUT OF LUCK.
THEY JUMPED THE WRONG WAY WHEN WE WENT IN. IT WAS COMPLETELY RANDOM, WE COULD JUST AS EASILY HAVE GONE OFF THE EDGE WITH THEM.
BUT...
PRUITT, PLEASE: STOP THIS. I PROMISE YOU, YOU'VE GOT ENOUGH PROBLEMS AS IT IS.
OKAY?
...
...
...D-DKK...D-D-DKK...
...D-D-D-D-DKK...
...

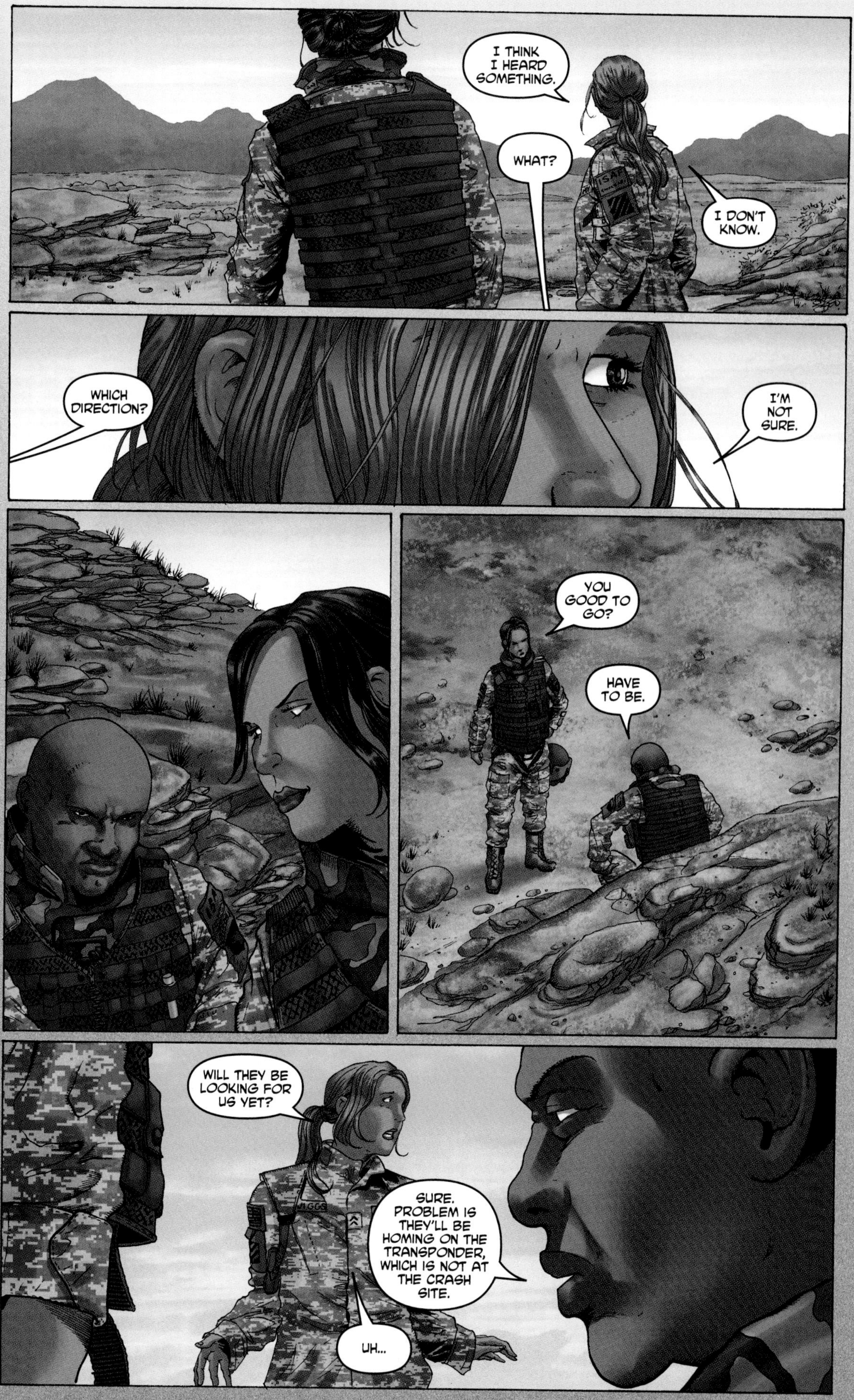
I THINK I HEARD SOMETHING.
WHAT?
I DON'T KNOW.
WHICH DIRECTION?
I'M NOT SURE.
YOU GOOD TO GO?
HAVE TO BE.
WILL THEY BE LOOKING FOR US YET?
SURE. PROBLEM IS THEY'LL BE HOMING ON THE TRANSPONDER, WHICH IS NOT AT THE CRASH SITE.
UH...

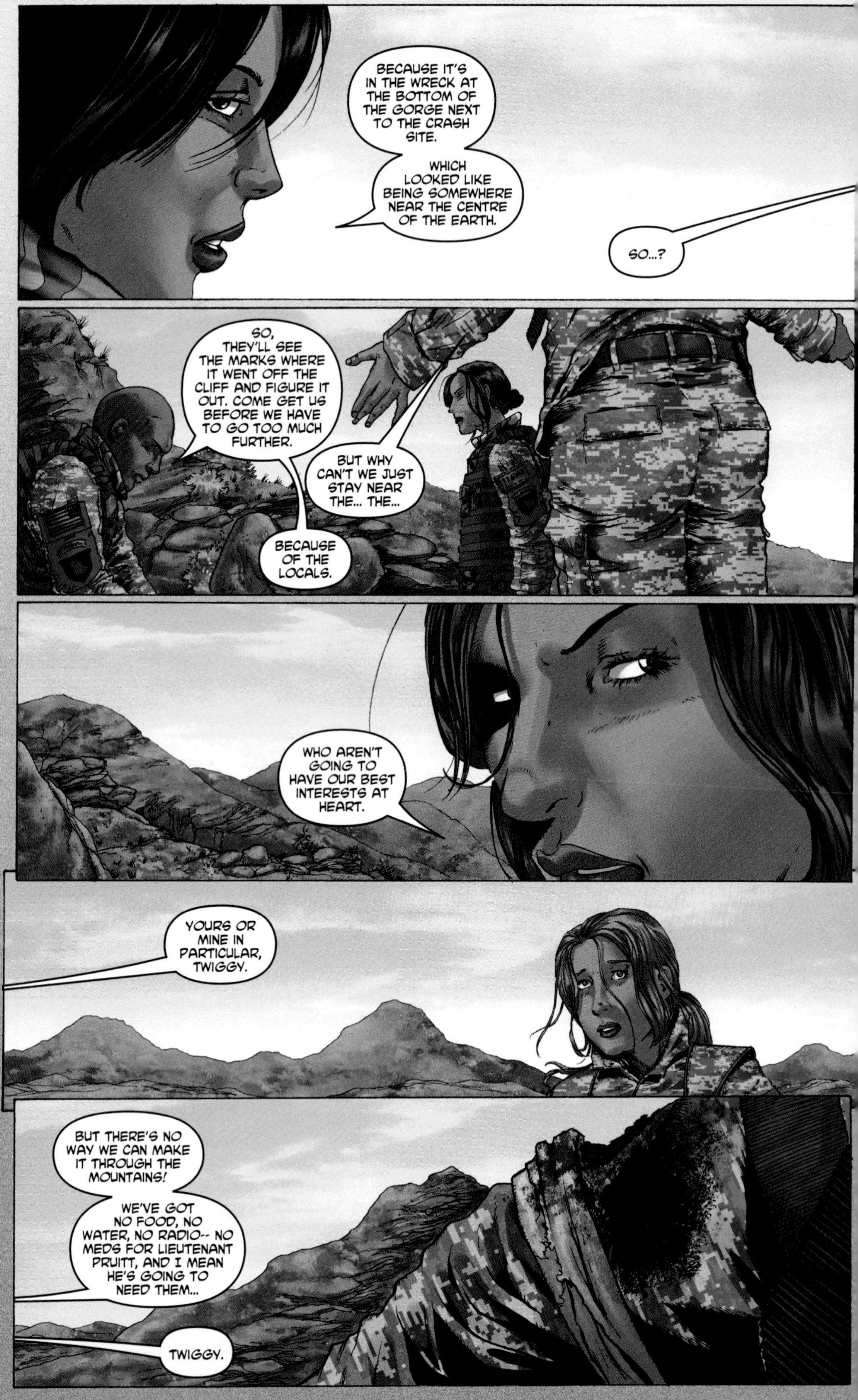

BECAUSE IT'S IN THE WRECK AT THE BOTTOM OF THE GORGE NEXT TO THE CRASH SITE.
WHICH LOOKED LIKE BEING SOMEWHERE NEAR THE CENTRE OF THE EARTH.
SO...?
SO, THEY'LL SEE THE MARKS WHERE IT WENT OFF THE CLIFF AND FIGURE IT OUT. COME GET US BEFORE WE HAVE TO GO TOO MUCH FURTHER.
BUT WHY CAN'T WE JUST STAY NEAR THE... THE...
BECAUSE OF THE LOCALS.
WHO AREN'T GOING TO HAVE OUR BEST INTERESTS AT HEART.
YOURS OR MINE IN PARTICULAR, TWIGGY.
BUT THERE'S NO WAY WE CAN MAKE IT THROUGH THE MOUNTAINS!
WE'VE GOT NO FOOD, NO WATER, NO RADIO-- NO MEDS FOR LIEUTENANT PRUITT, AND I MEAN HE'S GOING TO NEED THEM...
TWIGGY.

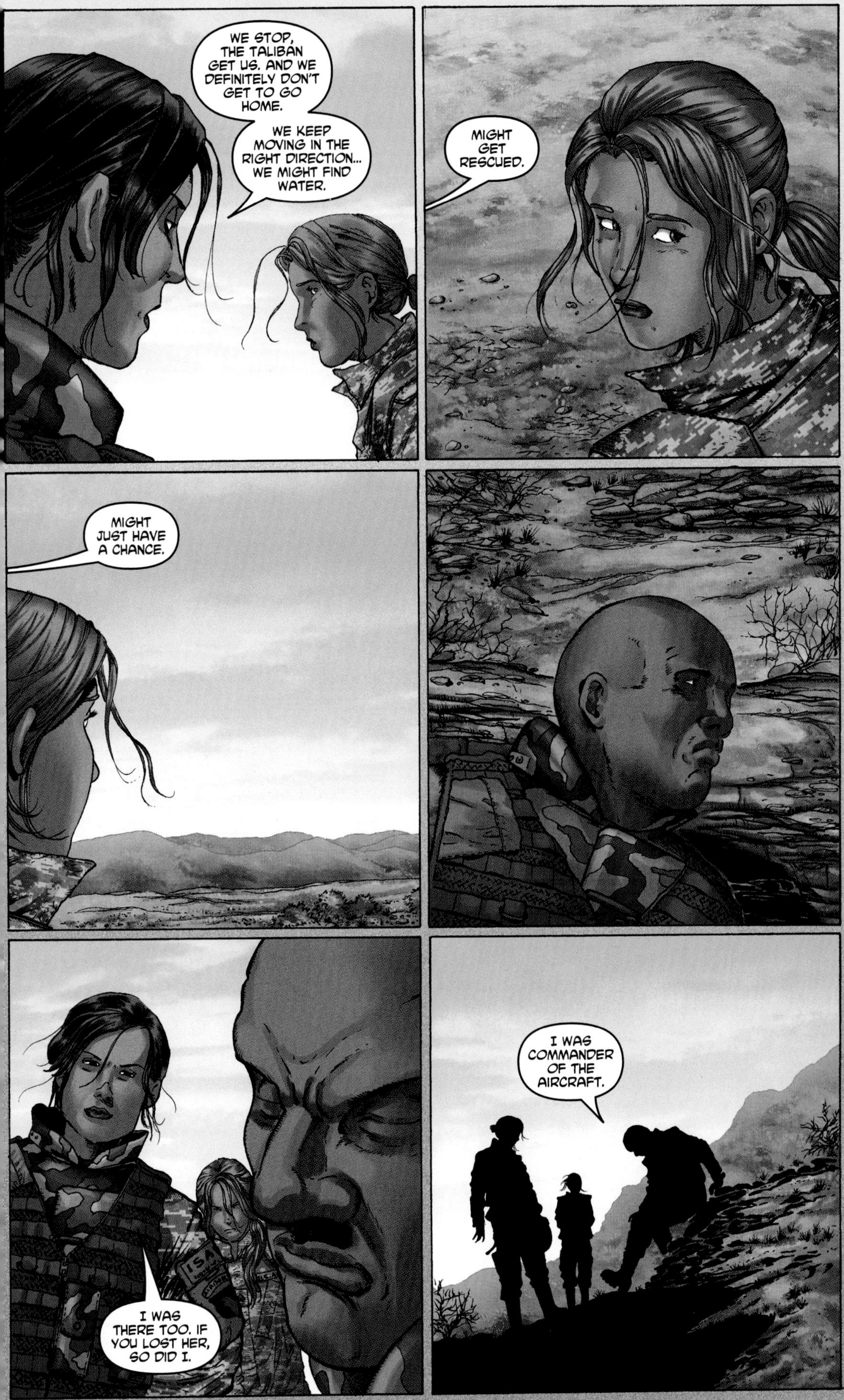

WE STOP, THE TALIBAN GET US. AND WE DEFINITELY DON'T GET TO GO HOME.
WE KEEP MOVING IN THE RIGHT DIRECTION... WE MIGHT FIND WATER.
MIGHT GET RESCUED.
MIGHT JUST HAVE A CHANCE.
I WAS THERE TOO. IF YOU LOST HER, SO DID I.
I WAS COMMANDER OF THE AIRCRAFT.

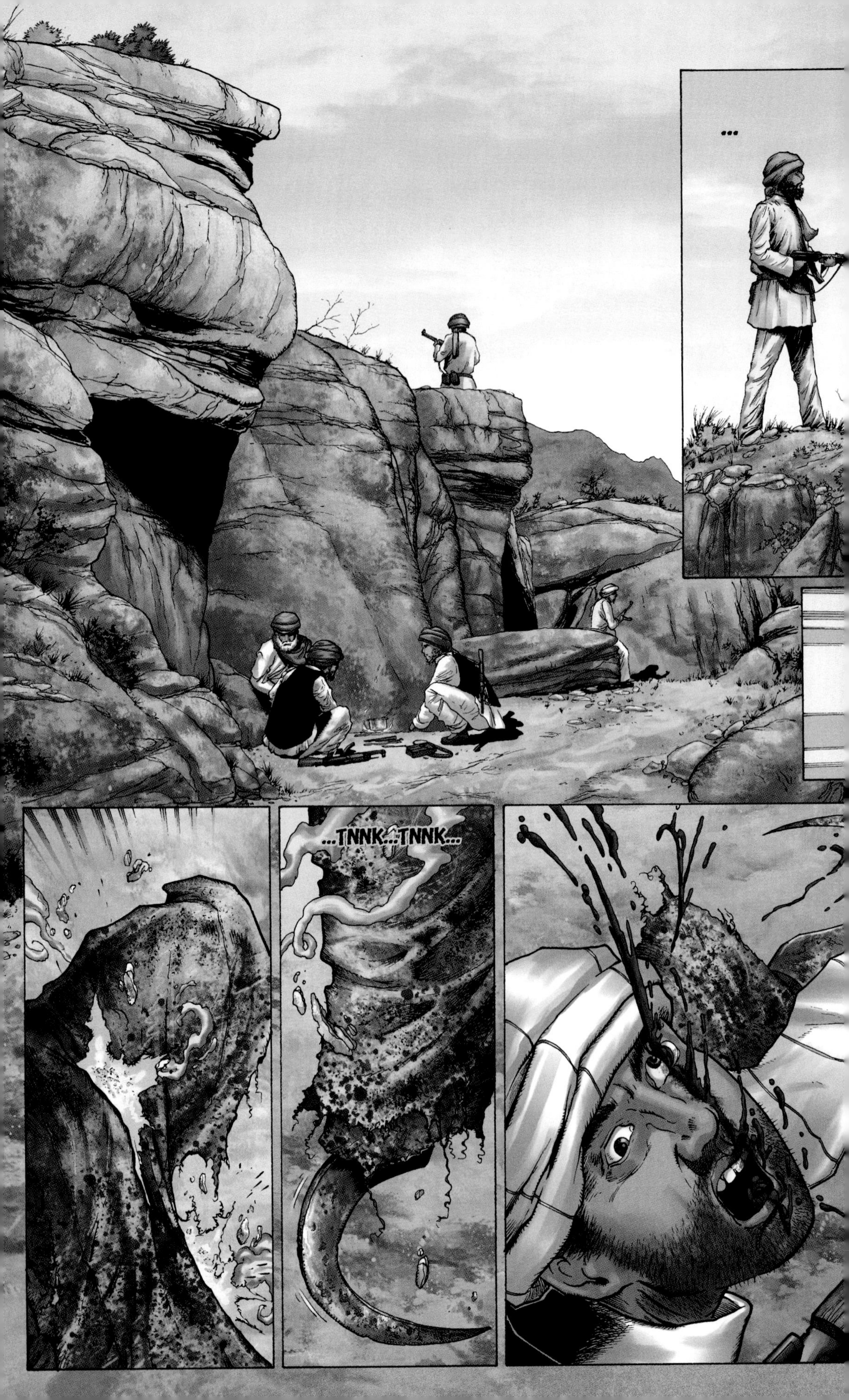
...
...TNNK...TNNK...

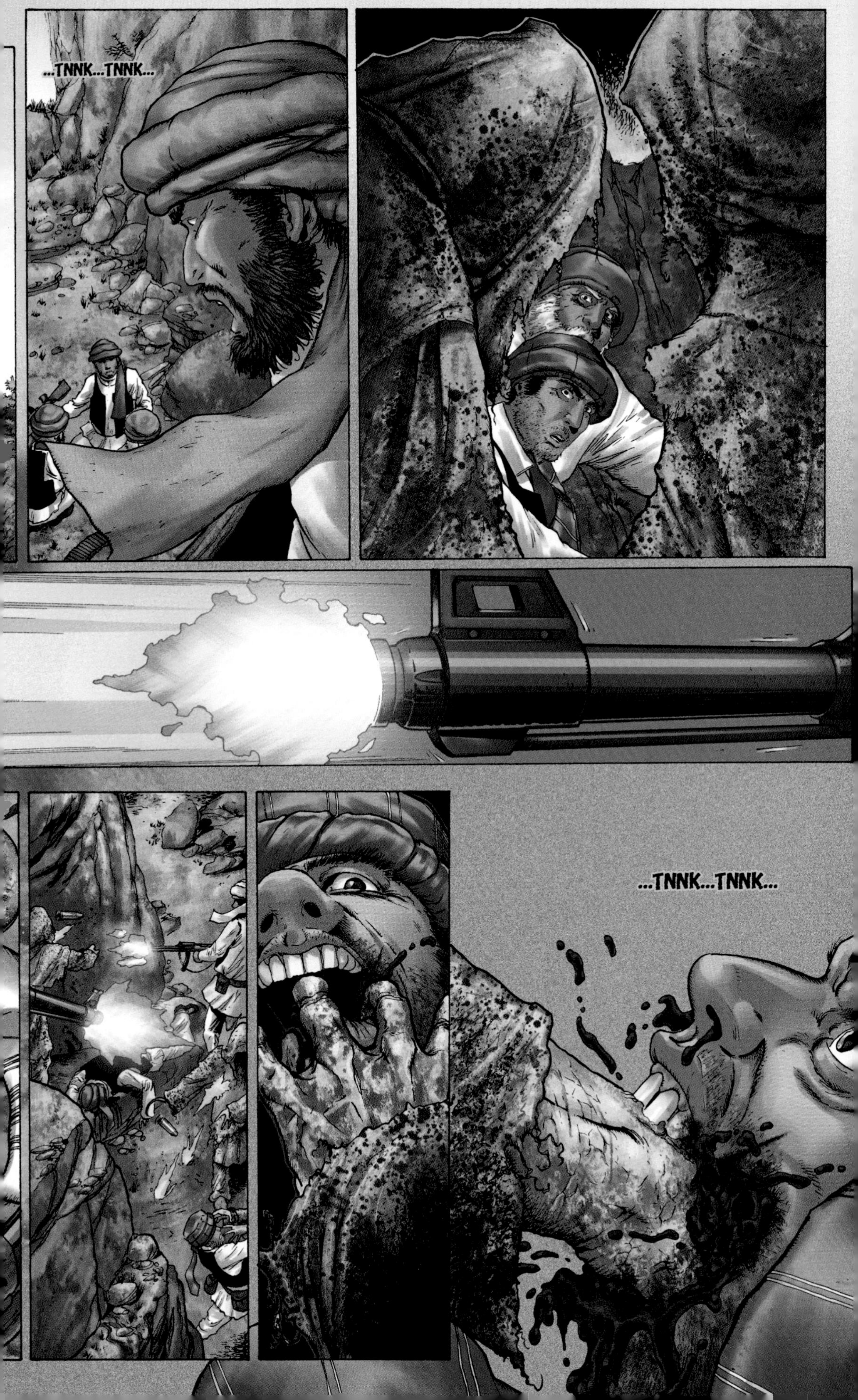
...TNNK...TNNK...
...TNNK...TNNK...

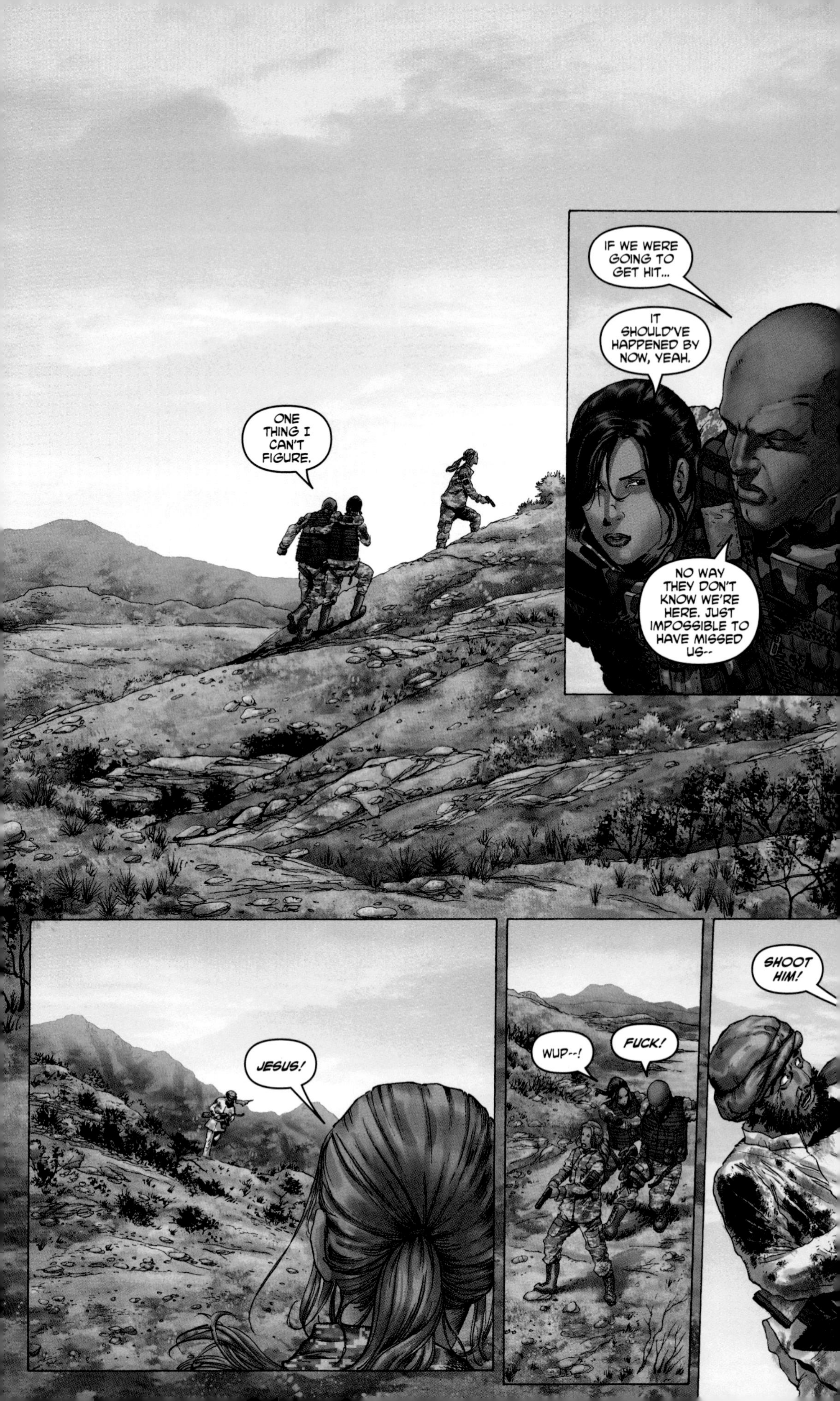
ONE THING I CAN'T FIGURE.
IF WE WERE GOING TO GET HIT...
IT SHOULD'VE HAPPENED BY NOW, YEAH.
NO WAY THEY DON'T KNOW WE'RE HERE. JUST IMPOSSIBLE TO HAVE MISSED US--
JESUS!
WUP--!
FUCK!
SHOOT HIM!

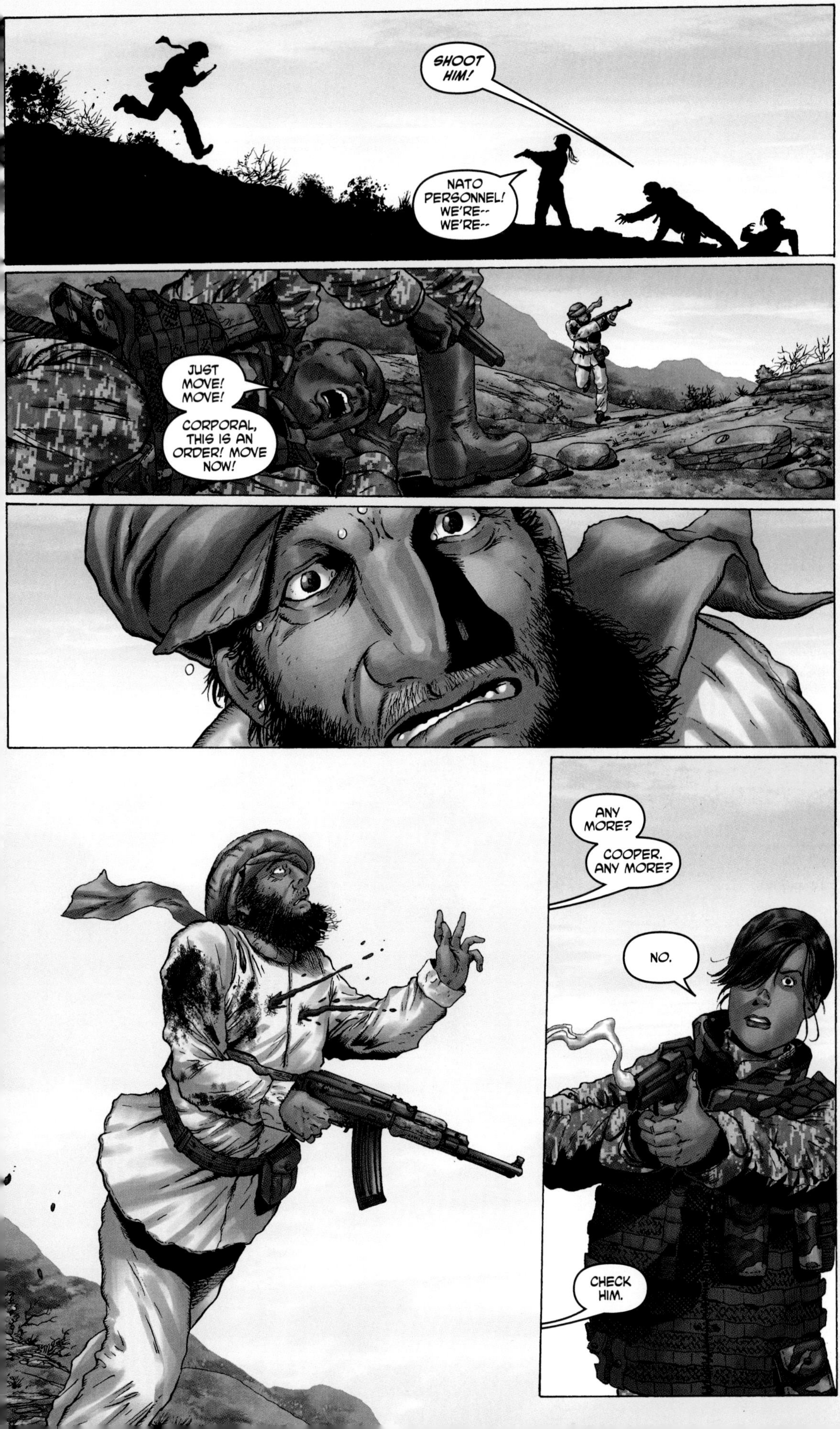
SHOOT HIM!
NATO PERSONNEL! WE'RE-- WE'RE--
JUST MOVE! MOVE!
CORPORAL, THIS IS AN ORDER! MOVE NOW!
ANY MORE?
COOPER. ANY MORE?
NO.
CHECK HIM.

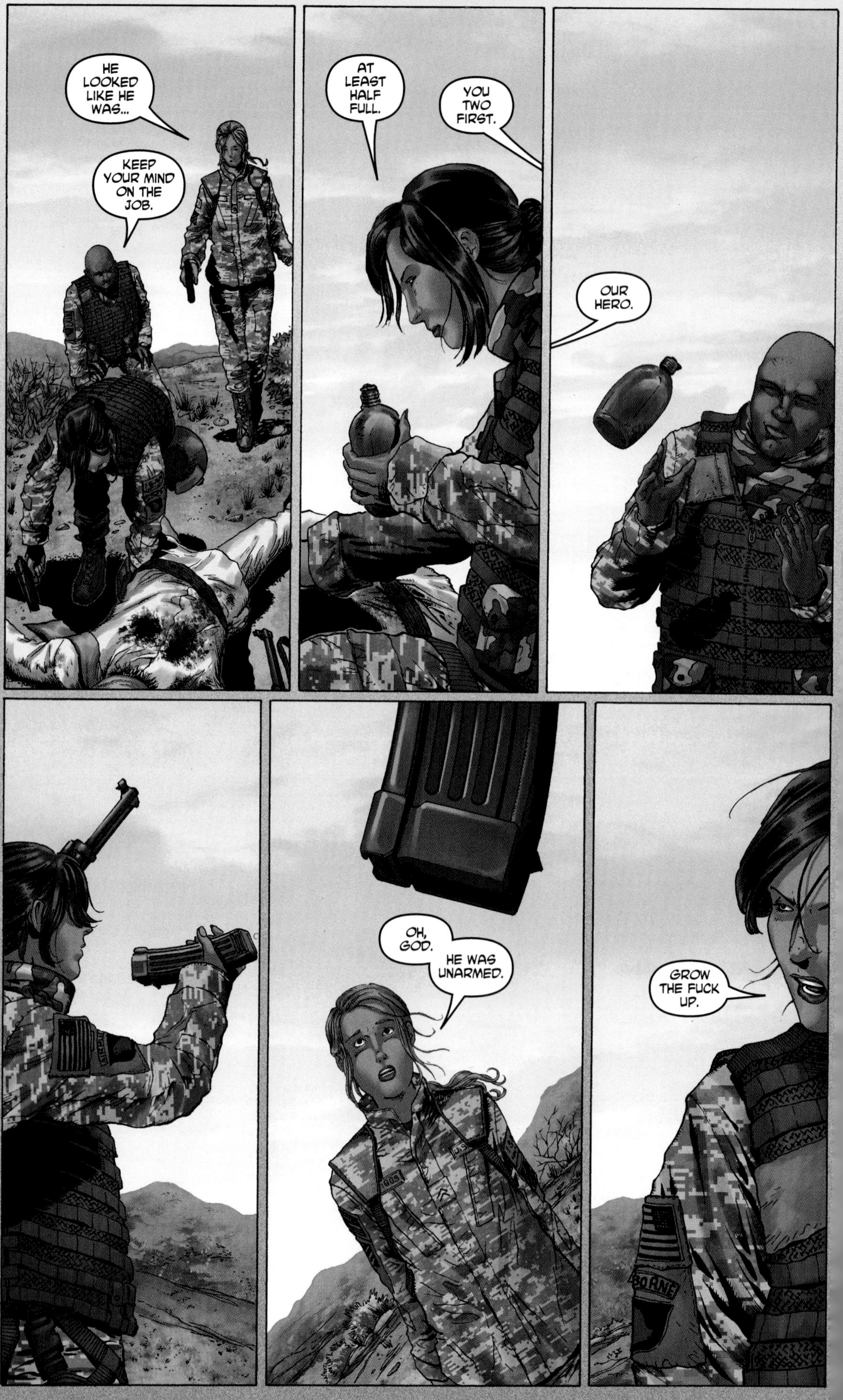
HE LOOKED LIKE HE WAS...
KEEP YOUR MIND ON THE JOB.
AT LEAST HALF FULL.
YOU TWO FIRST.
OUR HERO.
OH, GOD.
HE WAS UNARMED.
GROW THE FUCK UP.

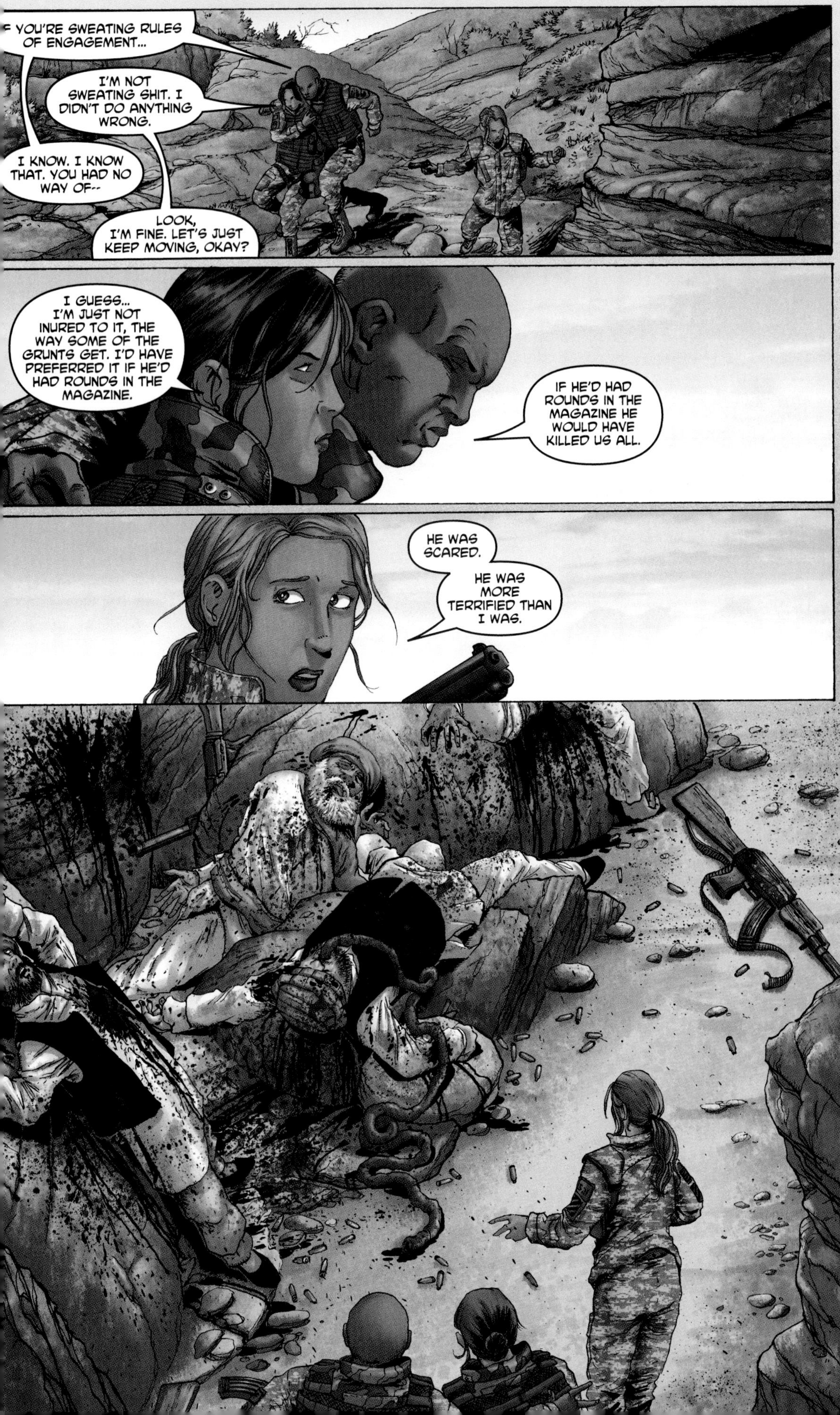
F YOU'RE SWEATING RULES OF ENGAGEMENT...
I'M NOT SWEATING SHIT. I DIDN'T DO ANYTHING WRONG.
I KNOW. I KNOW THAT. YOU HAD NO WAY OF--
LOOK, I'M FINE. LET'S JUST KEEP MOVING, OKAY?
I GUESS... I'M JUST NOT INURED TO IT, THE WAY SOME OF THE GRUNTS GET. I'D HAVE PREFERRED IT IF HE'D HAD ROUNDS IN THE MAGAZINE.
IF HE'D HAD ROUNDS IN THE MAGAZINE HE WOULD HAVE KILLED US ALL.
HE WAS SCARED.
HE WAS MORE TERRIFIED THAN I WAS.

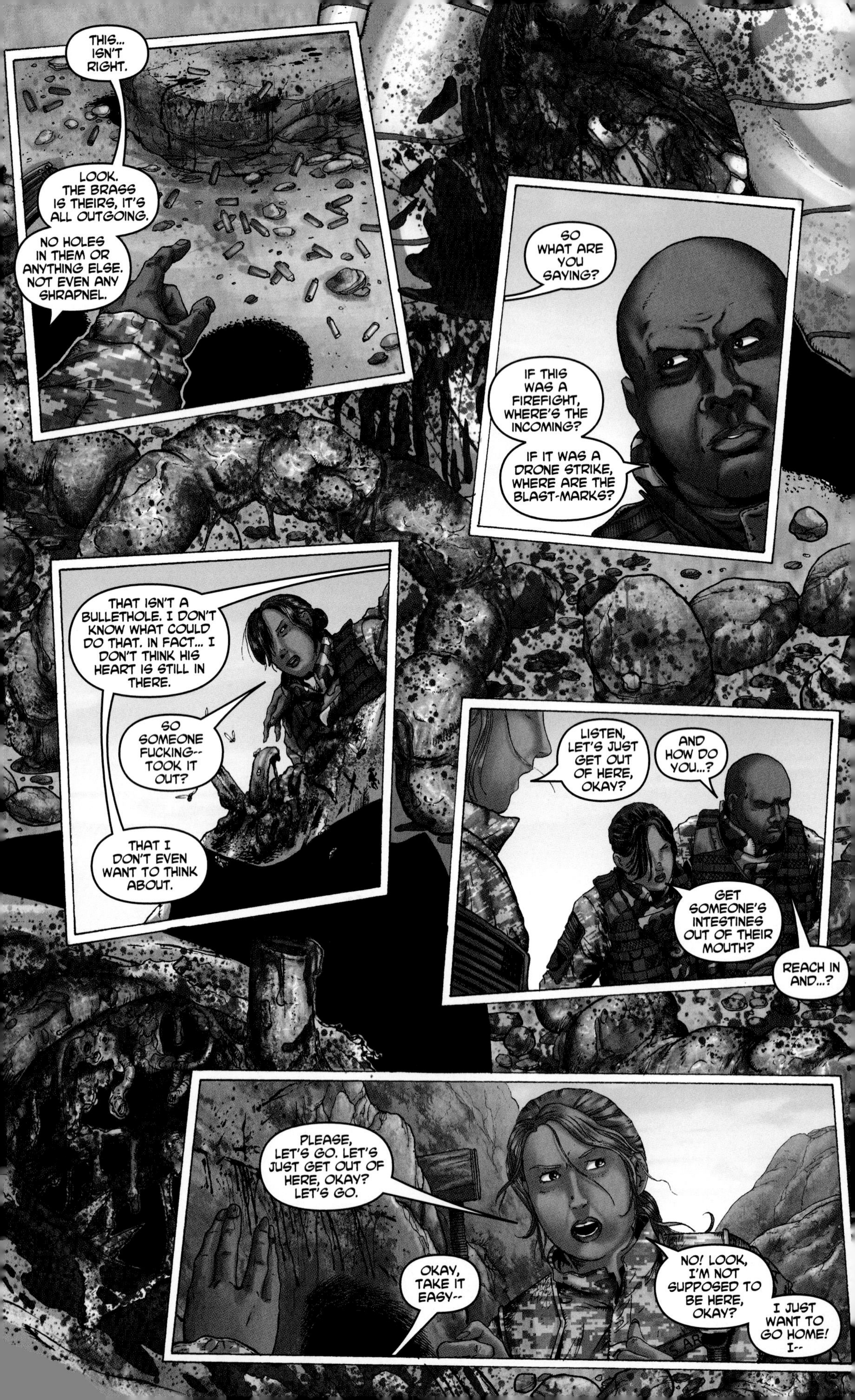

THIS... ISN'T RIGHT.
LOOK. THE BRASS IS THEIRS, IT'S ALL OUTGOING.
NO HOLES IN THEM OR ANYTHING ELSE. NOT EVEN ANY SHRAPNEL.
SO WHAT ARE YOU SAYING?
IF THIS WAS A FIREFIGHT, WHERE'S THE INCOMING?
IF IT WAS A DRONE STRIKE, WHERE ARE THE BLAST-MARKS?
THAT ISN'T A BULLETHOLE. I DON'T KNOW WHAT COULD DO THAT. IN FACT... I DON'T THINK HIS HEART IS STILL IN THERE.
SO SOMEONE FUCKING-- TOOK IT OUT?
THAT I DON'T EVEN WANT TO THINK ABOUT.
LISTEN, LET'S JUST GET OUT OF HERE, OKAY?
AND HOW DO YOU...?
GET SOMEONE'S INTESTINES OUT OF THEIR MOUTH?
REACH IN AND...?
PLEASE, LET'S GO. LET'S JUST GET OUT OF HERE, OKAY? LET'S GO.
OKAY, TAKE IT EASY--
NO! LOOK, I'M NOT SUPPOSED TO BE HERE, OKAY?
I JUST WANT TO GO HOME! I--

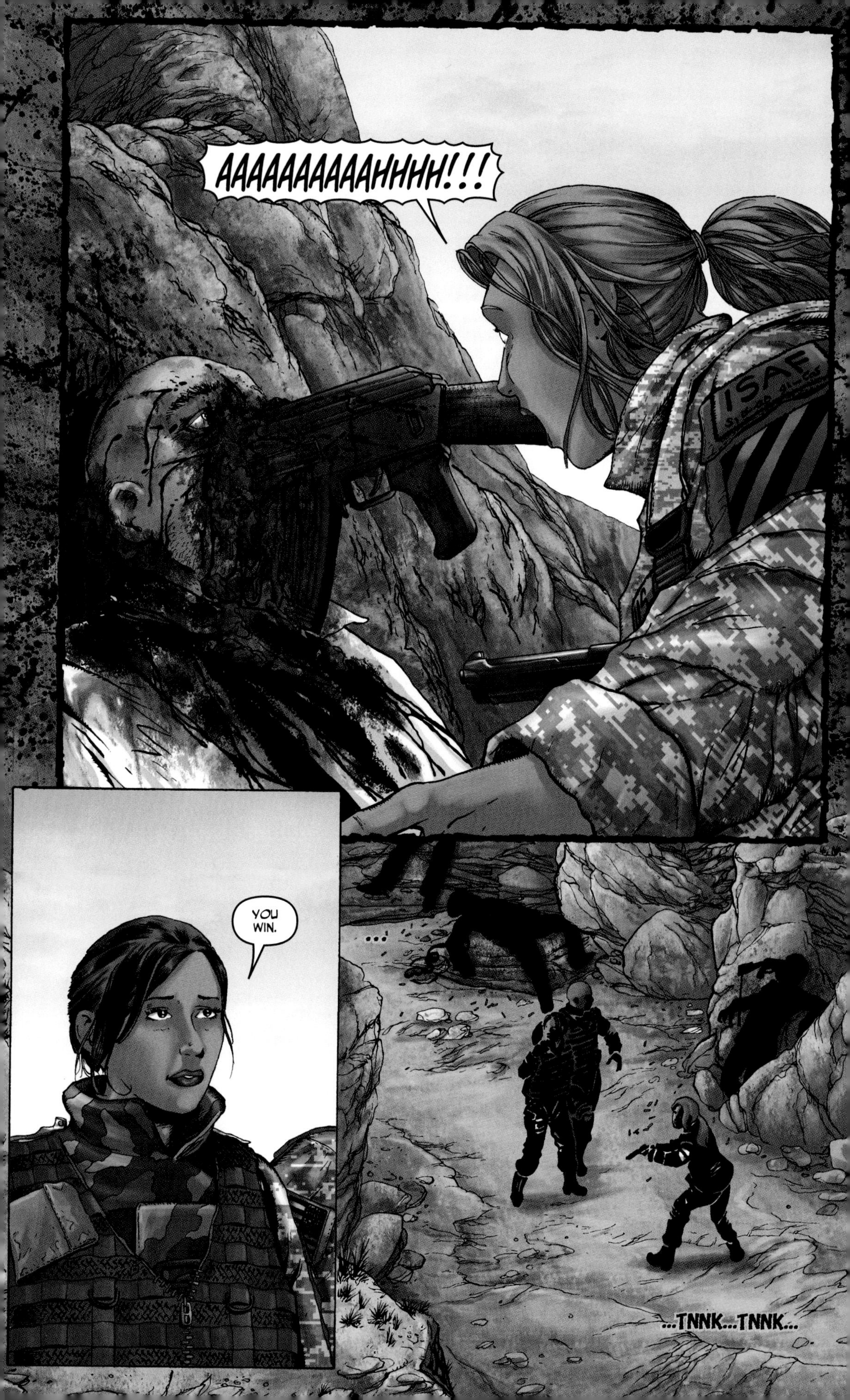
AAAAAAAAAAHHHH!!!
YOU WIN.
...TNNK...TNNK...

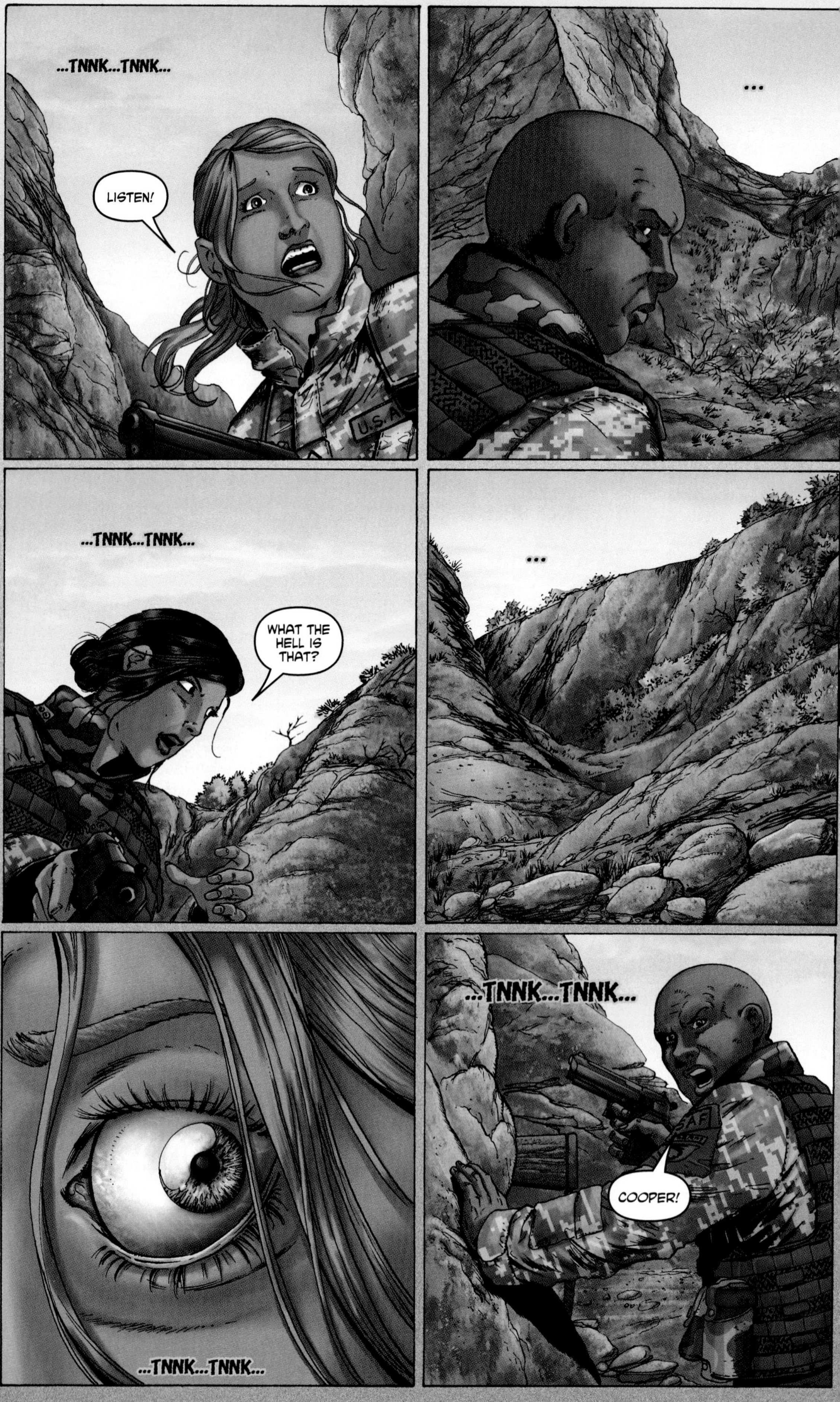
...TNNK...TNNK...
LISTEN!
...
...TNNK...TNNK...
WHAT THE HELL IS THAT?
...
...TNNK...TNNK...
...TNNK...TNNK...
COOPER!

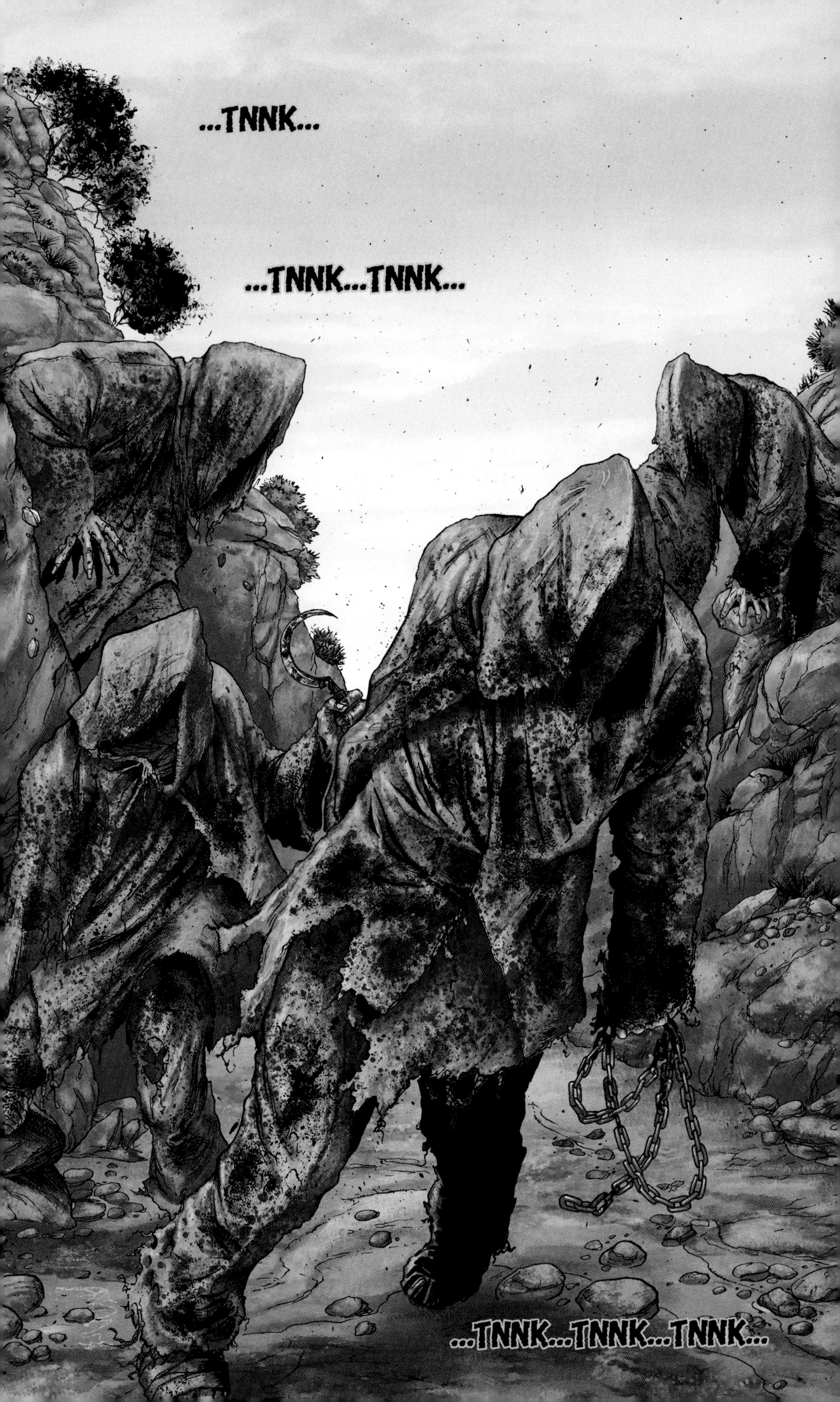
...TNNK...
...TNNK...TNNK...
...TNNK...TNNK...TNNK...

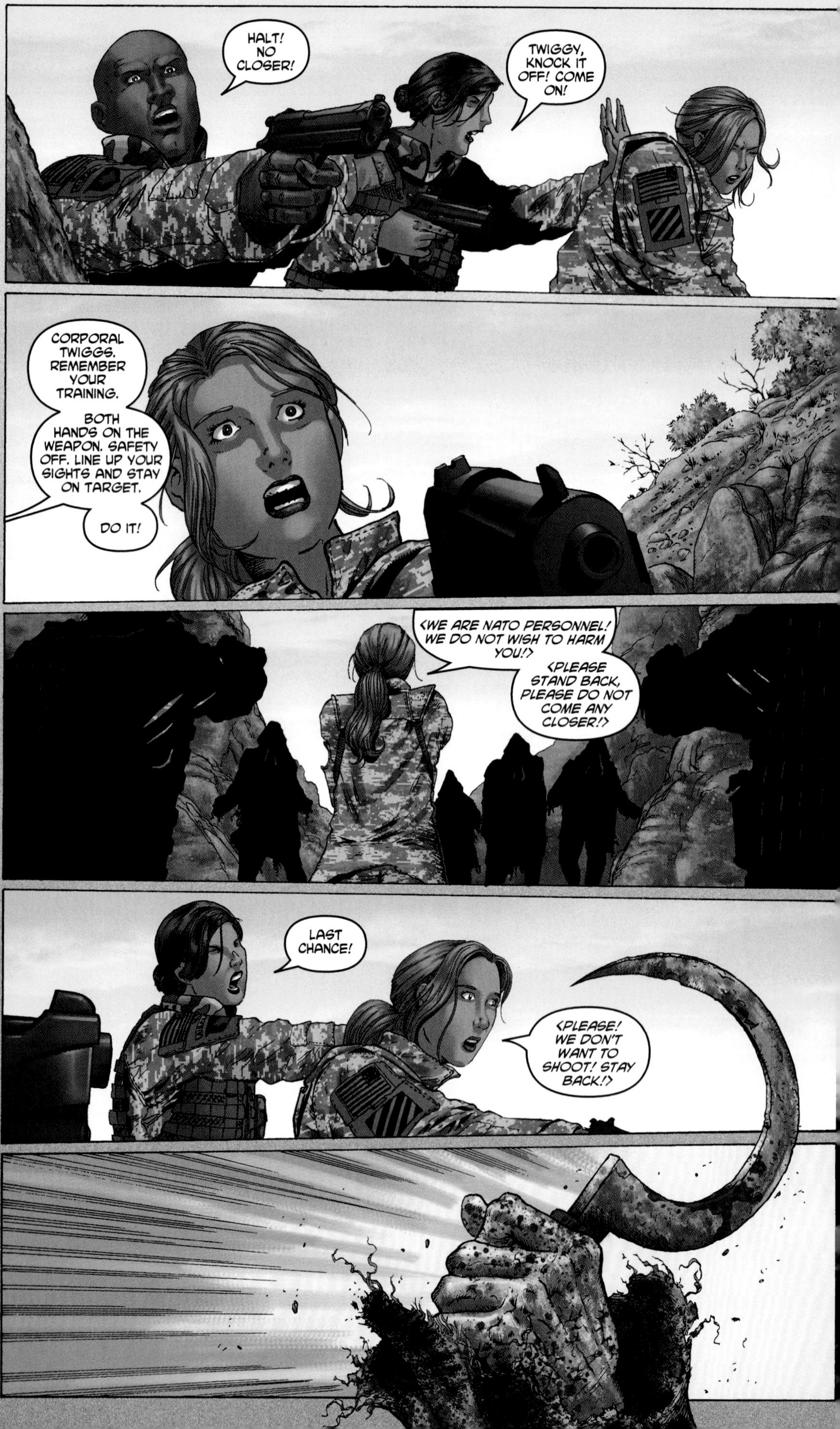
HALT! NO CLOSER!
TWIGGY, KNOCK IT OFF! COME ON!
CORPORAL TWIGGS. REMEMBER YOUR TRAINING.
BOTH HANDS ON THE WEAPON. SAFETY OFF. LINE UP YOUR SIGHTS AND STAY ON TARGET.
DO IT!
<WE ARE NATO PERSONNEL! WE DO NOT WISH TO HARM YOU!>
<PLEASE STAND BACK, PLEASE DO NOT COME ANY CLOSER!>
LAST CHANCE!
<PLEASE! WE DON'T WANT TO SHOOT! STAY BACK!>

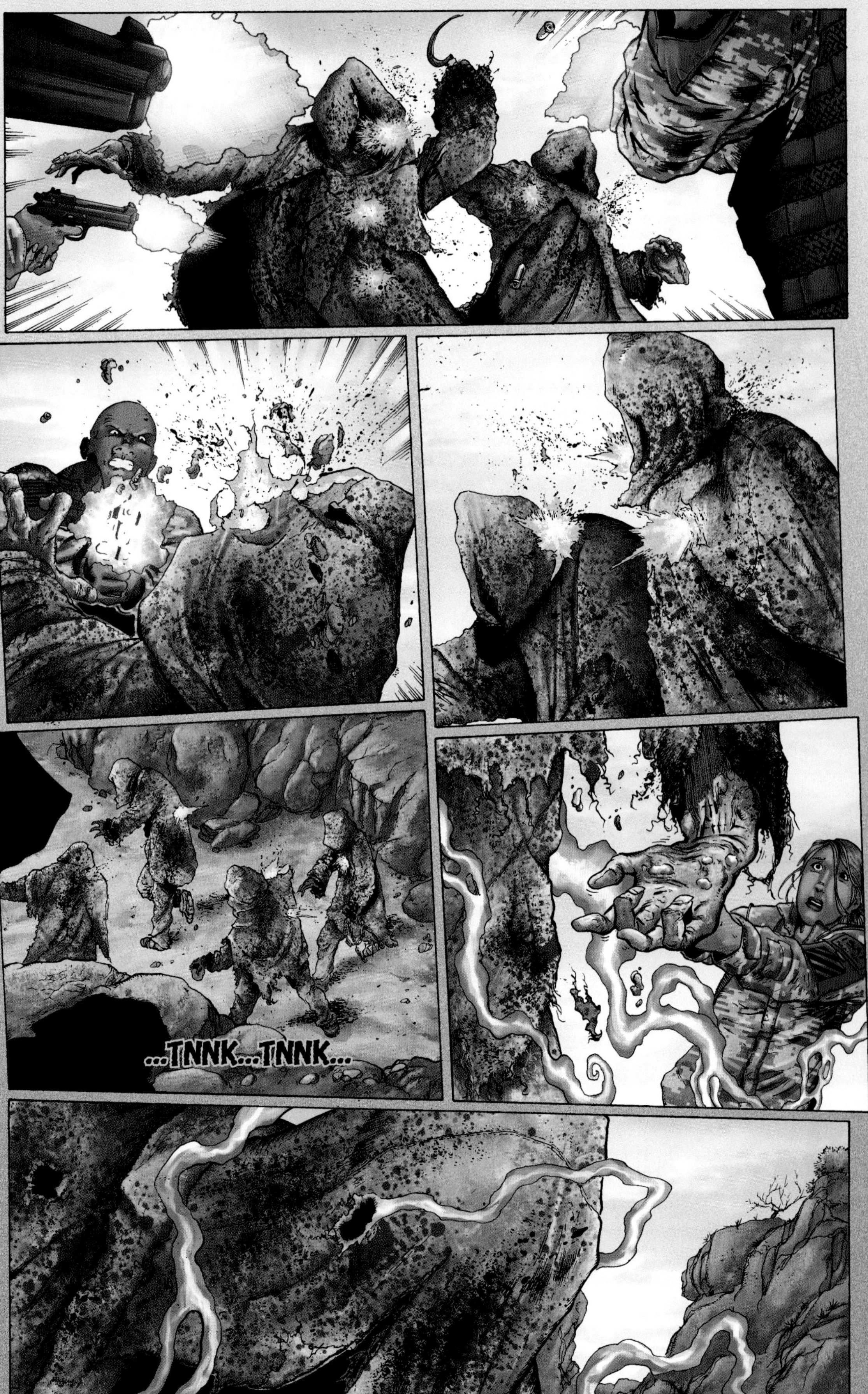
...TNNK...TNNK...

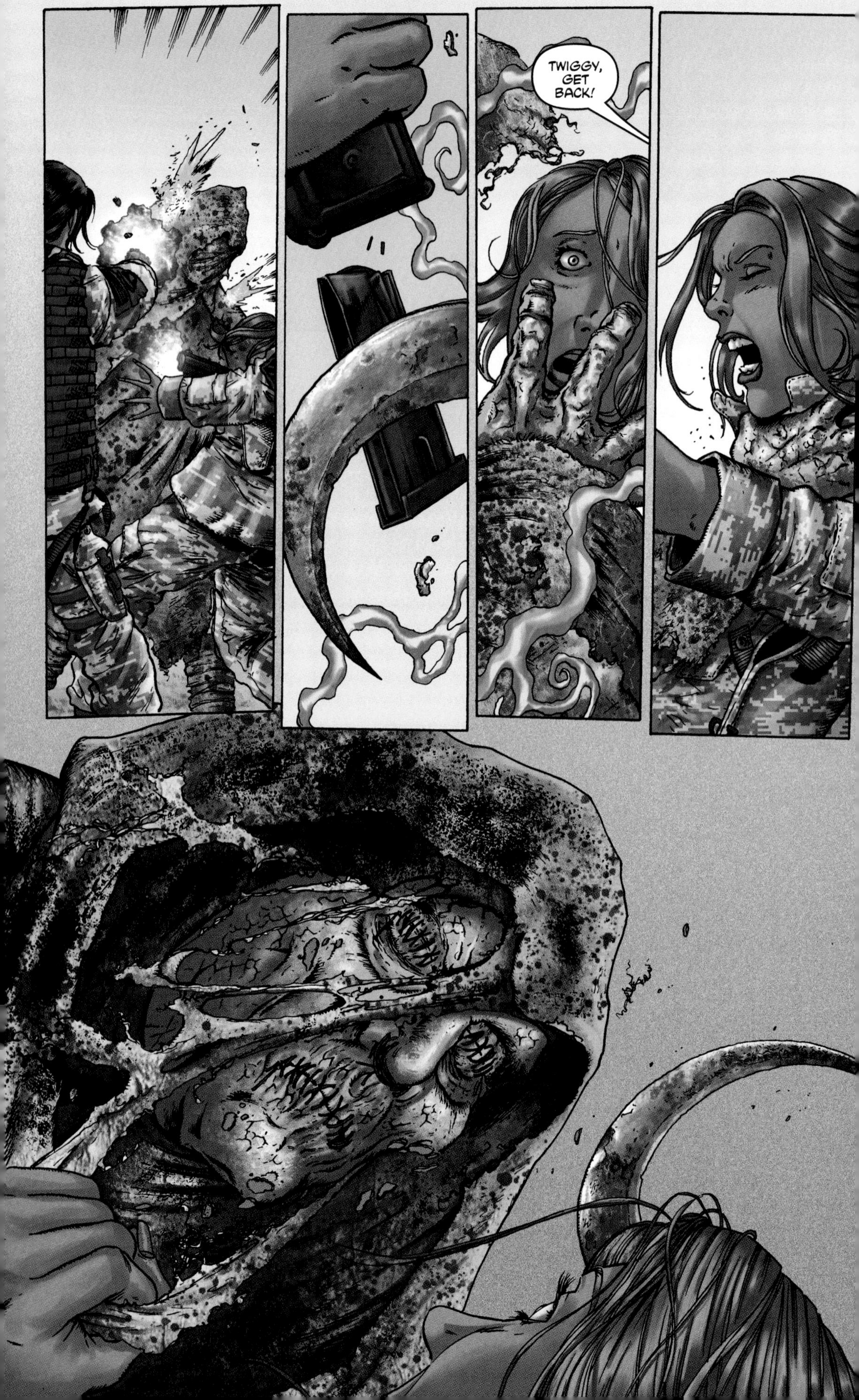
TWIGGY, GET BACK!

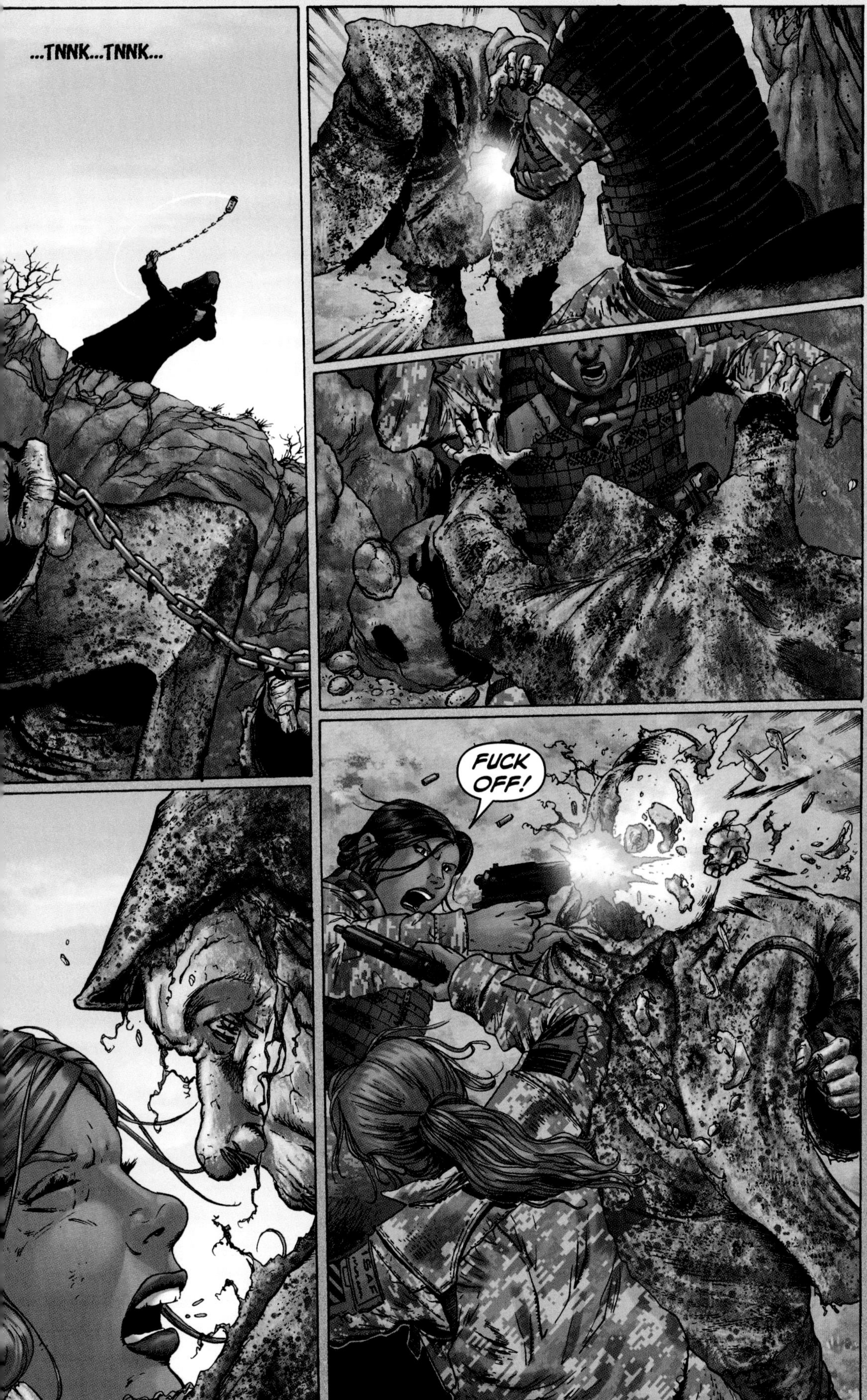
...TNNK...TNNK...
FUCK OFF!

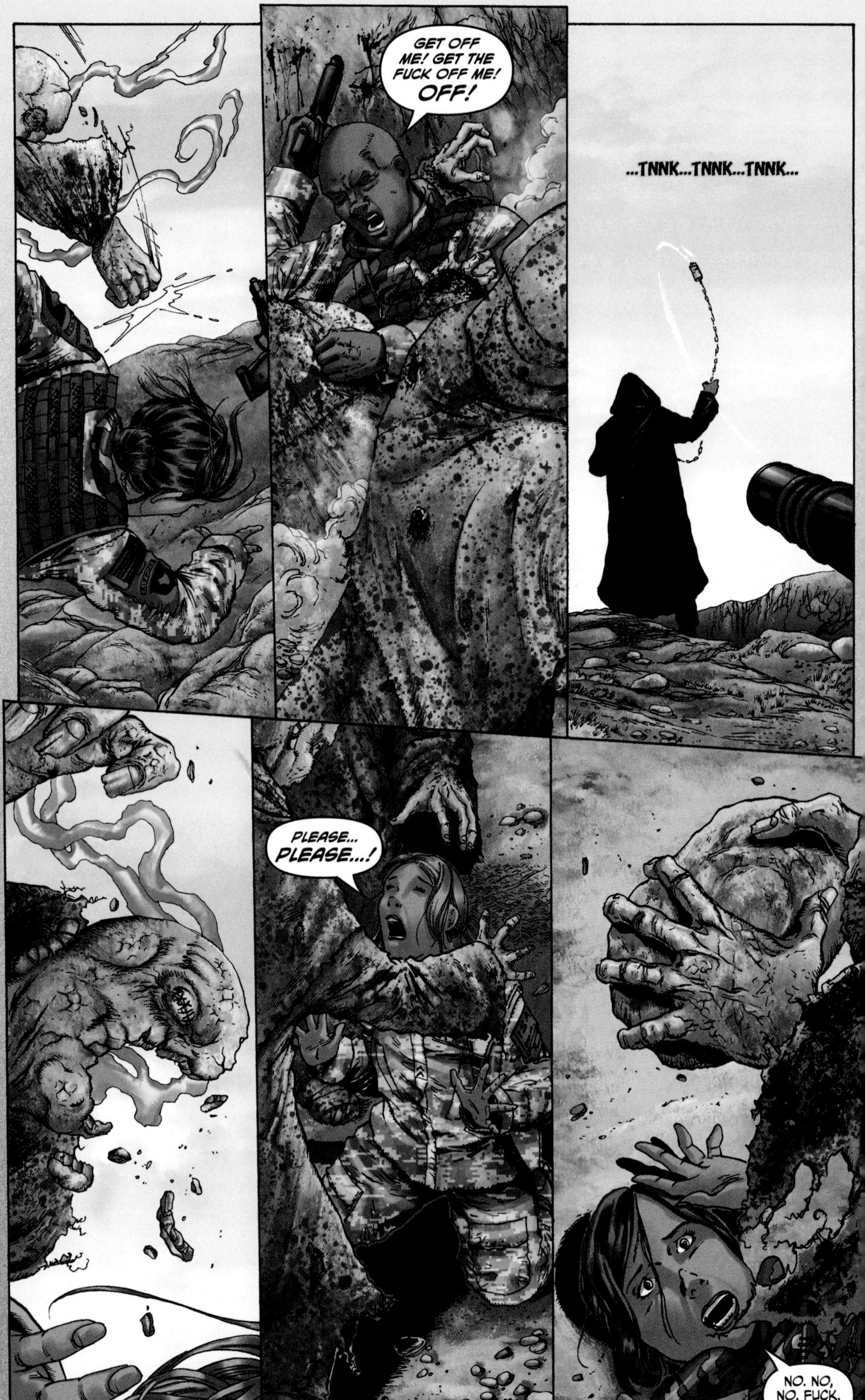
GET OFF ME! GET THE FUCK OFF ME! OFF!
...TNNK...TNNK...TNNK...
PLEASE... PLEASE...!
NO. NO, NO, FUCK, NO...!

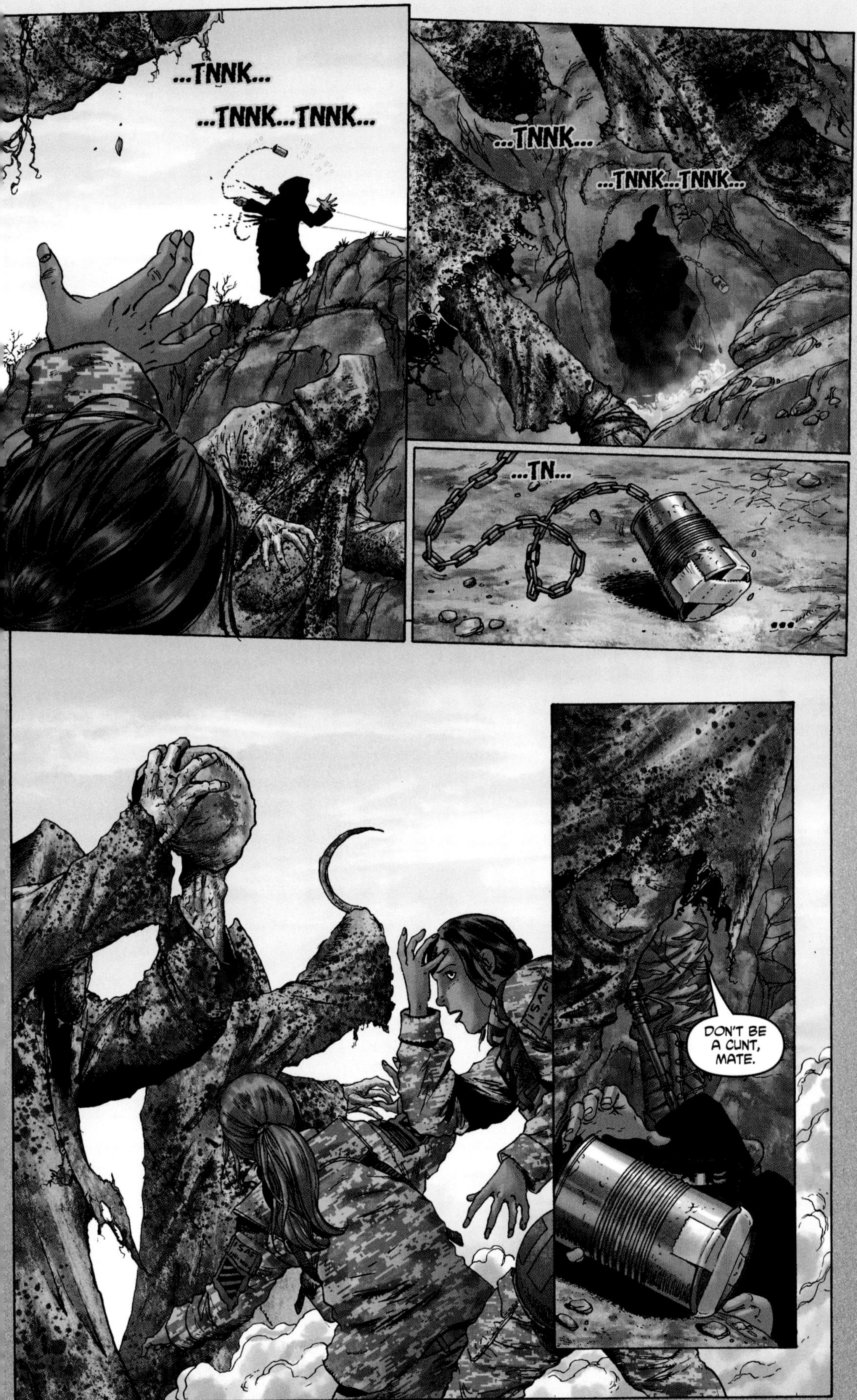
...TNNK...
...TNNK...TNNK...
...TNNK...
...TNNK...TNNK...
...TN...
...
DON'T BE A CUNT, MATE.

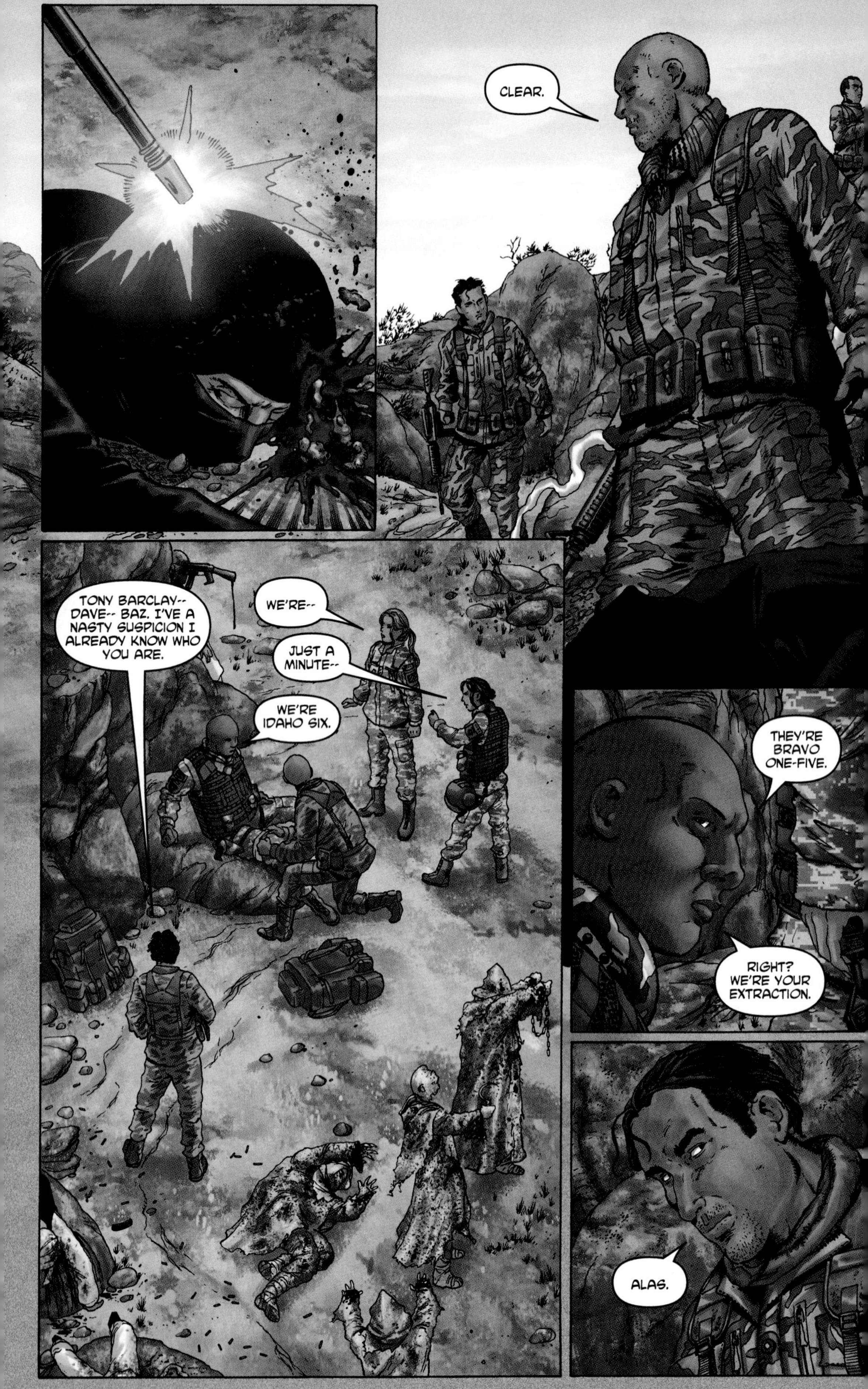
CLEAR.
TONY BARCLAY-- DAVE-- BAZ. I'VE A NASTY SUSPICION I ALREADY KNOW WHO YOU ARE.
WE'RE--
JUST A MINUTE--
WE'RE IDAHO SIX.
THEY'RE BRAVO ONE-FIVE.
RIGHT? WE'RE YOUR EXTRACTION.
ALAS.

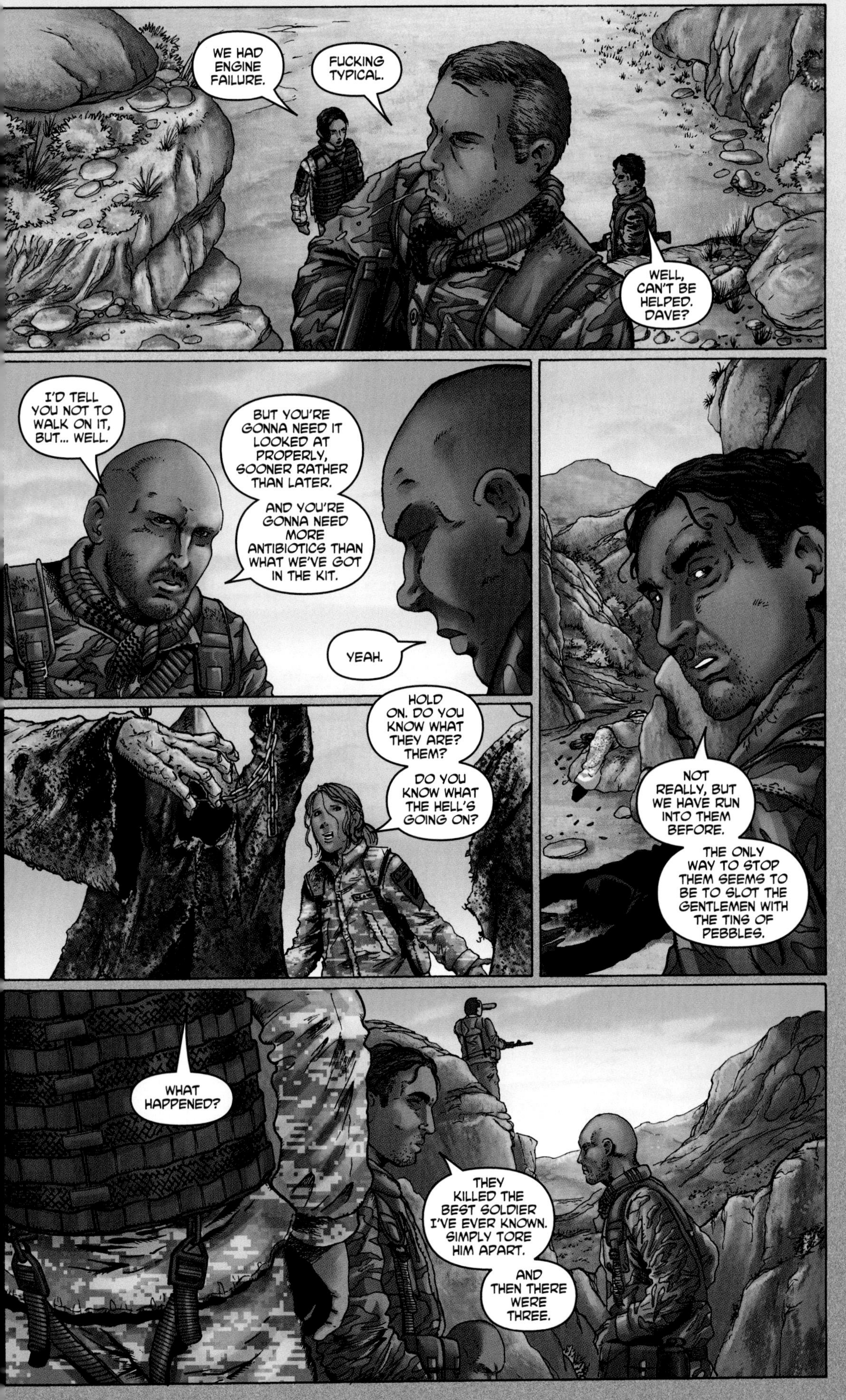
WE HAD ENGINE FAILURE.
FUCKING TYPICAL.
WELL, CAN'T BE HELPED. DAVE?
I'D TELL YOU NOT TO WALK ON IT, BUT... WELL.
BUT YOU'RE GONNA NEED IT LOOKED AT PROPERLY, SOONER RATHER THAN LATER.
AND YOU'RE GONNA NEED MORE ANTIBIOTICS THAN WHAT WE'VE GOT IN THE KIT.
YEAH.
HOLD ON. DO YOU KNOW WHAT THEY ARE? THEM?
DO YOU KNOW WHAT THE HELL'S GOING ON?
NOT REALLY, BUT WE HAVE RUN INTO THEM BEFORE.
THE ONLY WAY TO STOP THEM SEEMS TO BE TO SLOT THE GENTLEMEN WITH THE TINS OF PEBBLES.
WHAT HAPPENED?
THEY KILLED THE BEST SOLDIER I'VE EVER KNOWN. SIMPLY TORE HIM APART.
AND THEN THERE WERE THREE.

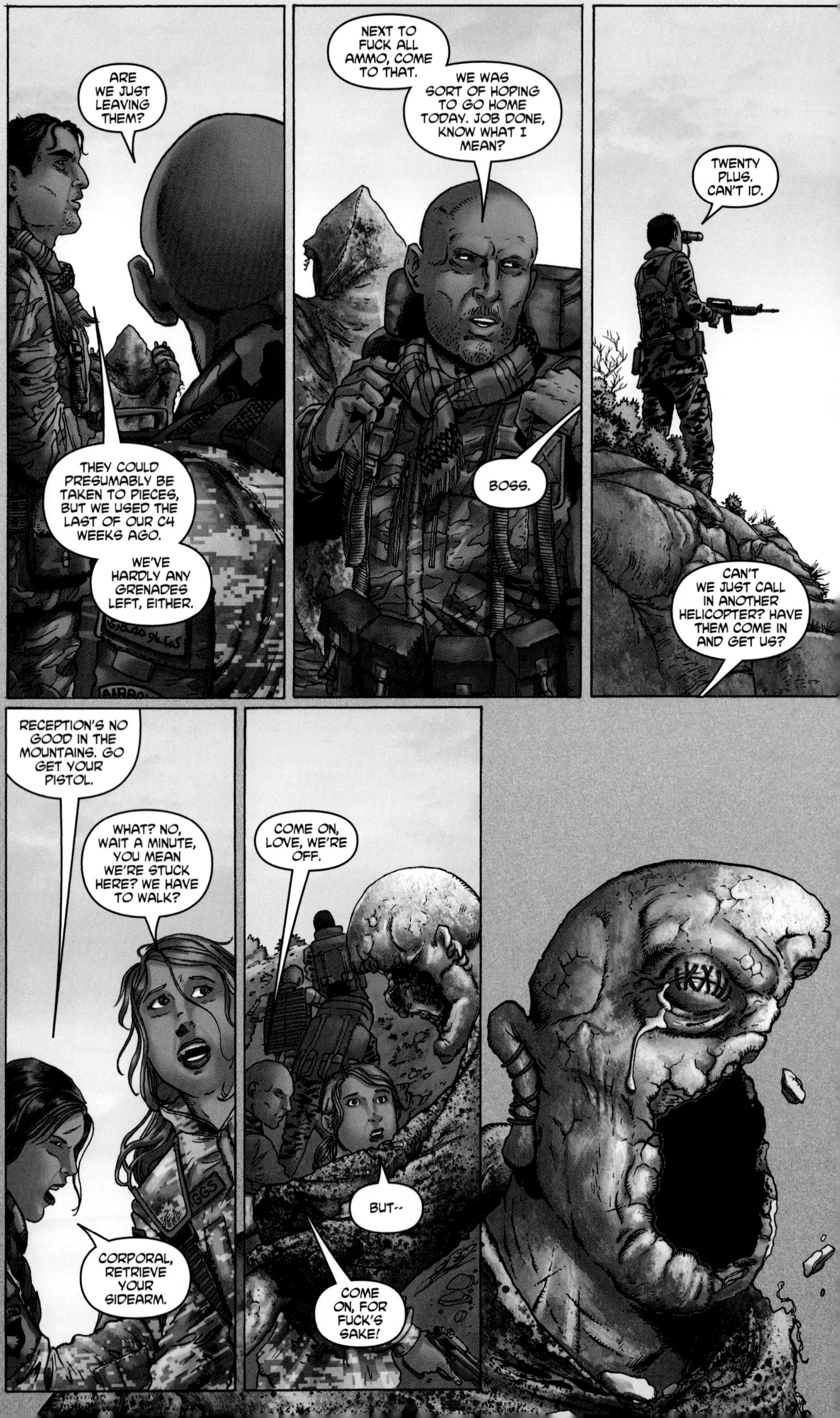

ARE WE JUST LEAVING THEM?
THEY COULD PRESUMABLY BE TAKEN TO PIECES, BUT WE USED THE LAST OF OUR C4 WEEKS AGO.
WE'VE HARDLY ANY GRENADES LEFT, EITHER.
NEXT TO FUCK ALL AMMO, COME TO THAT.
WE WAS SORT OF HOPING TO GO HOME TODAY. JOB DONE, KNOW WHAT I MEAN?
BOSS.
TWENTY PLUS. CAN'T ID.
CAN'T WE JUST CALL IN ANOTHER HELICOPTER? HAVE THEM COME IN AND GET US?
RECEPTION'S NO GOOD IN THE MOUNTAINS. GO GET YOUR PISTOL.
WHAT? NO, WAIT A MINUTE, YOU MEAN WE'RE STUCK HERE? WE HAVE TO WALK?
CORPORAL, RETRIEVE YOUR SIDEARM.
COME ON, LOVE, WE'RE OFF.
BUT--
COME ON, FOR FUCK'S SAKE!

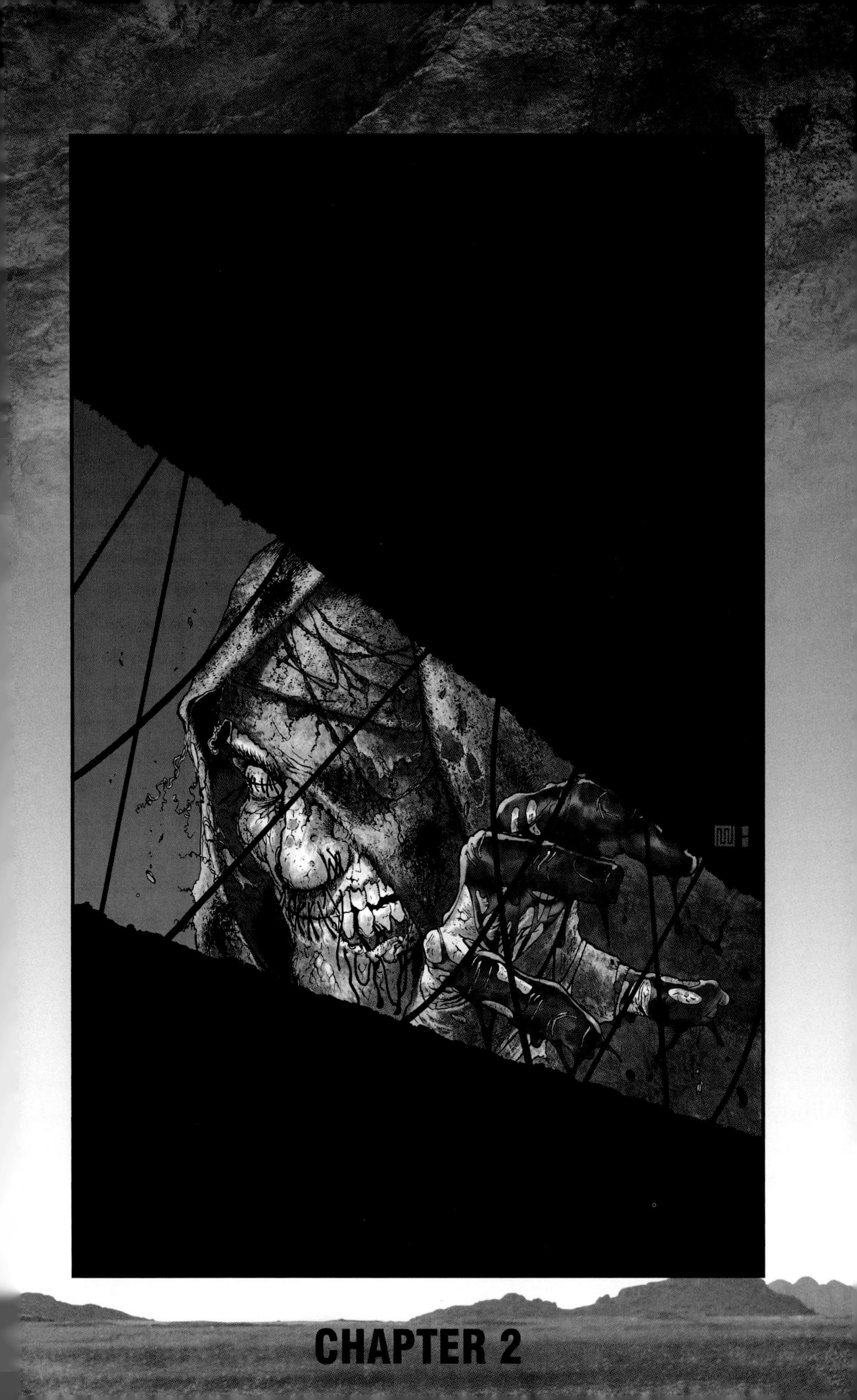

CHAPTER 2

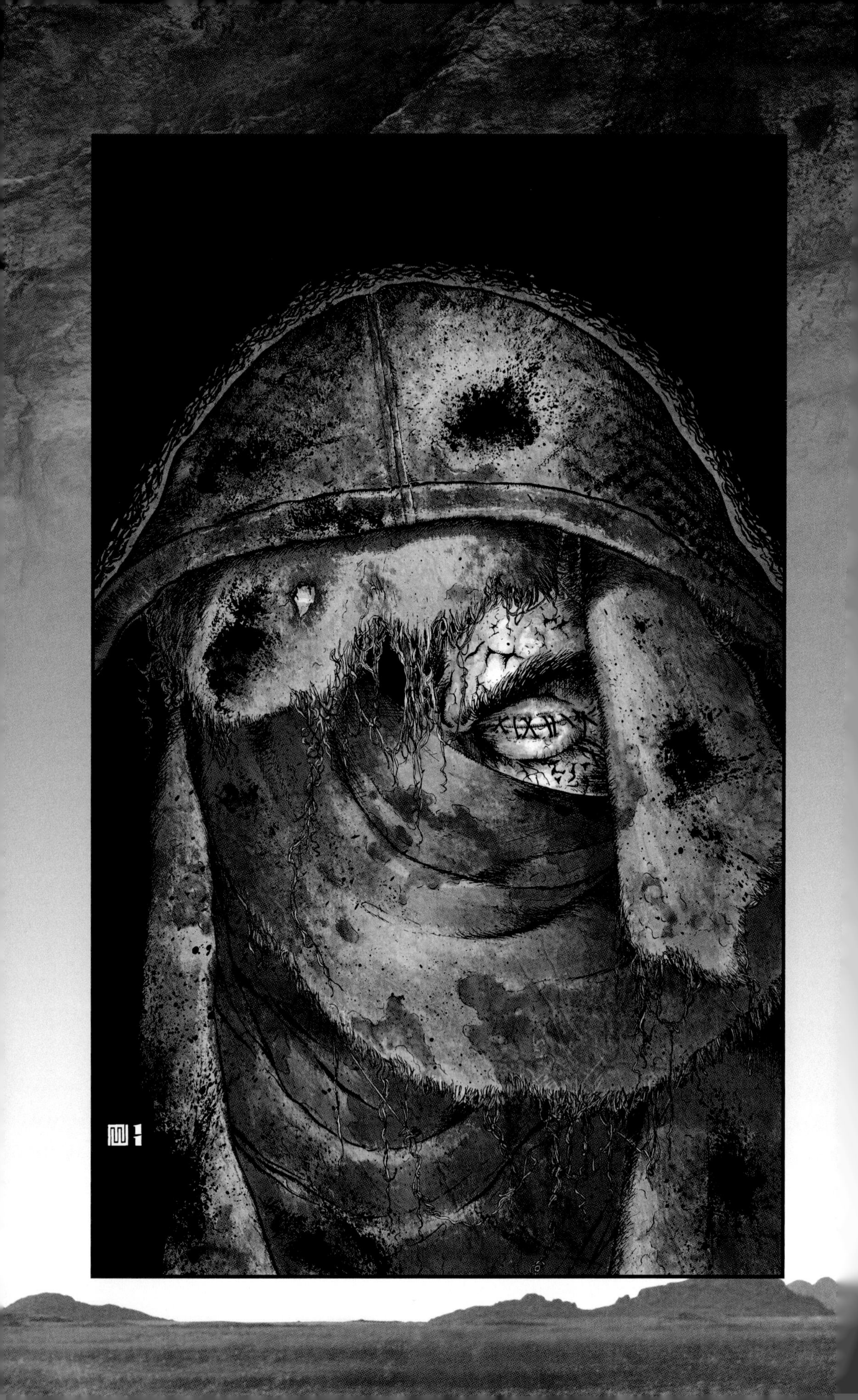

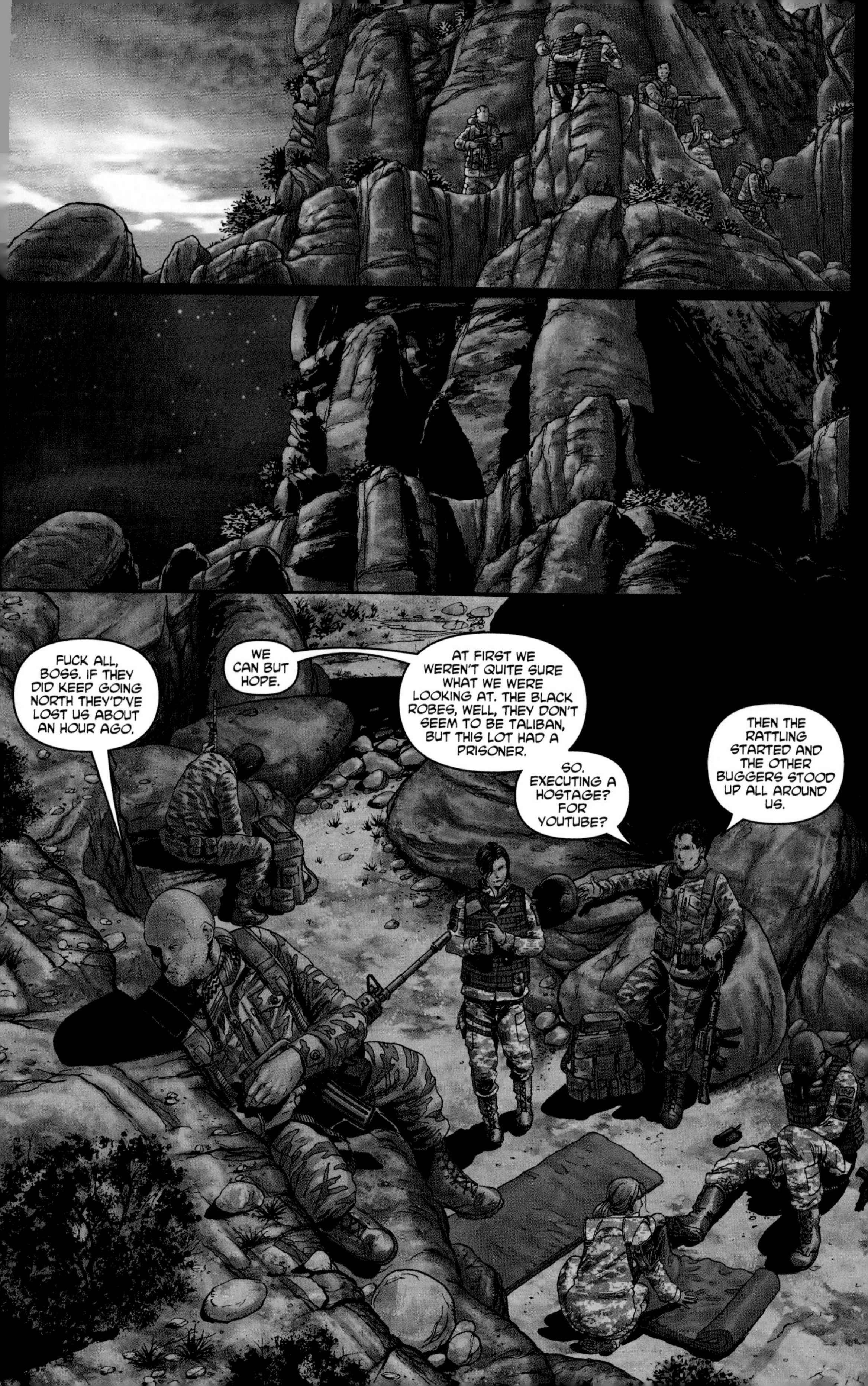
FUCK ALL, BOSS. IF THEY DID KEEP GOING NORTH THEY'D'VE LOST US ABOUT AN HOUR AGO.
WE CAN BUT HOPE.
AT FIRST WE WEREN'T QUITE SURE WHAT WE WERE LOOKING AT. THE BLACK ROBES, WELL, THEY DON'T SEEM TO BE TALIBAN, BUT THIS LOT HAD A PRISONER.
SO. EXECUTING A HOSTAGE? FOR YOUTUBE?
THEN THE RATTLING STARTED AND THE OTHER BUGGERS STOOD UP ALL AROUND US.

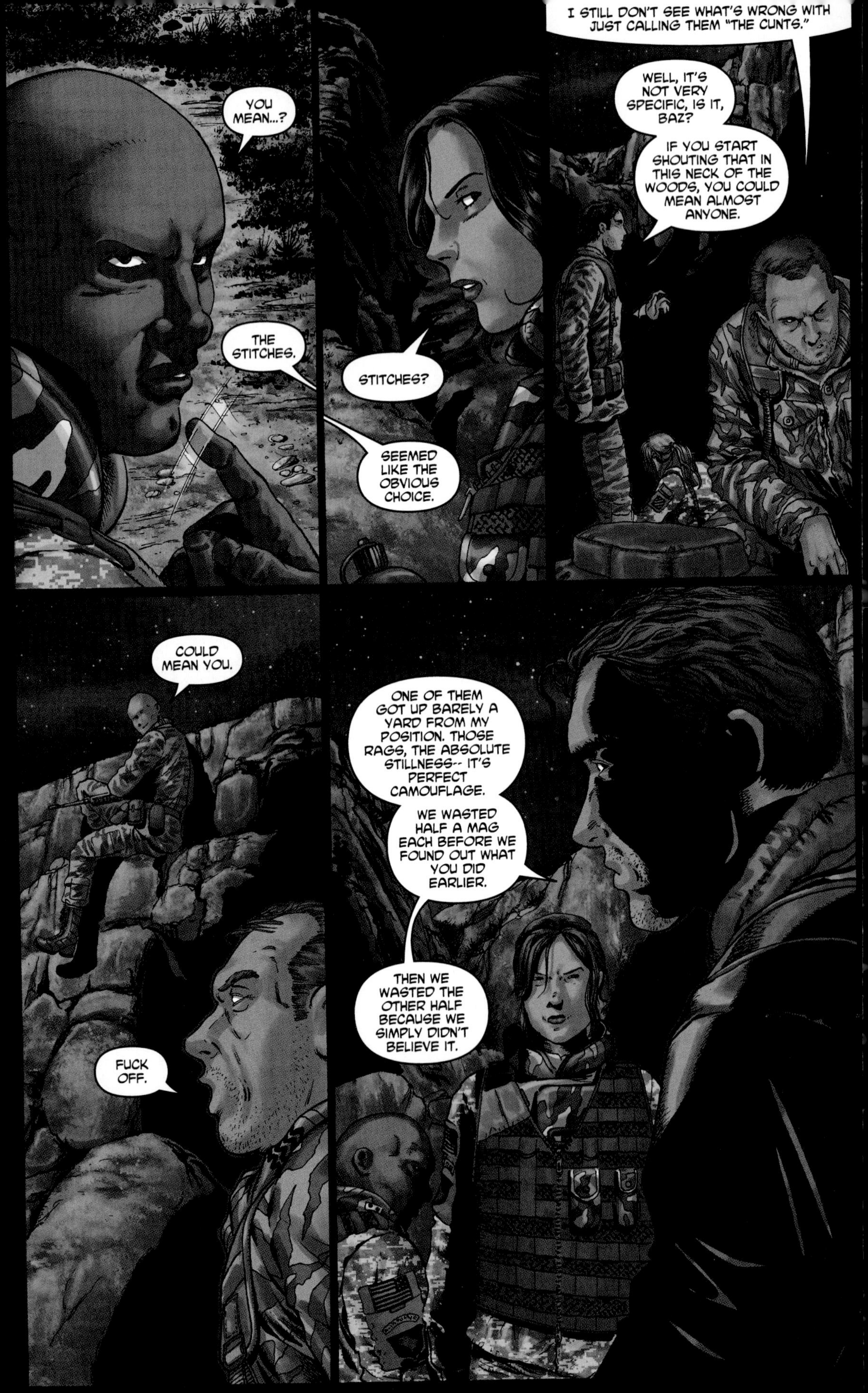
YOU MEAN...?
THE STITCHES.
STITCHES?
SEEMED LIKE THE OBVIOUS CHOICE.
I STILL DON'T SEE WHAT'S WRONG WITH JUST CALLING THEM "THE CUNTS."
WELL, IT'S NOT VERY SPECIFIC, IS IT, BAZ?
IF YOU START SHOUTING THAT IN THIS NECK OF THE WOODS, YOU COULD MEAN ALMOST ANYONE.
COULD MEAN YOU.
FUCK OFF.
ONE OF THEM GOT UP BARELY A YARD FROM MY POSITION. THOSE RAGS, THE ABSOLUTE STILLNESS-- IT'S PERFECT CAMOUFLAGE.
WE WASTED HALF A MAG EACH BEFORE WE FOUND OUT WHAT YOU DID EARLIER.
THEN WE WASTED THE OTHER HALF BECAUSE WE SIMPLY DIDN'T BELIEVE IT.

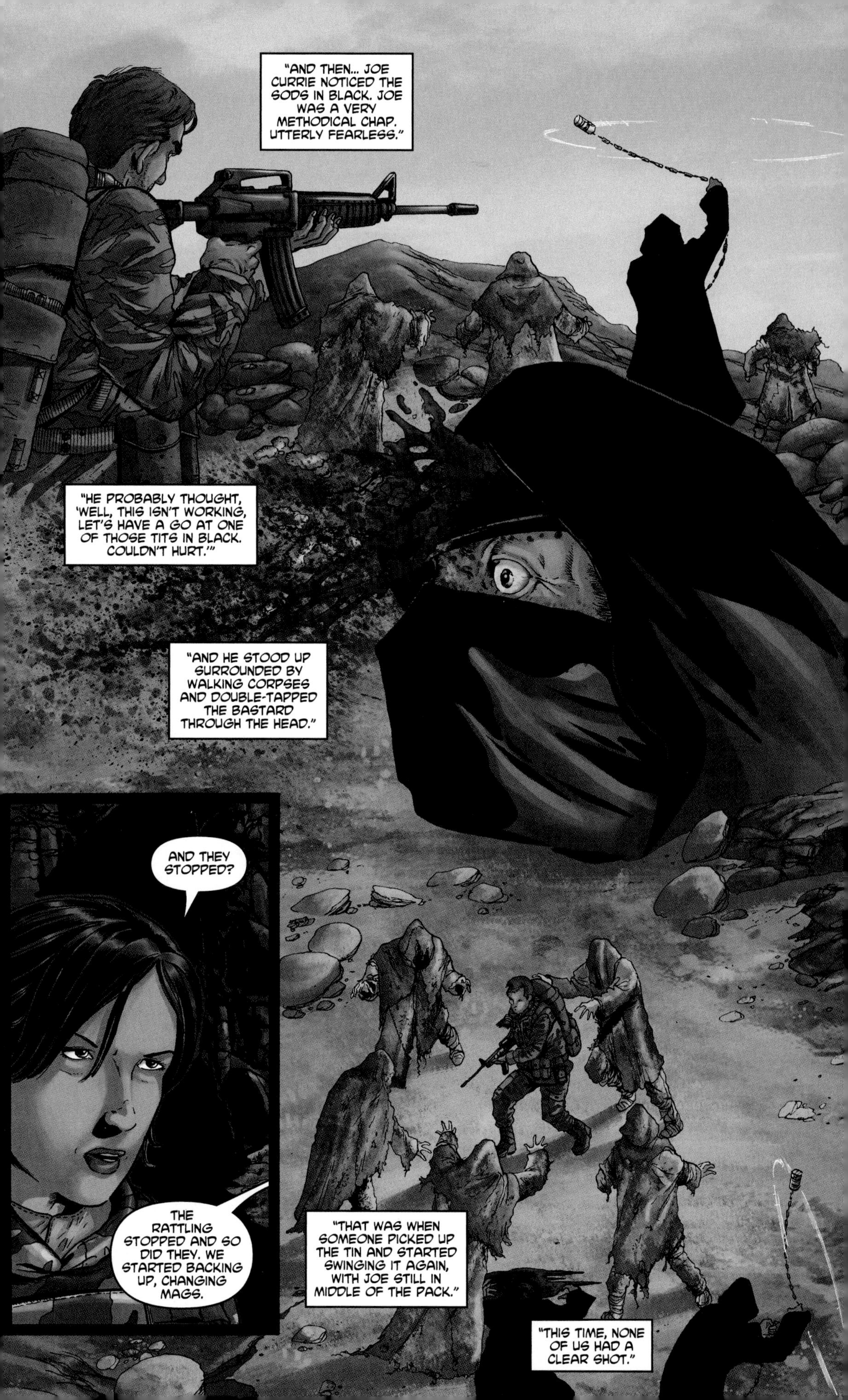
"AND THEN... JOE CURRIE NOTICED THE SODS IN BLACK. JOE WAS A VERY METHODICAL CHAP. UTTERLY FEARLESS."
"HE PROBABLY THOUGHT, 'WELL, THIS ISN'T WORKING, LET'S HAVE A GO AT ONE OF THOSE TITS IN BLACK. COULDN'T HURT.'"
"AND HE STOOD UP SURROUNDED BY WALKING CORPSES AND DOUBLE-TAPPED THE BASTARD THROUGH THE HEAD."
AND THEY STOPPED?
THE RATTLING STOPPED AND SO DID THEY. WE STARTED BACKING UP, CHANGING MAGS.
"THAT WAS WHEN SOMEONE PICKED UP THE TIN AND STARTED SWINGING IT AGAIN, WITH JOE STILL IN MIDDLE OF THE PACK."
"THIS TIME, NONE OF US HAD A CLEAR SHOT."

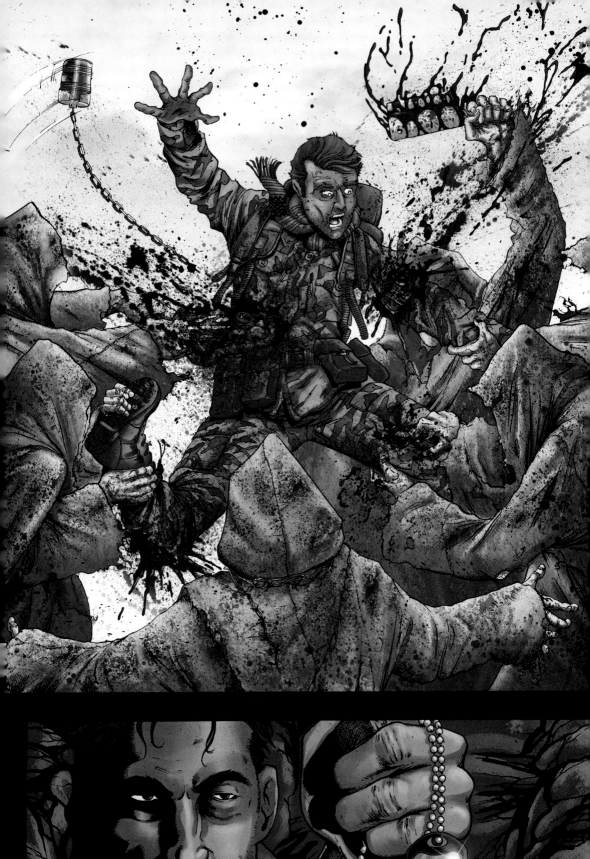

I TOOK
THESE OFF
WHAT LANDED
AT MY FEET.

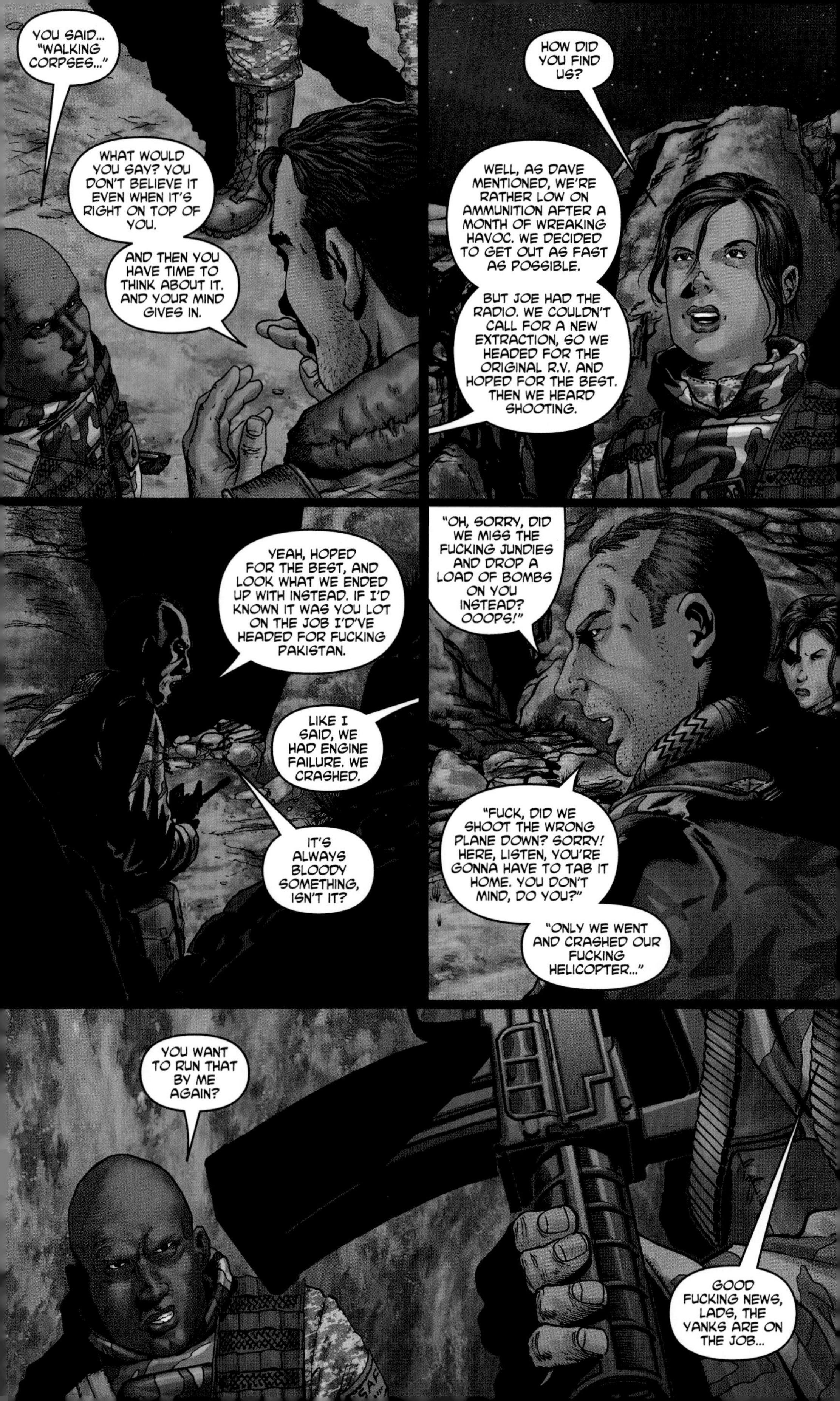

YOU SAID... "WALKING CORPSES..."
WHAT WOULD YOU SAY? YOU DON'T BELIEVE IT EVEN WHEN IT'S RIGHT ON TOP OF YOU.
AND THEN YOU HAVE TIME TO THINK ABOUT IT. AND YOUR MIND GIVES IN.
HOW DID YOU FIND US?
WELL, AS DAVE MENTIONED, WE'RE RATHER LOW ON AMMUNITION AFTER A MONTH OF WREAKING HAVOC. WE DECIDED TO GET OUT AS FAST AS POSSIBLE.
BUT JOE HAD THE RADIO. WE COULDN'T CALL FOR A NEW EXTRACTION, SO WE HEADED FOR THE ORIGINAL R.V. AND HOPED FOR THE BEST. THEN WE HEARD SHOOTING.
YEAH, HOPED FOR THE BEST, AND LOOK WHAT WE ENDED UP WITH INSTEAD. IF I'D KNOWN IT WAS YOU LOT ON THE JOB I'D'VE HEADED FOR FUCKING PAKISTAN.
LIKE I SAID, WE HAD ENGINE FAILURE. WE CRASHED.
IT'S ALWAYS BLOODY SOMETHING, ISN'T IT?
"OH, SORRY, DID WE MISS THE FUCKING JUNDIES AND DROP A LOAD OF BOMBS ON YOU INSTEAD? OOOPS!"
"FUCK, DID WE SHOOT THE WRONG PLANE DOWN? SORRY! HERE, LISTEN, YOU'RE GONNA HAVE TO TAB IT HOME. YOU DON'T MIND, DO YOU?"
"ONLY WE WENT AND CRASHED OUR FUCKING HELICOPTER..."
YOU WANT TO RUN THAT BY ME AGAIN?
GOOD FUCKING NEWS, LADS, THE YANKS ARE ON THE JOB...

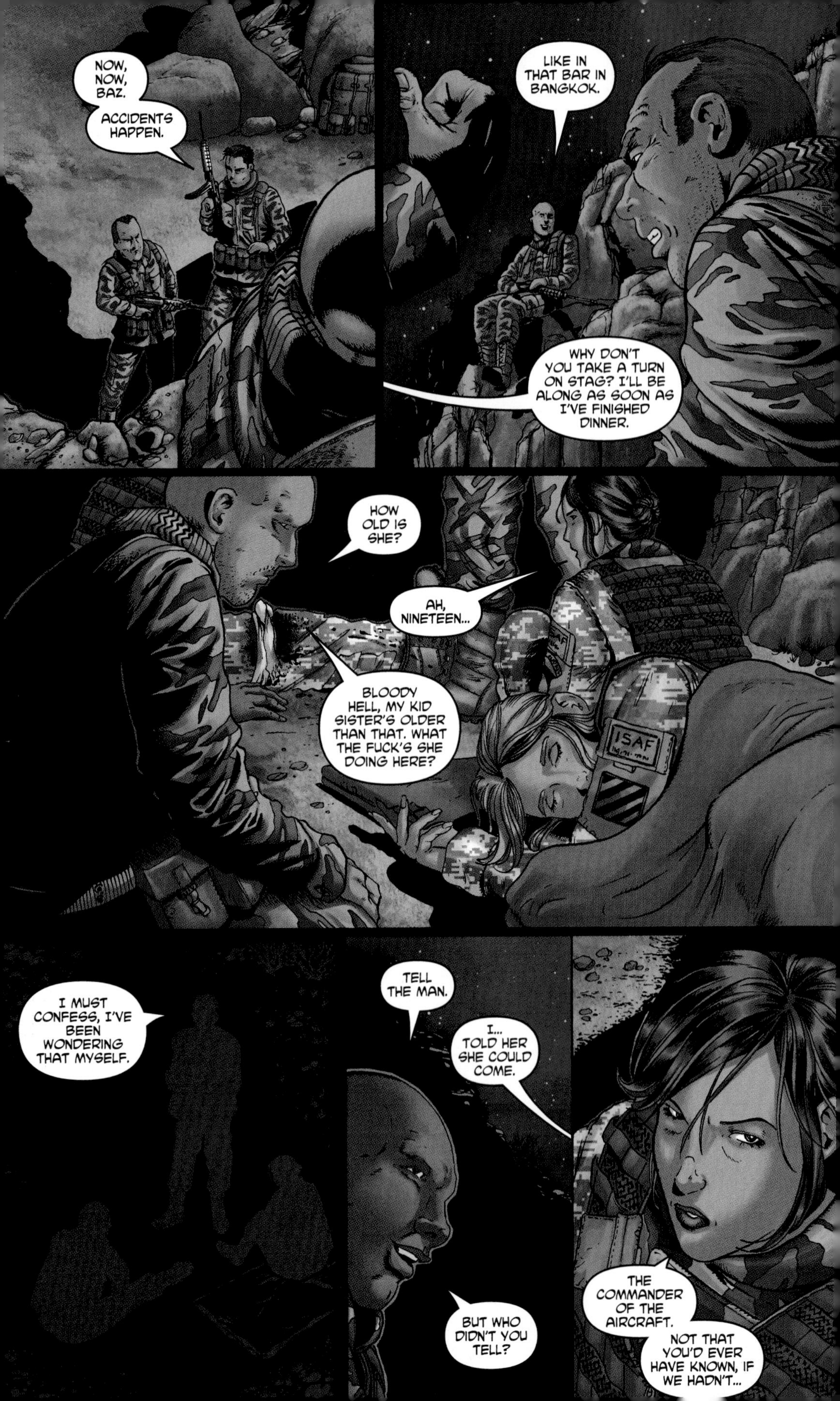
NOW, NOW, BAZ.
ACCIDENTS HAPPEN.
LIKE IN THAT BAR IN BANGKOK.
WHY DON'T YOU TAKE A TURN ON STAG? I'LL BE ALONG AS SOON AS I'VE FINISHED DINNER.
HOW OLD IS SHE?
AH, NINETEEN...
BLOODY HELL, MY KID SISTER'S OLDER THAN THAT. WHAT THE FUCK'S SHE DOING HERE?
ISAF
ISAF
I MUST CONFESS, I'VE BEEN WONDERING THAT MYSELF.
TELL THE MAN.
I... TOLD HER SHE COULD COME.
BUT WHO DIDN'T YOU TELL?
THE COMMANDER OF THE AIRCRAFT.
NOT THAT YOU'D EVER HAVE KNOWN, IF WE HADN'T...

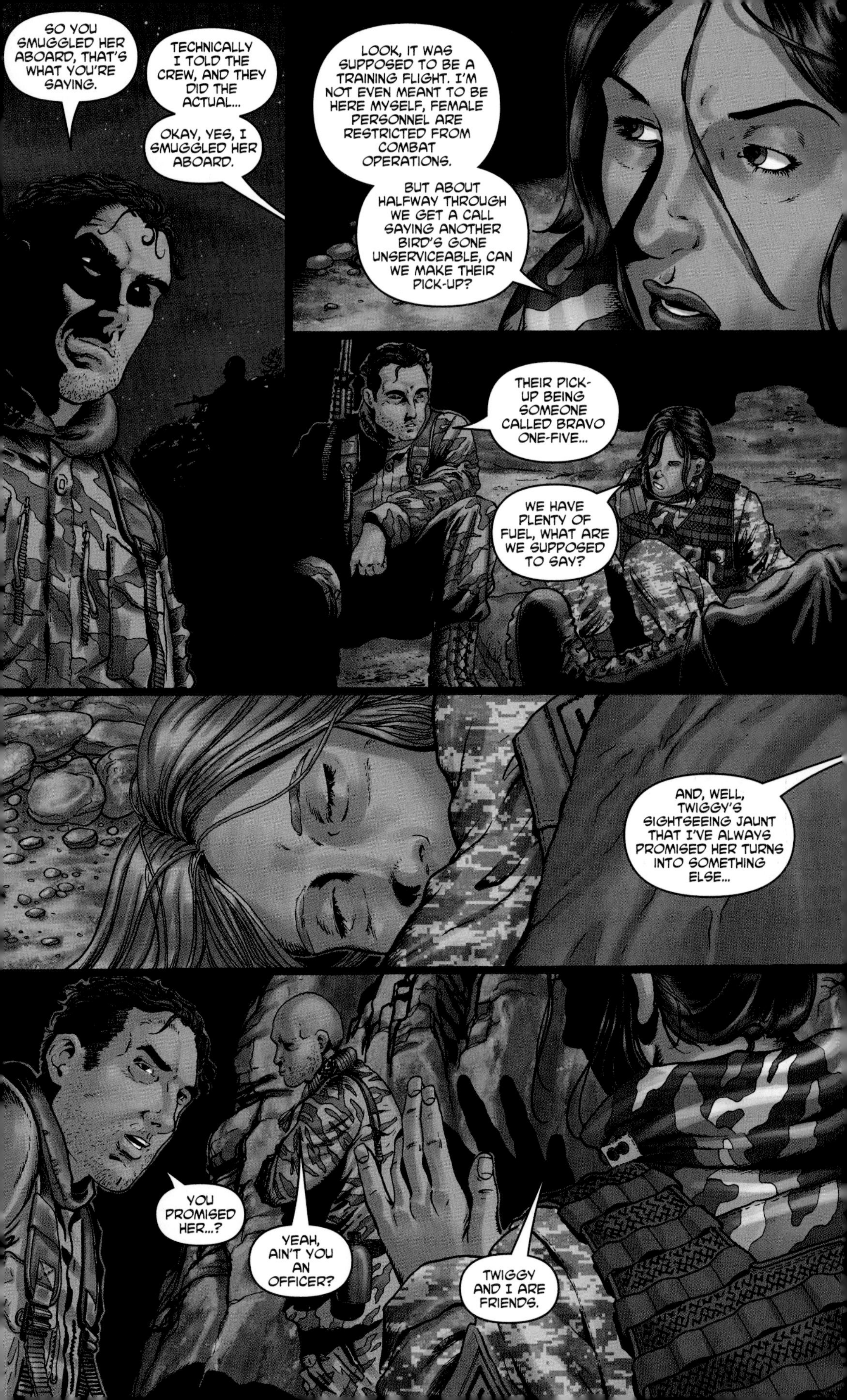
SO YOU SMUGGLED HER ABOARD, THAT'S WHAT YOU'RE SAYING.
TECHNICALLY I TOLD THE CREW, AND THEY DID THE ACTUAL...
OKAY, YES, I SMUGGLED HER ABOARD.
LOOK, IT WAS SUPPOSED TO BE A TRAINING FLIGHT. I'M NOT EVEN MEANT TO BE HERE MYSELF, FEMALE PERSONNEL ARE RESTRICTED FROM COMBAT OPERATIONS.
BUT ABOUT HALFWAY THROUGH WE GET A CALL SAYING ANOTHER BIRD'S GONE UNSERVICEABLE, CAN WE MAKE THEIR PICK-UP?
THEIR PICK-UP BEING SOMEONE CALLED BRAVO ONE-FIVE...
WE HAVE PLENTY OF FUEL, WHAT ARE WE SUPPOSED TO SAY?
AND, WELL, TWIGGY'S SIGHTSEEING JAUNT THAT I'VE ALWAYS PROMISED HER TURNS INTO SOMETHING ELSE...
YOU PROMISED HER...?
YEAH, AIN'T YOU AN OFFICER?
TWIGGY AND I ARE FRIENDS.

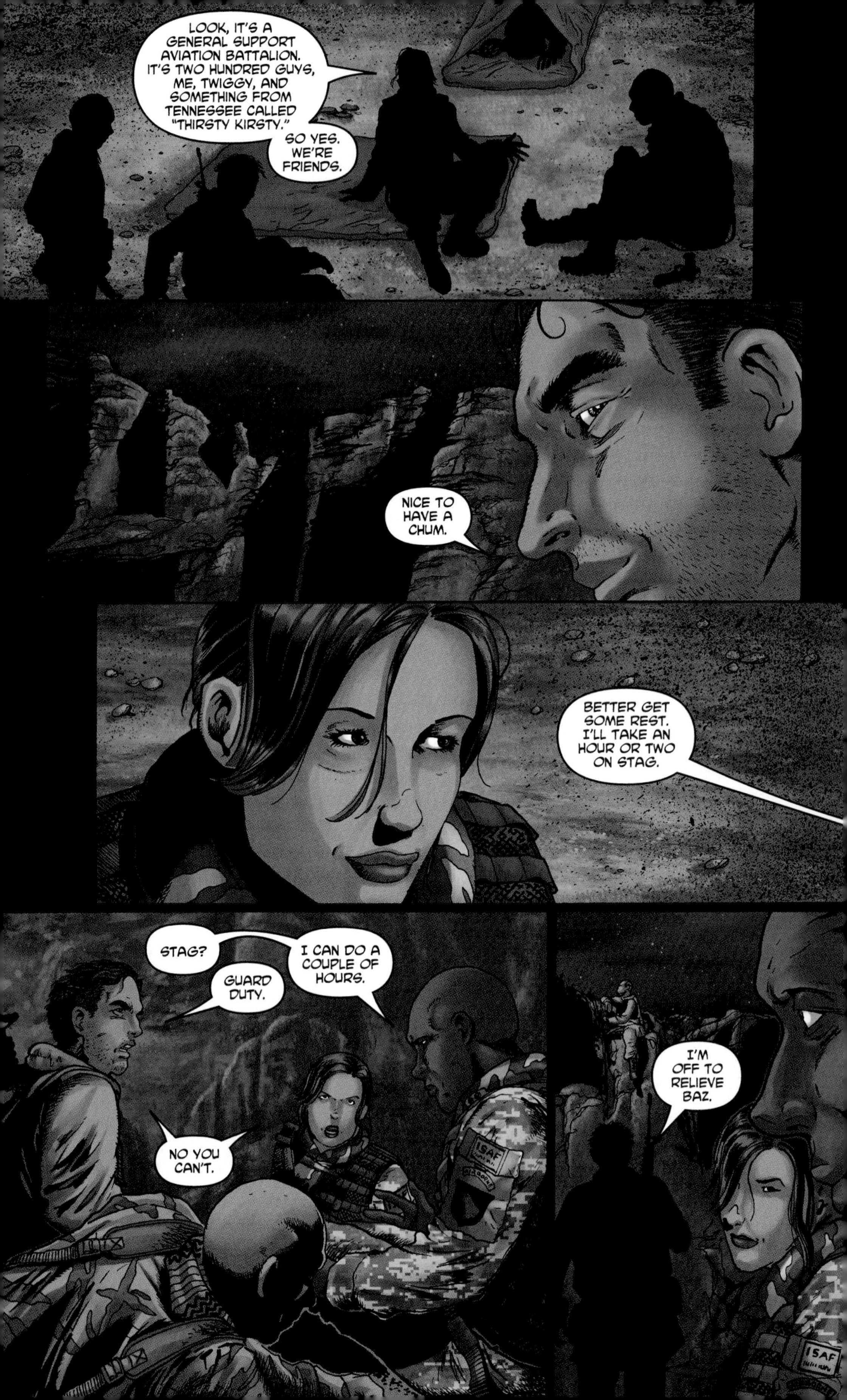
LOOK, IT'S A GENERAL SUPPORT AVIATION BATTALION. IT'S TWO HUNDRED GUYS, ME, TWIGGY, AND SOMETHING FROM TENNESSEE CALLED "THIRSTY KIRSTY."
SO YES. WE'RE FRIENDS.
NICE TO HAVE A CHUM.
BETTER GET SOME REST. I'LL TAKE AN HOUR OR TWO ON STAG.
STAG?
GUARD DUTY.
I CAN DO A COUPLE OF HOURS.
NO YOU CAN'T.
I'M OFF TO RELIEVE BAZ.
ISAF
ISAF

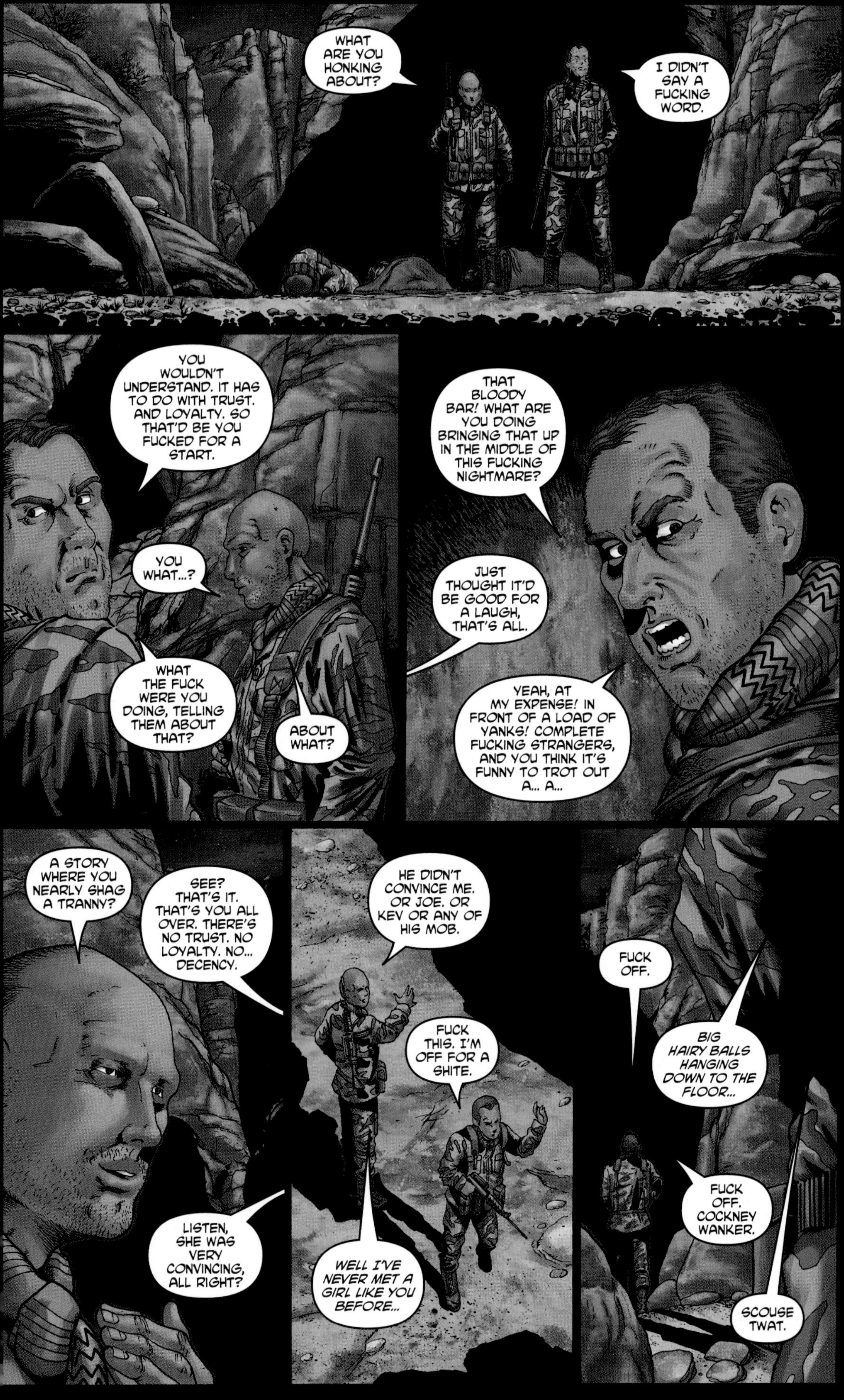
WHAT ARE YOU HONKING ABOUT?
I DIDN'T SAY A FUCKING WORD.
YOU WOULDN'T UNDERSTAND. IT HAS TO DO WITH TRUST. AND LOYALTY. SO THAT'D BE YOU FUCKED FOR A START.
YOU WHAT...?
WHAT THE FUCK WERE YOU DOING, TELLING THEM ABOUT THAT?
ABOUT WHAT?
THAT BLOODY BAR! WHAT ARE YOU DOING BRINGING THAT UP IN THE MIDDLE OF THIS FUCKING NIGHTMARE?
JUST THOUGHT IT'D BE GOOD FOR A LAUGH, THAT'S ALL.
YEAH, AT MY EXPENSE! IN FRONT OF A LOAD OF YANKS! COMPLETE FUCKING STRANGERS, AND YOU THINK IT'S FUNNY TO TROT OUT A... A...
A STORY WHERE YOU NEARLY SHAG A TRANNY?
SEE? THAT'S IT. THAT'S YOU ALL OVER. THERE'S NO TRUST. NO LOYALTY. NO... DECENCY.
LISTEN, SHE WAS VERY CONVINCING, ALL RIGHT?
HE DIDN'T CONVINCE ME. OR JOE. OR KEV OR ANY OF HIS MOB.
FUCK THIS. I'M OFF FOR A SHITE.
WELL I'VE NEVER MET A GIRL LIKE YOU BEFORE...
FUCK OFF.
BIG HAIRY BALLS HANGING DOWN TO THE FLOOR...
FUCK OFF. COCKNEY WANKER.
SCOUSE TWAT.

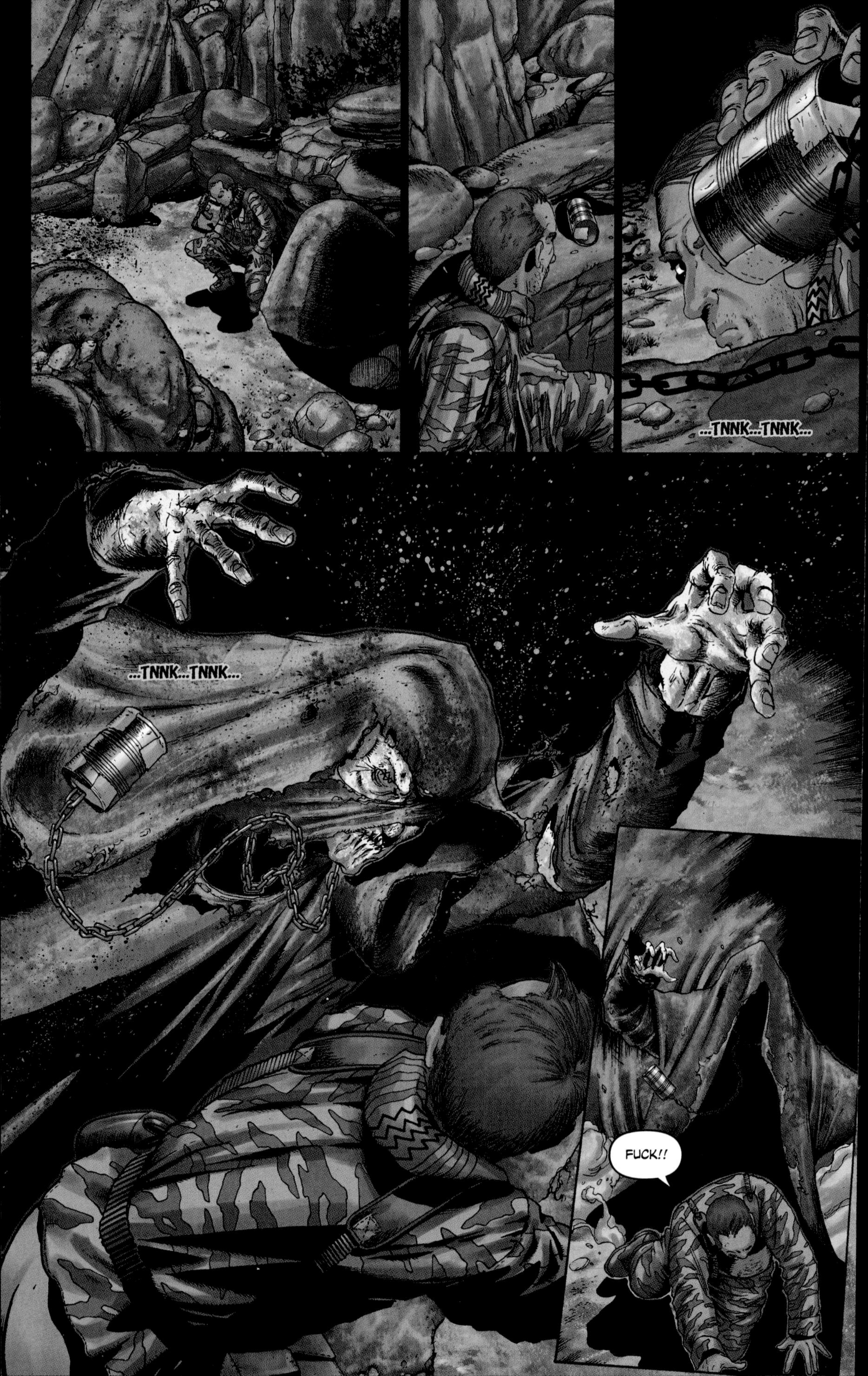
...TNNK...TNNK...
...TNNK...TNNK...
FUCK!!

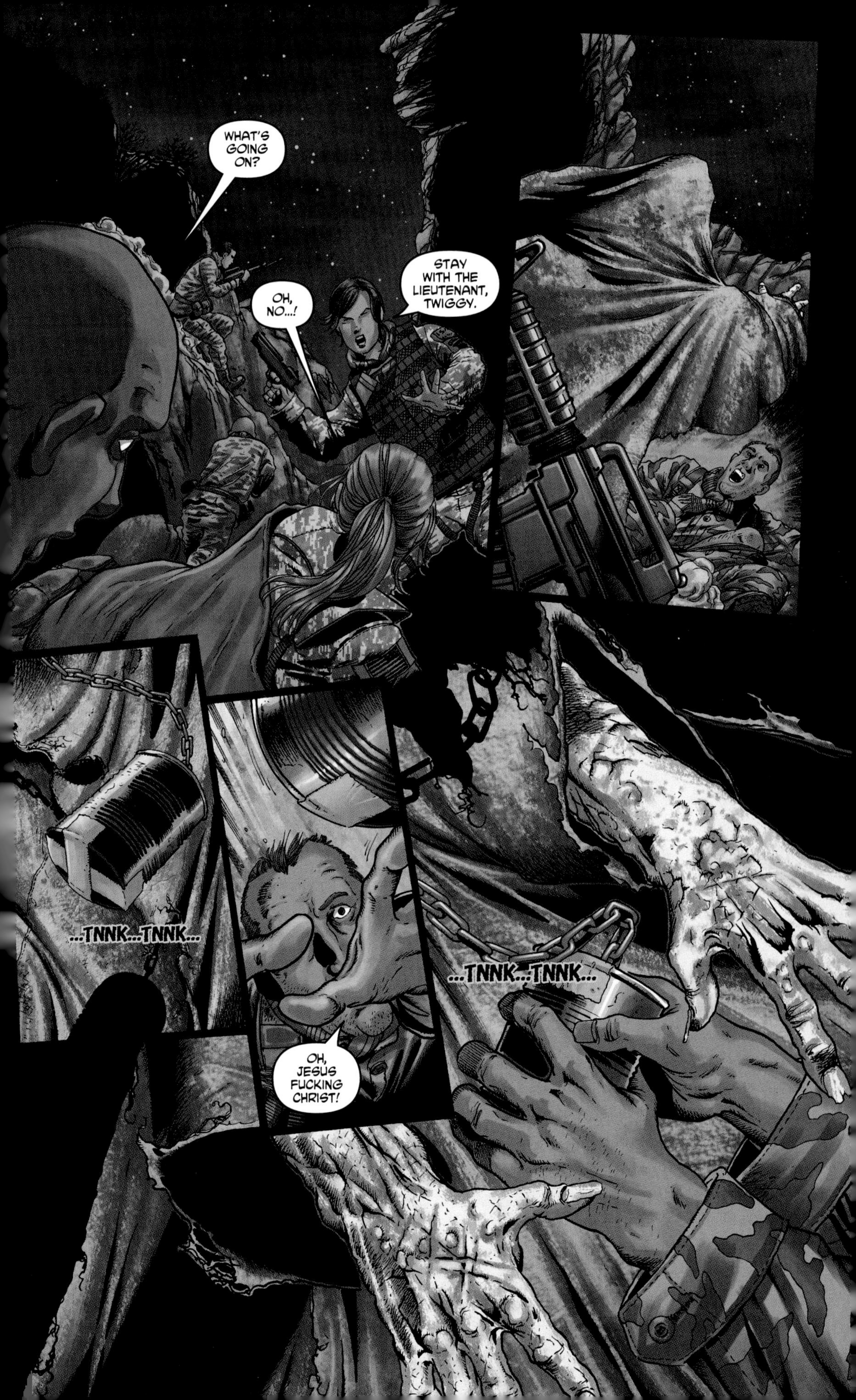
WHAT'S GOING ON?
OH, NO...!
STAY WITH THE LIEUTENANT, TWIGGY.
...TNNK...TNNK...
OH, JESUS FUCKING CHRIST!
...TNNK...TNNK...

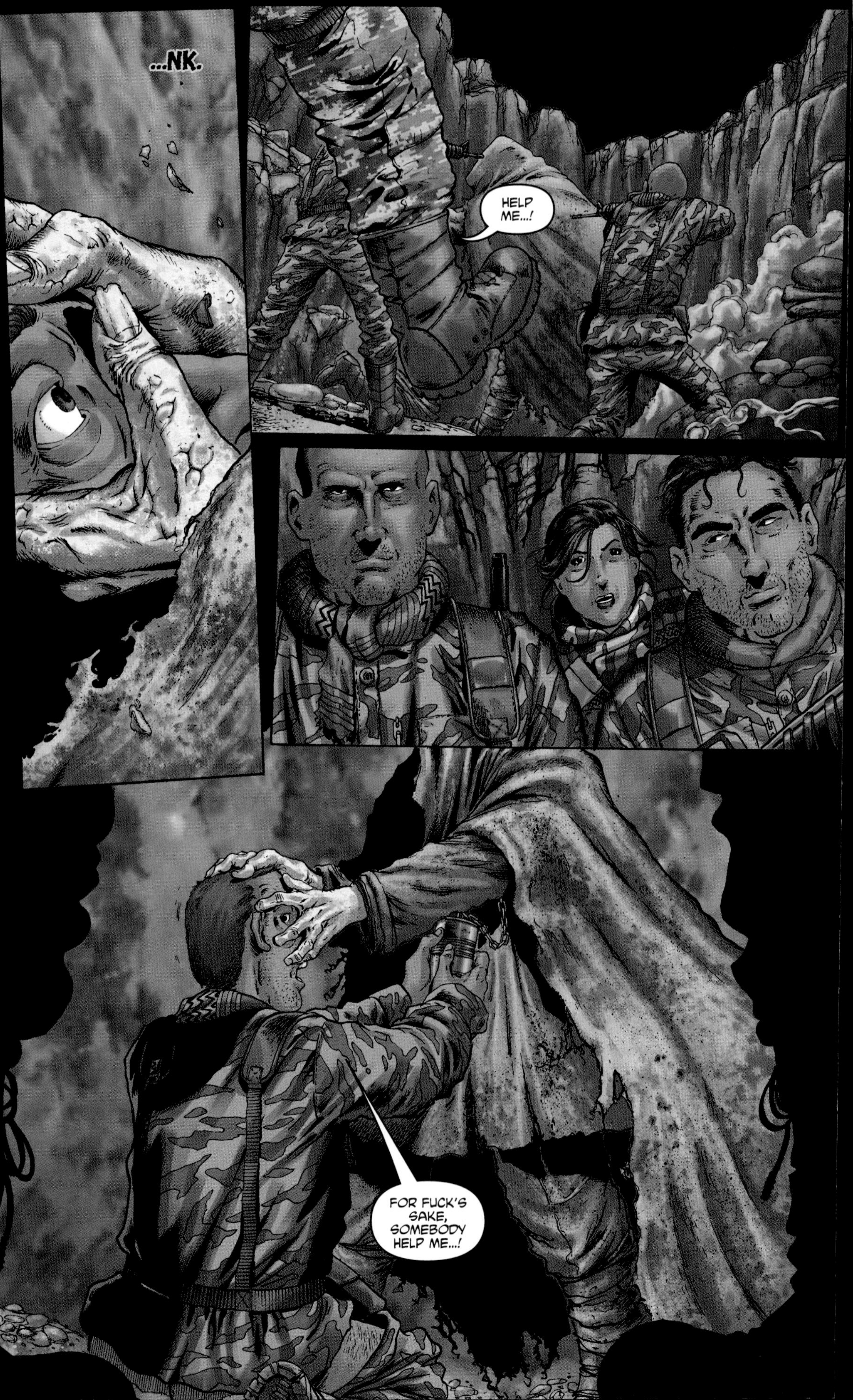
...NK.
HELP ME...!
FOR FUCK'S SAKE, SOMEBODY HELP ME...!

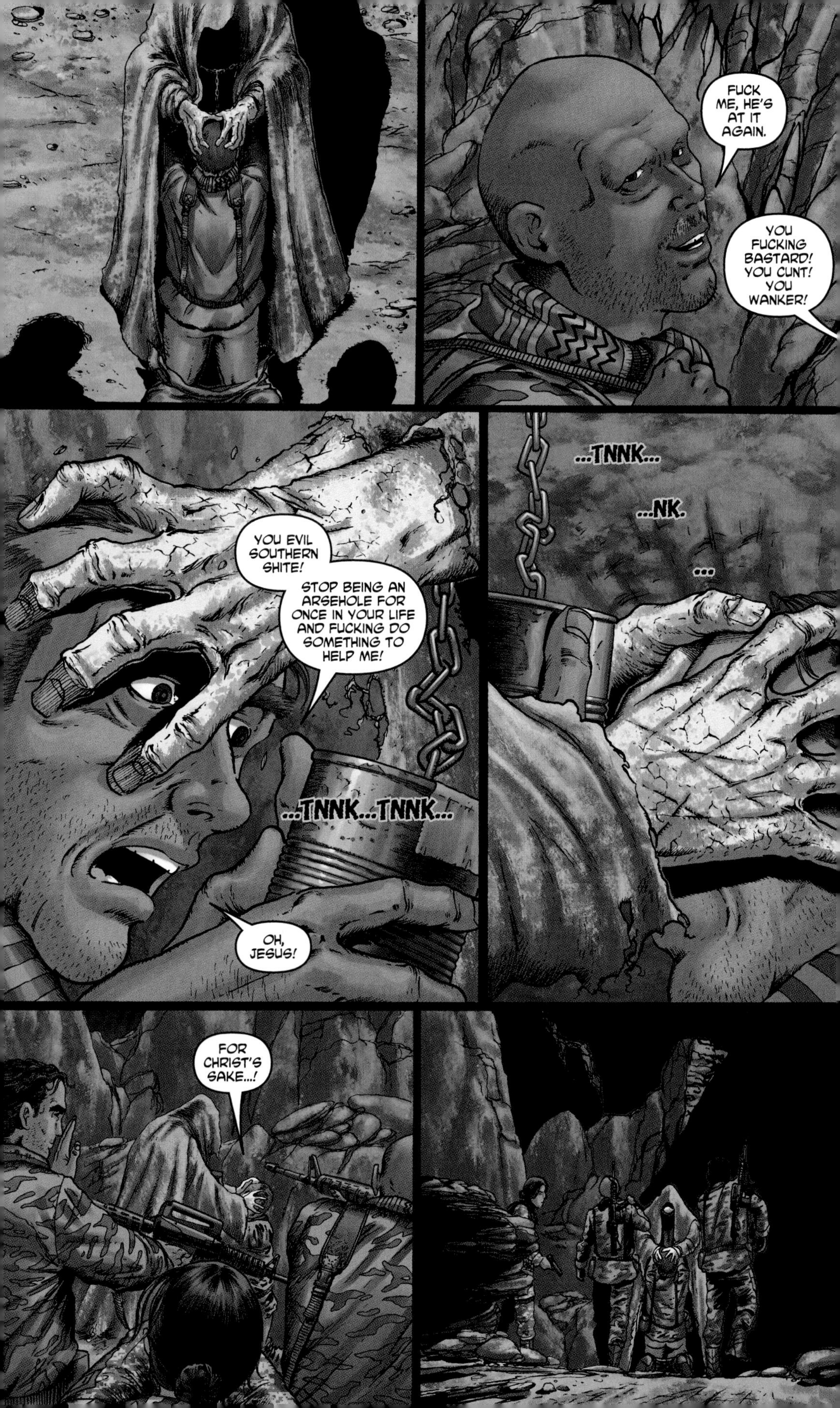
FUCK ME, HE'S AT IT AGAIN.
YOU FUCKING BASTARD! YOU CUNT! YOU WANKER!
YOU EVIL SOUTHERN SHITE!
STOP BEING AN ARSEHOLE FOR ONCE IN YOUR LIFE AND FUCKING DO SOMETHING TO HELP ME!
...TNNK...TNNK...
OH, JESUS!
...TNNK...
...NK.
...
FOR CHRIST'S SAKE...!

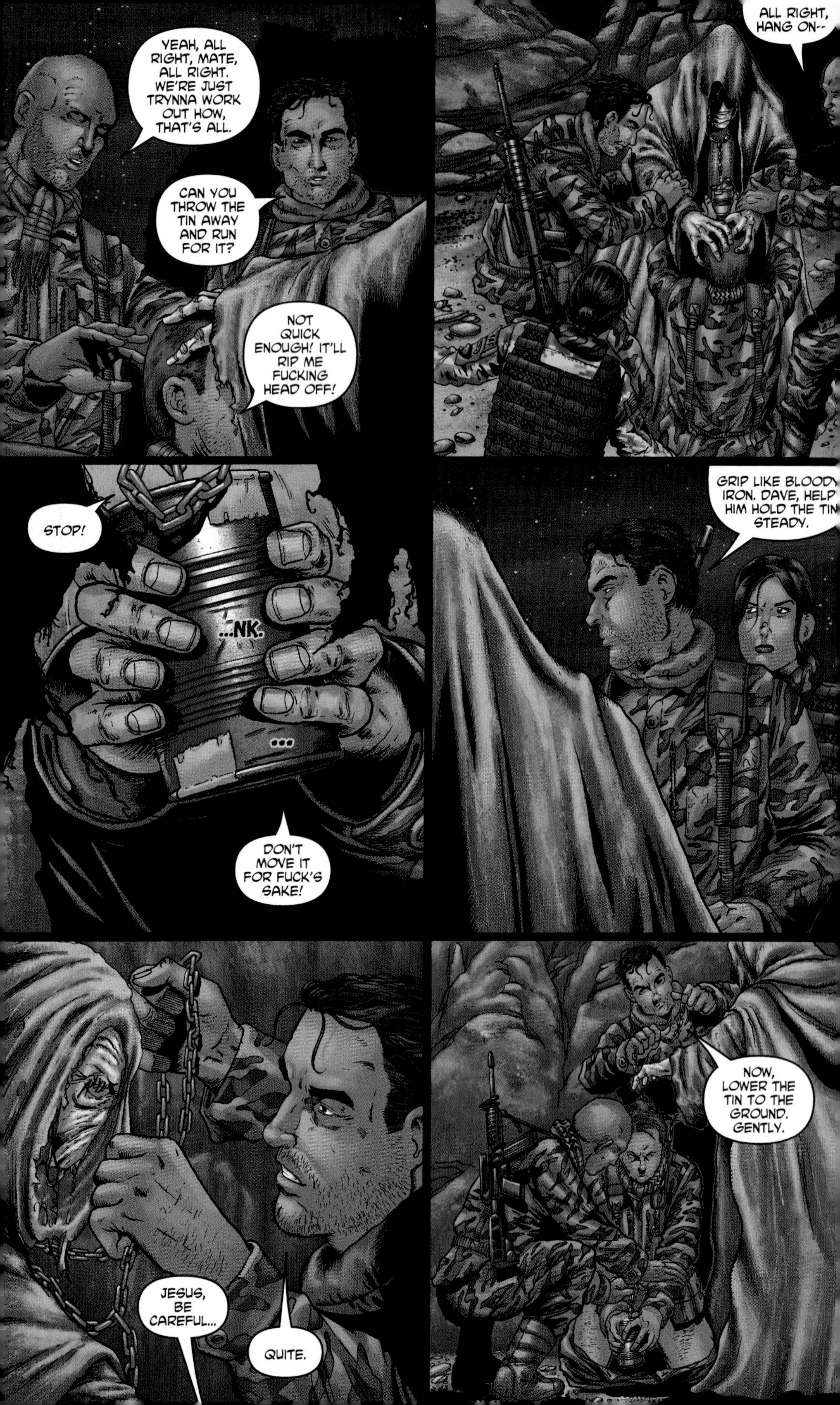
YEAH, ALL RIGHT, MATE, ALL RIGHT. WE'RE JUST TRYNNA WORK OUT HOW, THAT'S ALL.
CAN YOU THROW THE TIN AWAY AND RUN FOR IT?
NOT QUICK ENOUGH! IT'LL RIP ME FUCKING HEAD OFF!
ALL RIGHT, HANG ON--
STOP!
...NK.
...
DON'T MOVE IT FOR FUCK'S SAKE!
GRIP LIKE BLOODY IRON. DAVE, HELP HIM HOLD THE TIN STEADY.
JESUS, BE CAREFUL...
QUITE.
NOW, LOWER THE TIN TO THE GROUND. GENTLY.

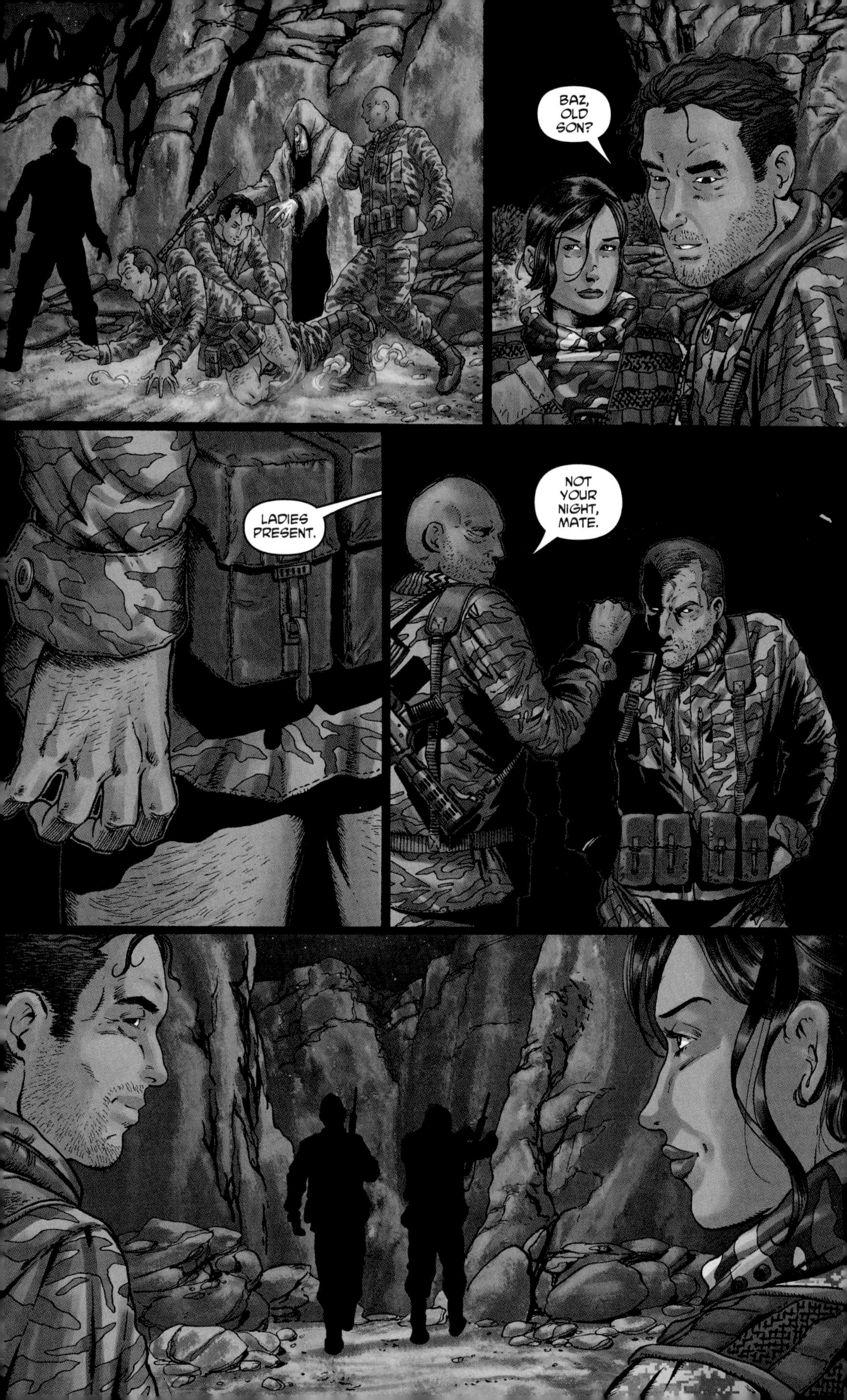
BAZ, OLD SON?
LADIES PRESENT.
NOT YOUR NIGHT, MATE.

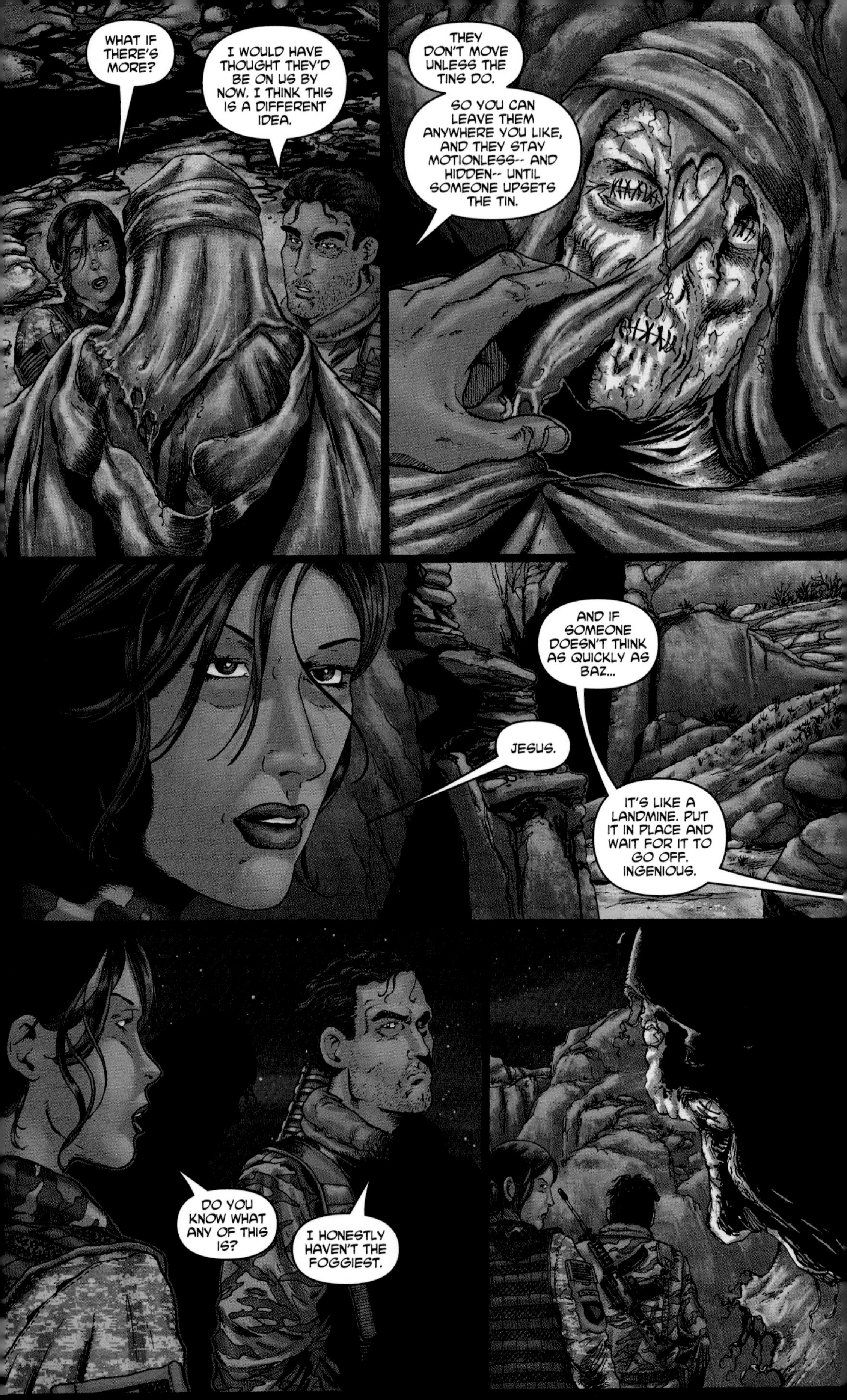
WHAT IF THERE'S MORE?
I WOULD HAVE THOUGHT THEY'D BE ON US BY NOW. I THINK THIS IS A DIFFERENT IDEA.
THEY DON'T MOVE UNLESS THE TINS DO.
SO YOU CAN LEAVE THEM ANYWHERE YOU LIKE, AND THEY STAY MOTIONLESS-- AND HIDDEN-- UNTIL SOMEONE UPSETS THE TIN.
AND IF SOMEONE DOESN'T THINK AS QUICKLY AS BAZ...
JESUS.
IT'S LIKE A LANDMINE. PUT IT IN PLACE AND WAIT FOR IT TO GO OFF. INGENIOUS.
DO YOU KNOW WHAT ANY OF THIS IS?
I HONESTLY HAVEN'T THE FOGGIEST.

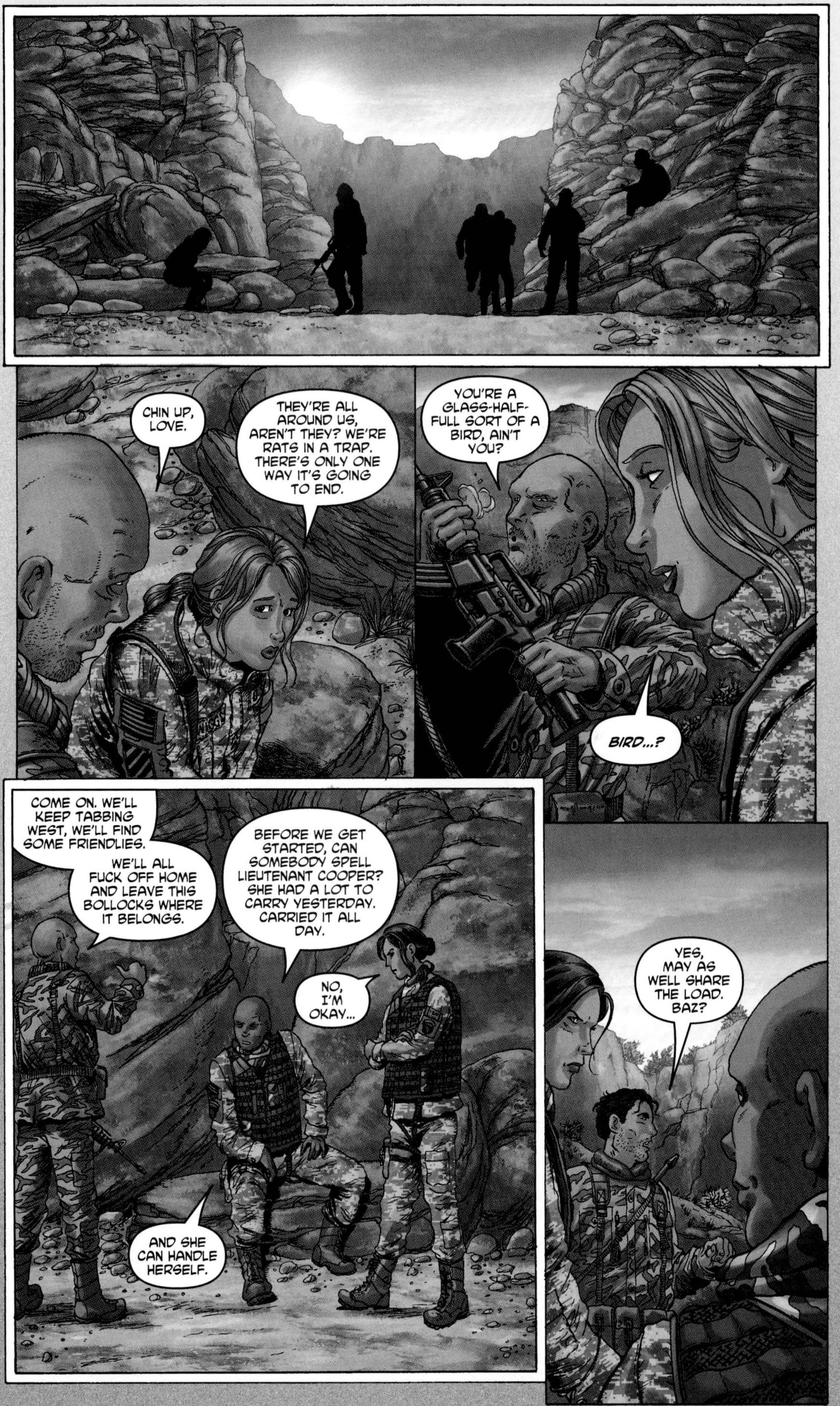
CHIN UP, LOVE.
THEY'RE ALL AROUND US, AREN'T THEY? WE'RE RATS IN A TRAP. THERE'S ONLY ONE WAY IT'S GOING TO END.
YOU'RE A GLASS-HALF-FULL SORT OF A BIRD, AIN'T YOU?
BIRD...?
COME ON. WE'LL KEEP TABBING WEST, WE'LL FIND SOME FRIENDLIES.
WE'LL ALL FUCK OFF HOME AND LEAVE THIS BOLLOCKS WHERE IT BELONGS.
BEFORE WE GET STARTED, CAN SOMEBODY SPELL LIEUTENANT COOPER? SHE HAD A LOT TO CARRY YESTERDAY. CARRIED IT ALL DAY.
NO, I'M OKAY...
AND SHE CAN HANDLE HERSELF.
YES, MAY AS WELL SHARE THE LOAD. BAZ?

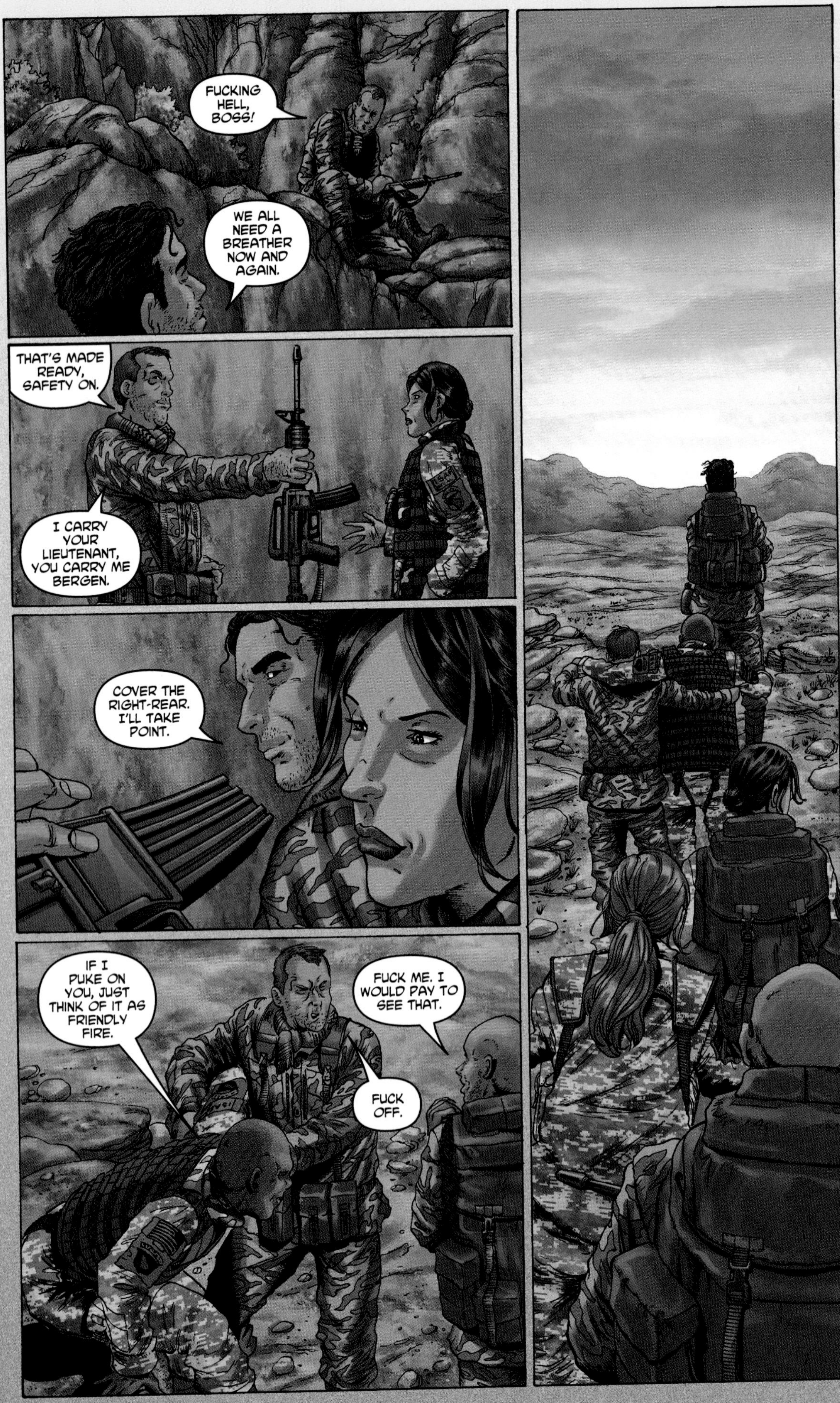
FUCKING HELL, BOSS!
WE ALL NEED A BREATHER NOW AND AGAIN.
THAT'S MADE READY, SAFETY ON.
I CARRY YOUR LIEUTENANT, YOU CARRY ME BERGEN.
COVER THE RIGHT-REAR. I'LL TAKE POINT.
IF I PUKE ON YOU, JUST THINK OF IT AS FRIENDLY FIRE.
FUCK ME. I WOULD PAY TO SEE THAT.
FUCK OFF.

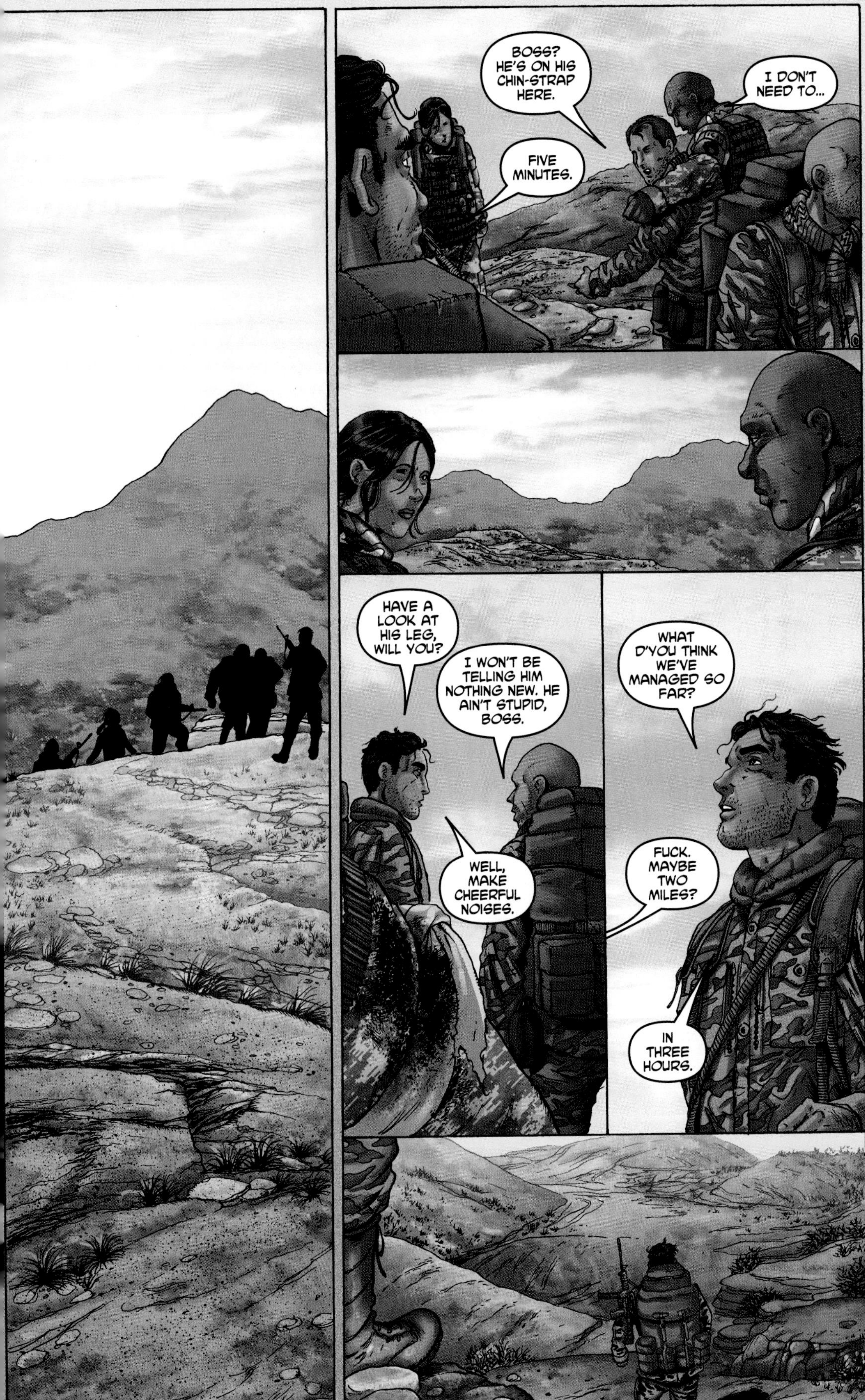
BOSS? HE'S ON HIS CHIN-STRAP HERE.
I DON'T NEED TO...
FIVE MINUTES.
HAVE A LOOK AT HIS LEG, WILL YOU?
I WON'T BE TELLING HIM NOTHING NEW. HE AIN'T STUPID, BOSS.
WELL, MAKE CHEERFUL NOISES.
WHAT D'YOU THINK WE'VE MANAGED SO FAR?
FUCK. MAYBE TWO MILES?
IN THREE HOURS.

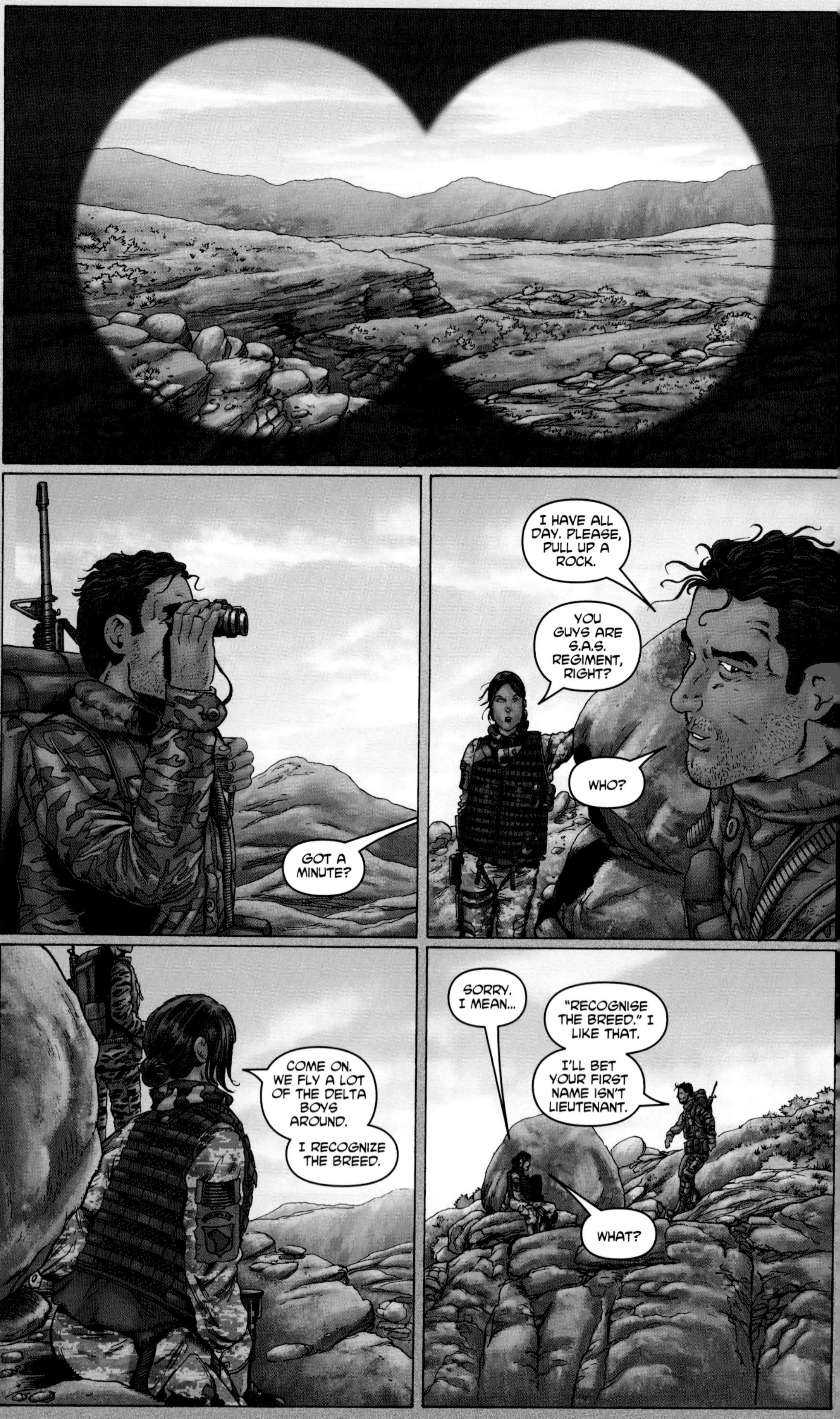

GOT A MINUTE?
I HAVE ALL DAY. PLEASE, PULL UP A ROCK.
YOU GUYS ARE S.A.S. REGIMENT, RIGHT?
WHO?
COME ON. WE FLY A LOT OF THE DELTA BOYS AROUND.
I RECOGNIZE THE BREED.
SORRY. I MEAN...
"RECOGNISE THE BREED." I LIKE THAT.
I'LL BET YOUR FIRST NAME ISN'T LIEUTENANT.
WHAT?

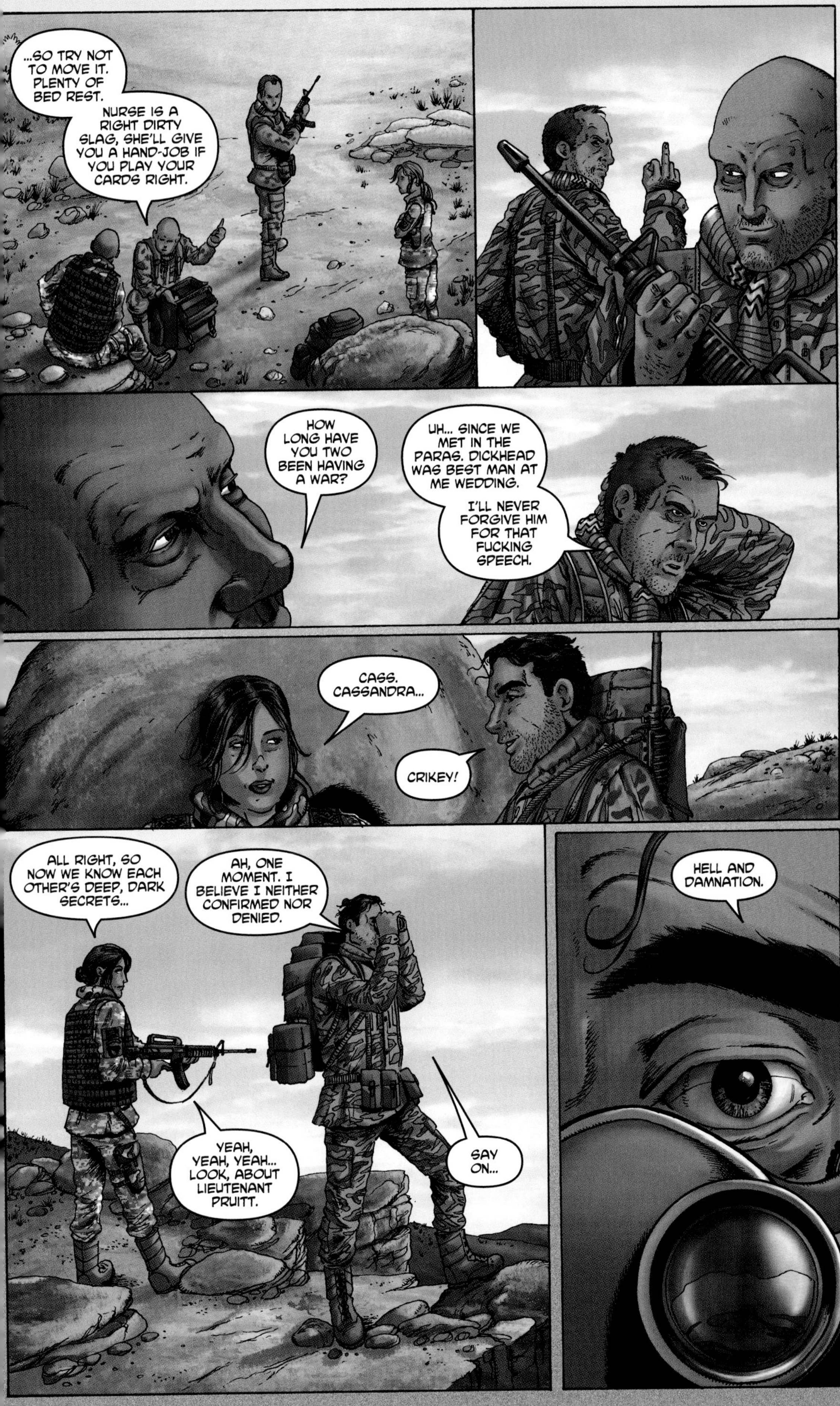
...SO TRY NOT TO MOVE IT. PLENTY OF BED REST.
NURSE IS A RIGHT DIRTY SLAG, SHE'LL GIVE YOU A HAND-JOB IF YOU PLAY YOUR CARDS RIGHT.
HOW LONG HAVE YOU TWO BEEN HAVING A WAR?
UH... SINCE WE MET IN THE PARAS. DICKHEAD WAS BEST MAN AT ME WEDDING.
I'LL NEVER FORGIVE HIM FOR THAT FUCKING SPEECH.
CASS. CASSANDRA...
CRIKEY!
ALL RIGHT, SO NOW WE KNOW EACH OTHER'S DEEP, DARK SECRETS...
AH, ONE MOMENT. I BELIEVE I NEITHER CONFIRMED NOR DENIED.
YEAH, YEAH, YEAH... LOOK, ABOUT LIEUTENANT PRUITT.
SAY ON...
HELL AND DAMNATION.

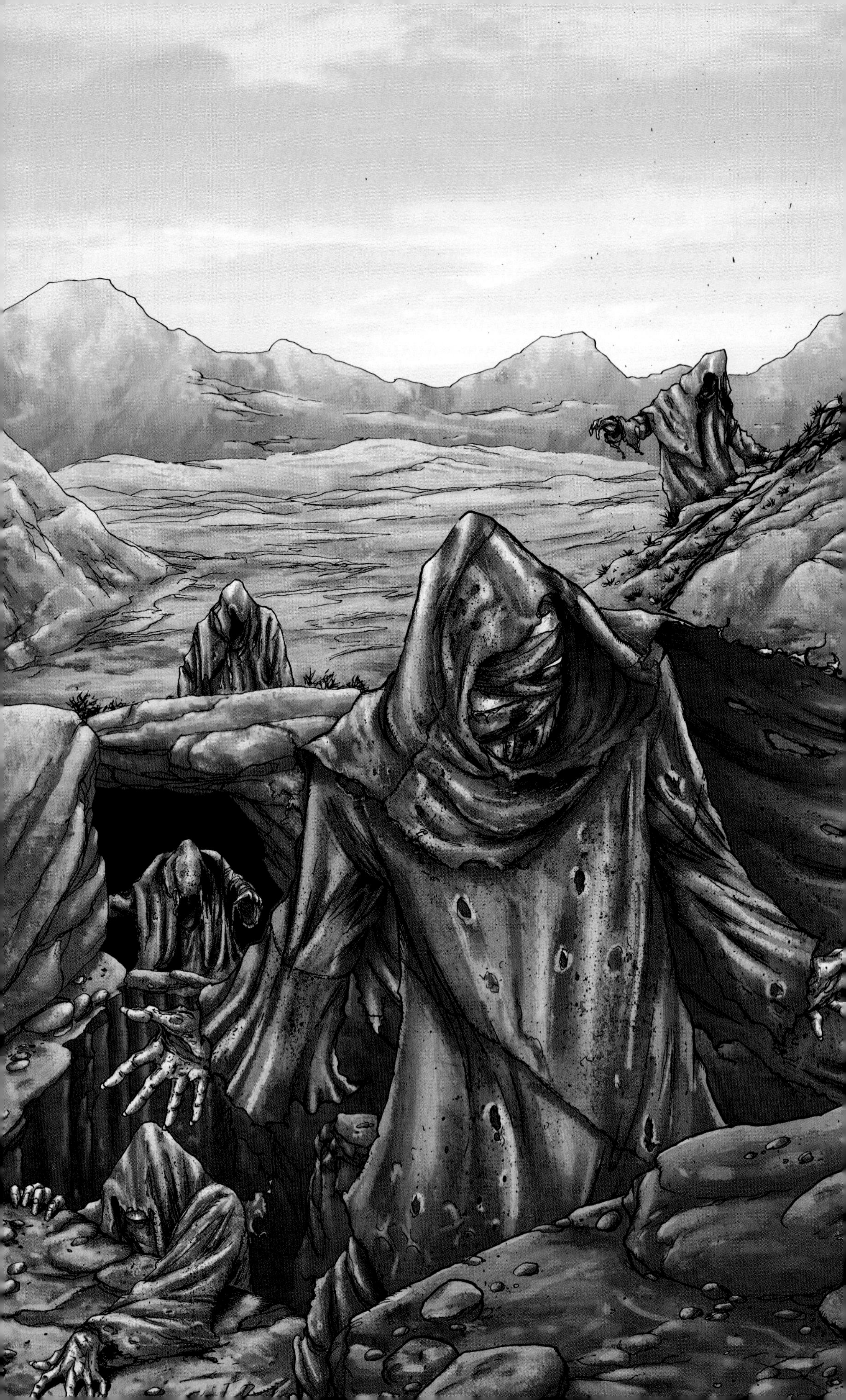

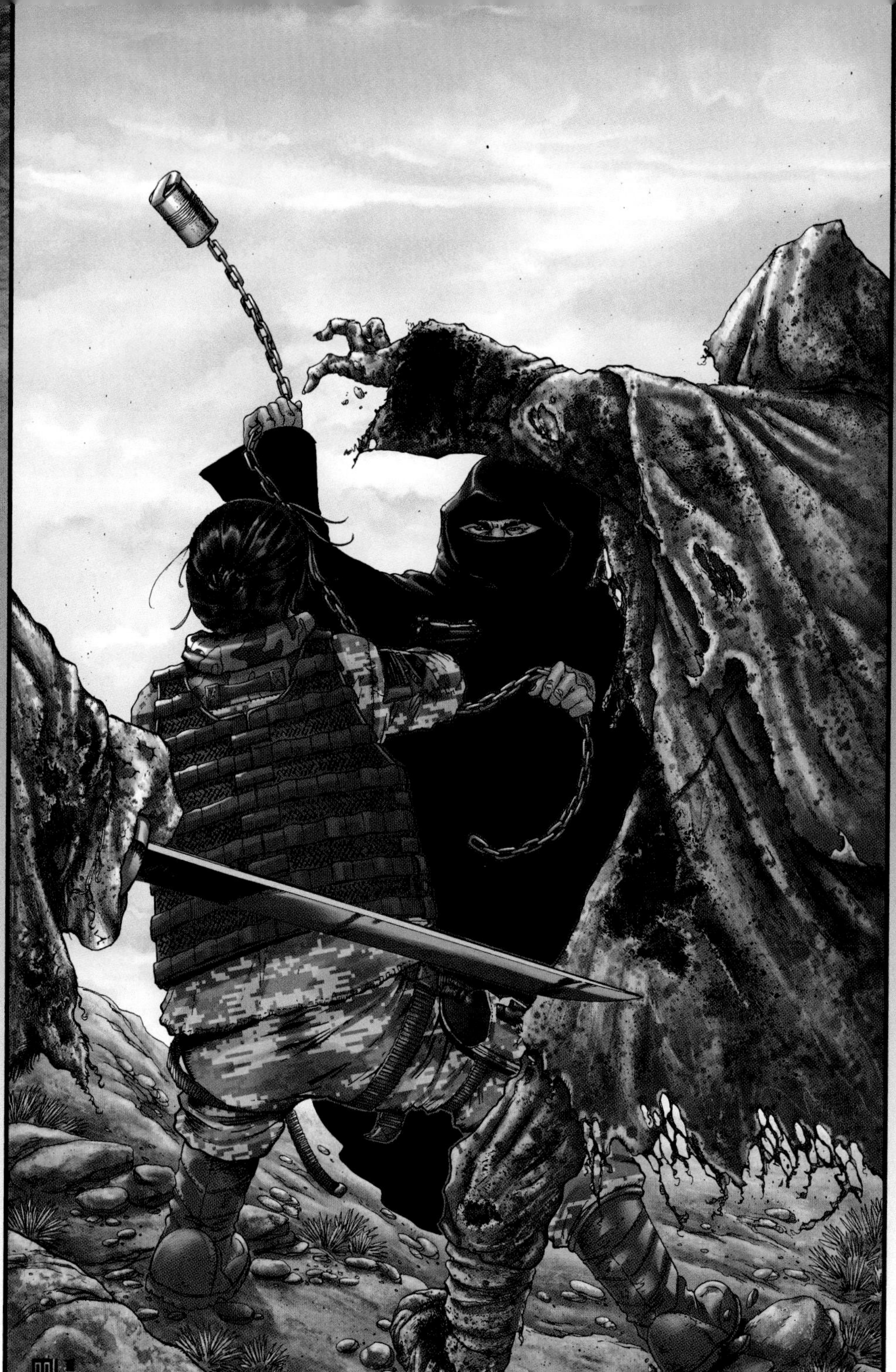

CHAPTER 3

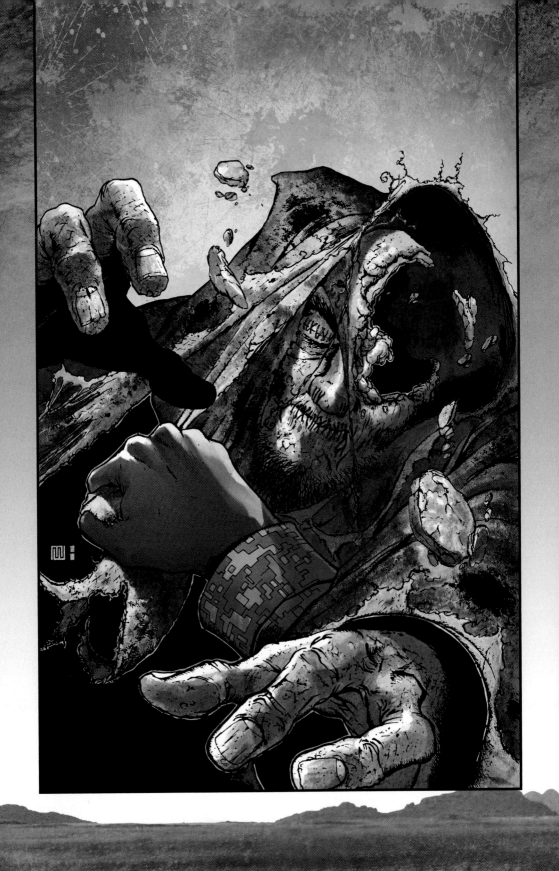

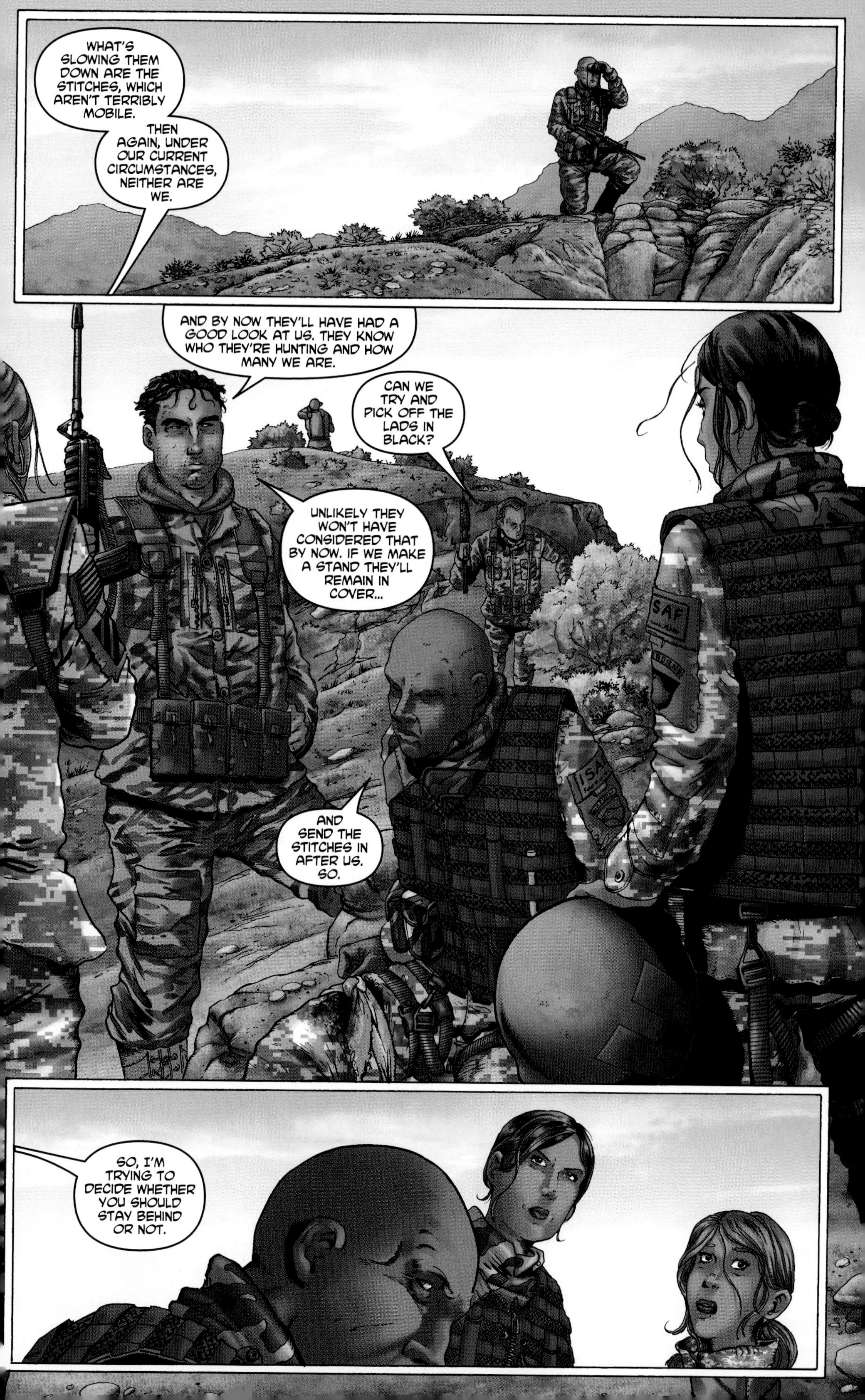
WHAT'S SLOWING THEM DOWN ARE THE STITCHES, WHICH AREN'T TERRIBLY MOBILE.
THEN AGAIN, UNDER OUR CURRENT CIRCUMSTANCES, NEITHER ARE WE.
AND BY NOW THEY'LL HAVE HAD A GOOD LOOK AT US. THEY KNOW WHO THEY'RE HUNTING AND HOW MANY WE ARE.
CAN WE TRY AND PICK OFF THE LADS IN BLACK?
UNLIKELY THEY WON'T HAVE CONSIDERED THAT BY NOW. IF WE MAKE A STAND THEY'LL REMAIN IN COVER...
AND SEND THE STITCHES IN AFTER US. SO.
ISAF
ISAF
SO, I'M TRYING TO DECIDE WHETHER YOU SHOULD STAY BEHIND OR NOT.

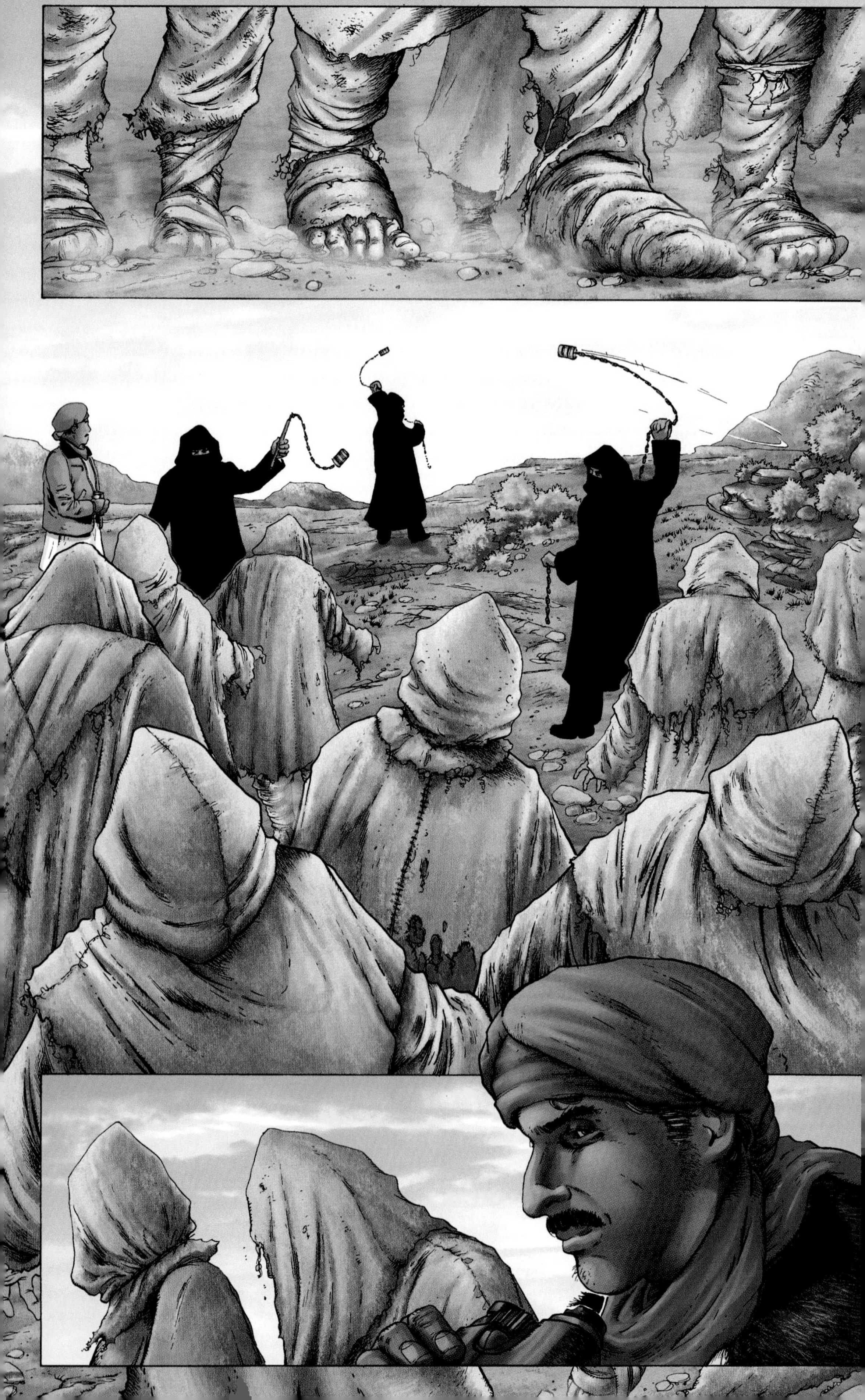

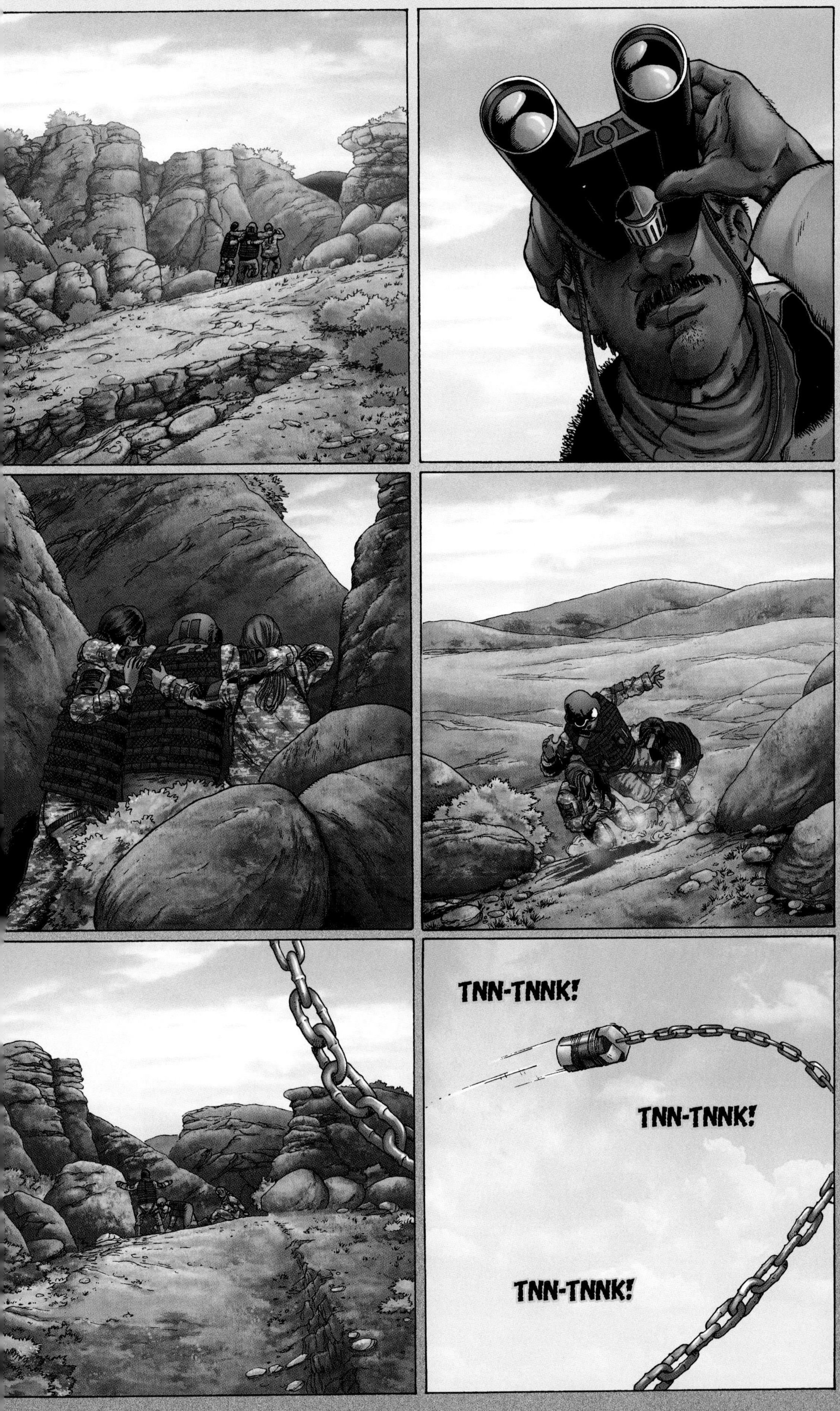
TNN-TNNK!
TNN-TNNK!
TNN-TNNK!

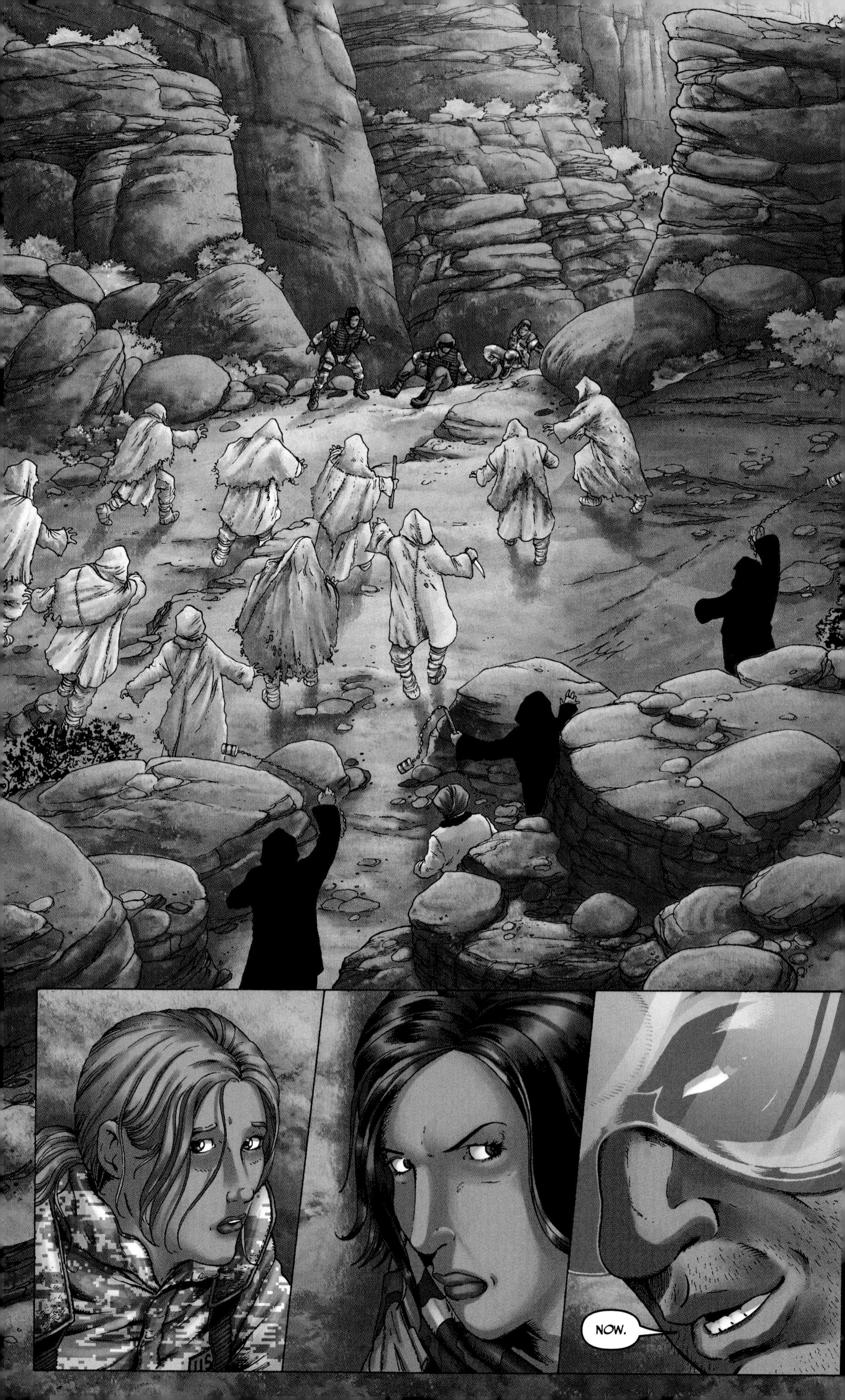
NOW.

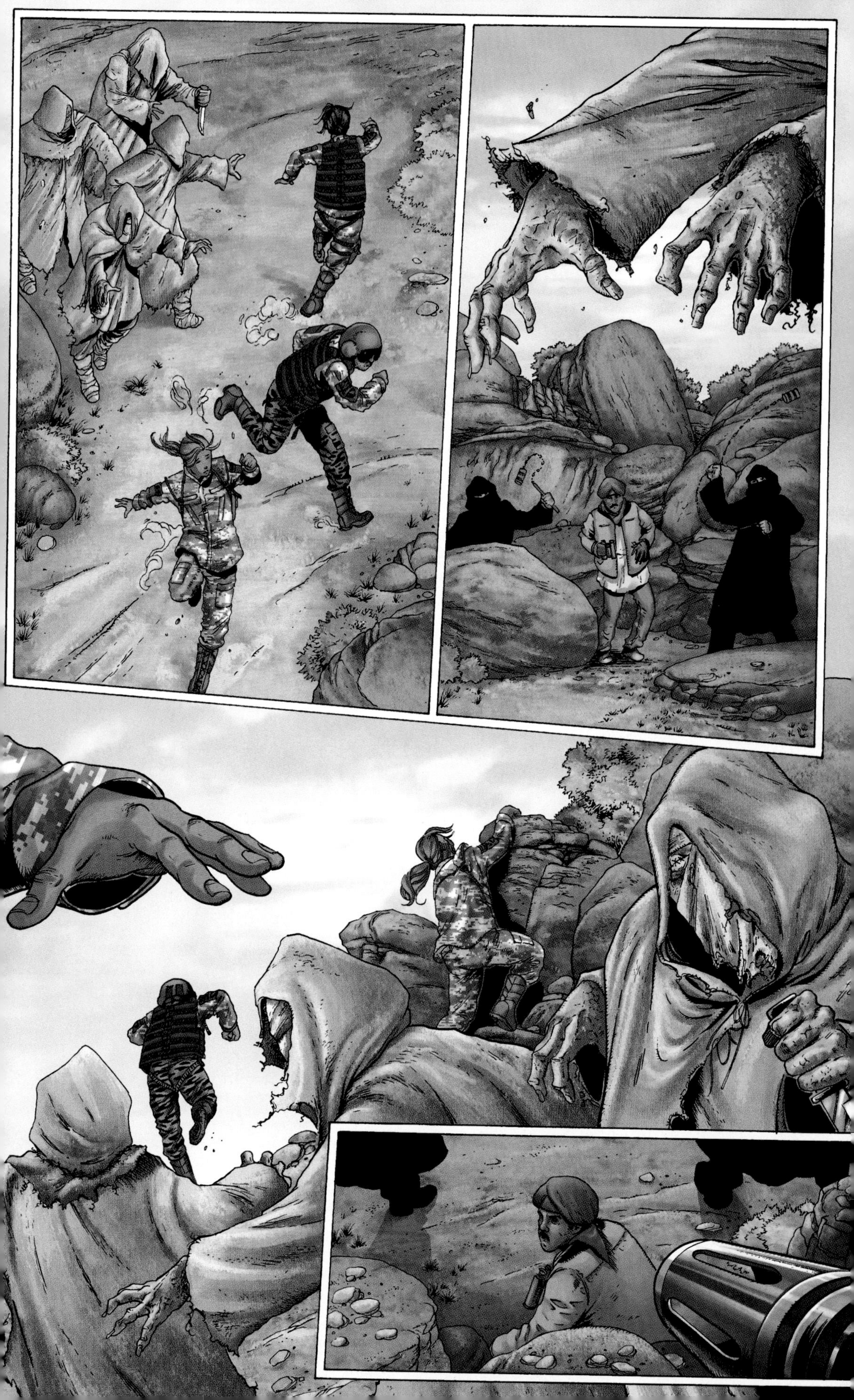

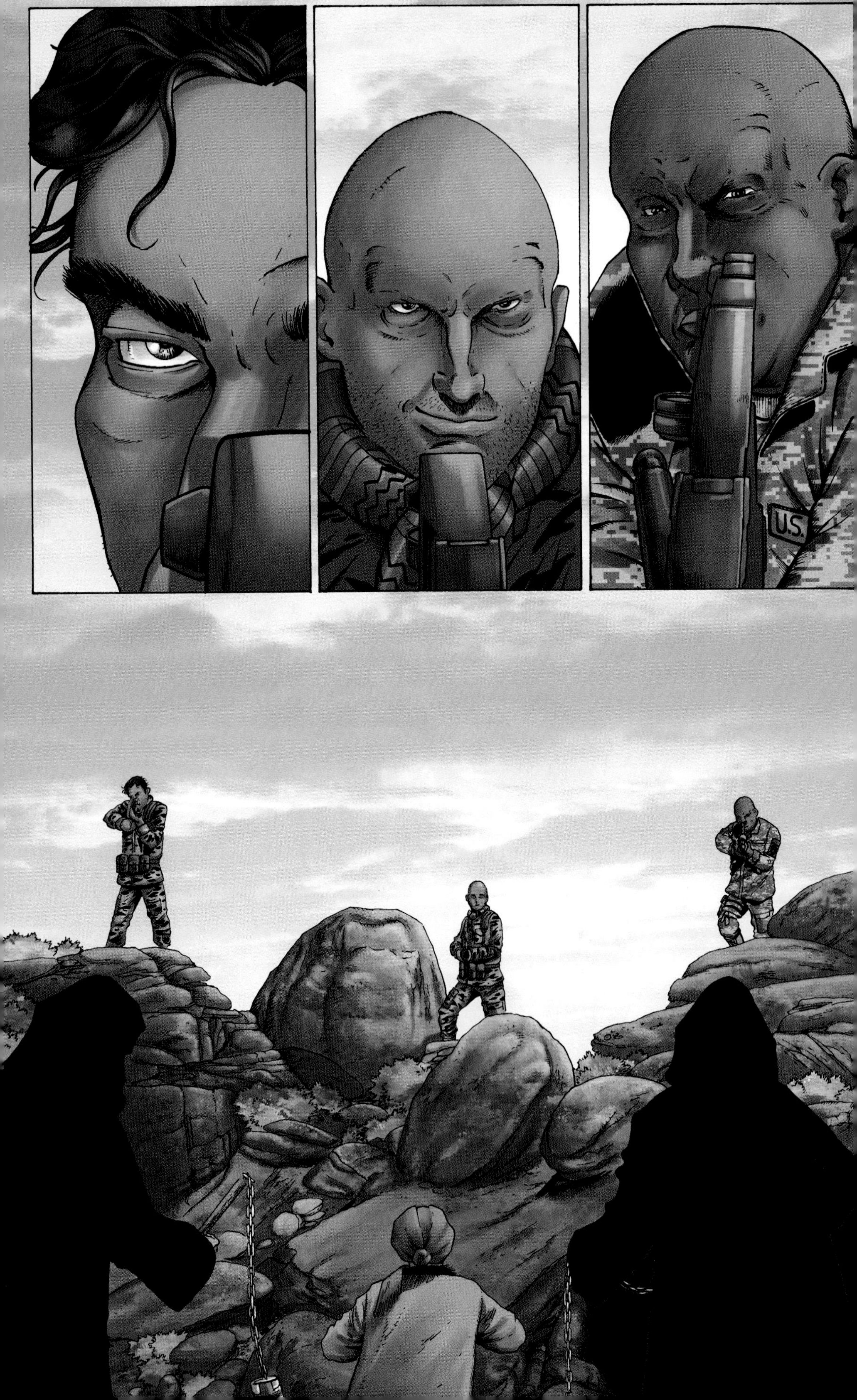
U.S.

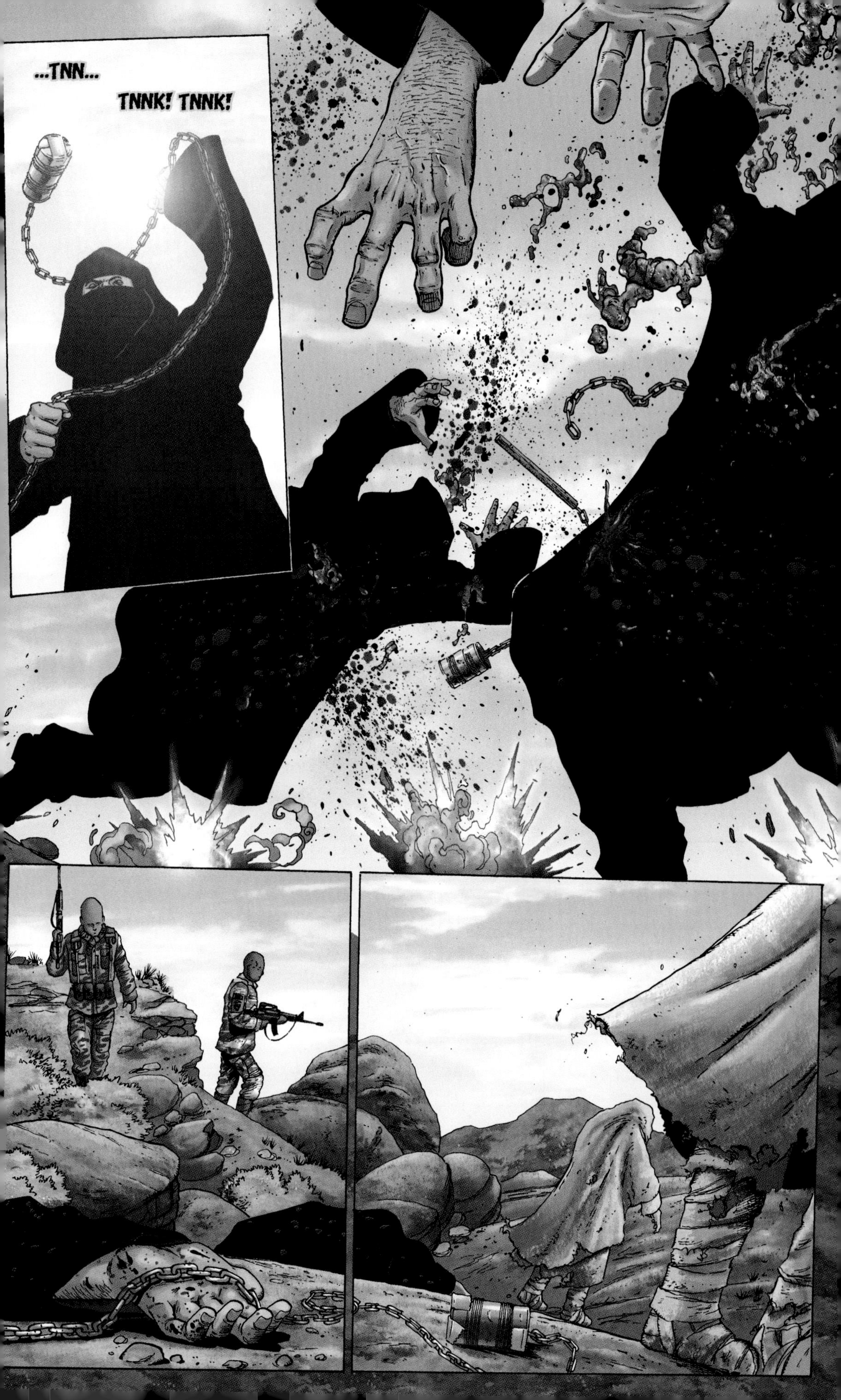
...TNN...
TNNK! TNNK!

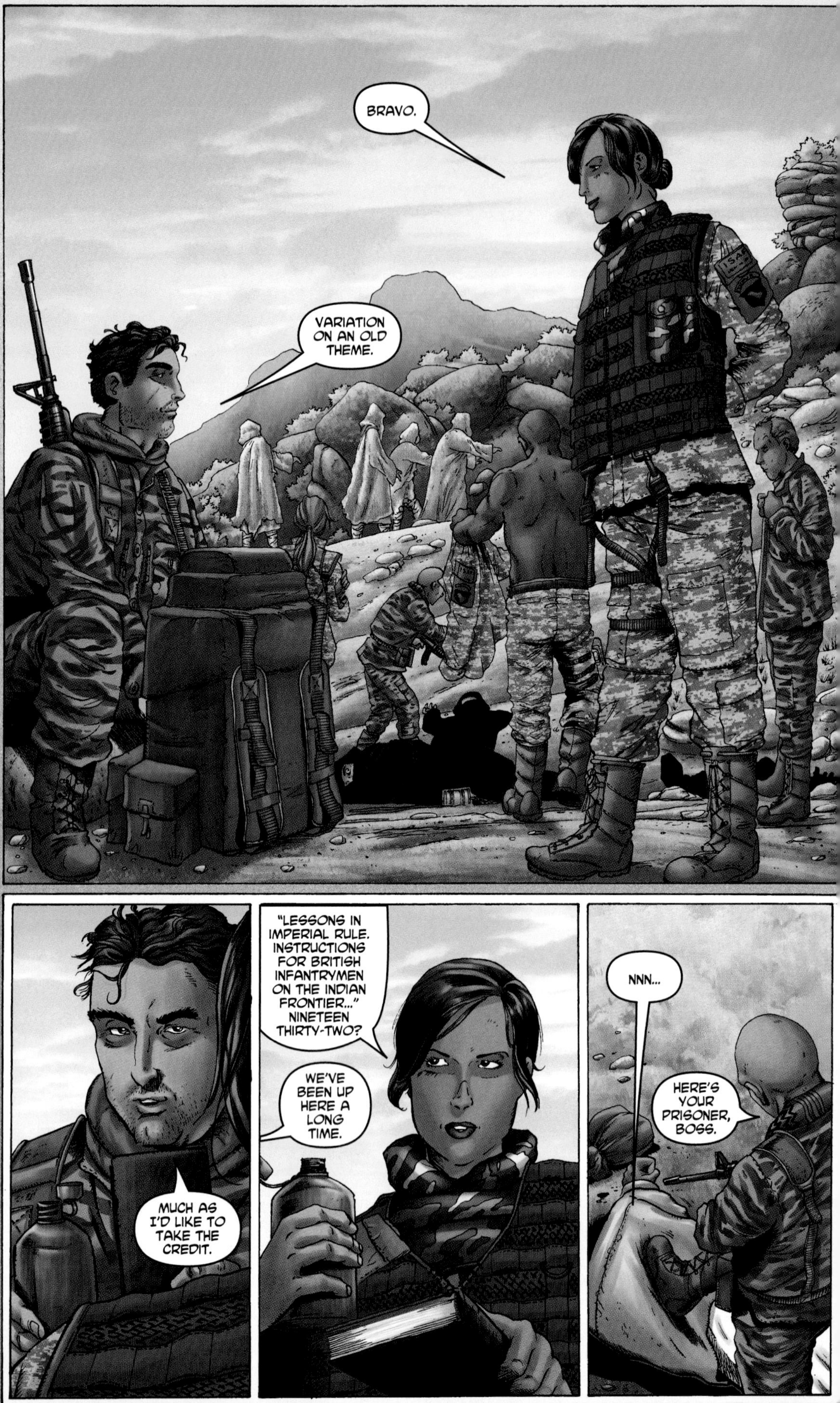
BRAVO.
VARIATION ON AN OLD THEME.
MUCH AS I'D LIKE TO TAKE THE CREDIT.
"LESSONS IN IMPERIAL RULE. INSTRUCTIONS FOR BRITISH INFANTRYMEN ON THE INDIAN FRONTIER..." NINETEEN THIRTY-TWO?
WE'VE BEEN UP HERE A LONG TIME.
NNN...
HERE'S YOUR PRISONER, BOSS.

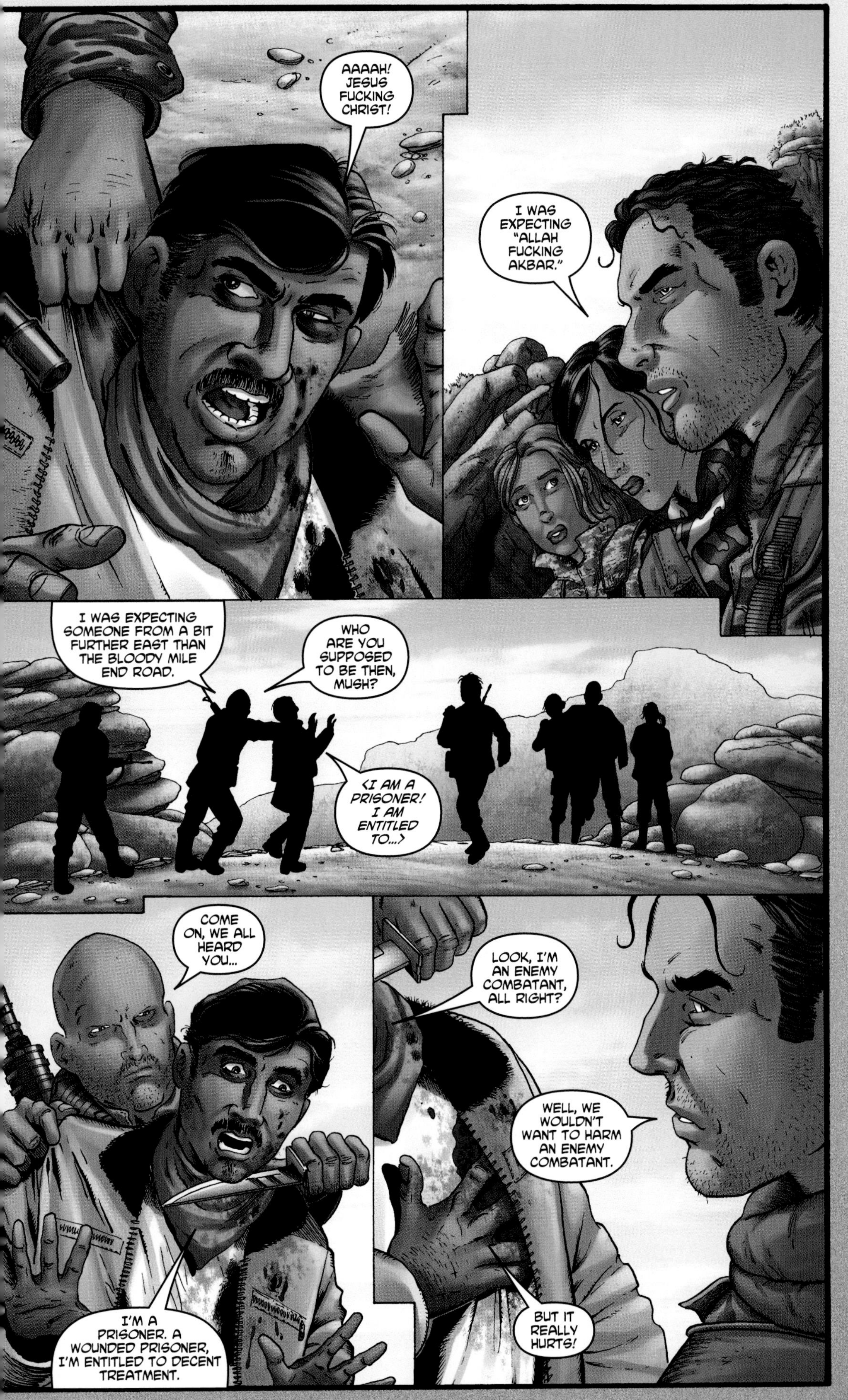
AAAAH! JESUS FUCKING CHRIST!
I WAS EXPECTING "ALLAH FUCKING AKBAR."
I WAS EXPECTING SOMEONE FROM A BIT FURTHER EAST THAN THE BLOODY MILE END ROAD.
WHO ARE YOU SUPPOSED TO BE THEN, MUSH?
<I AM A PRISONER! I AM ENTITLED TO...>
COME ON, WE ALL HEARD YOU...
I'M A PRISONER. A WOUNDED PRISONER, I'M ENTITLED TO DECENT TREATMENT.
LOOK, I'M AN ENEMY COMBATANT, ALL RIGHT?
WELL, WE WOULDN'T WANT TO HARM AN ENEMY COMBATANT.
BUT IT REALLY HURTS!

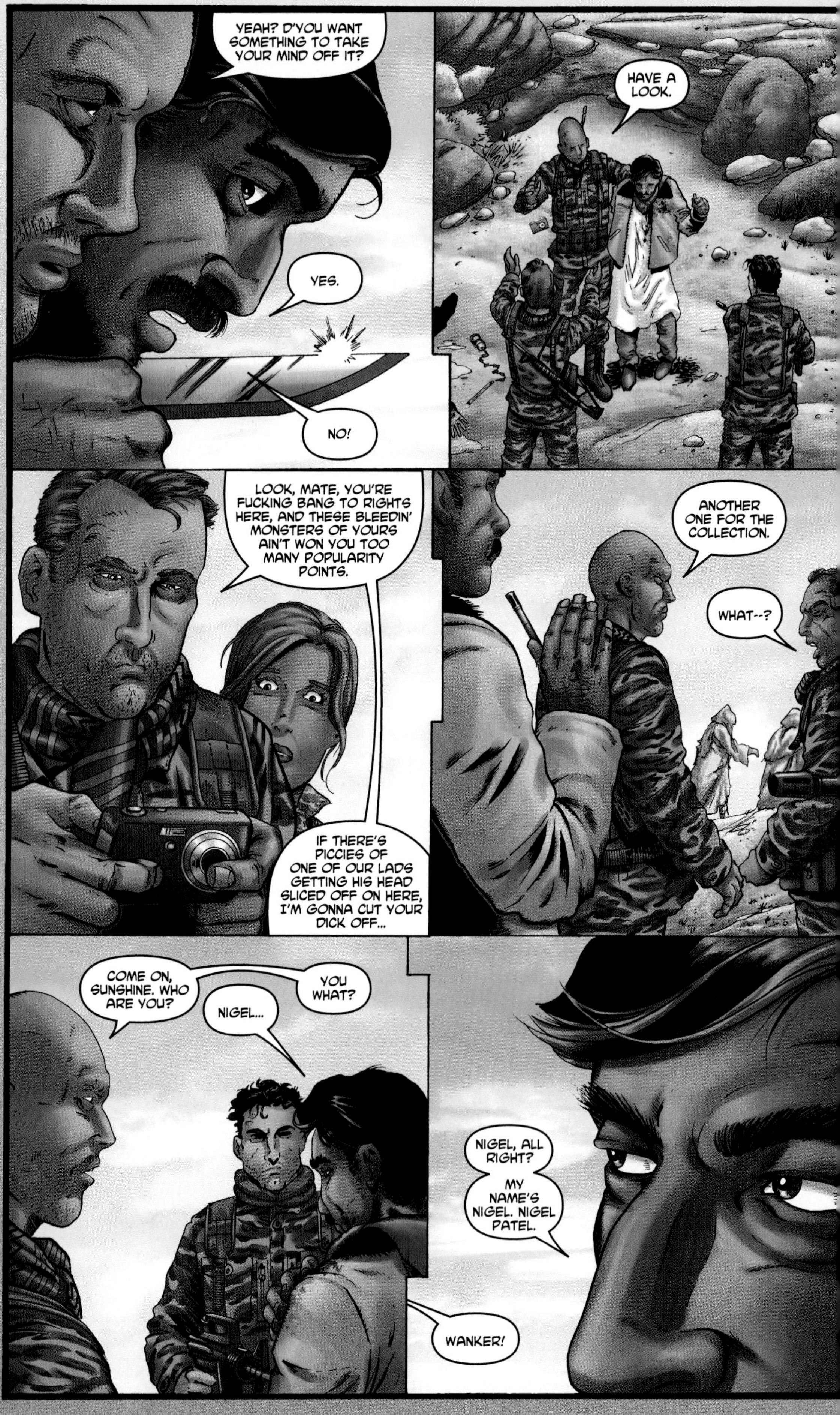
YEAH? D'YOU WANT SOMETHING TO TAKE YOUR MIND OFF IT?
YES.
NO!
HAVE A LOOK.
LOOK, MATE, YOU'RE FUCKING BANG TO RIGHTS HERE, AND THESE BLEEDIN' MONSTERS OF YOURS AIN'T WON YOU TOO MANY POPULARITY POINTS.
IF THERE'S PICCIES OF ONE OF OUR LADS GETTING HIS HEAD SLICED OFF ON HERE, I'M GONNA CUT YOUR DICK OFF...
ANOTHER ONE FOR THE COLLECTION.
WHAT--?
COME ON, SUNSHINE. WHO ARE YOU?
YOU WHAT?
NIGEL...
WANKER!
NIGEL, ALL RIGHT?
MY NAME'S NIGEL. NIGEL PATEL.

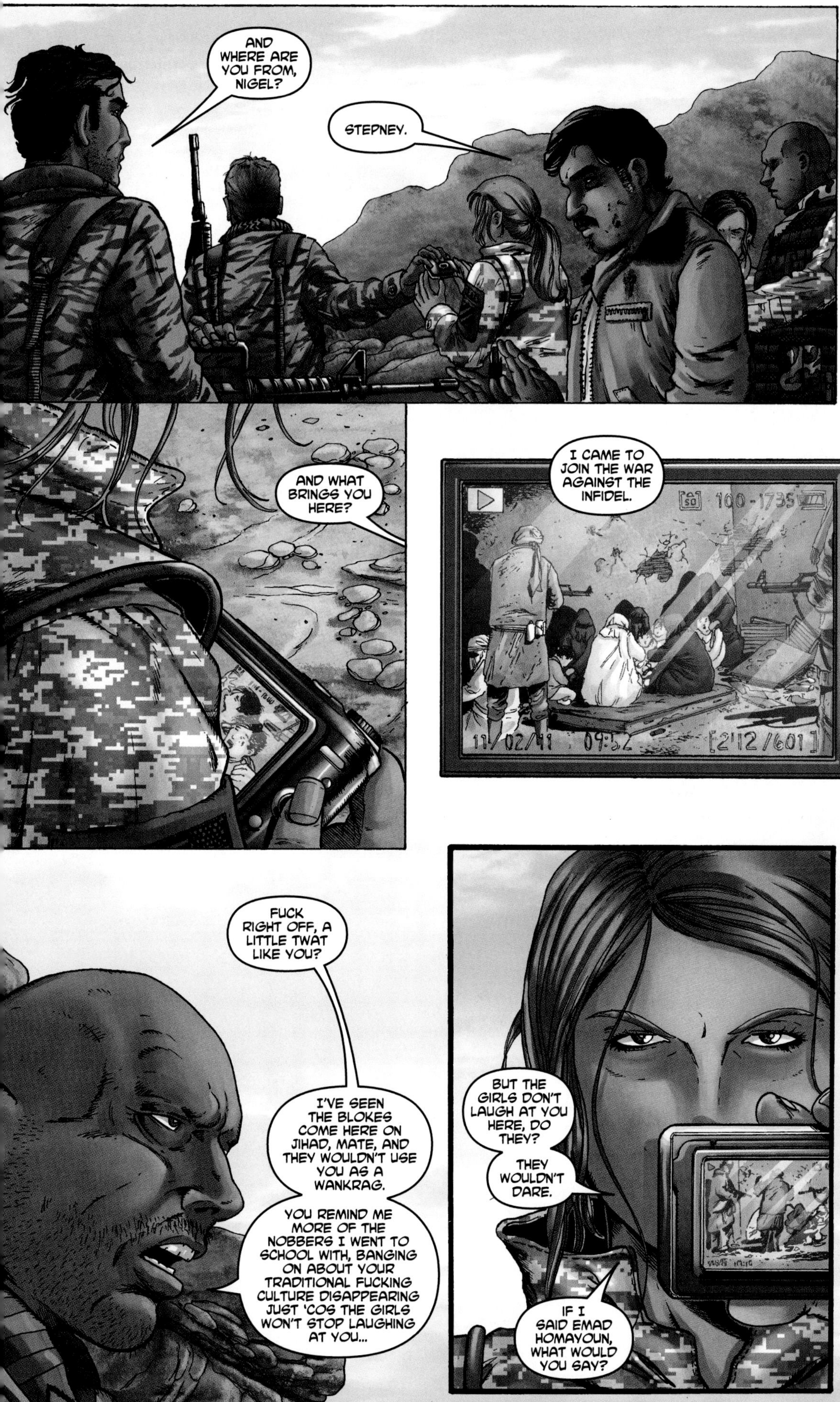
AND WHERE ARE YOU FROM, NIGEL?
STEPNEY.
AND WHAT BRINGS YOU HERE?
I CAME TO JOIN THE WAR AGAINST THE INFIDEL.
FUCK RIGHT OFF, A LITTLE TWAT LIKE YOU?
I'VE SEEN THE BLOKES COME HERE ON JIHAD, MATE, AND THEY WOULDN'T USE YOU AS A WANKRAG.
YOU REMIND ME MORE OF THE NOBBERS I WENT TO SCHOOL WITH, BANGING ON ABOUT YOUR TRADITIONAL FUCKING CULTURE DISAPPEARING JUST 'COS THE GIRLS WON'T STOP LAUGHING AT YOU...
BUT THE GIRLS DON'T LAUGH AT YOU HERE, DO THEY?
THEY WOULDN'T DARE.
IF I SAID EMAD HOMAYOUN, WHAT WOULD YOU SAY?

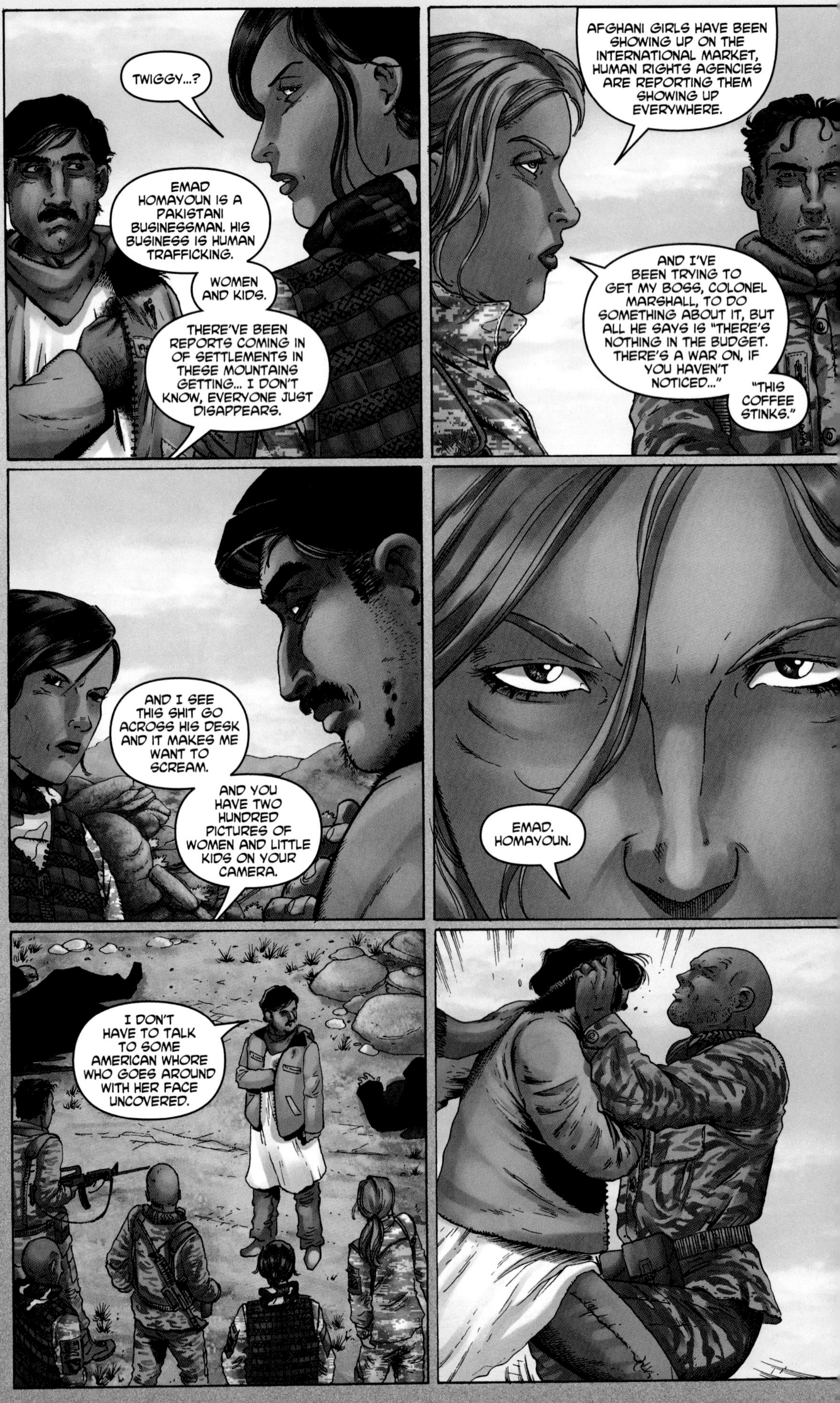

TWIGGY...?
EMAD HOMAYOUN IS A PAKISTANI BUSINESSMAN. HIS BUSINESS IS HUMAN TRAFFICKING.
WOMEN AND KIDS.
THERE'VE BEEN REPORTS COMING IN OF SETTLEMENTS IN THESE MOUNTAINS GETTING... I DON'T KNOW, EVERYONE JUST DISAPPEARS.
AFGHANI GIRLS HAVE BEEN SHOWING UP ON THE INTERNATIONAL MARKET, HUMAN RIGHTS AGENCIES ARE REPORTING THEM SHOWING UP EVERYWHERE.
AND I'VE BEEN TRYING TO GET MY BOSS, COLONEL MARSHALL, TO DO SOMETHING ABOUT IT, BUT ALL HE SAYS IS "THERE'S NOTHING IN THE BUDGET. THERE'S A WAR ON, IF YOU HAVEN'T NOTICED..."
"THIS COFFEE STINKS."
AND I SEE THIS SHIT GO ACROSS HIS DESK AND IT MAKES ME WANT TO SCREAM.
AND YOU HAVE TWO HUNDRED PICTURES OF WOMEN AND LITTLE KIDS ON YOUR CAMERA.
EMAD. HOMAYOUN.
I DON'T HAVE TO TALK TO SOME AMERICAN WHORE WHO GOES AROUND WITH HER FACE UNCOVERED.

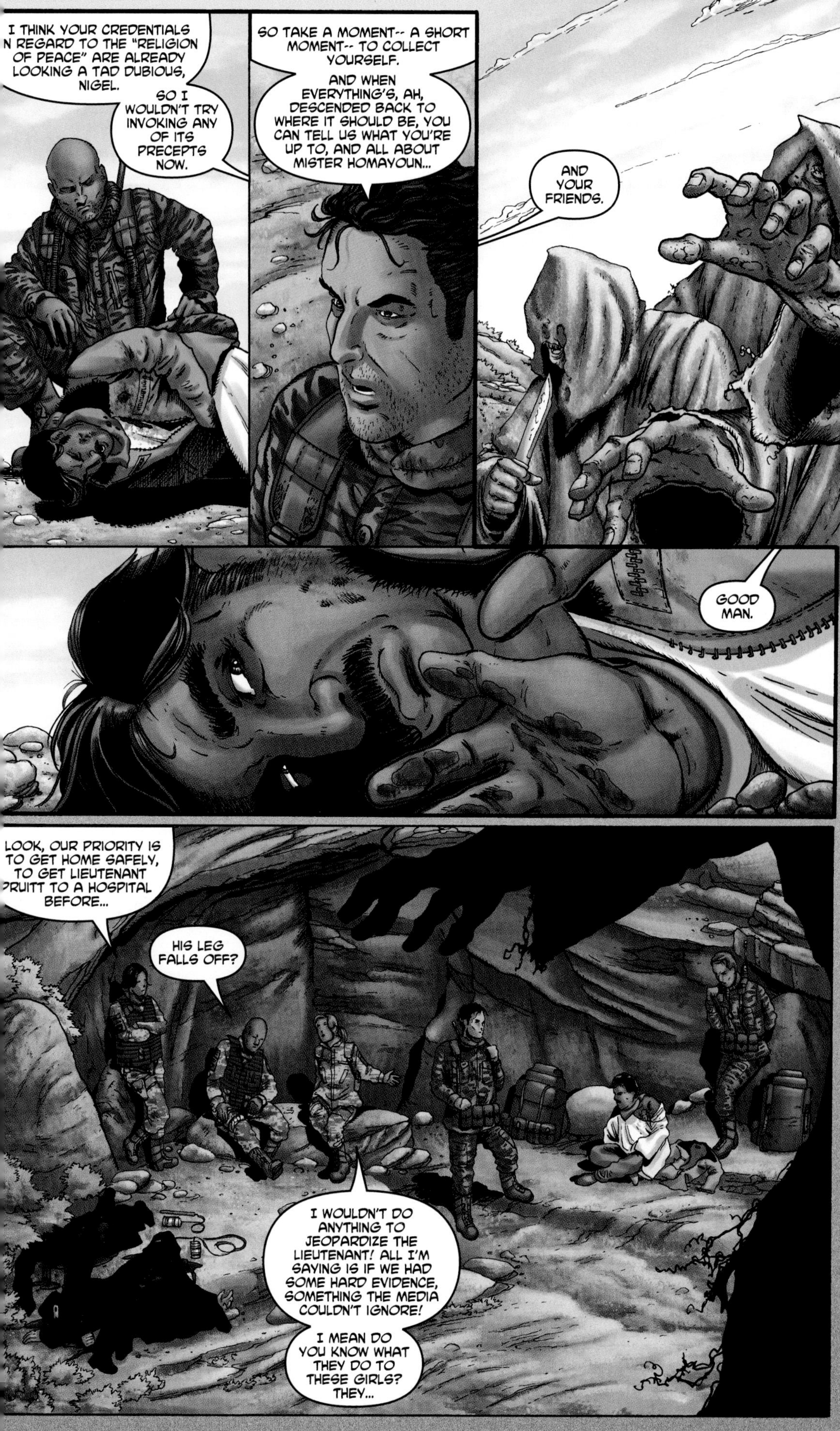
I THINK YOUR CREDENTIALS N REGARD TO THE "RELIGION OF PEACE" ARE ALREADY LOOKING A TAD DUBIOUS, NIGEL.
SO I WOULDN'T TRY INVOKING ANY OF ITS PRECEPTS NOW.
SO TAKE A MOMENT-- A SHORT MOMENT-- TO COLLECT YOURSELF.
AND WHEN EVERYTHING'S, AH, DESCENDED BACK TO WHERE IT SHOULD BE, YOU CAN TELL US WHAT YOU'RE UP TO, AND ALL ABOUT MISTER HOMAYOUN...
AND YOUR FRIENDS.
GOOD MAN.
LOOK, OUR PRIORITY IS TO GET HOME SAFELY, TO GET LIEUTENANT PRUITT TO A HOSPITAL BEFORE...
HIS LEG FALLS OFF?
I WOULDN'T DO ANYTHING TO JEOPARDIZE THE LIEUTENANT! ALL I'M SAYING IS IF WE HAD SOME HARD EVIDENCE, SOMETHING THE MEDIA COULDN'T IGNORE!
I MEAN DO YOU KNOW WHAT THEY DO TO THESE GIRLS? THEY...

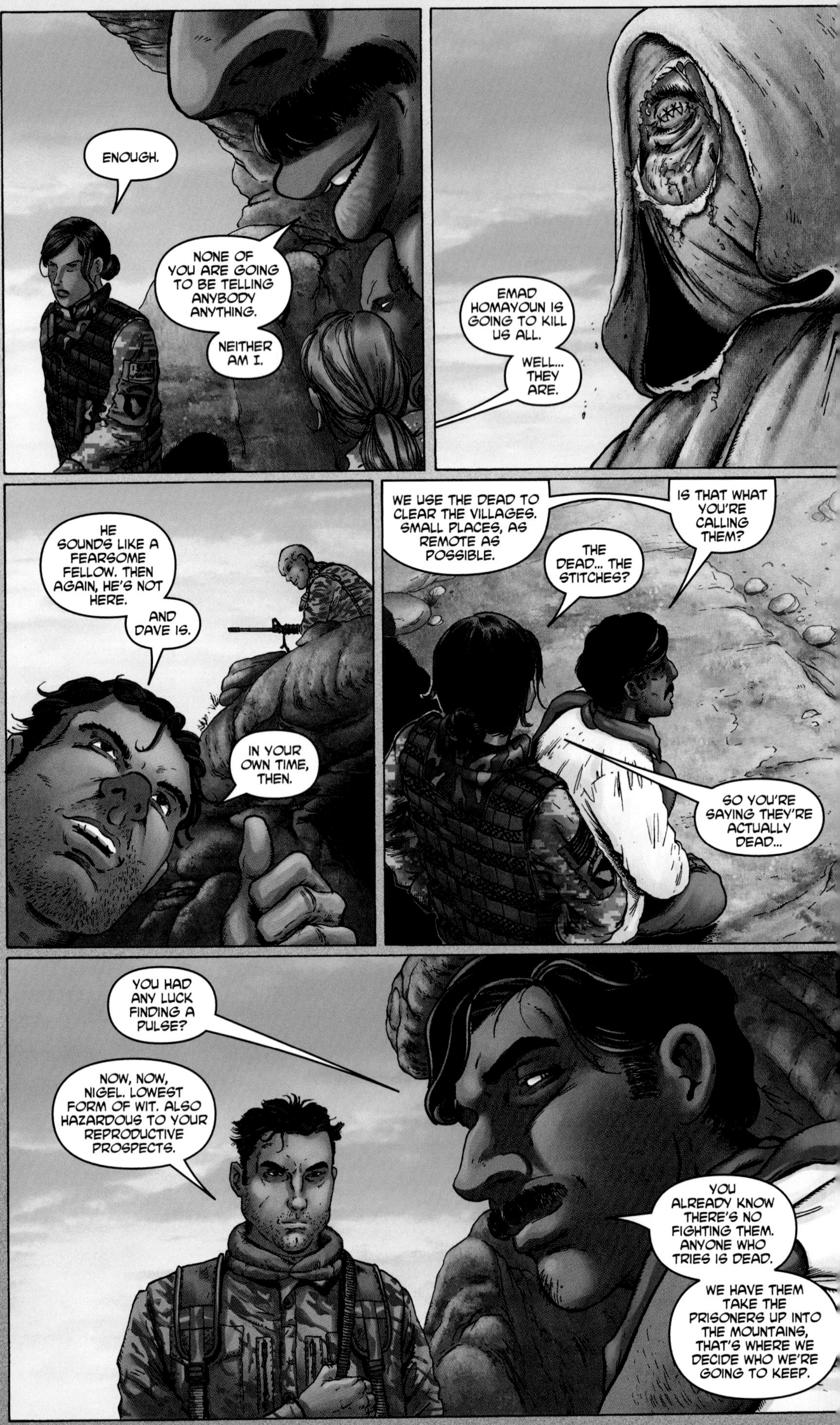
ENOUGH.
NONE OF YOU ARE GOING TO BE TELLING ANYBODY ANYTHING.
NEITHER AM I.
EMAD HOMAYOUN IS GOING TO KILL US ALL.
WELL... THEY ARE.
HE SOUNDS LIKE A FEARSOME FELLOW. THEN AGAIN, HE'S NOT HERE.
AND DAVE IS.
IN YOUR OWN TIME, THEN.
WE USE THE DEAD TO CLEAR THE VILLAGES. SMALL PLACES, AS REMOTE AS POSSIBLE.
IS THAT WHAT YOU'RE CALLING THEM?
THE DEAD... THE STITCHES?
SO YOU'RE SAYING THEY'RE ACTUALLY DEAD...
YOU HAD ANY LUCK FINDING A PULSE?
NOW, NOW, NIGEL. LOWEST FORM OF WIT. ALSO HAZARDOUS TO YOUR REPRODUCTIVE PROSPECTS.
YOU ALREADY KNOW THERE'S NO FIGHTING THEM. ANYONE WHO TRIES IS DEAD.
WE HAVE THEM TAKE THE PRISONERS UP INTO THE MOUNTAINS, THAT'S WHERE WE DECIDE WHO WE'RE GOING TO KEEP.

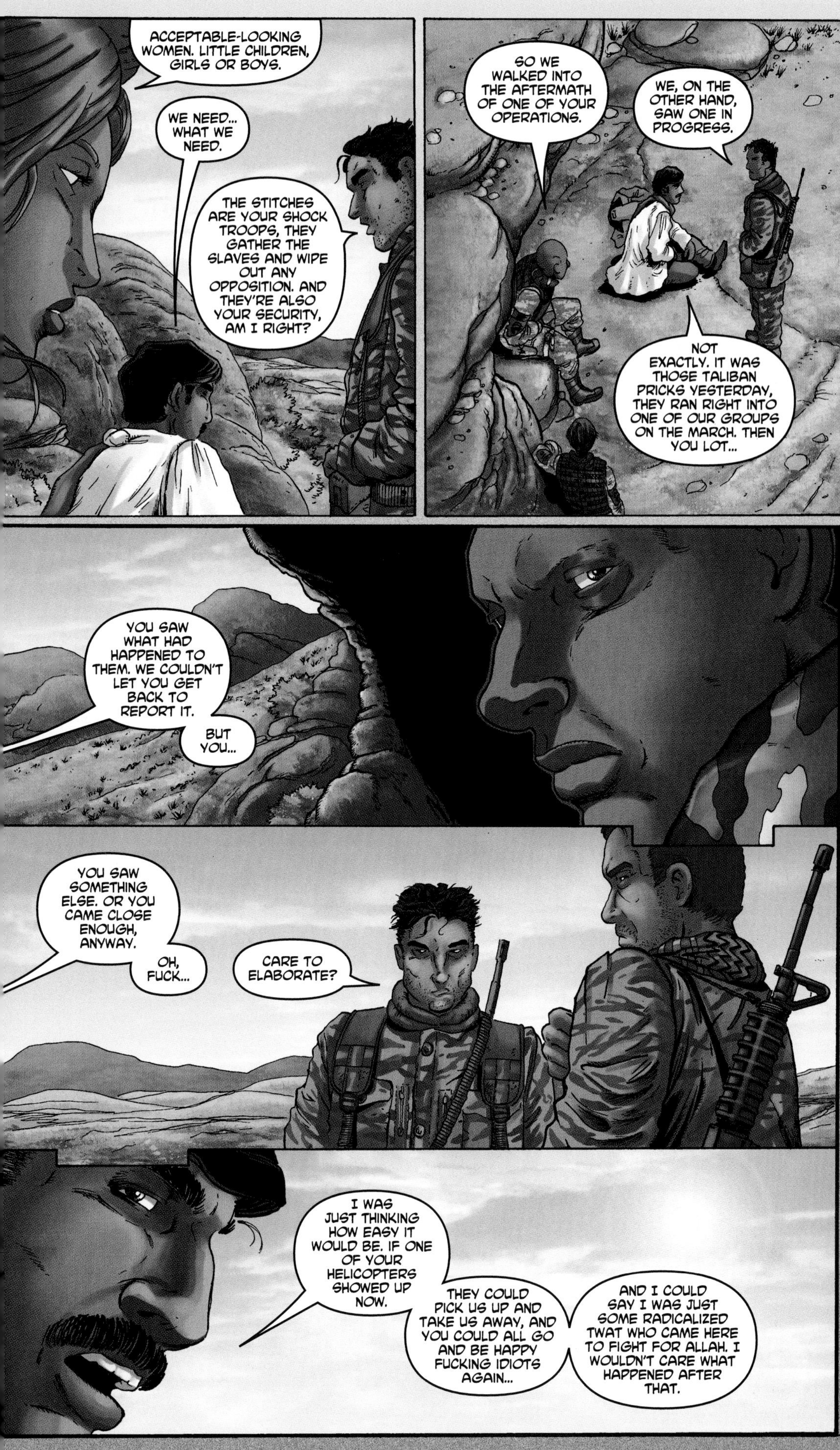
ACCEPTABLE-LOOKING WOMEN. LITTLE CHILDREN, GIRLS OR BOYS.
WE NEED... WHAT WE NEED.
THE STITCHES ARE YOUR SHOCK TROOPS, THEY GATHER THE SLAVES AND WIPE OUT ANY OPPOSITION. AND THEY'RE ALSO YOUR SECURITY, AM I RIGHT?
SO WE WALKED INTO THE AFTERMATH OF ONE OF YOUR OPERATIONS.
WE, ON THE OTHER HAND, SAW ONE IN PROGRESS.
NOT EXACTLY. IT WAS THOSE TALIBAN PRICKS YESTERDAY, THEY RAN RIGHT INTO ONE OF OUR GROUPS ON THE MARCH. THEN YOU LOT...
YOU SAW WHAT HAD HAPPENED TO THEM. WE COULDN'T LET YOU GET BACK TO REPORT IT.
BUT YOU...
YOU SAW SOMETHING ELSE. OR YOU CAME CLOSE ENOUGH, ANYWAY.
OH, FUCK...
CARE TO ELABORATE?
I WAS JUST THINKING HOW EASY IT WOULD BE. IF ONE OF YOUR HELICOPTERS SHOWED UP NOW.
THEY COULD PICK US UP AND TAKE US AWAY, AND YOU COULD ALL GO AND BE HAPPY FUCKING IDIOTS AGAIN...
AND I COULD SAY I WAS JUST SOME RADICALIZED TWAT WHO CAME HERE TO FIGHT FOR ALLAH. I WOULDN'T CARE WHAT HAPPENED AFTER THAT.

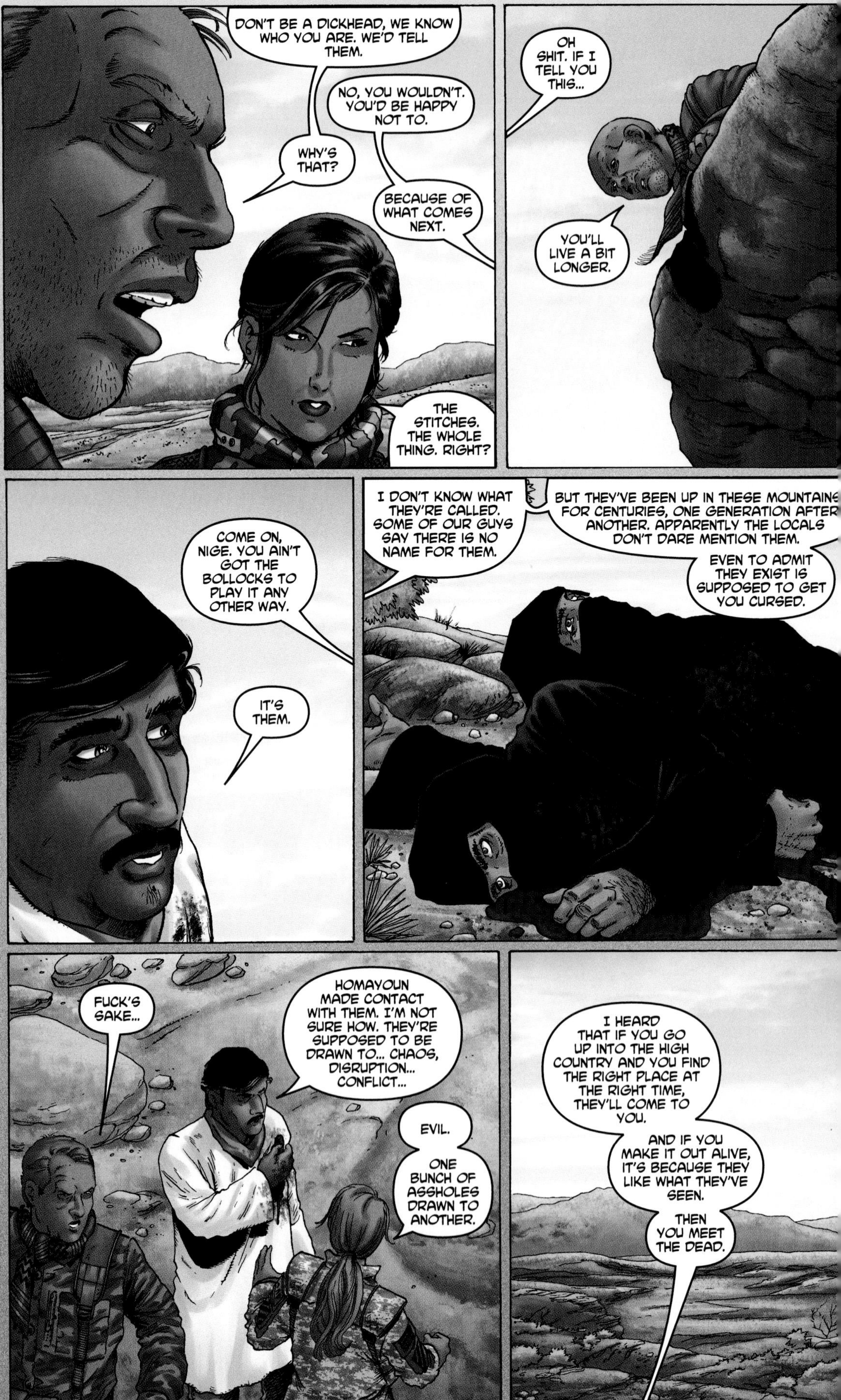
DON'T BE A DICKHEAD, WE KNOW WHO YOU ARE. WE'D TELL THEM.
NO, YOU WOULDN'T. YOU'D BE HAPPY NOT TO.
WHY'S THAT?
BECAUSE OF WHAT COMES NEXT.
THE STITCHES. THE WHOLE THING. RIGHT?
OH SHIT. IF I TELL YOU THIS...
YOU'LL LIVE A BIT LONGER.
COME ON, NIGE. YOU AIN'T GOT THE BOLLOCKS TO PLAY IT ANY OTHER WAY.
IT'S THEM.
I DON'T KNOW WHAT THEY'RE CALLED. SOME OF OUR GUYS SAY THERE IS NO NAME FOR THEM.
BUT THEY'VE BEEN UP IN THESE MOUNTAINS FOR CENTURIES, ONE GENERATION AFTER ANOTHER. APPARENTLY THE LOCALS DON'T DARE MENTION THEM.
EVEN TO ADMIT THEY EXIST IS SUPPOSED TO GET YOU CURSED.
FUCK'S SAKE...
HOMAYOUN MADE CONTACT WITH THEM. I'M NOT SURE HOW. THEY'RE SUPPOSED TO BE DRAWN TO... CHAOS, DISRUPTION... CONFLICT...
EVIL.
ONE BUNCH OF ASSHOLES DRAWN TO ANOTHER.
I HEARD THAT IF YOU GO UP INTO THE HIGH COUNTRY AND YOU FIND THE RIGHT PLACE AT THE RIGHT TIME, THEY'LL COME TO YOU.
AND IF YOU MAKE IT OUT ALIVE, IT'S BECAUSE THEY LIKE WHAT THEY'VE SEEN.
THEN YOU MEET THE DEAD.

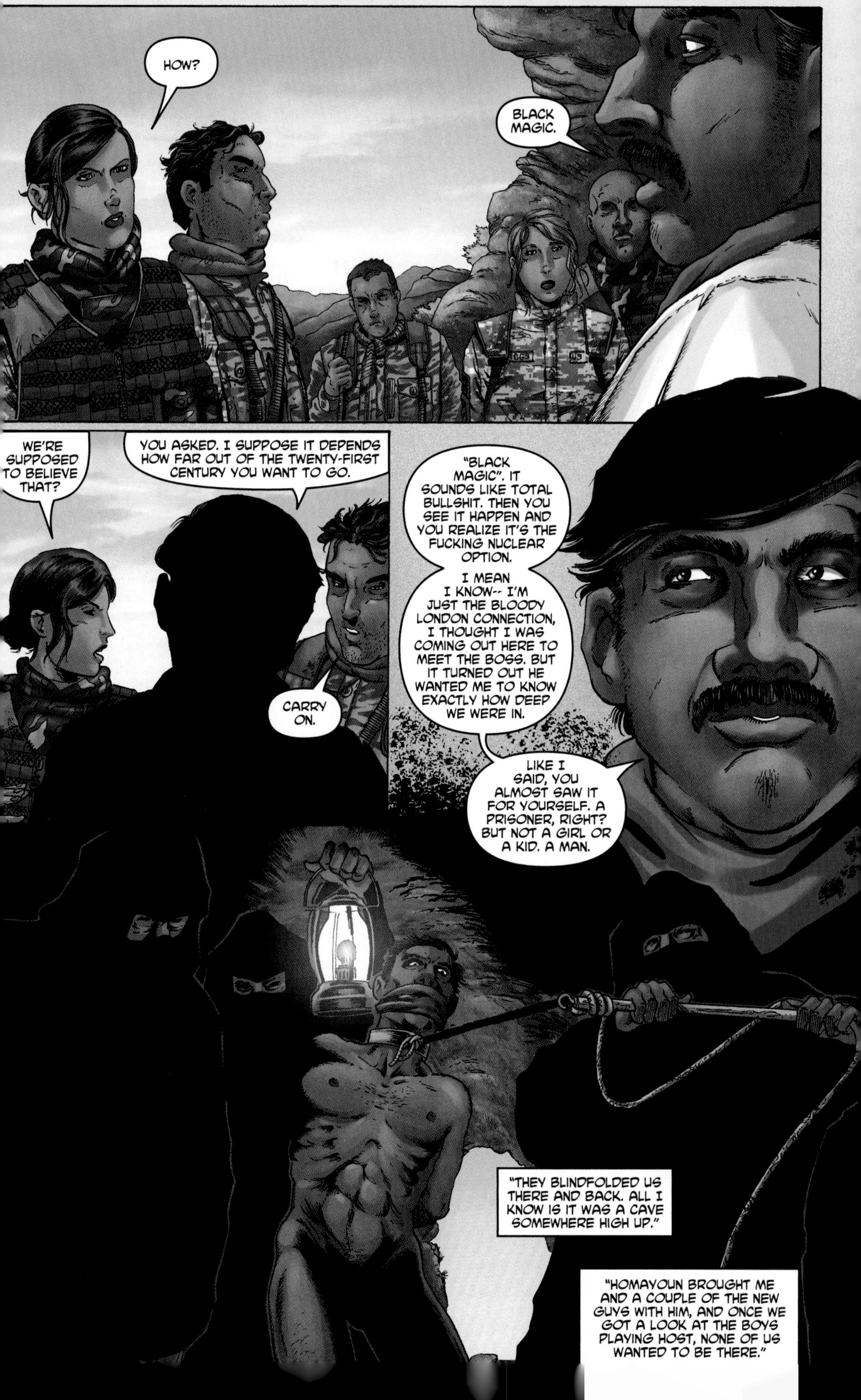

HOW?
BLACK MAGIC.
WE'RE SUPPOSED TO BELIEVE THAT?
YOU ASKED. I SUPPOSE IT DEPENDS HOW FAR OUT OF THE TWENTY-FIRST CENTURY YOU WANT TO GO.
CARRY ON.
"BLACK MAGIC". IT SOUNDS LIKE TOTAL BULLSHIT. THEN YOU SEE IT HAPPEN AND YOU REALIZE IT'S THE FUCKING NUCLEAR OPTION.
I MEAN I KNOW-- I'M JUST THE BLOODY LONDON CONNECTION, I THOUGHT I WAS COMING OUT HERE TO MEET THE BOSS. BUT IT TURNED OUT HE WANTED ME TO KNOW EXACTLY HOW DEEP WE WERE IN.
LIKE I SAID, YOU ALMOST SAW IT FOR YOURSELF. A PRISONER, RIGHT? BUT NOT A GIRL OR A KID. A MAN.
"THEY BLINDFOLDED US THERE AND BACK. ALL I KNOW IS IT WAS A CAVE SOMEWHERE HIGH UP."
"HOMAYOUN BROUGHT ME AND A COUPLE OF THE NEW GUYS WITH HIM, AND ONCE WE GOT A LOOK AT THE BOYS PLAYING HOST, NONE OF US WANTED TO BE THERE."

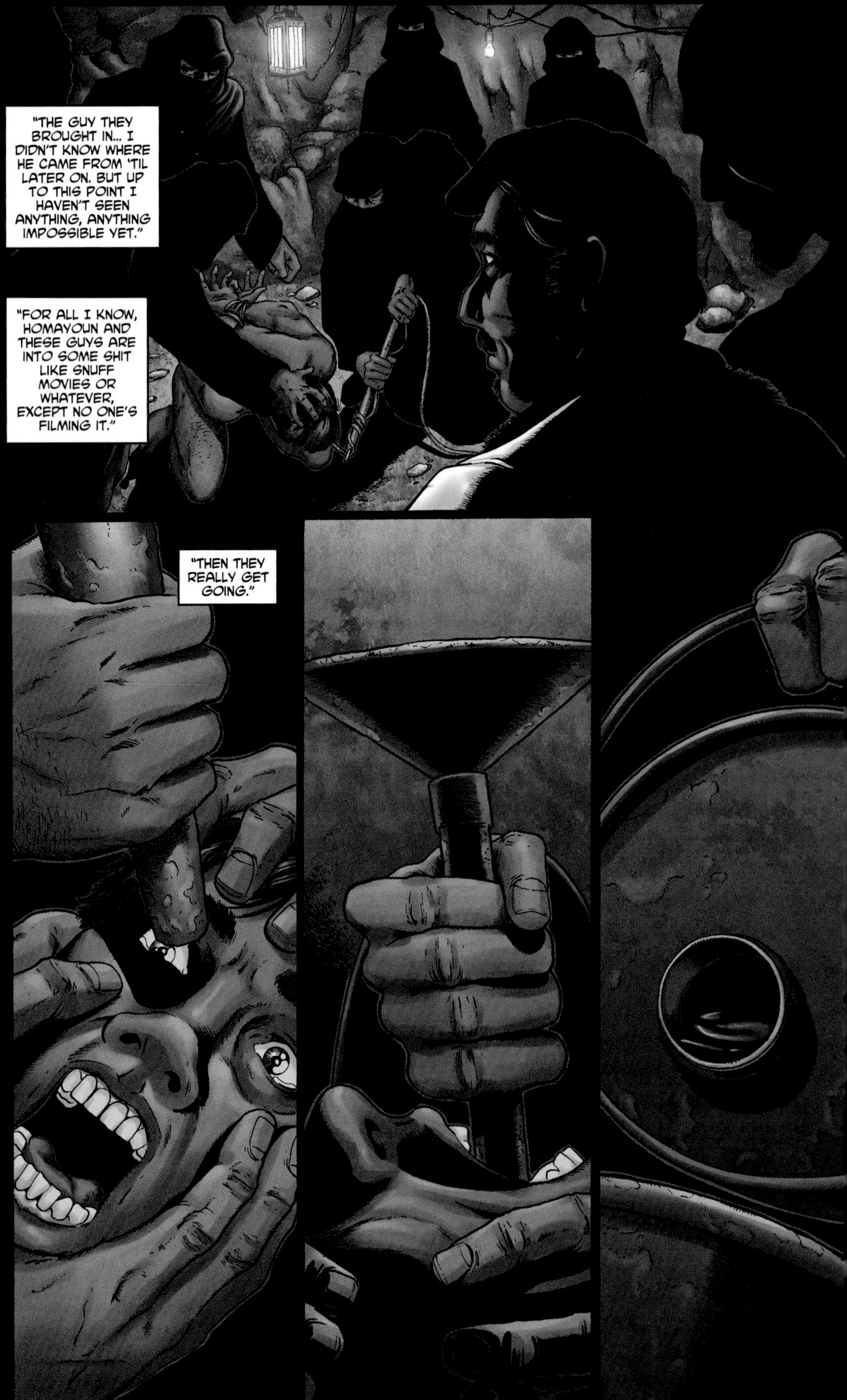
"THE GUY THEY BROUGHT IN... I DIDN'T KNOW WHERE HE CAME FROM 'TIL LATER ON. BUT UP TO THIS POINT I HAVEN'T SEEN ANYTHING, ANYTHING IMPOSSIBLE YET."
"FOR ALL I KNOW, HOMAYOUN AND THESE GUYS ARE INTO SOME SHIT LIKE SNUFF MOVIES OR WHATEVER, EXCEPT NO ONE'S FILMING IT."
"THEN THEY REALLY GET GOING."

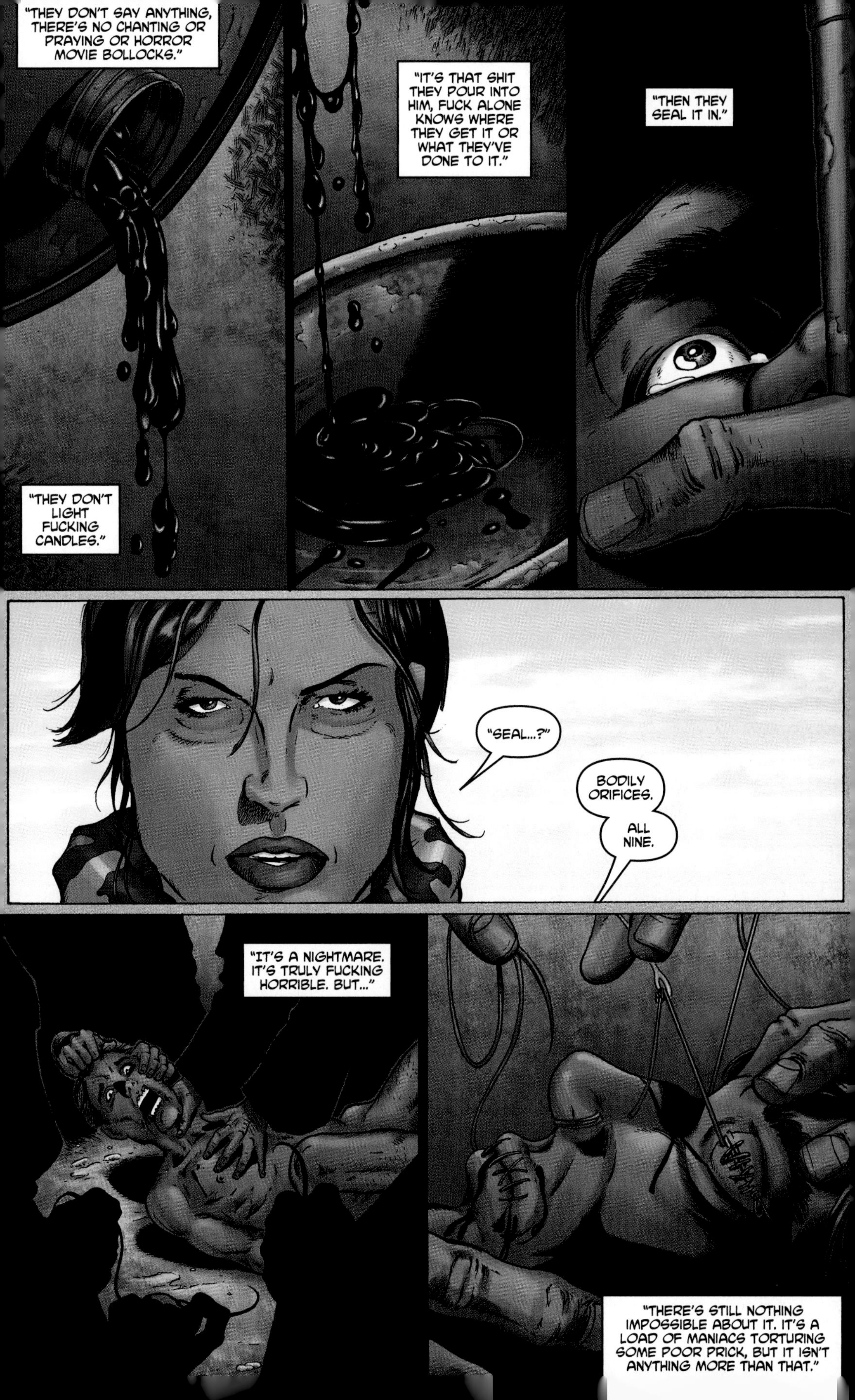
"THEY DON'T SAY ANYTHING, THERE'S NO CHANTING OR PRAYING OR HORROR MOVIE BOLLOCKS."
"THEY DON'T LIGHT FUCKING CANDLES."
"IT'S THAT SHIT THEY POUR INTO HIM, FUCK ALONE KNOWS WHERE THEY GET IT OR WHAT THEY'VE DONE TO IT."
"THEN THEY SEAL IT IN."
"SEAL...?"
BODILY ORIFICES.
ALL NINE.
"IT'S A NIGHTMARE. IT'S TRULY FUCKING HORRIBLE. BUT..."
"THERE'S STILL NOTHING IMPOSSIBLE ABOUT IT. IT'S A LOAD OF MANIACS TORTURING SOME POOR PRICK, BUT IT ISN'T ANYTHING MORE THAN THAT."

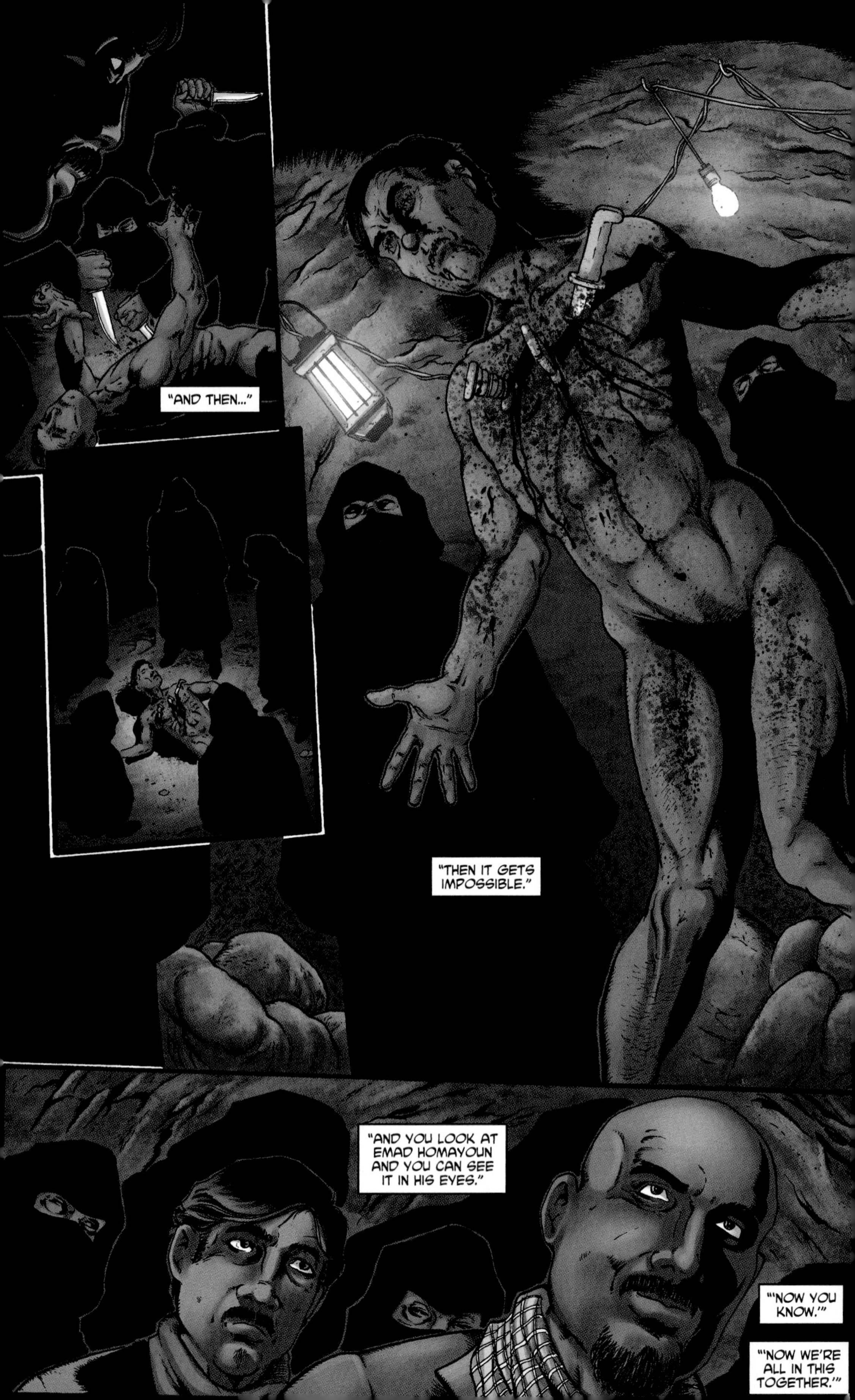
"AND THEN..."
"THEN IT GETS IMPOSSIBLE."
"AND YOU LOOK AT EMAD HOMAYOUN AND YOU CAN SEE IT IN HIS EYES."
"'NOW YOU KNOW.'"
"'NOW WE'RE ALL IN THIS TOGETHER.'"

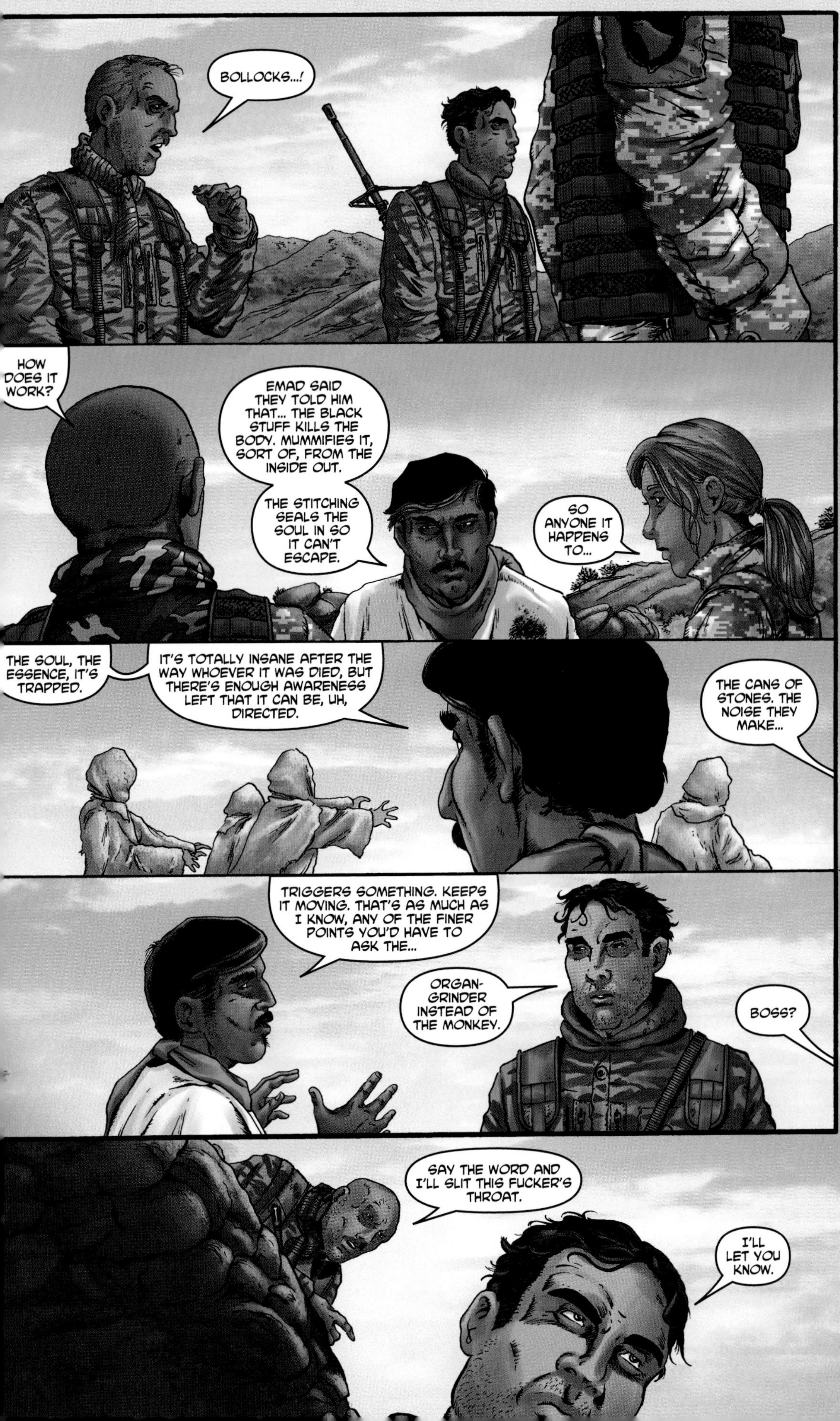
BOLLOCKS...!
HOW DOES IT WORK?
EMAD SAID THEY TOLD HIM THAT... THE BLACK STUFF KILLS THE BODY. MUMMIFIES IT, SORT OF, FROM THE INSIDE OUT.
THE STITCHING SEALS THE SOUL IN SO IT CAN'T ESCAPE.
SO ANYONE IT HAPPENS TO...
THE SOUL, THE ESSENCE, IT'S TRAPPED.
IT'S TOTALLY INSANE AFTER THE WAY WHOEVER IT WAS DIED, BUT THERE'S ENOUGH AWARENESS LEFT THAT IT CAN BE, UH, DIRECTED.
THE CANS OF STONES. THE NOISE THEY MAKE...
TRIGGERS SOMETHING. KEEPS IT MOVING. THAT'S AS MUCH AS I KNOW, ANY OF THE FINER POINTS YOU'D HAVE TO ASK THE...
ORGAN-GRINDER INSTEAD OF THE MONKEY.
BOSS?
SAY THE WORD AND I'LL SLIT THIS FUCKER'S THROAT.
I'LL LET YOU KNOW.

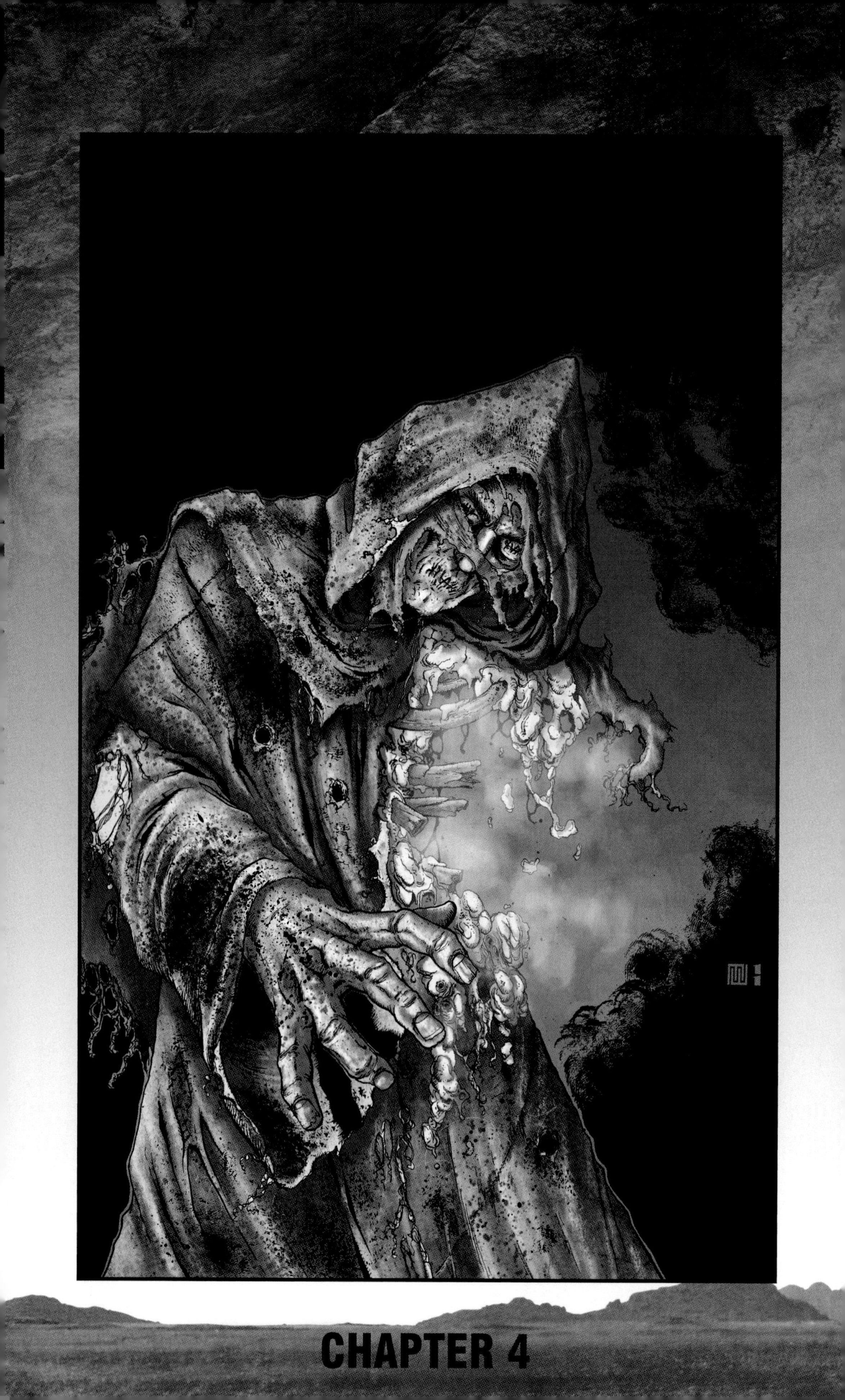

CHAPTER 4

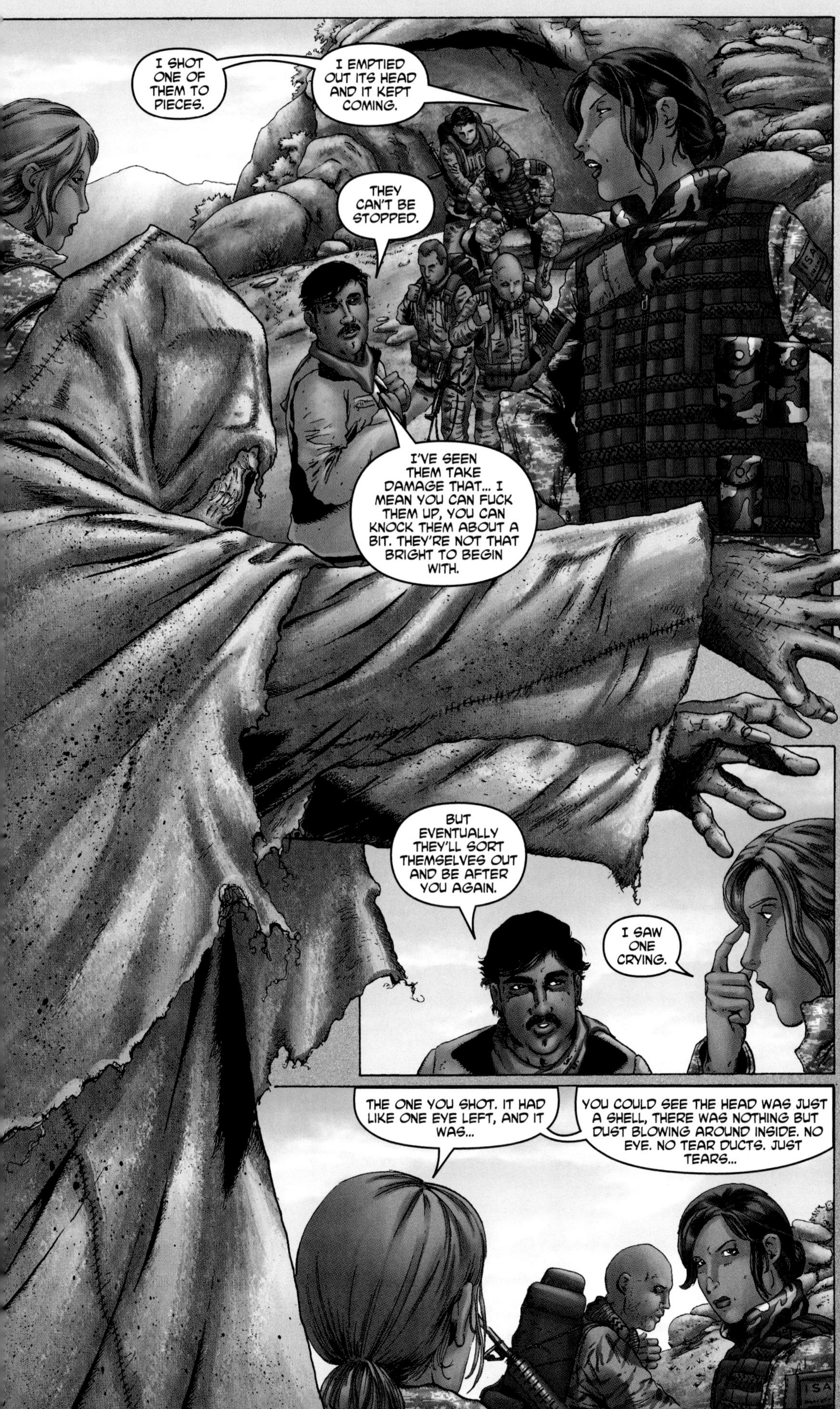
I SHOT ONE OF THEM TO PIECES.
I EMPTIED OUT ITS HEAD AND IT KEPT COMING.
THEY CAN'T BE STOPPED.
I'VE SEEN THEM TAKE DAMAGE THAT... I MEAN YOU CAN FUCK THEM UP, YOU CAN KNOCK THEM ABOUT A BIT. THEY'RE NOT THAT BRIGHT TO BEGIN WITH.
BUT EVENTUALLY THEY'LL SORT THEMSELVES OUT AND BE AFTER YOU AGAIN.
I SAW ONE CRYING.
THE ONE YOU SHOT. IT HAD LIKE ONE EYE LEFT, AND IT WAS...
YOU COULD SEE THE HEAD WAS JUST A SHELL, THERE WAS NOTHING BUT DUST BLOWING AROUND INSIDE. NO EYE. NO TEAR DUCTS. JUST TEARS...

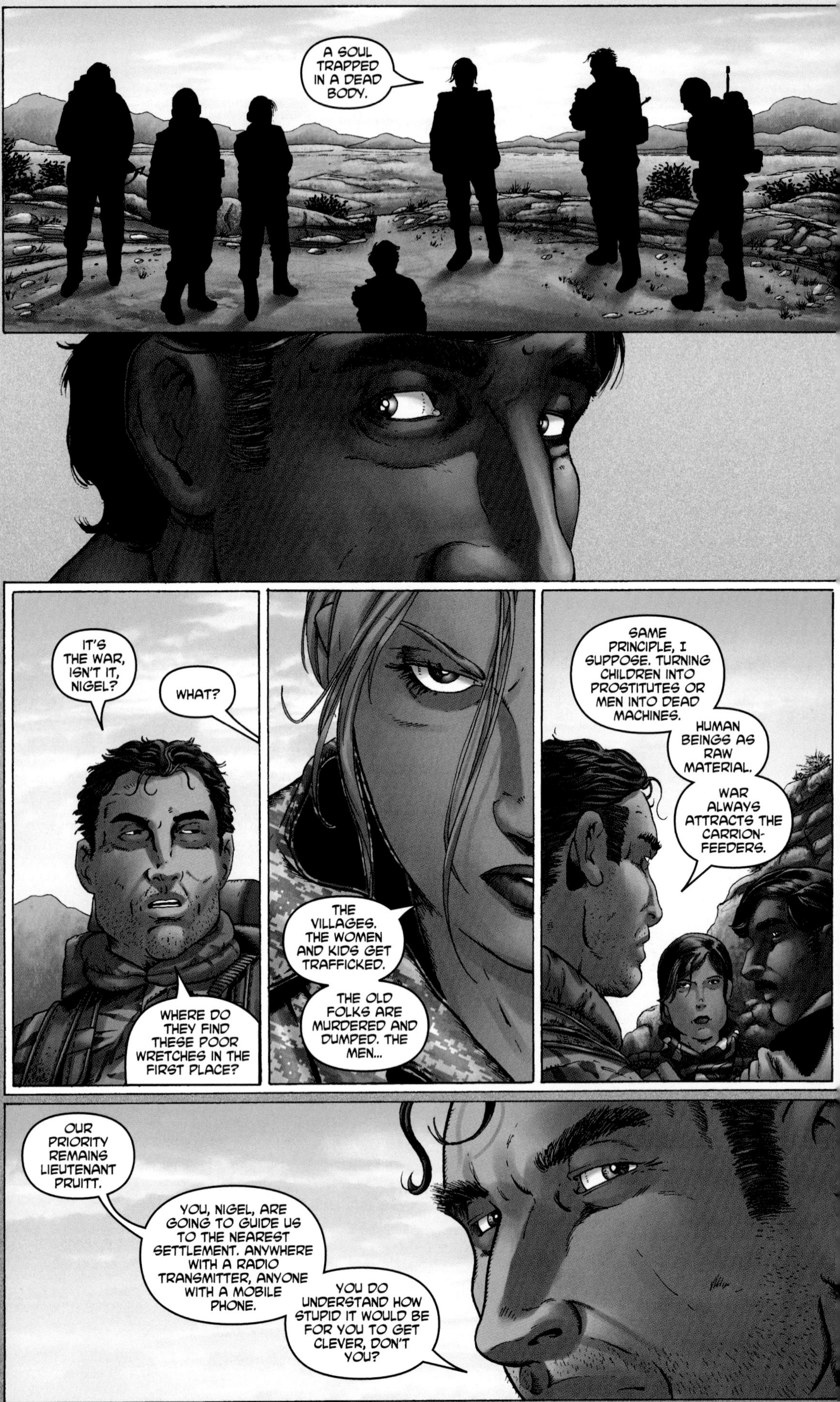
A SOUL TRAPPED IN A DEAD BODY.
IT'S THE WAR, ISN'T IT, NIGEL?
WHAT?
WHERE DO THEY FIND THESE POOR WRETCHES IN THE FIRST PLACE?
THE VILLAGES. THE WOMEN AND KIDS GET TRAFFICKED.
THE OLD FOLKS ARE MURDERED AND DUMPED. THE MEN...
SAME PRINCIPLE, I SUPPOSE. TURNING CHILDREN INTO PROSTITUTES OR MEN INTO DEAD MACHINES.
HUMAN BEINGS AS RAW MATERIAL.
WAR ALWAYS ATTRACTS THE CARRION-FEEDERS.
OUR PRIORITY REMAINS LIEUTENANT PRUITT.
YOU, NIGEL, ARE GOING TO GUIDE US TO THE NEAREST SETTLEMENT. ANYWHERE WITH A RADIO TRANSMITTER, ANYONE WITH A MOBILE PHONE.
YOU DO UNDERSTAND HOW STUPID IT WOULD BE FOR YOU TO GET CLEVER, DON'T YOU?

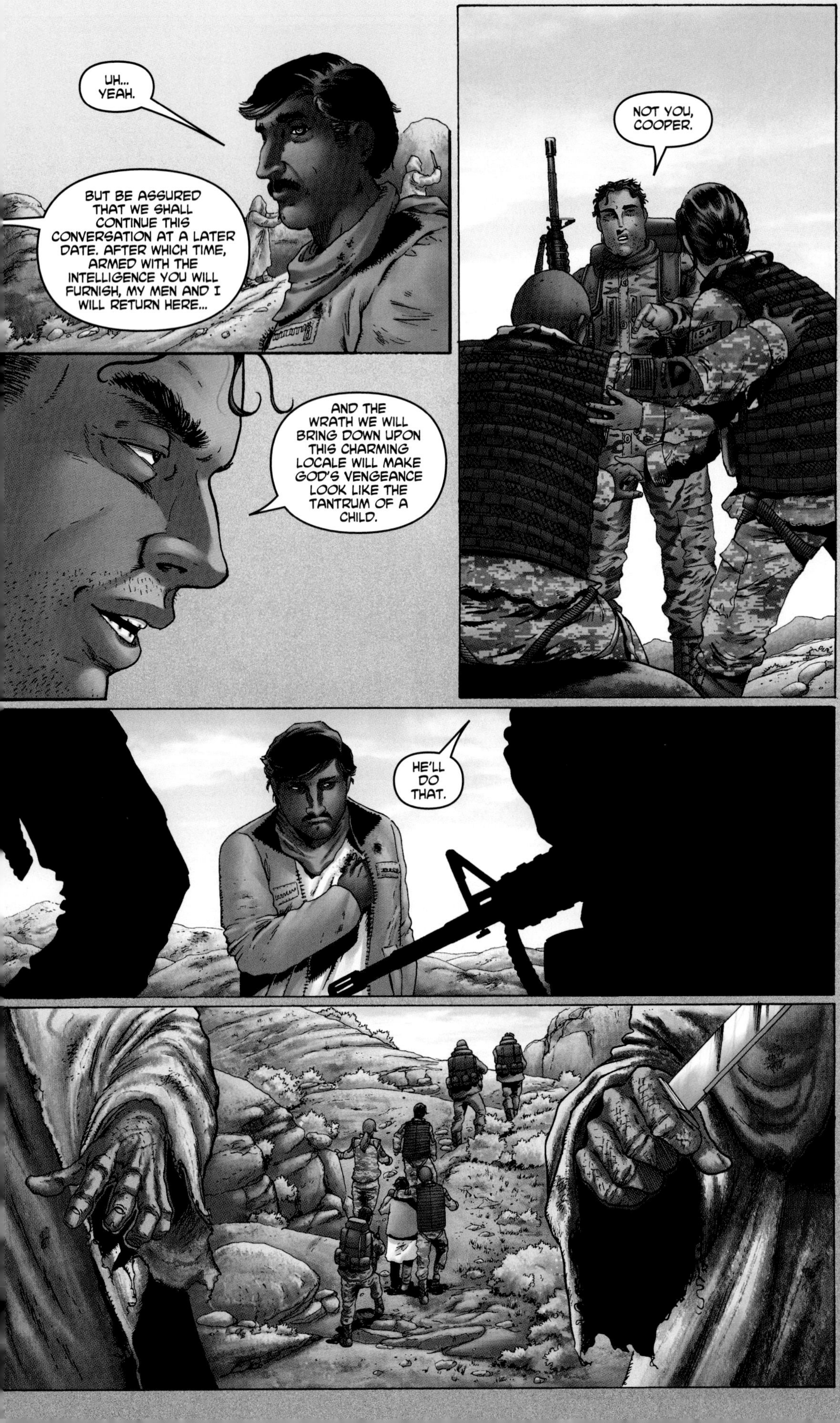
UH... YEAH.
BUT BE ASSURED THAT WE SHALL CONTINUE THIS CONVERSATION AT A LATER DATE. AFTER WHICH TIME, ARMED WITH THE INTELLIGENCE YOU WILL FURNISH, MY MEN AND I WILL RETURN HERE...
AND THE WRATH WE WILL BRING DOWN UPON THIS CHARMING LOCALE WILL MAKE GOD'S VENGEANCE LOOK LIKE THE TANTRUM OF A CHILD.
NOT YOU, COOPER.
HE'LL DO THAT.

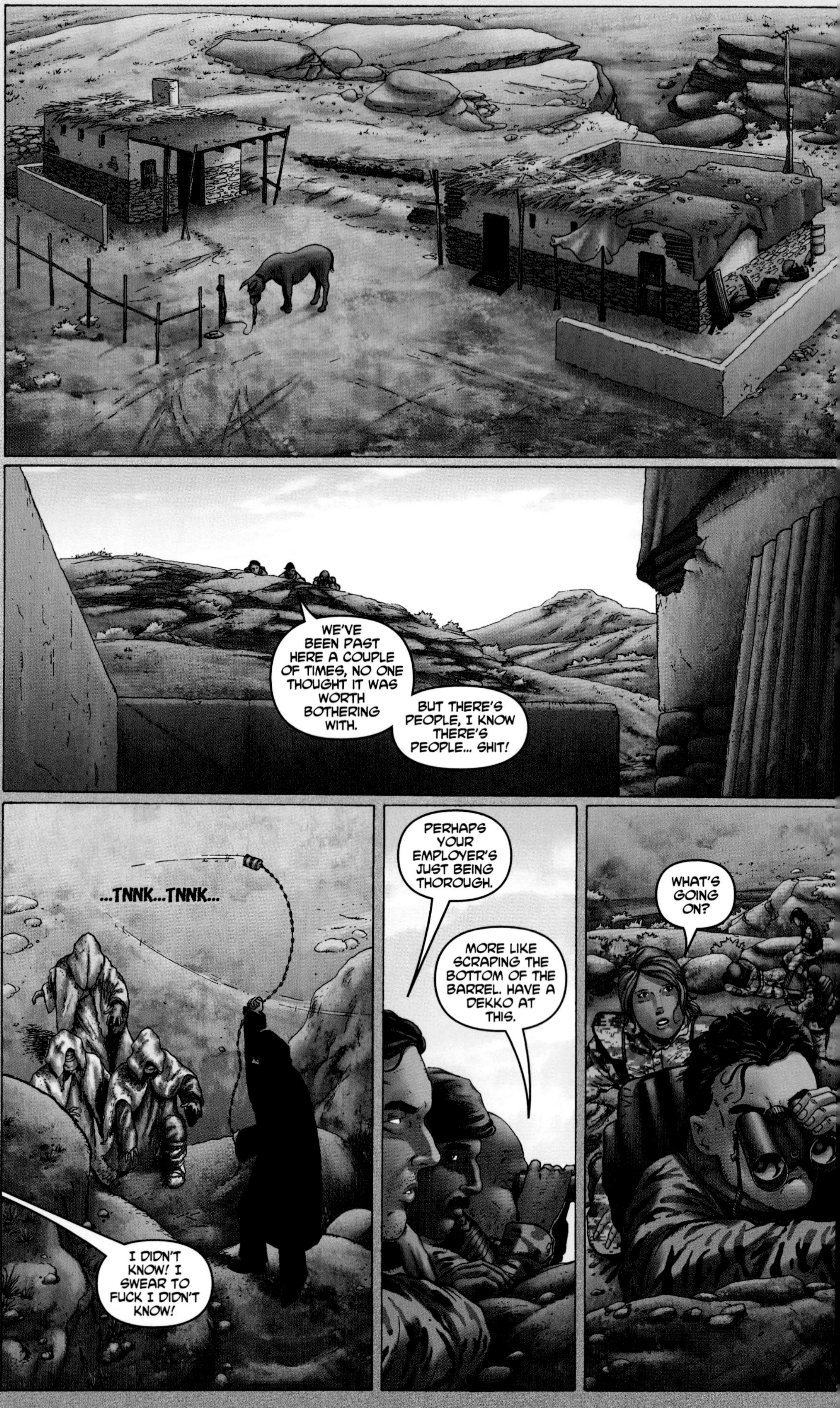
WE'VE BEEN PAST HERE A COUPLE OF TIMES, NO ONE THOUGHT IT WAS WORTH BOTHERING WITH.
BUT THERE'S PEOPLE, I KNOW THERE'S PEOPLE... SHIT!
...TNNK...TNNK...
I DIDN'T KNOW! I SWEAR TO FUCK I DIDN'T KNOW!
PERHAPS YOUR EMPLOYER'S JUST BEING THOROUGH.
MORE LIKE SCRAPING THE BOTTOM OF THE BARREL. HAVE A DEKKO AT THIS.
WHAT'S GOING ON?

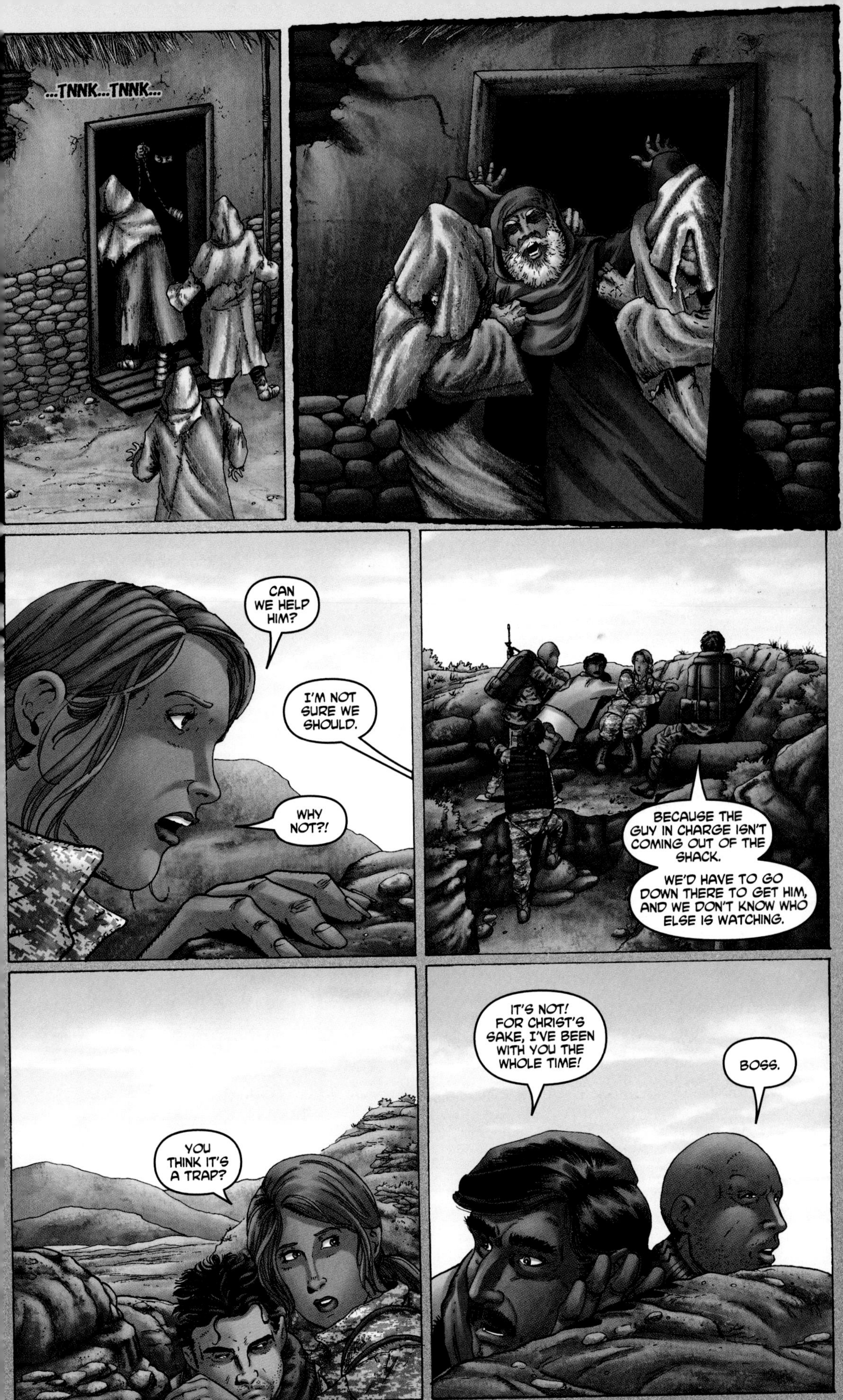

...TNNK...TNNK...
CAN WE HELP HIM?
I'M NOT SURE WE SHOULD.
WHY NOT?!
BECAUSE THE GUY IN CHARGE ISN'T COMING OUT OF THE SHACK.
WE'D HAVE TO GO DOWN THERE TO GET HIM, AND WE DON'T KNOW WHO ELSE IS WATCHING.
YOU THINK IT'S A TRAP?
IT'S NOT! FOR CHRIST'S SAKE, I'VE BEEN WITH YOU THE WHOLE TIME!
BOSS.

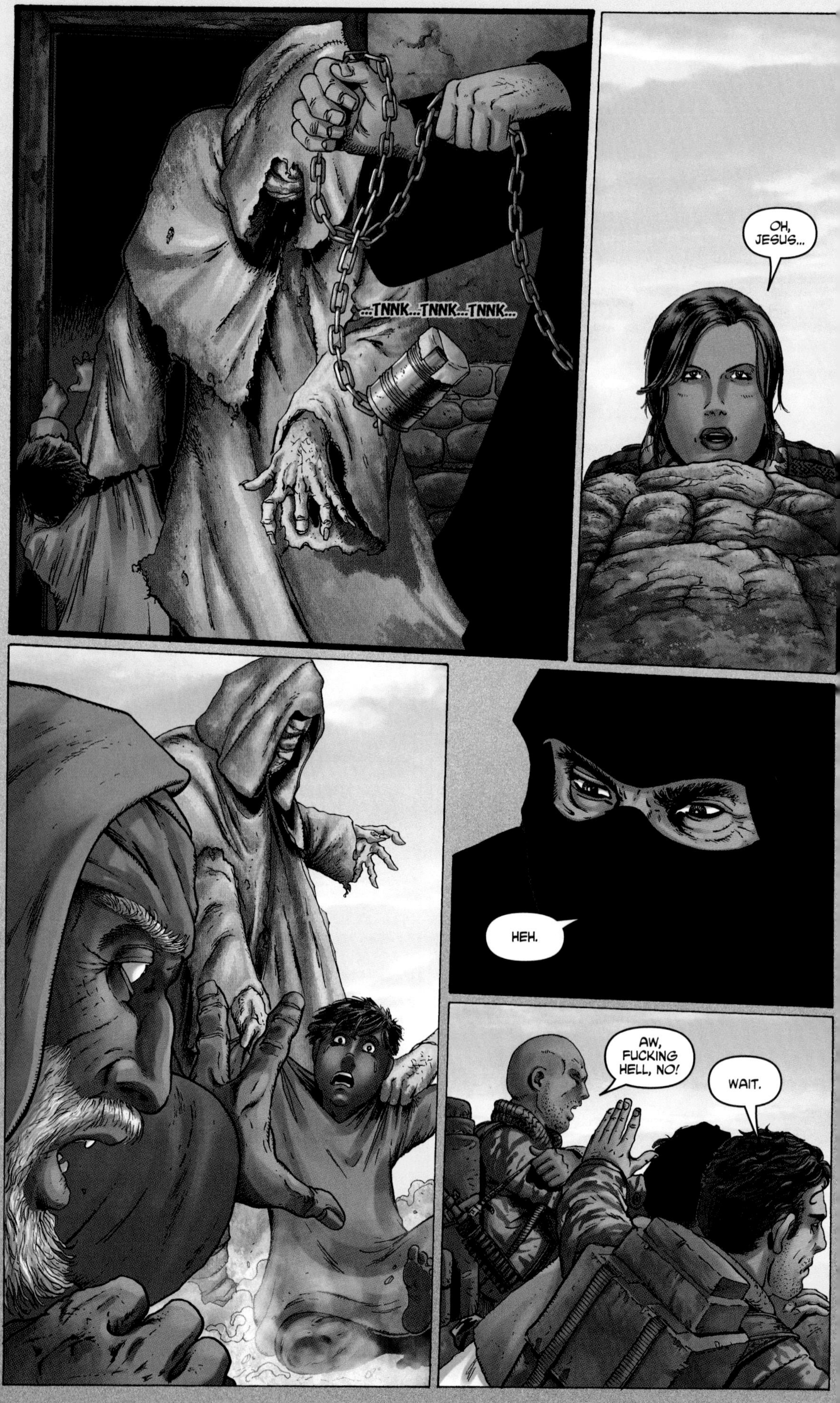
...TNNK...TNNK...TNNK...
OH, JESUS...
HEH.
AW, FUCKING HELL, NO!
WAIT.

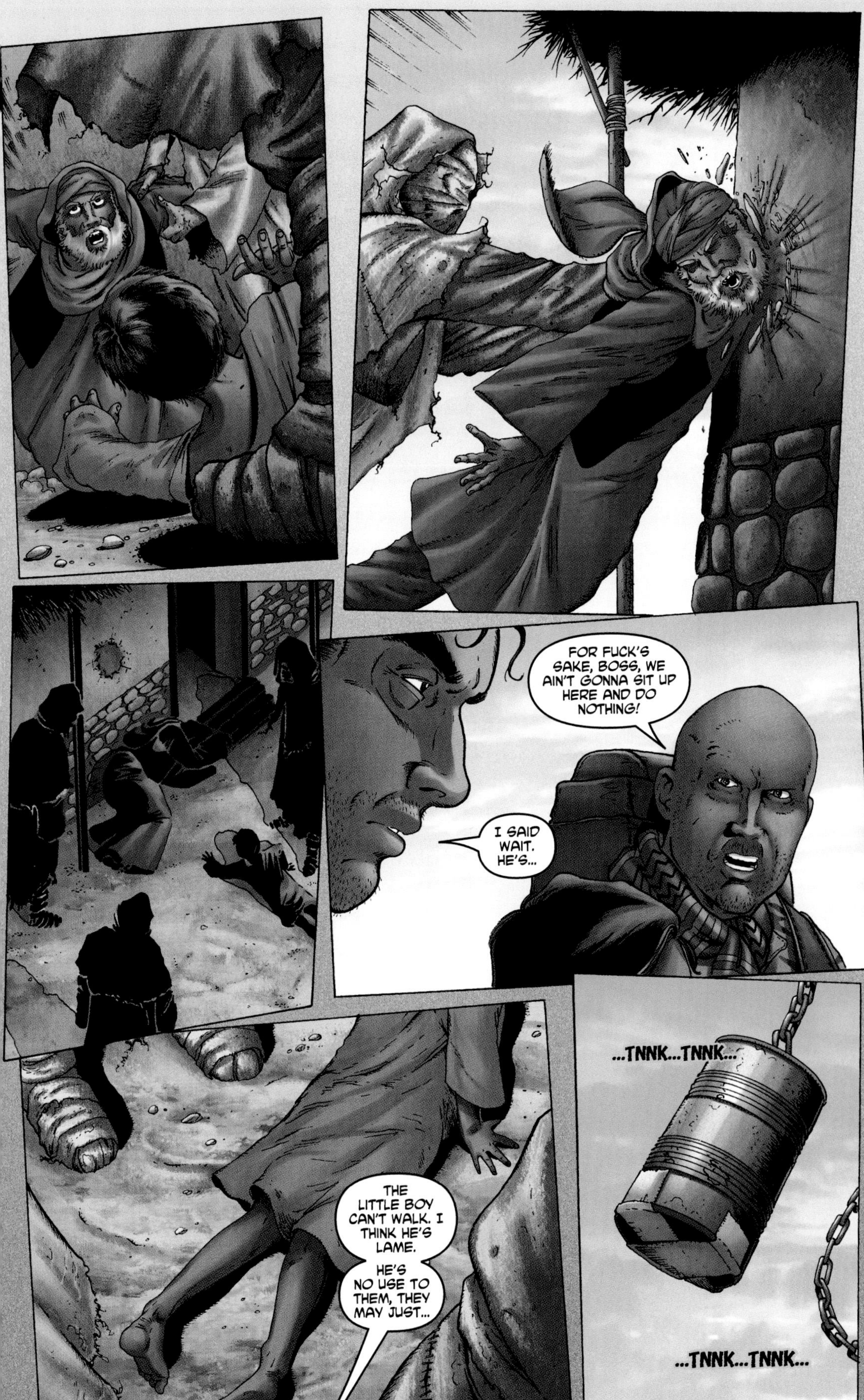
FOR FUCK'S SAKE, BOSS, WE AIN'T GONNA SIT UP HERE AND DO NOTHING!
I SAID WAIT. HE'S...
THE LITTLE BOY CAN'T WALK. I THINK HE'S LAME.
HE'S NO USE TO THEM, THEY MAY JUST...
...TNNK...TNNK...
...TNNK...TNNK...

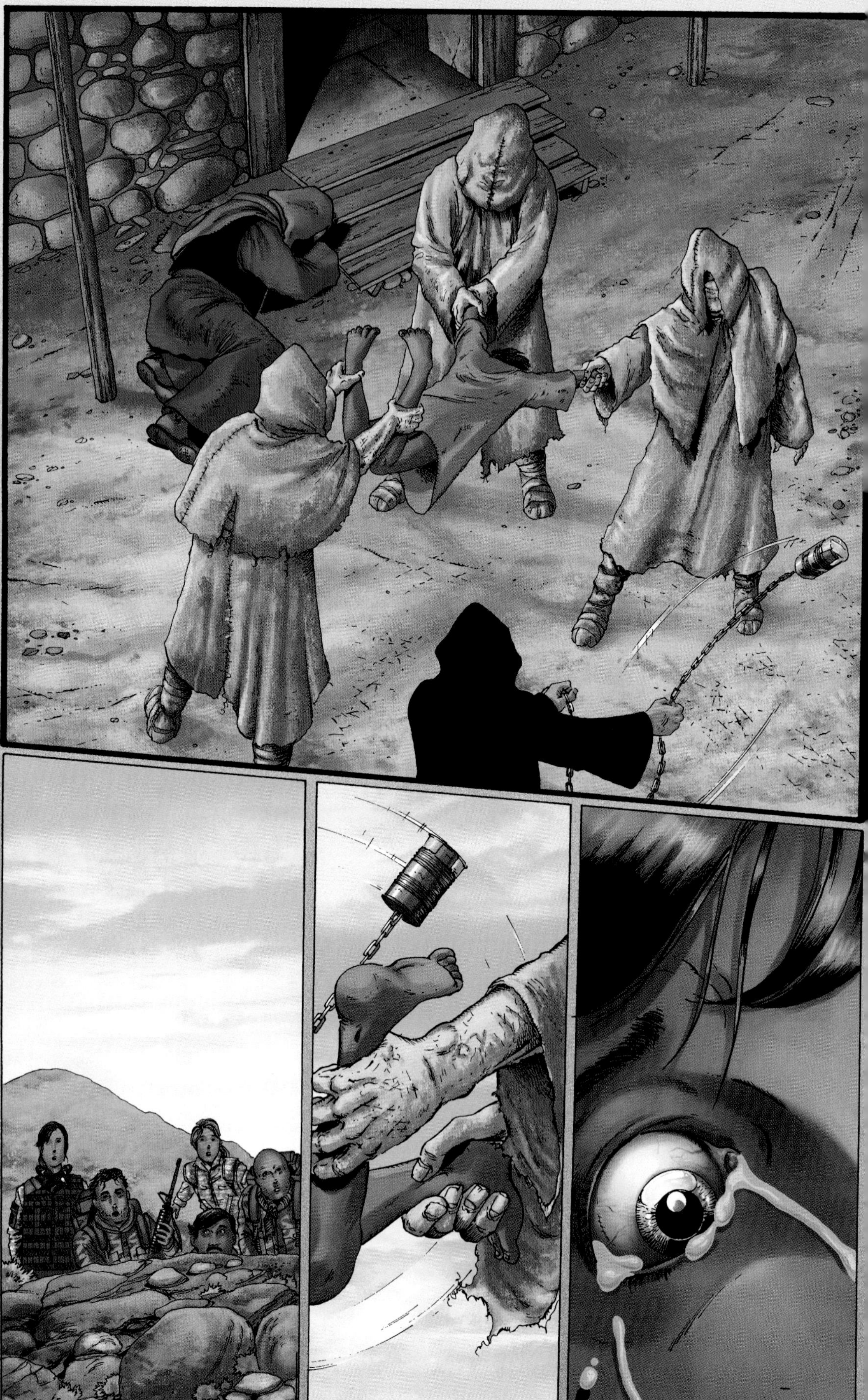

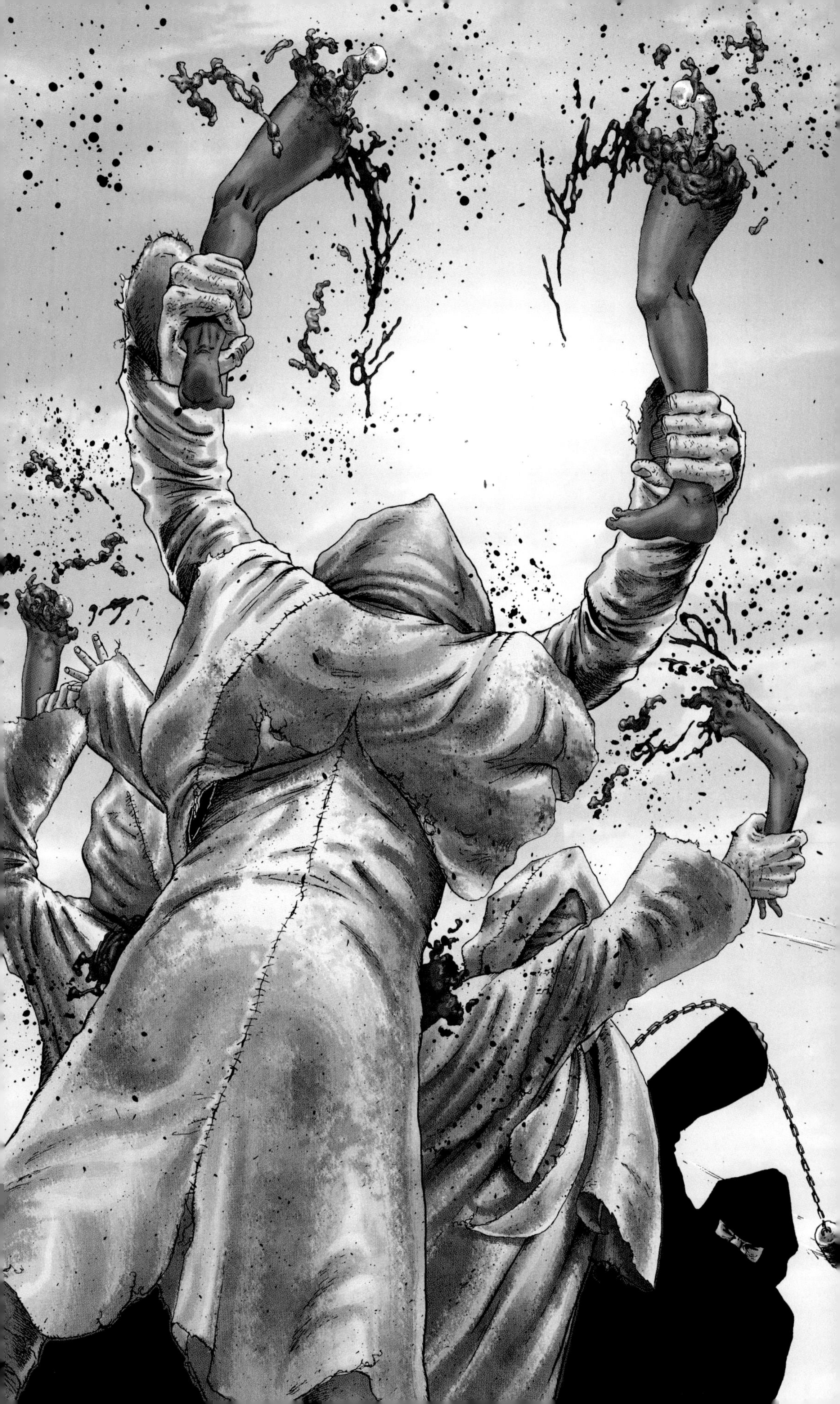

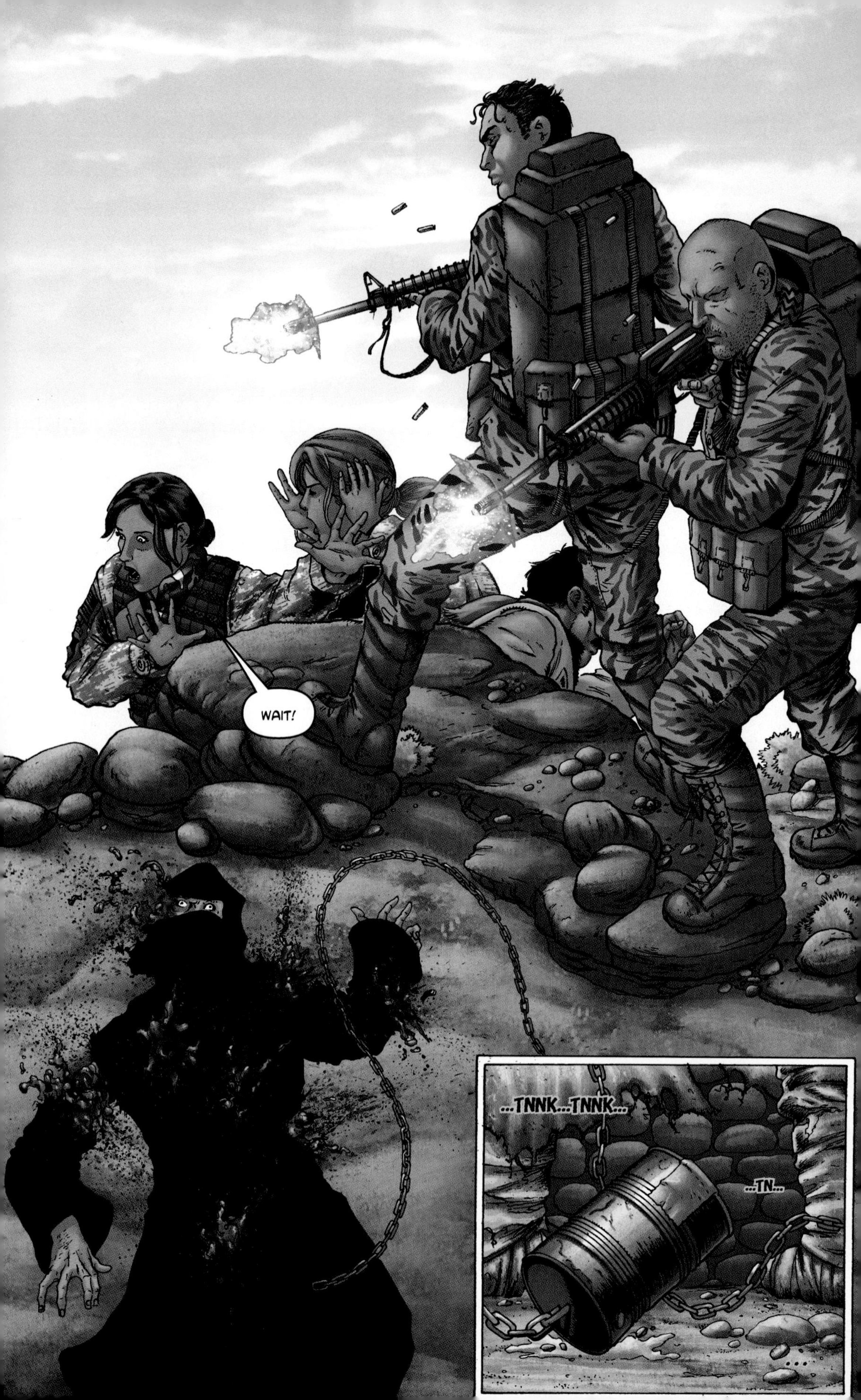
WAIT!
...TNNK...TNNK...
...TN...

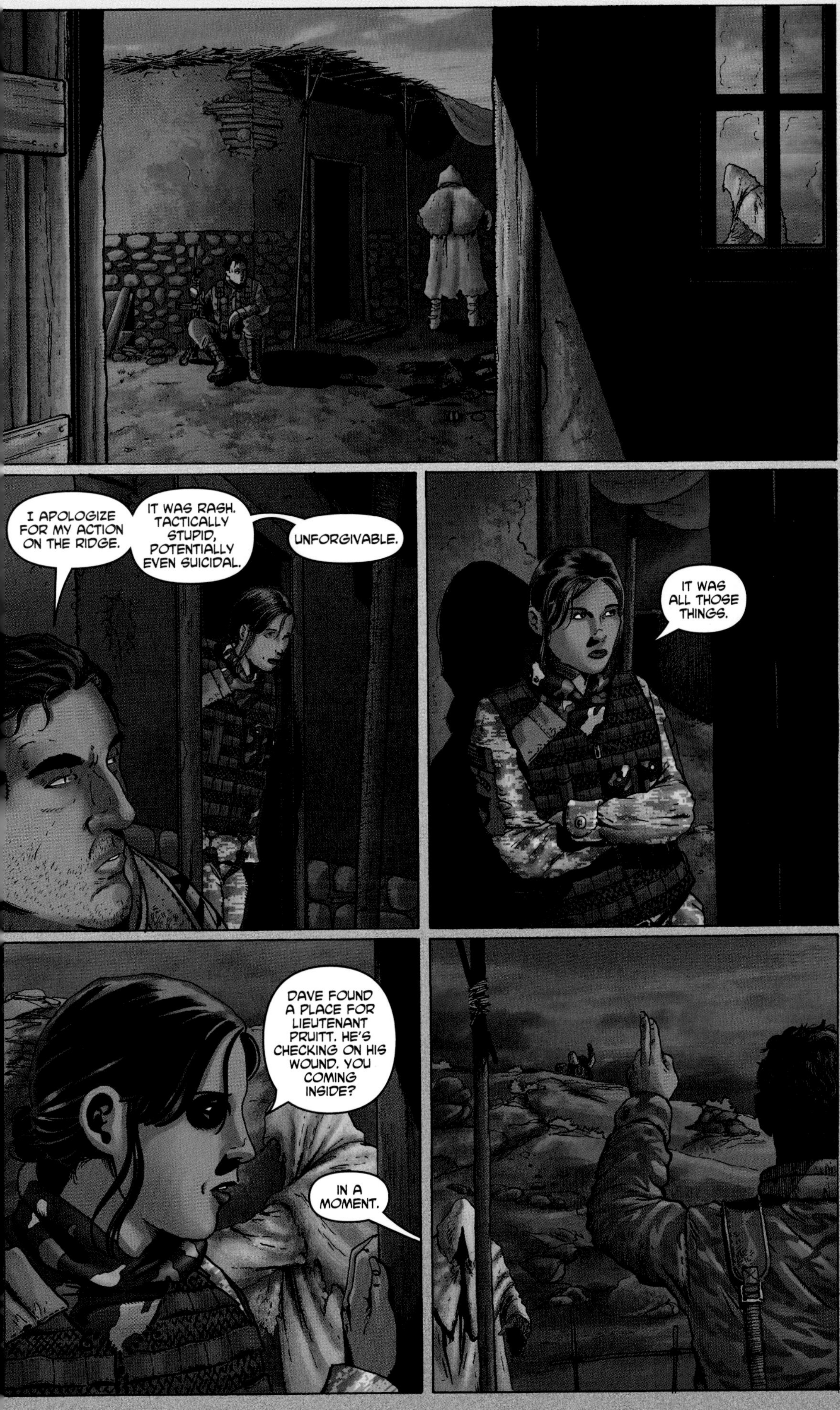
I APOLOGIZE FOR MY ACTION ON THE RIDGE.
IT WAS RASH. TACTICALLY STUPID, POTENTIALLY EVEN SUICIDAL.
UNFORGIVABLE.
IT WAS ALL THOSE THINGS.
DAVE FOUND A PLACE FOR LIEUTENANT PRUITT. HE'S CHECKING ON HIS WOUND. YOU COMING INSIDE?
IN A MOMENT.

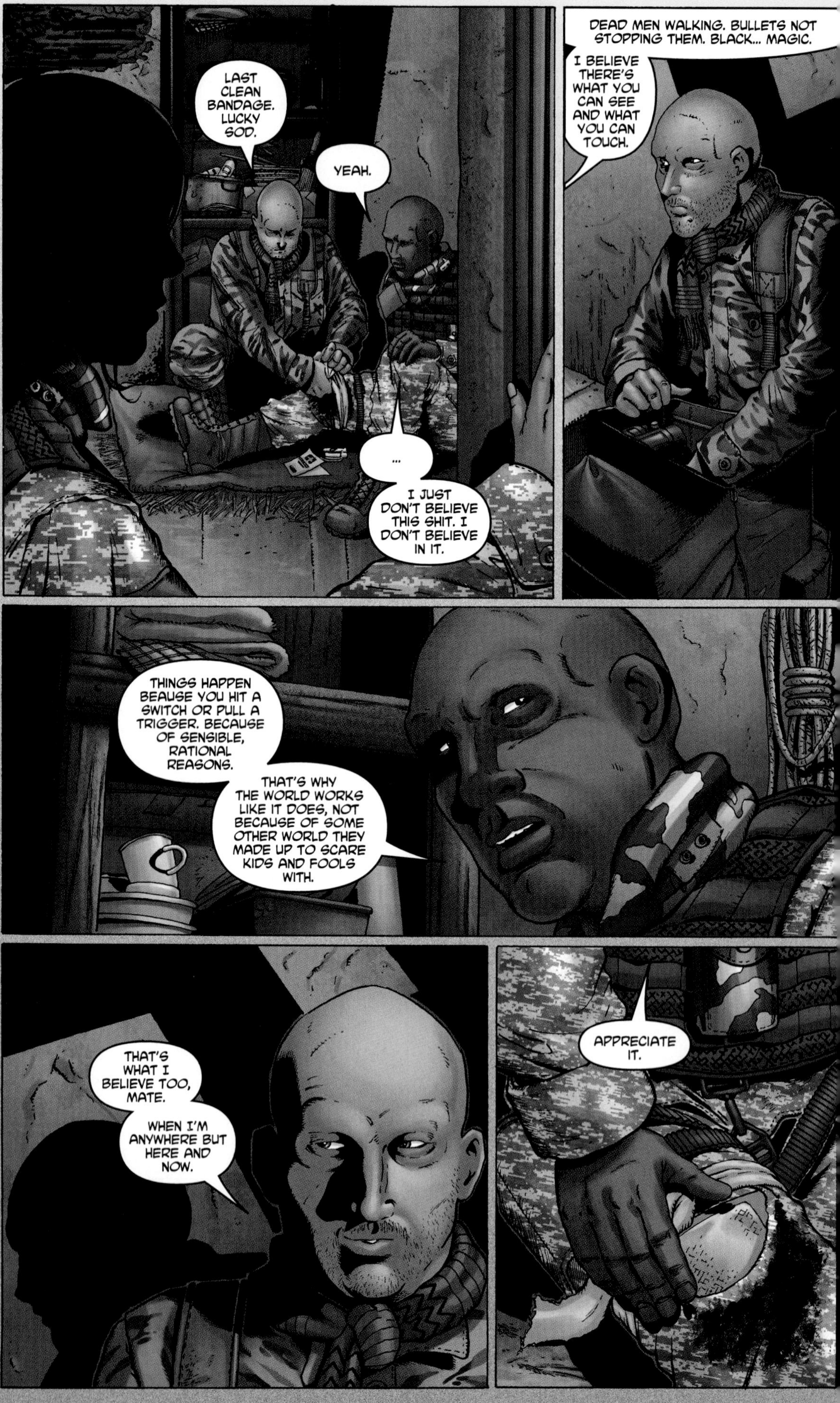
LAST CLEAN BANDAGE. LUCKY SOD.
YEAH.
...
I JUST DON'T BELIEVE THIS SHIT. I DON'T BELIEVE IN IT.
DEAD MEN WALKING. BULLETS NOT STOPPING THEM. BLACK... MAGIC.
I BELIEVE THERE'S WHAT YOU CAN SEE AND WHAT YOU CAN TOUCH.
THINGS HAPPEN BEAUSE YOU HIT A SWITCH OR PULL A TRIGGER. BECAUSE OF SENSIBLE, RATIONAL REASONS.
THAT'S WHY THE WORLD WORKS LIKE IT DOES, NOT BECAUSE OF SOME OTHER WORLD THEY MADE UP TO SCARE KIDS AND FOOLS WITH.
THAT'S WHAT I BELIEVE TOO, MATE.
WHEN I'M ANYWHERE BUT HERE AND NOW.
APPRECIATE IT.

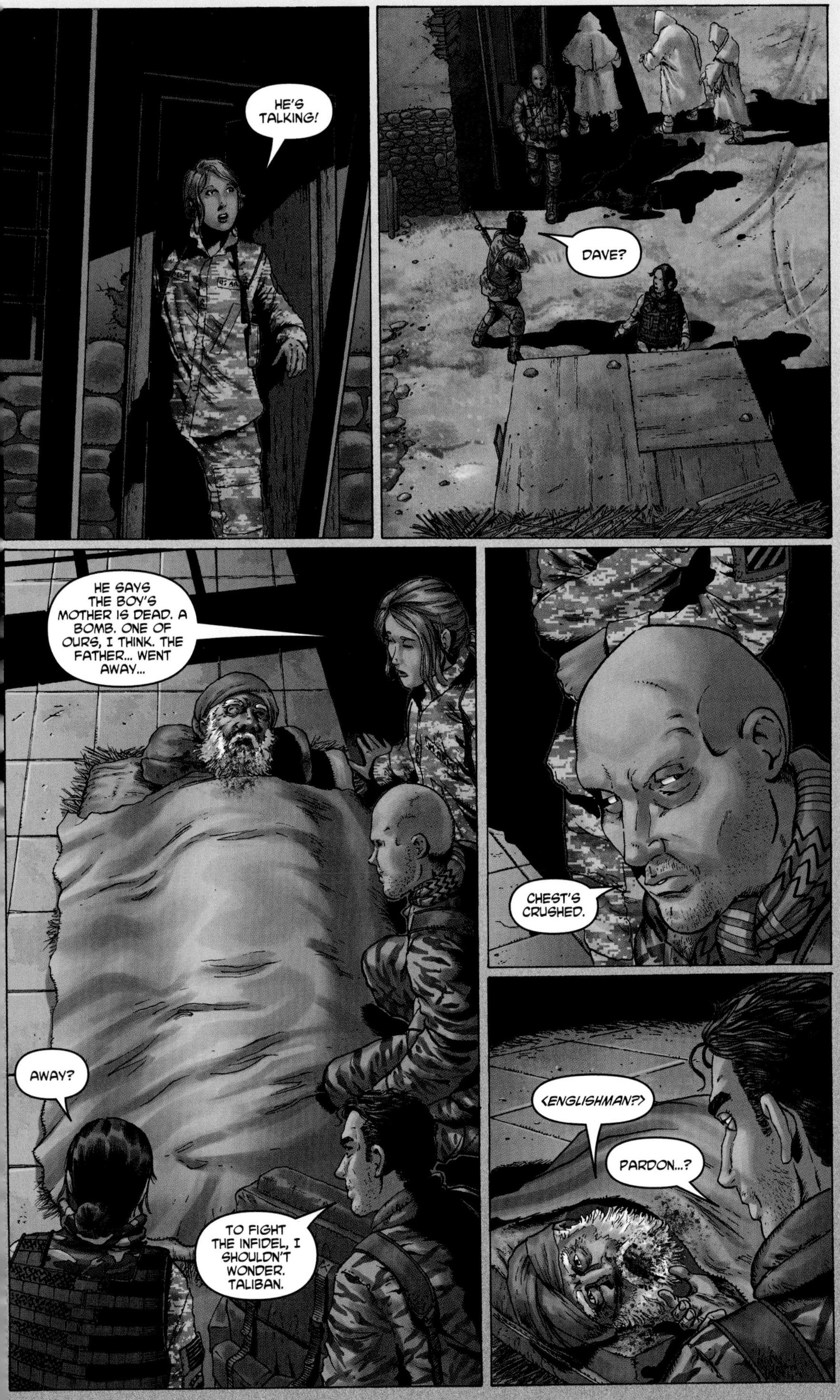
HE'S TALKING!
DAVE?
HE SAYS THE BOY'S MOTHER IS DEAD. A BOMB. ONE OF OURS, I THINK. THE FATHER... WENT AWAY...
AWAY?
TO FIGHT THE INFIDEL, I SHOULDN'T WONDER. TALIBAN.
CHEST'S CRUSHED.
<ENGLISHMAN?>
PARDON...?

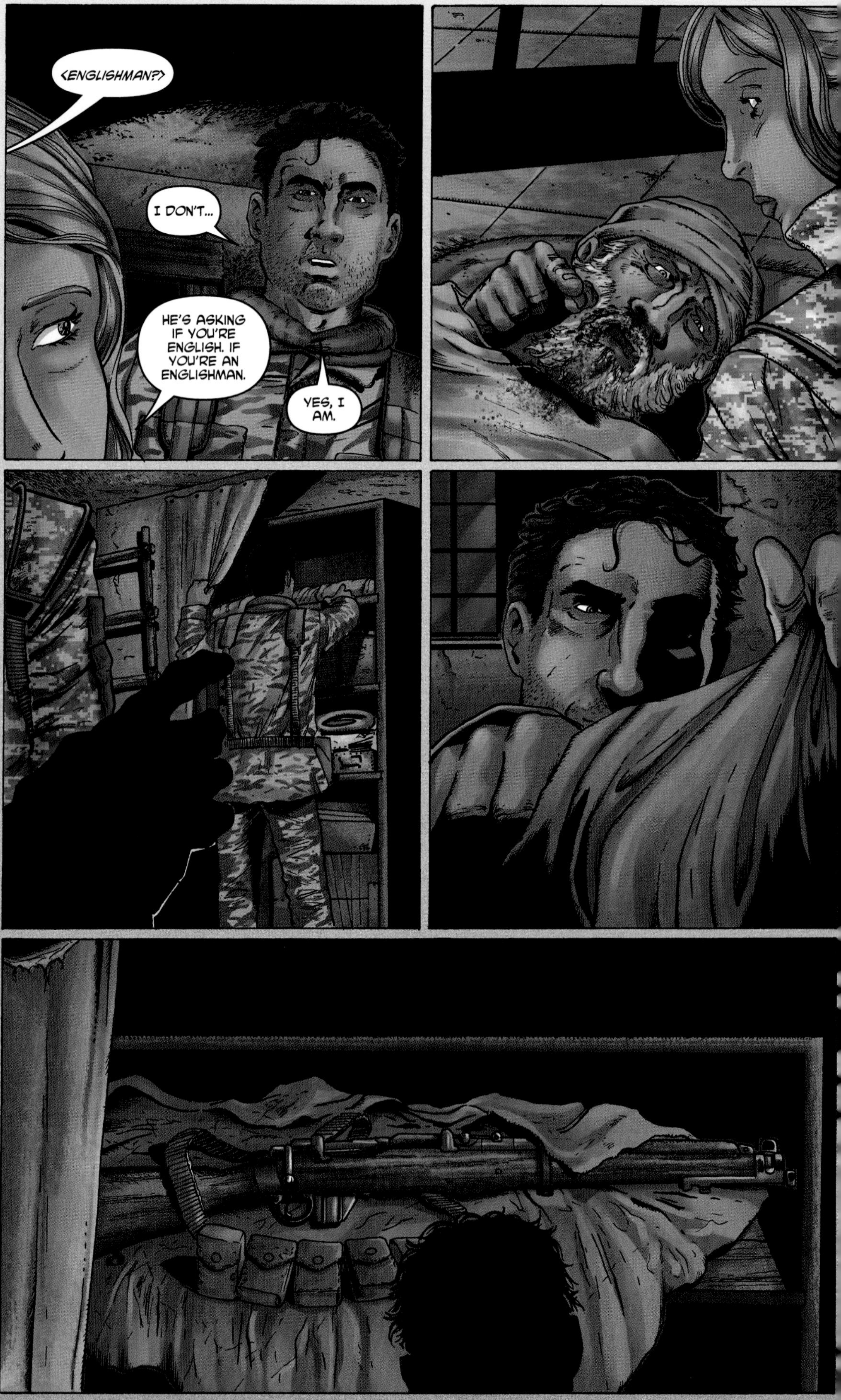
<ENGLISHMAN?>
I DON'T...
HE'S ASKING IF YOU'RE ENGLISH. IF YOU'RE AN ENGLISHMAN.
YES, I AM.

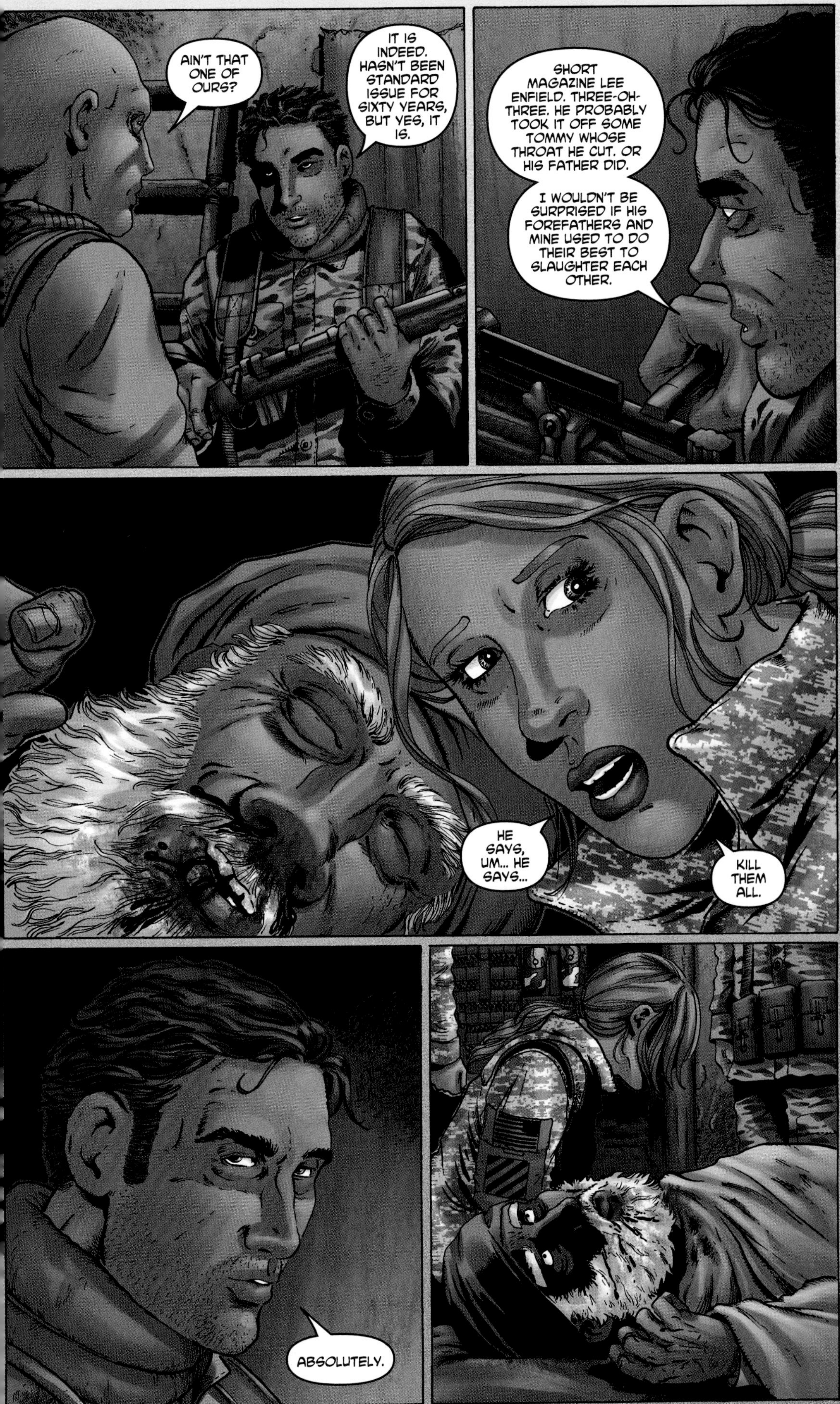
AIN'T THAT ONE OF OURS?
IT IS INDEED. HASN'T BEEN STANDARD ISSUE FOR SIXTY YEARS, BUT YES, IT IS.
SHORT MAGAZINE LEE ENFIELD. THREE-OH-THREE. HE PROBABLY TOOK IT OFF SOME TOMMY WHOSE THROAT HE CUT. OR HIS FATHER DID.
I WOULDN'T BE SURPRISED IF HIS FOREFATHERS AND MINE USED TO DO THEIR BEST TO SLAUGHTER EACH OTHER.
HE SAYS, UM... HE SAYS...
KILL THEM ALL.
ABSOLUTELY.

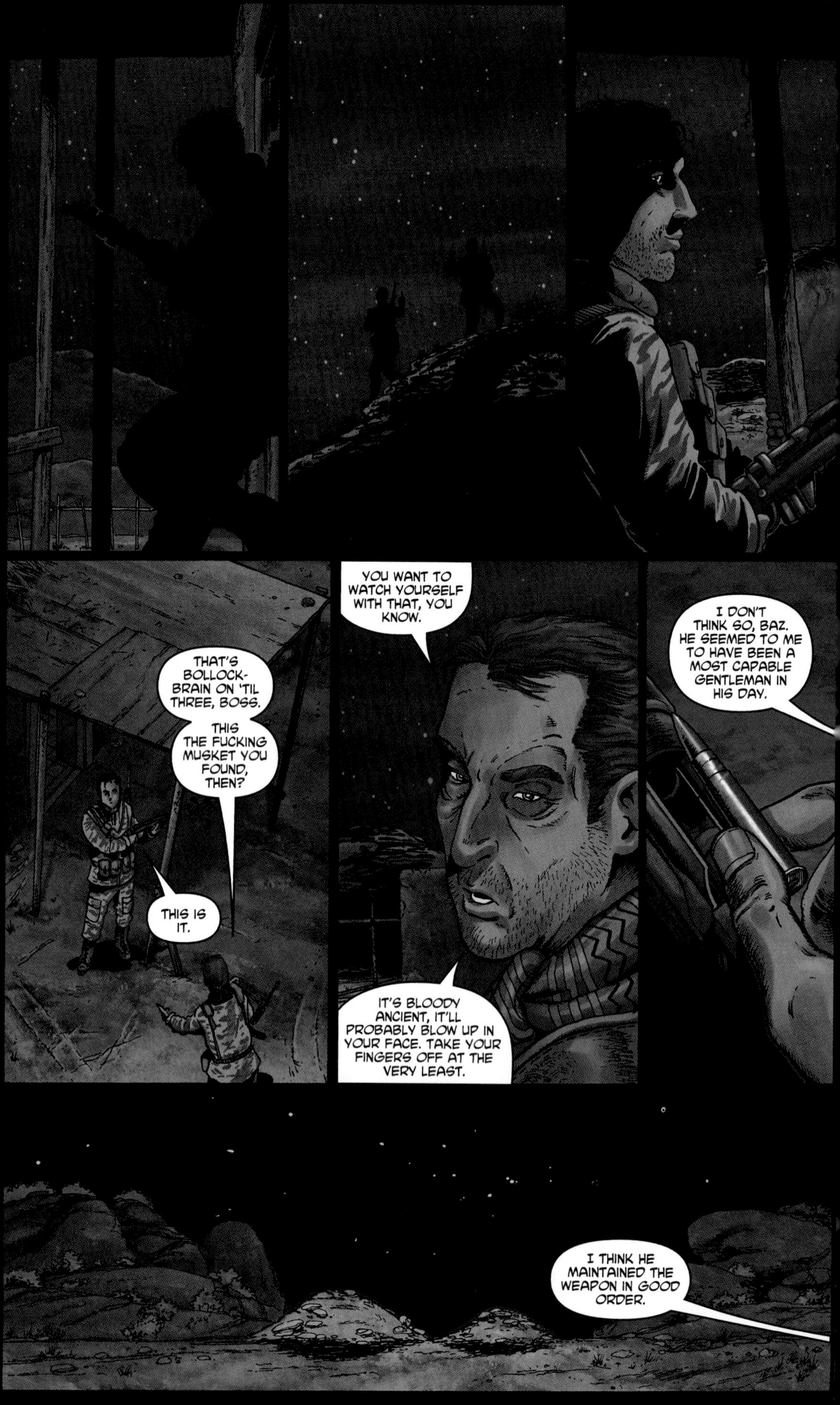
THAT'S BOLLOCK-BRAIN ON 'TIL THREE, BOSS.
THIS THE FUCKING MUSKET YOU FOUND, THEN?
THIS IS IT.
YOU WANT TO WATCH YOURSELF WITH THAT, YOU KNOW.
IT'S BLOODY ANCIENT, IT'LL PROBABLY BLOW UP IN YOUR FACE. TAKE YOUR FINGERS OFF AT THE VERY LEAST.
I DON'T THINK SO, BAZ. HE SEEMED TO ME TO HAVE BEEN A MOST CAPABLE GENTLEMAN IN HIS DAY.
I THINK HE MAINTAINED THE WEAPON IN GOOD ORDER.

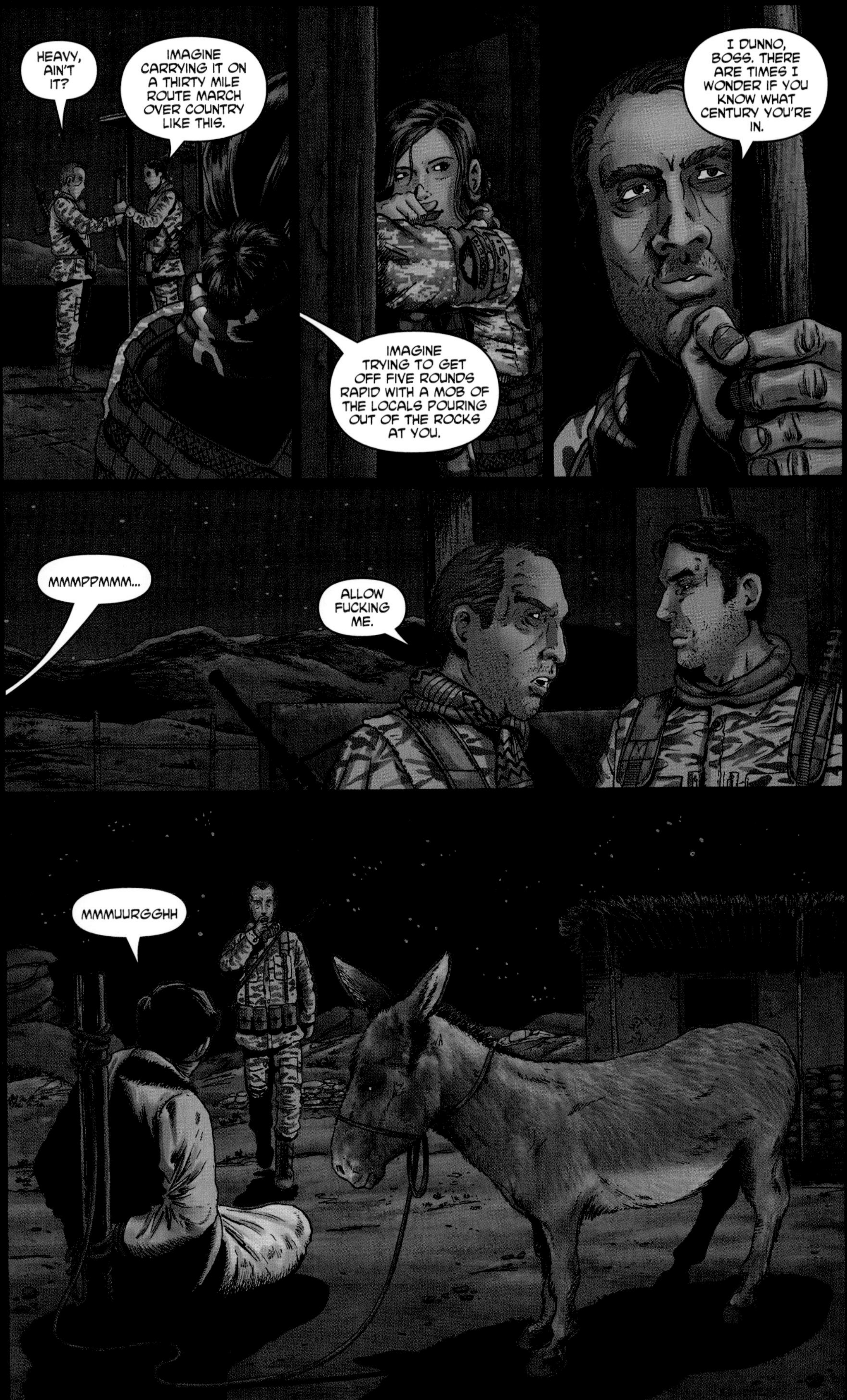
HEAVY, AIN'T IT?
IMAGINE CARRYING IT ON A THIRTY MILE ROUTE MARCH OVER COUNTRY LIKE THIS.
IMAGINE TRYING TO GET OFF FIVE ROUNDS RAPID WITH A MOB OF THE LOCALS POURING OUT OF THE ROCKS AT YOU.
I DUNNO, BOSS. THERE ARE TIMES I WONDER IF YOU KNOW WHAT CENTURY YOU'RE IN.
MMMPPMMM...
ALLOW FUCKING ME.
MMMUURGGHH

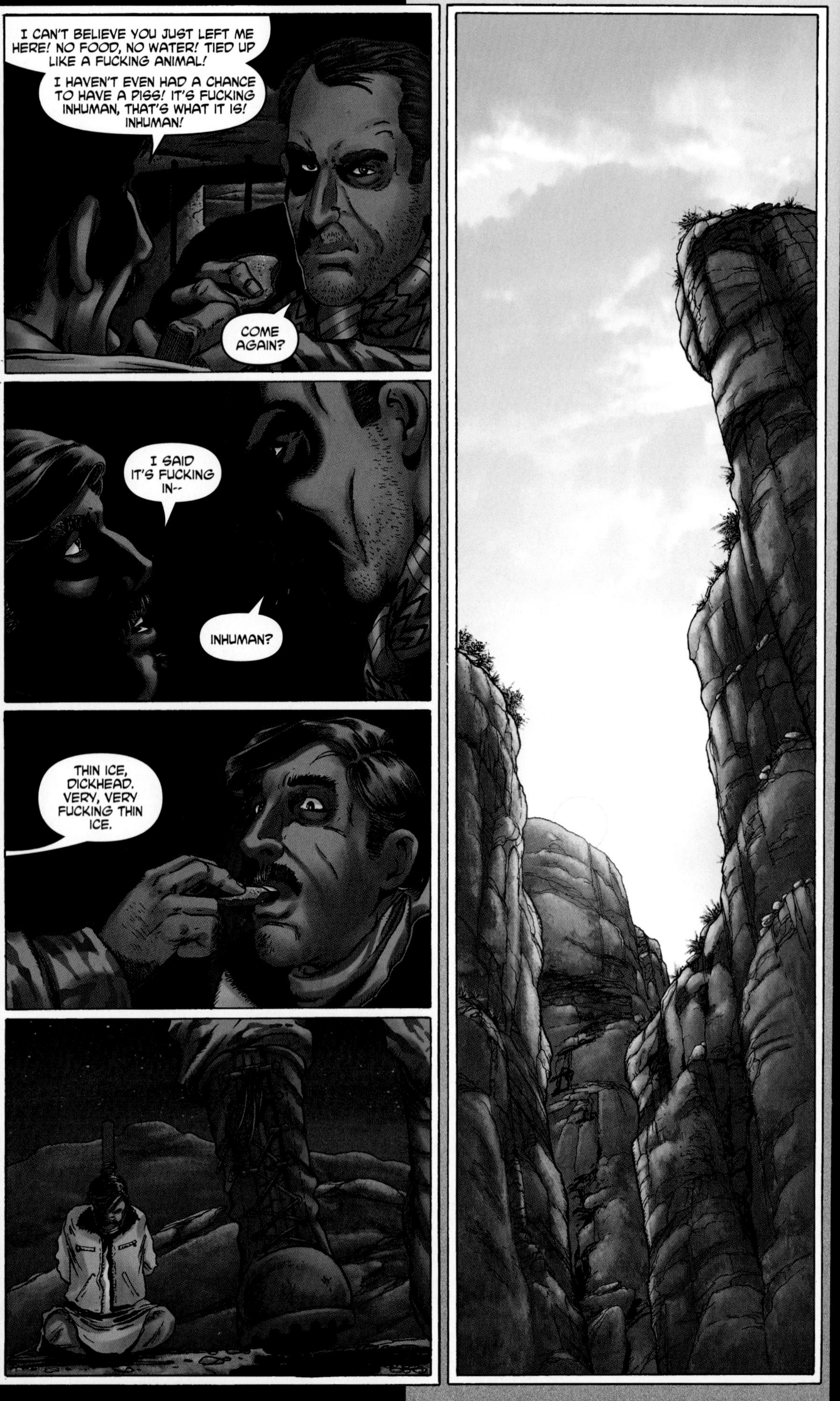
I CAN'T BELIEVE YOU JUST LEFT ME HERE! NO FOOD, NO WATER! TIED UP LIKE A FUCKING ANIMAL!
I HAVEN'T EVEN HAD A CHANCE TO HAVE A PISS! IT'S FUCKING INHUMAN, THAT'S WHAT IT IS! INHUMAN!
COME AGAIN?
I SAID IT'S FUCKING IN--
INHUMAN?
THIN ICE, DICKHEAD. VERY, VERY FUCKING THIN ICE.

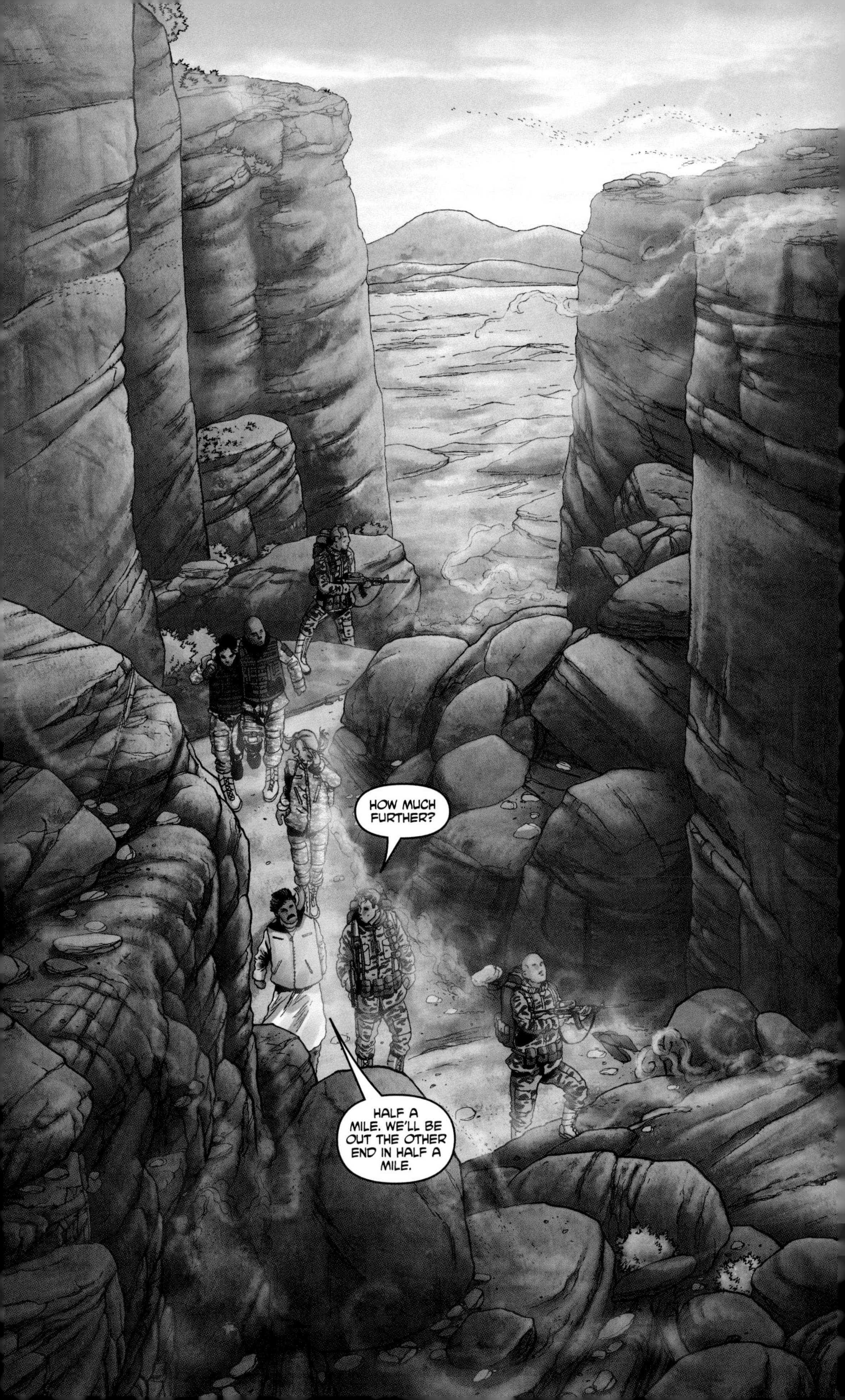
HOW MUCH FURTHER?
HALF A MILE. WE'LL BE OUT THE OTHER END IN HALF A MILE.

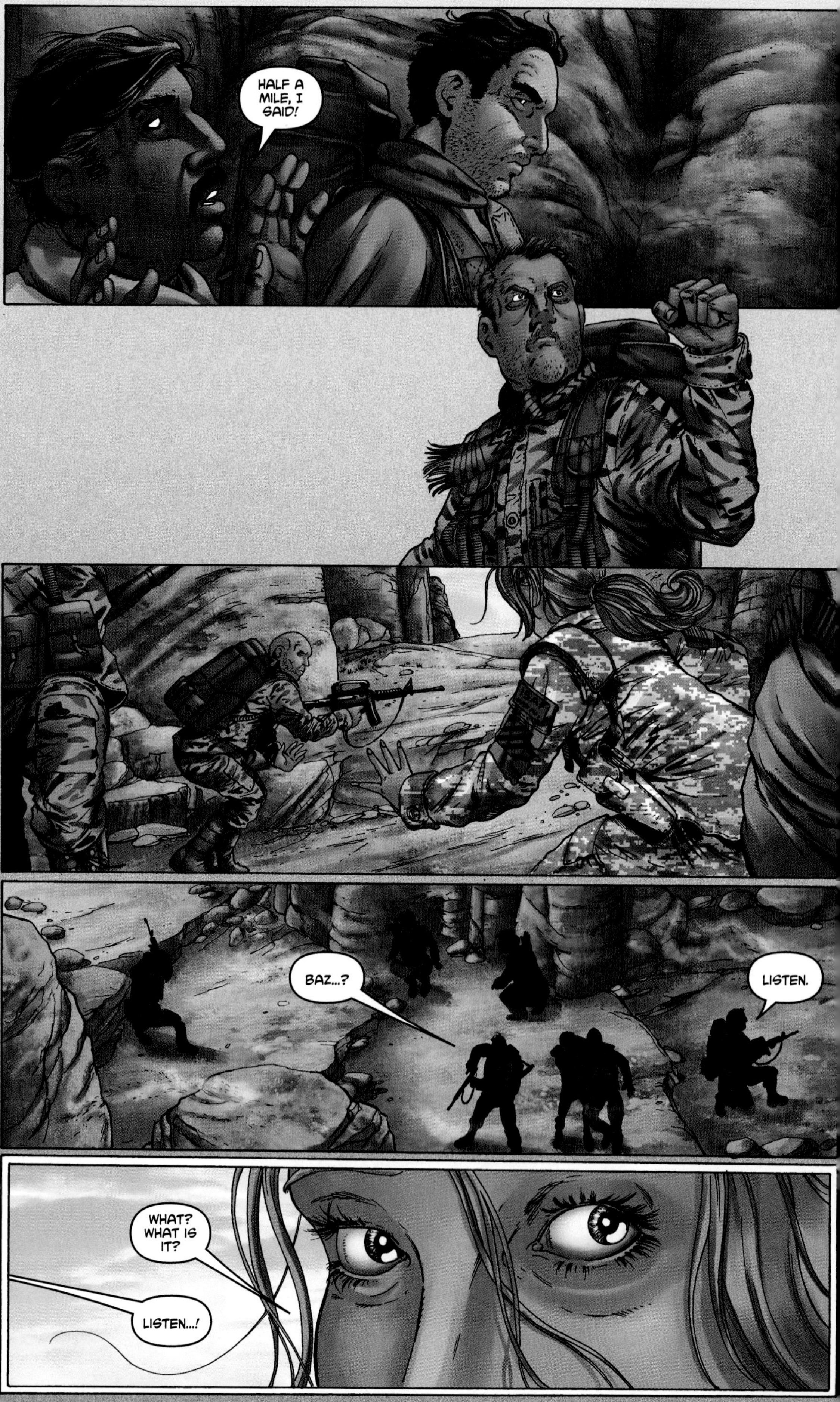
HALF A MILE, I SAID!
BAZ...?
LISTEN.
WHAT? WHAT IS IT?
LISTEN...!

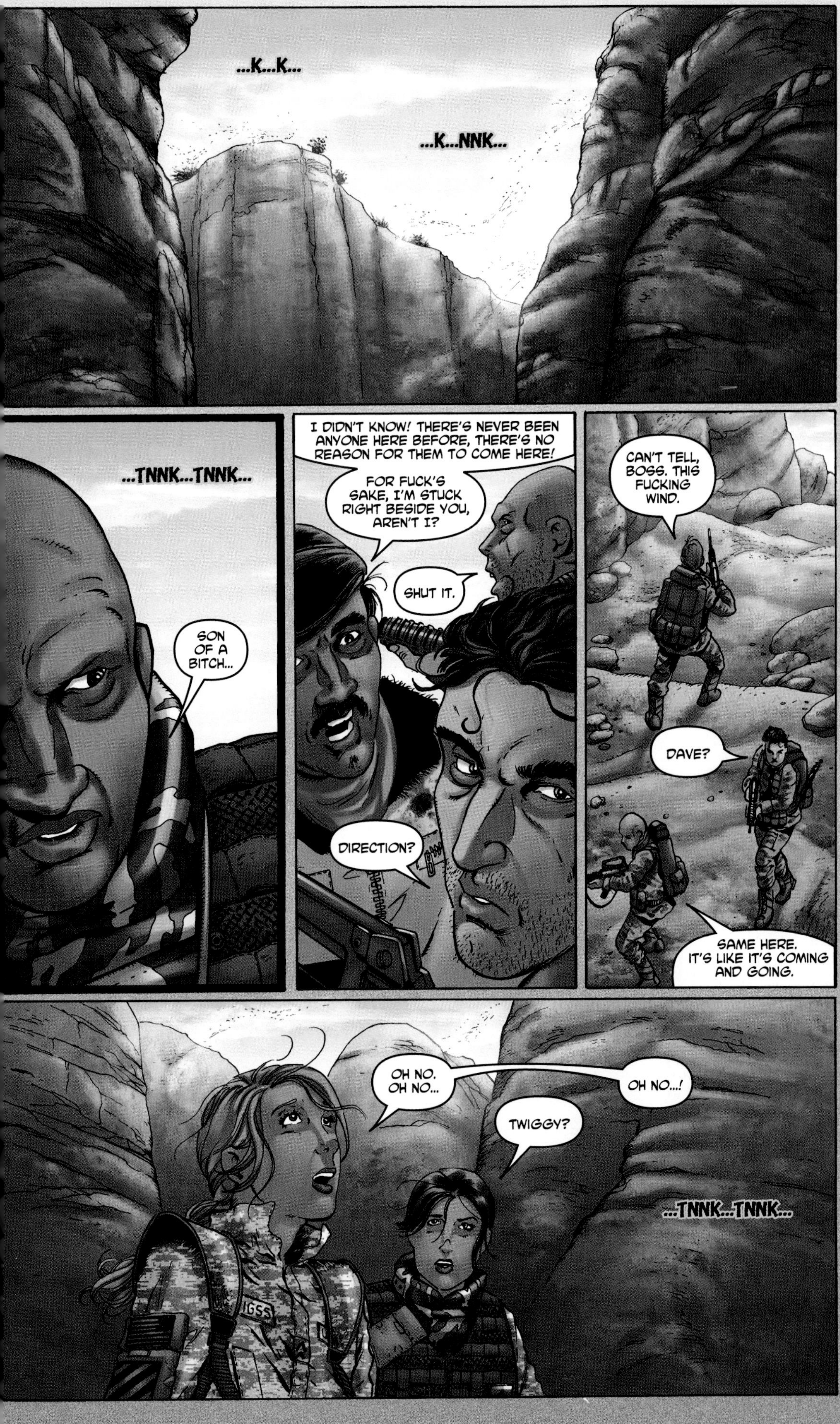
...K...K...
...K...NNK...
...TNNK...TNNK...
SON OF A BITCH...
I DIDN'T KNOW! THERE'S NEVER BEEN ANYONE HERE BEFORE, THERE'S NO REASON FOR THEM TO COME HERE!
FOR FUCK'S SAKE, I'M STUCK RIGHT BESIDE YOU, AREN'T I?
SHUT IT.
DIRECTION?
CAN'T TELL, BOSS. THIS FUCKING WIND.
DAVE?
SAME HERE. IT'S LIKE IT'S COMING AND GOING.
OH NO. OH NO...
OH NO...!
TWIGGY?
...TNNK...TNNK...

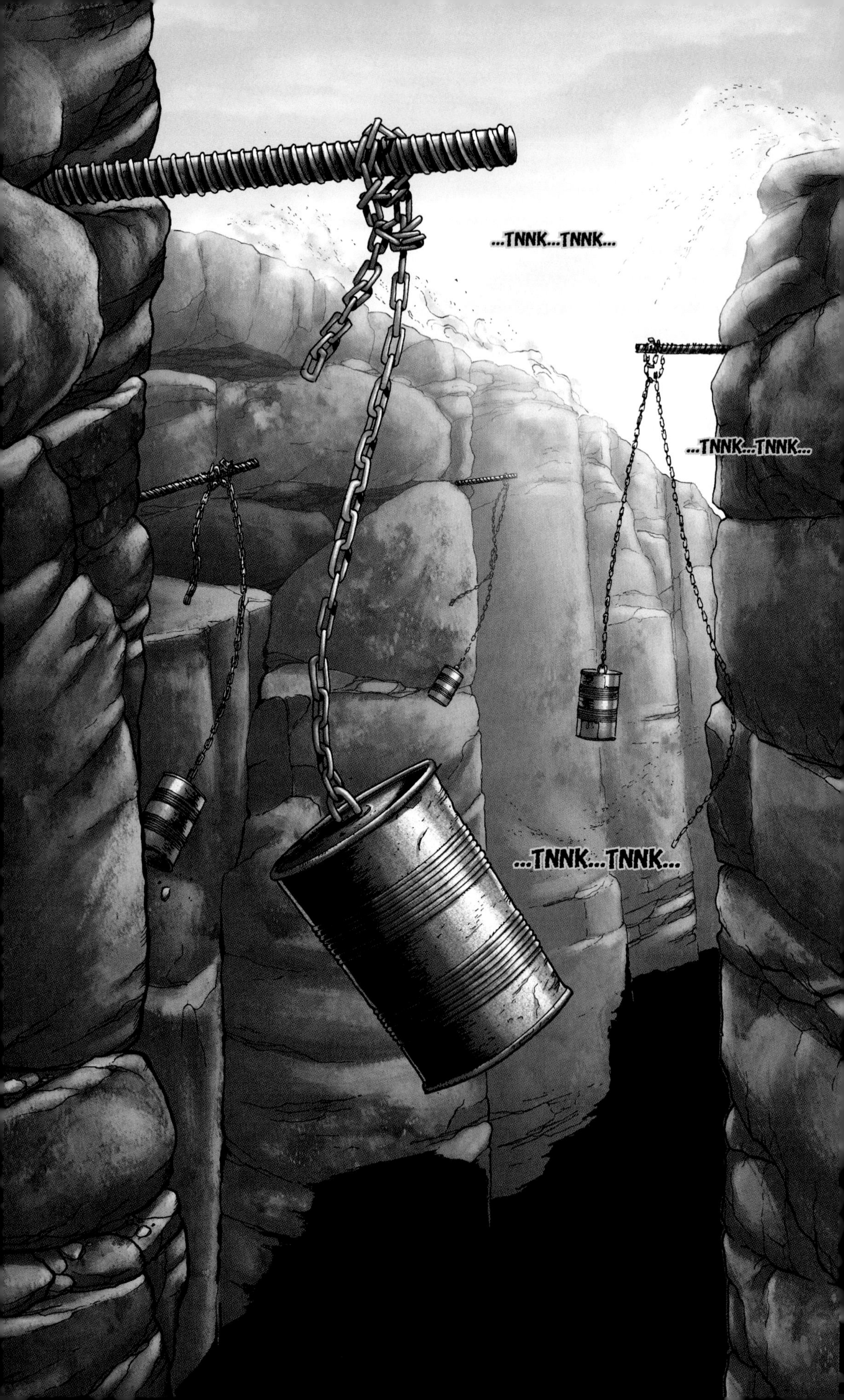
...TNNK...TNNK...
...TNNK...TNNK...
...TNNK...TNNK...

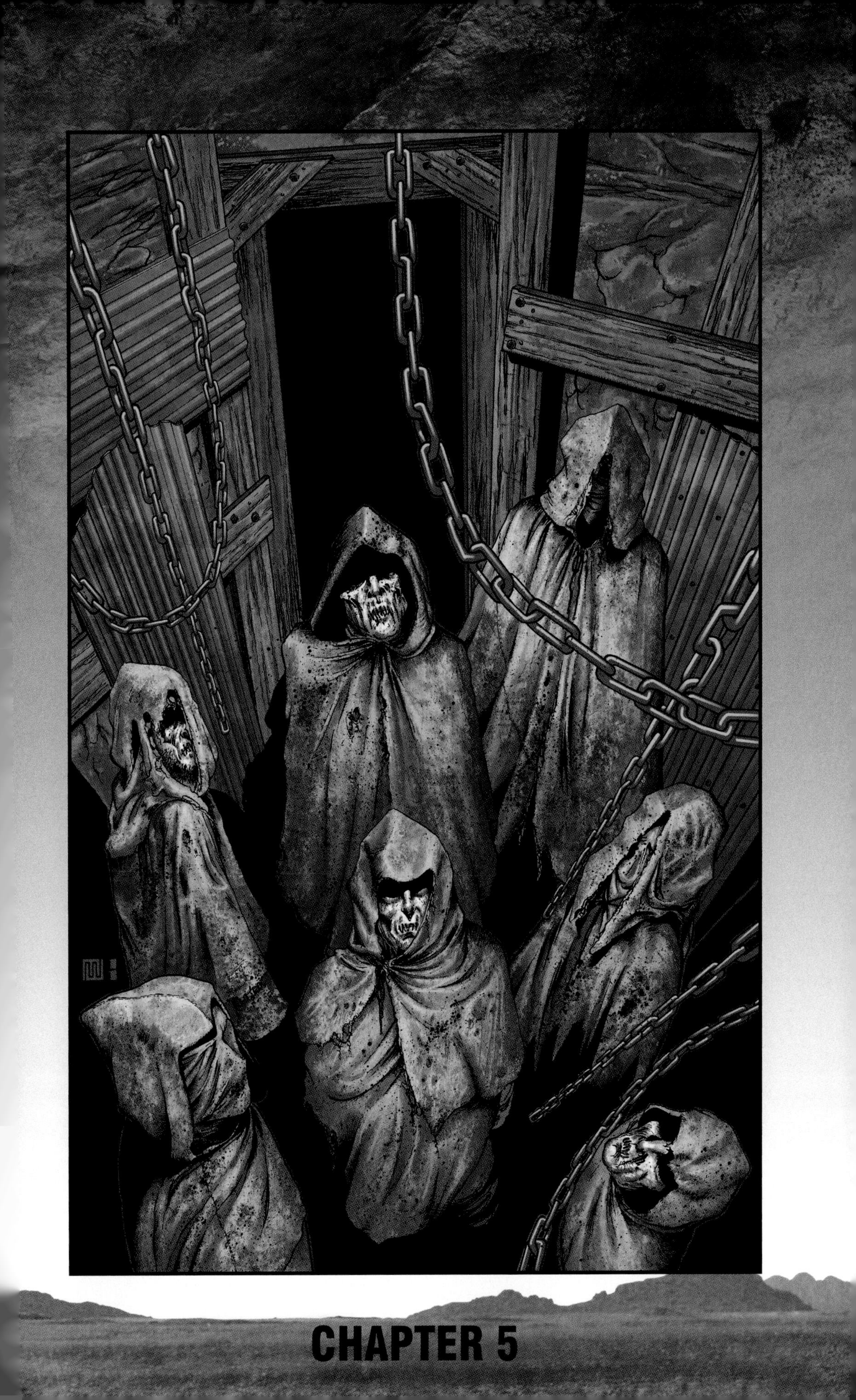

CHAPTER 5

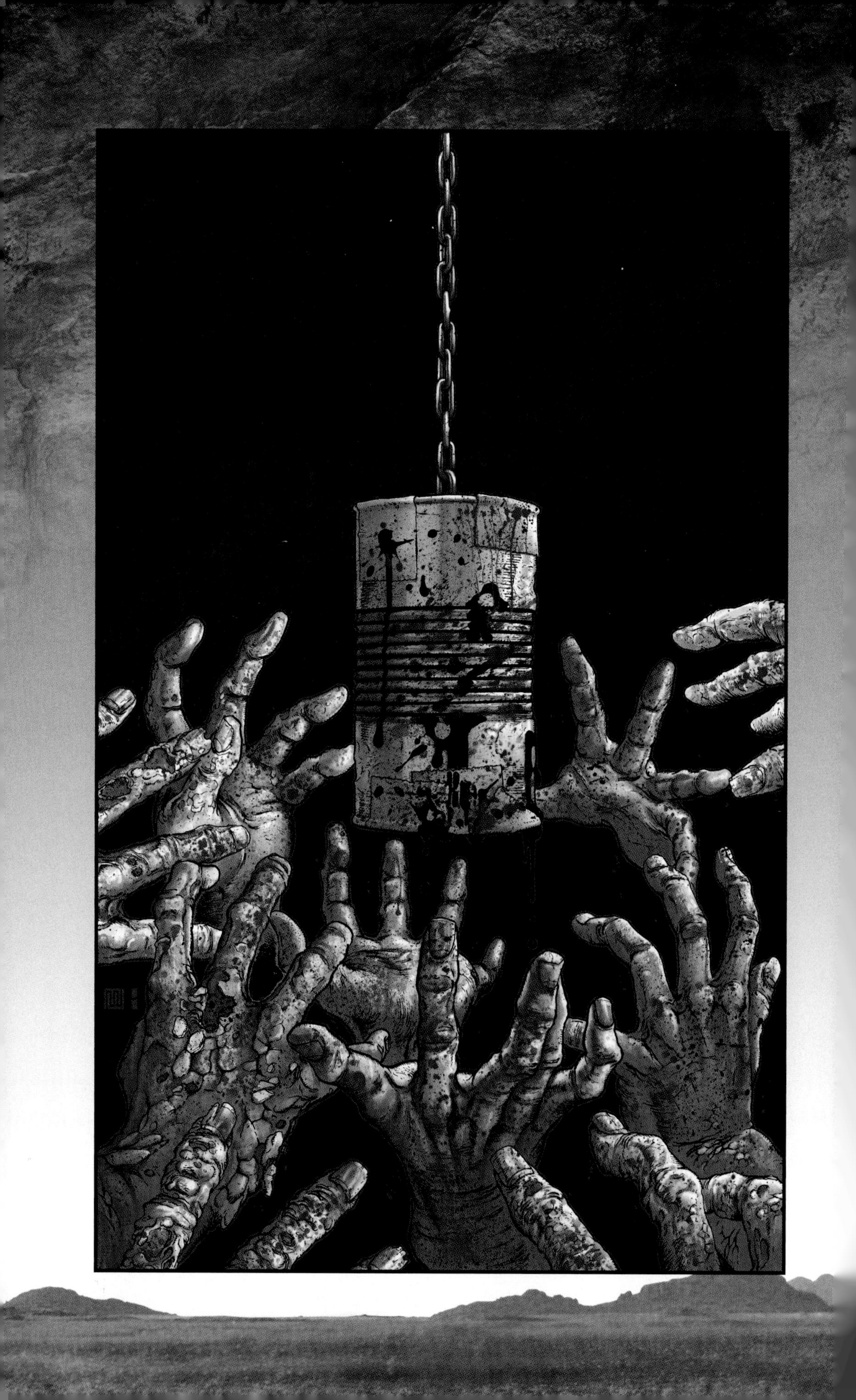

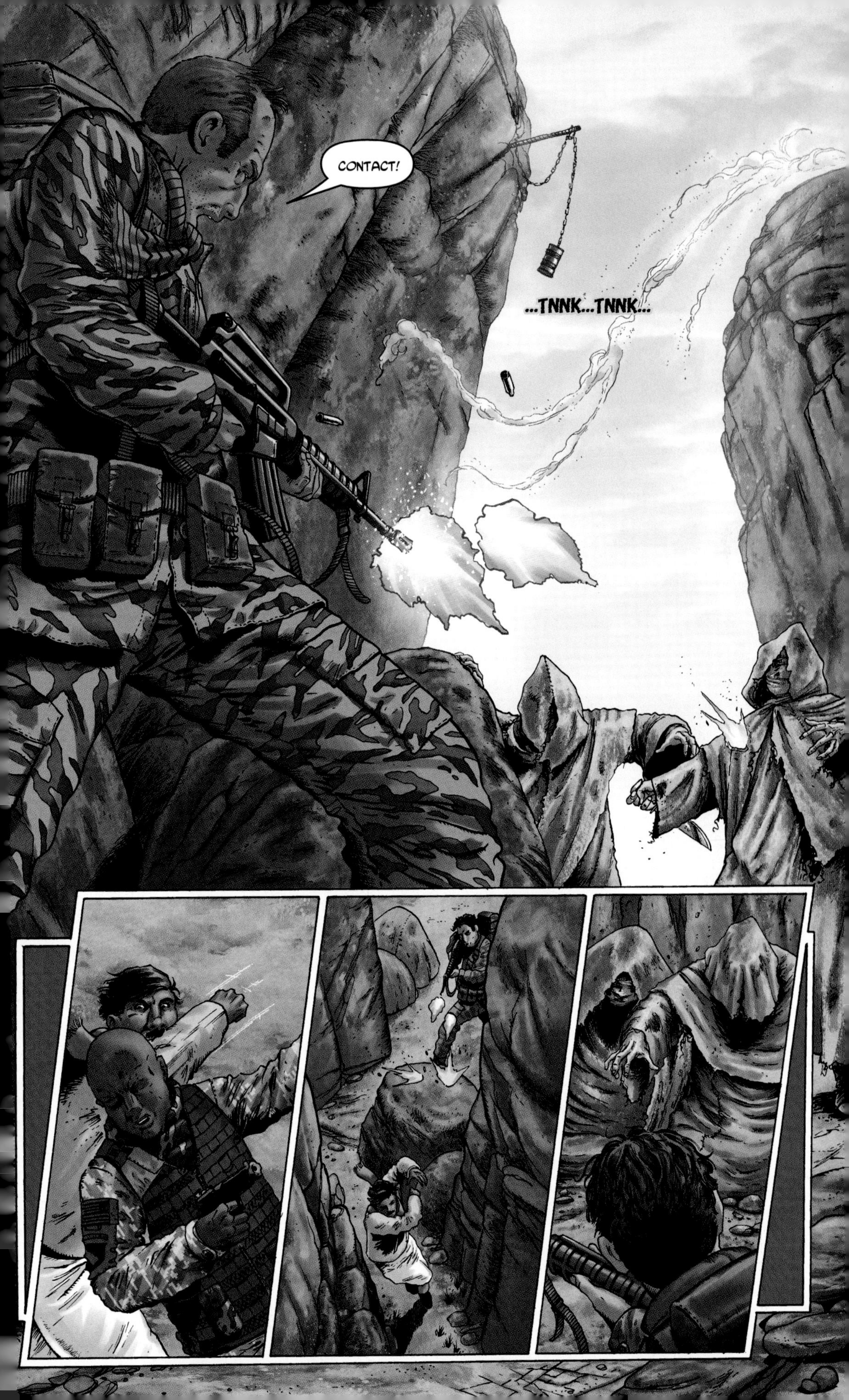
CONTACT!
...TNNK...TNNK...

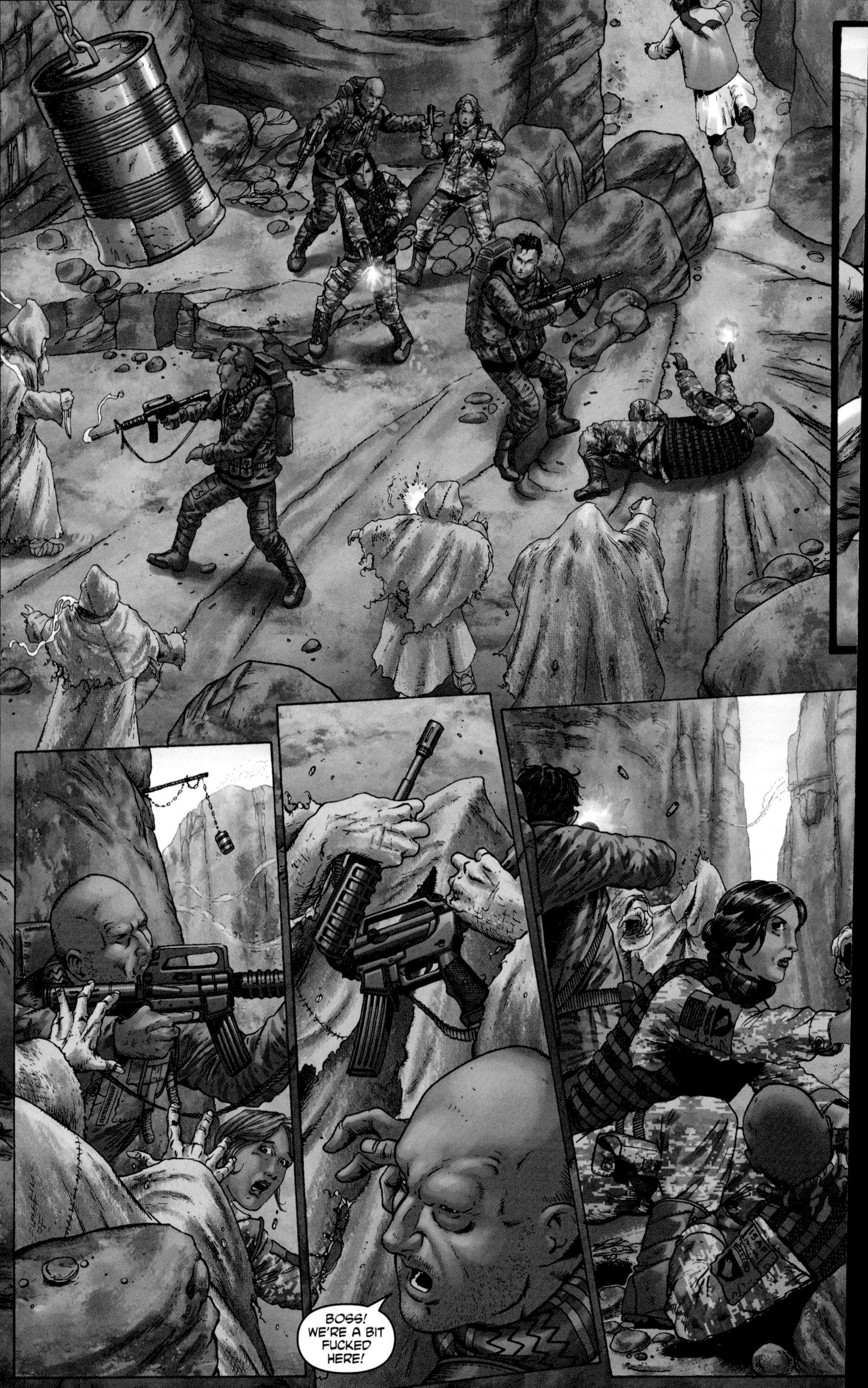
BOSS! WE'RE A BIT FUCKED HERE!

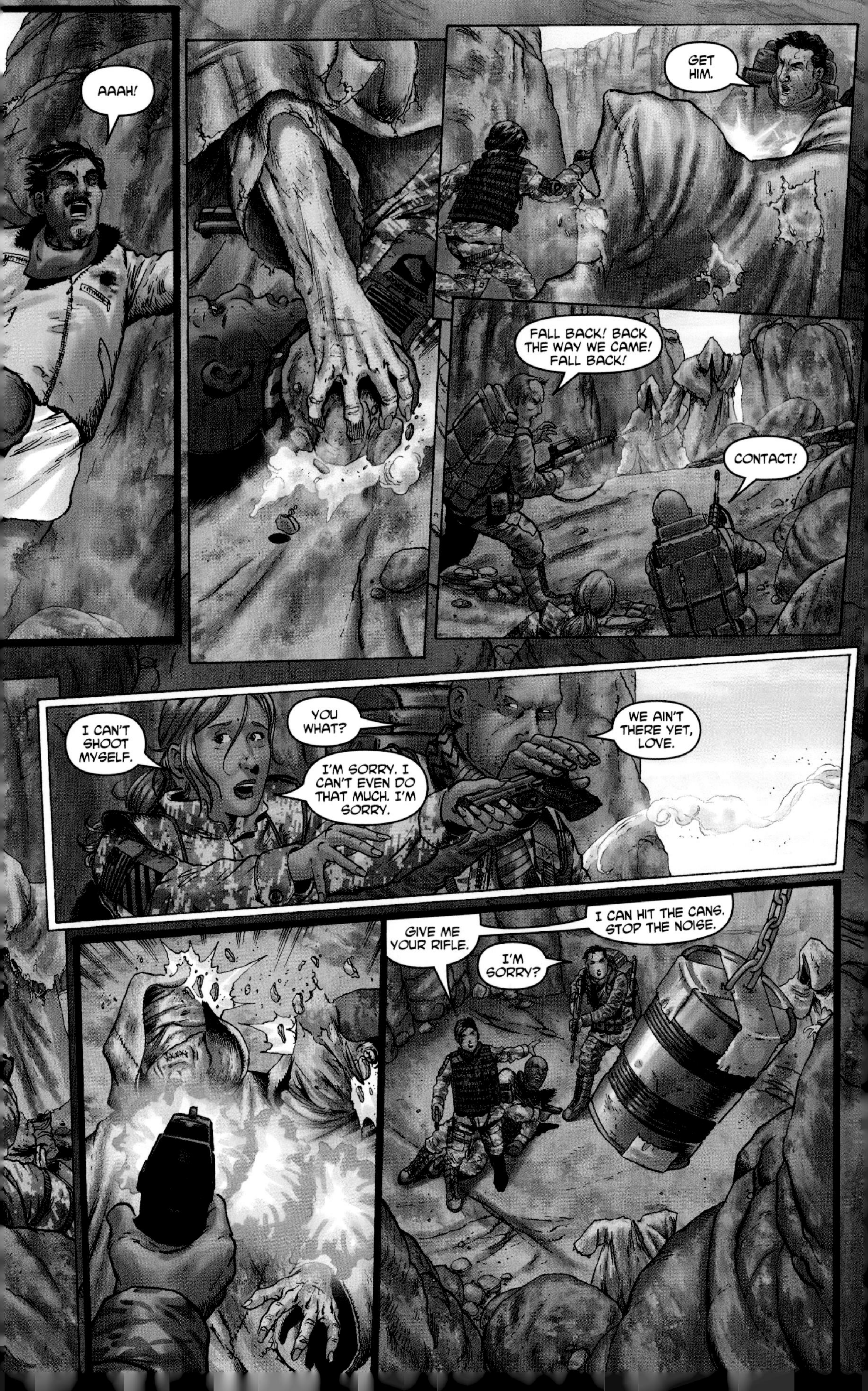
AAAH!
GET HIM.
FALL BACK! BACK THE WAY WE CAME! FALL BACK!
CONTACT!
I CAN'T SHOOT MYSELF.
YOU WHAT?
WE AIN'T THERE YET, LOVE.
I'M SORRY. I CAN'T EVEN DO THAT MUCH. I'M SORRY.
GIVE ME YOUR RIFLE.
I CAN HIT THE CANS. STOP THE NOISE.
I'M SORRY?

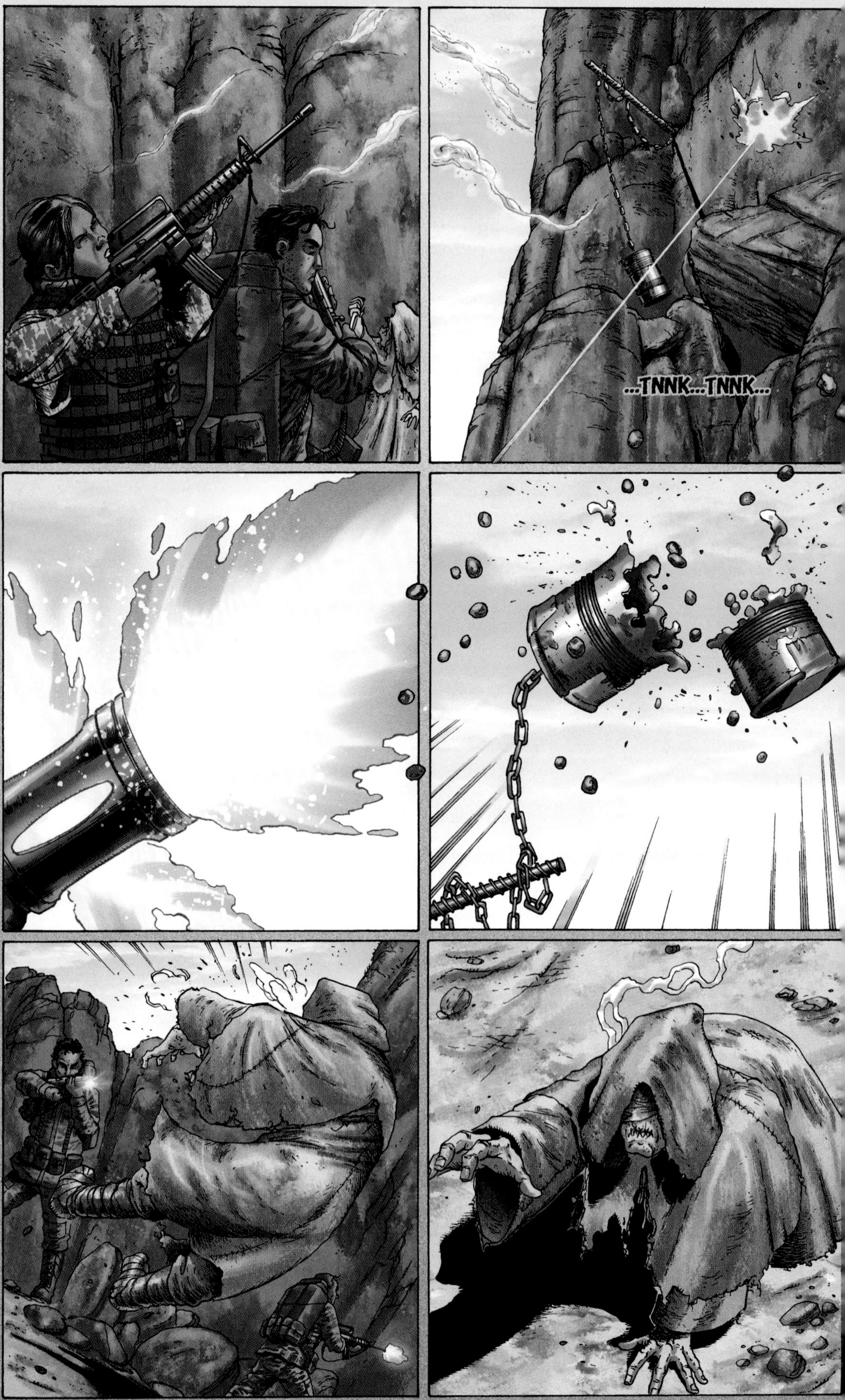
...TNNK...TNNK...

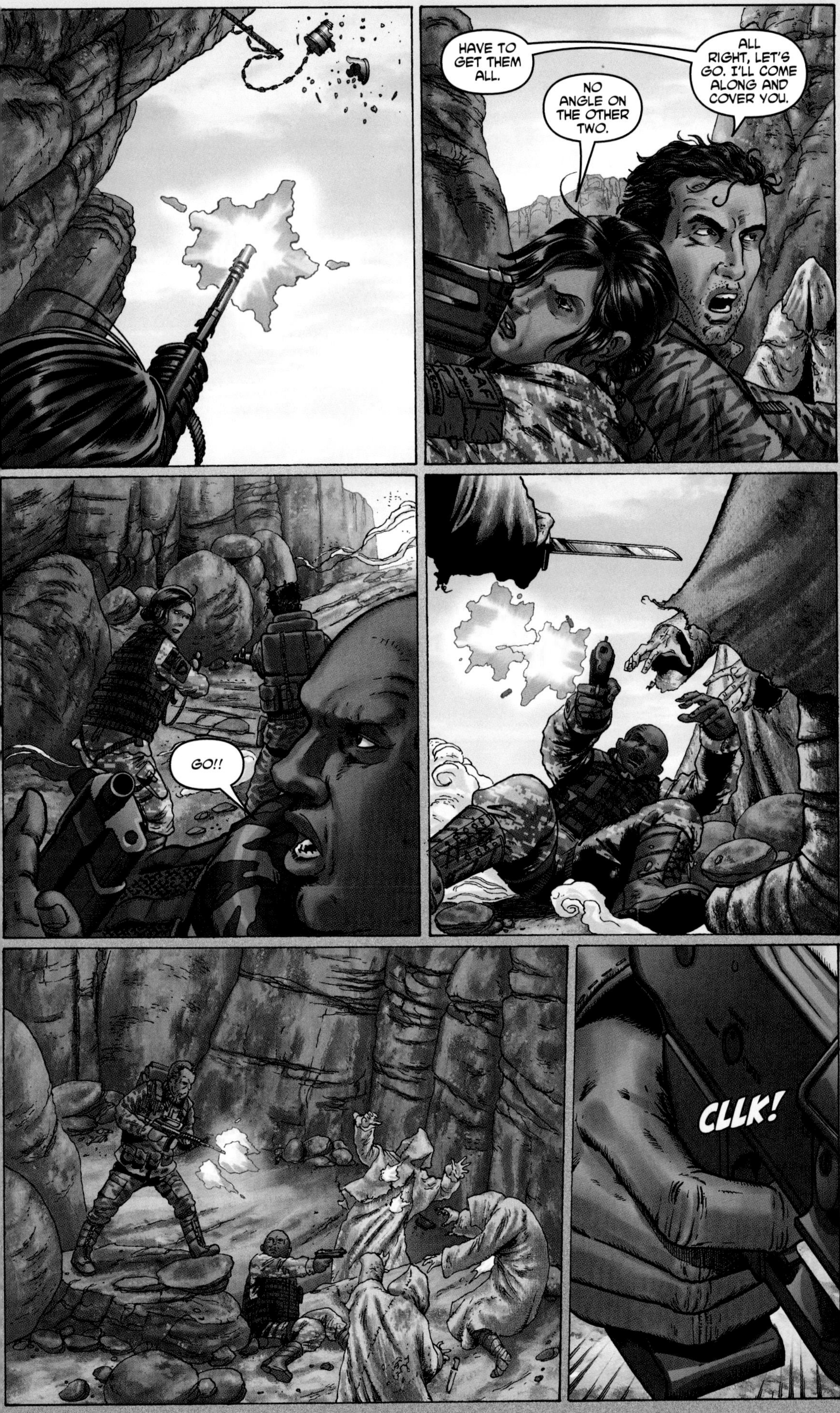
HAVE TO GET THEM ALL.
NO ANGLE ON THE OTHER TWO.
ALL RIGHT, LET'S GO. I'LL COME ALONG AND COVER YOU.
GO!!
CLLK!

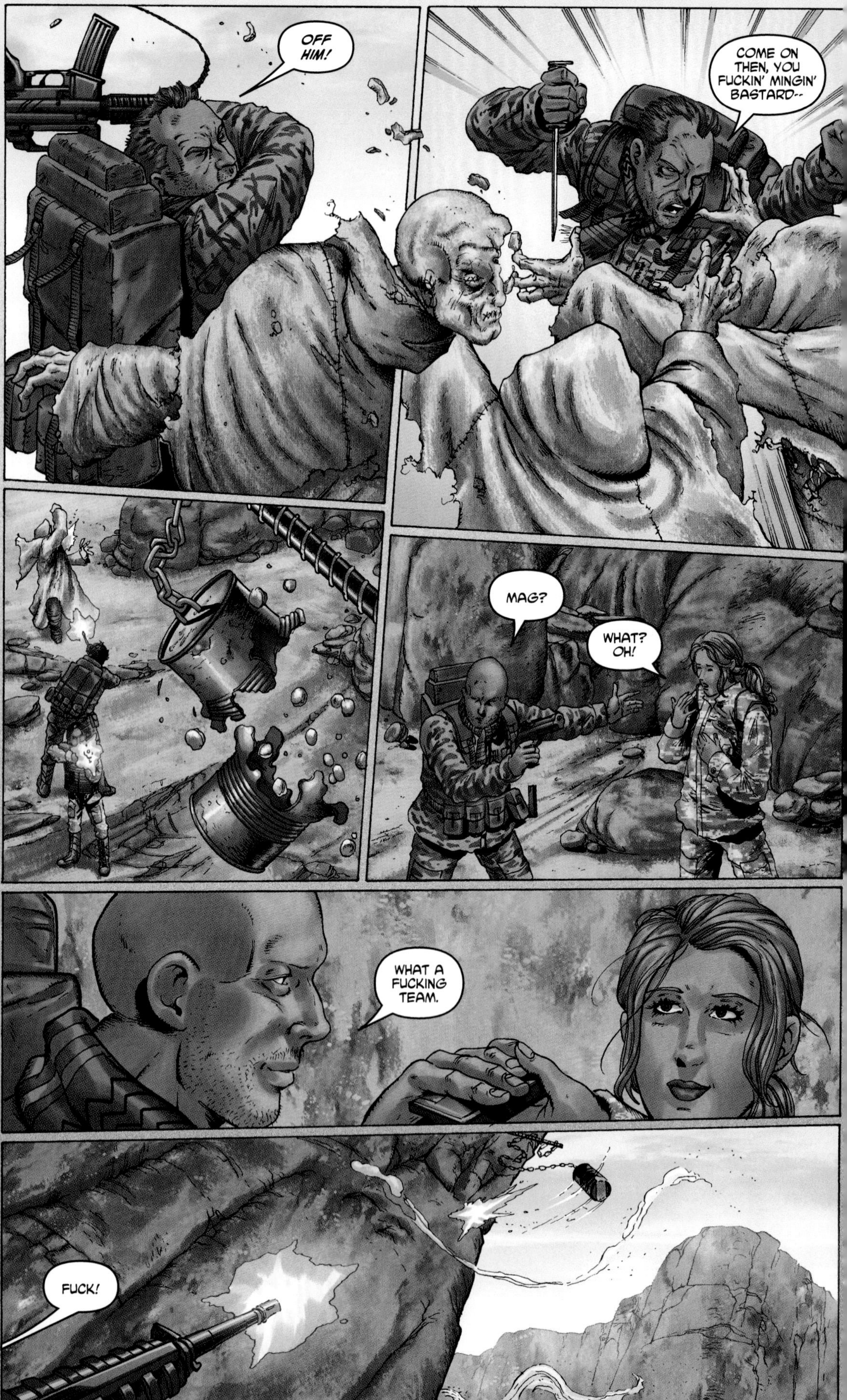
OFF HIM!
COME ON THEN, YOU FUCKIN' MINGIN' BASTARD--
MAG?
WHAT? OH!
WHAT A FUCKING TEAM.
FUCK!

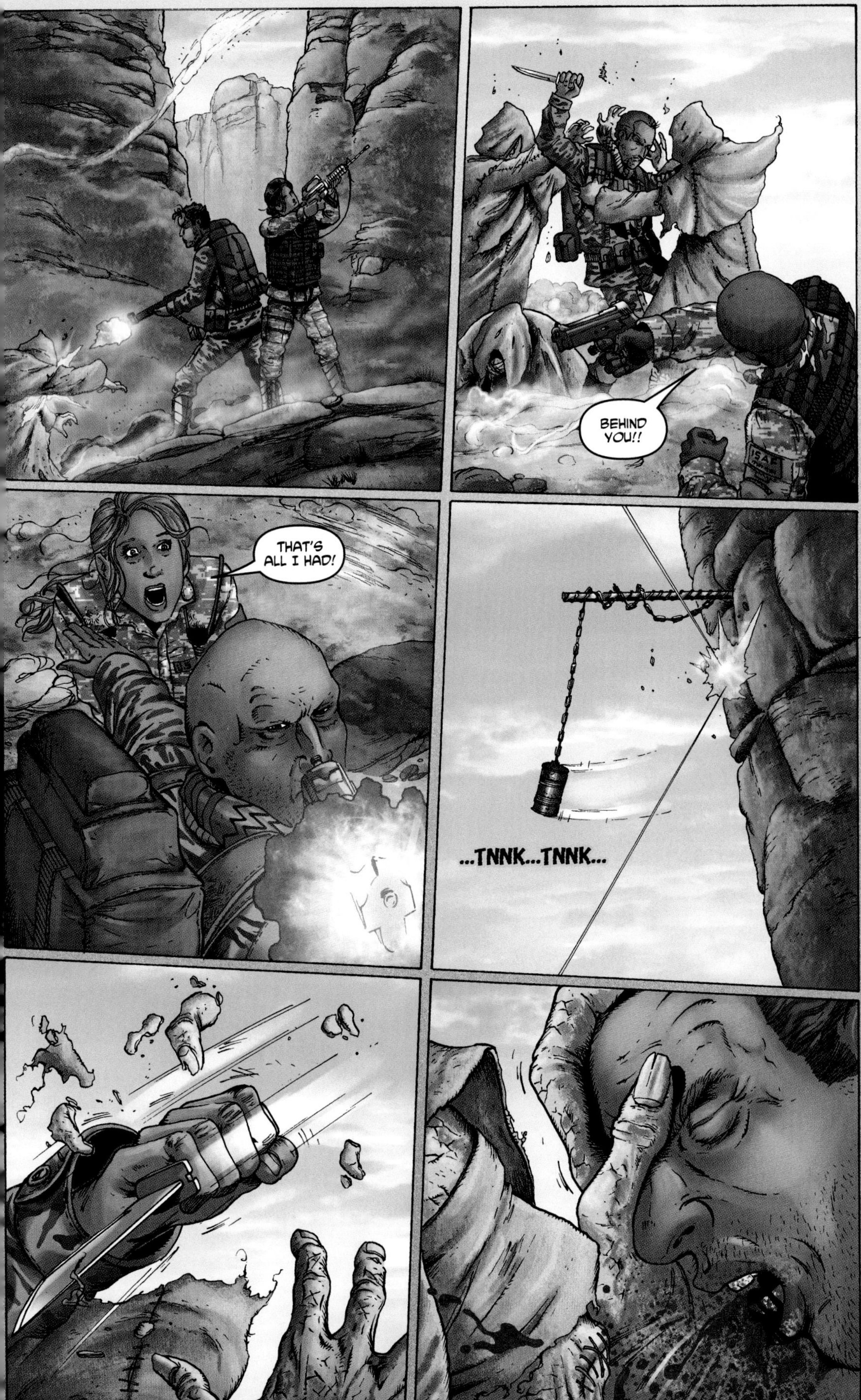
BEHIND YOU!!
THAT'S ALL I HAD!
...TNNK...TNNK...

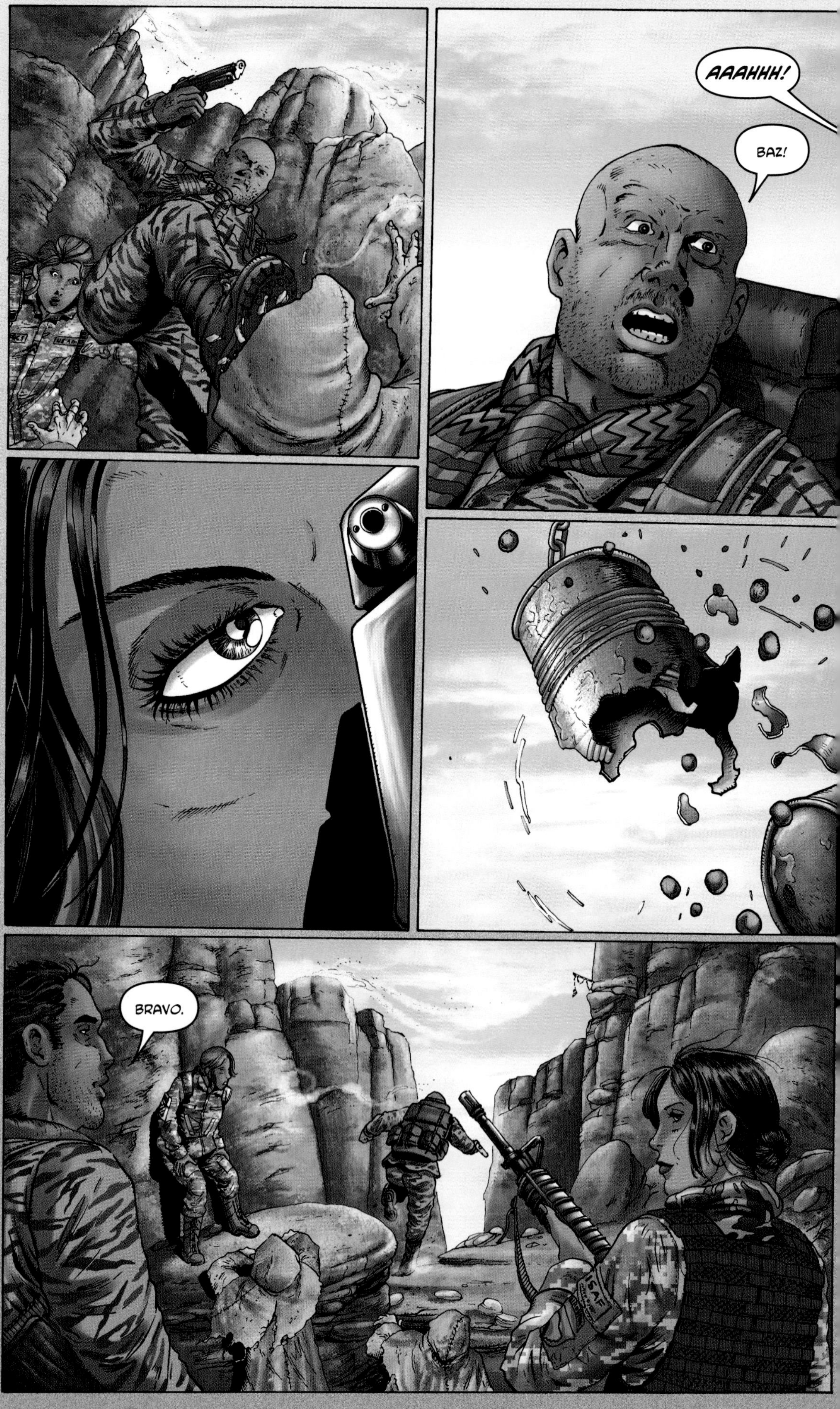
AAAHHH!
BAZ!
BRAVO.

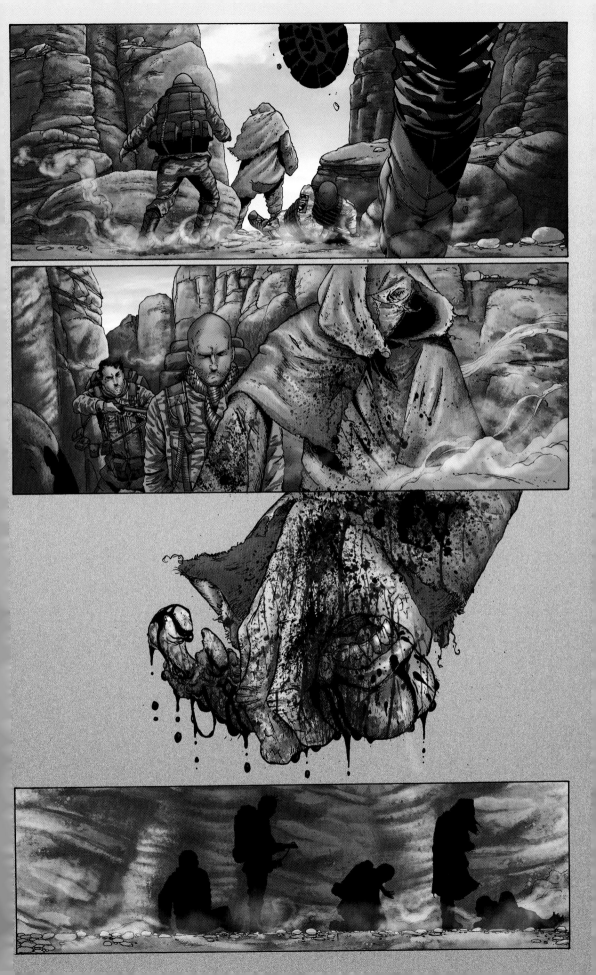

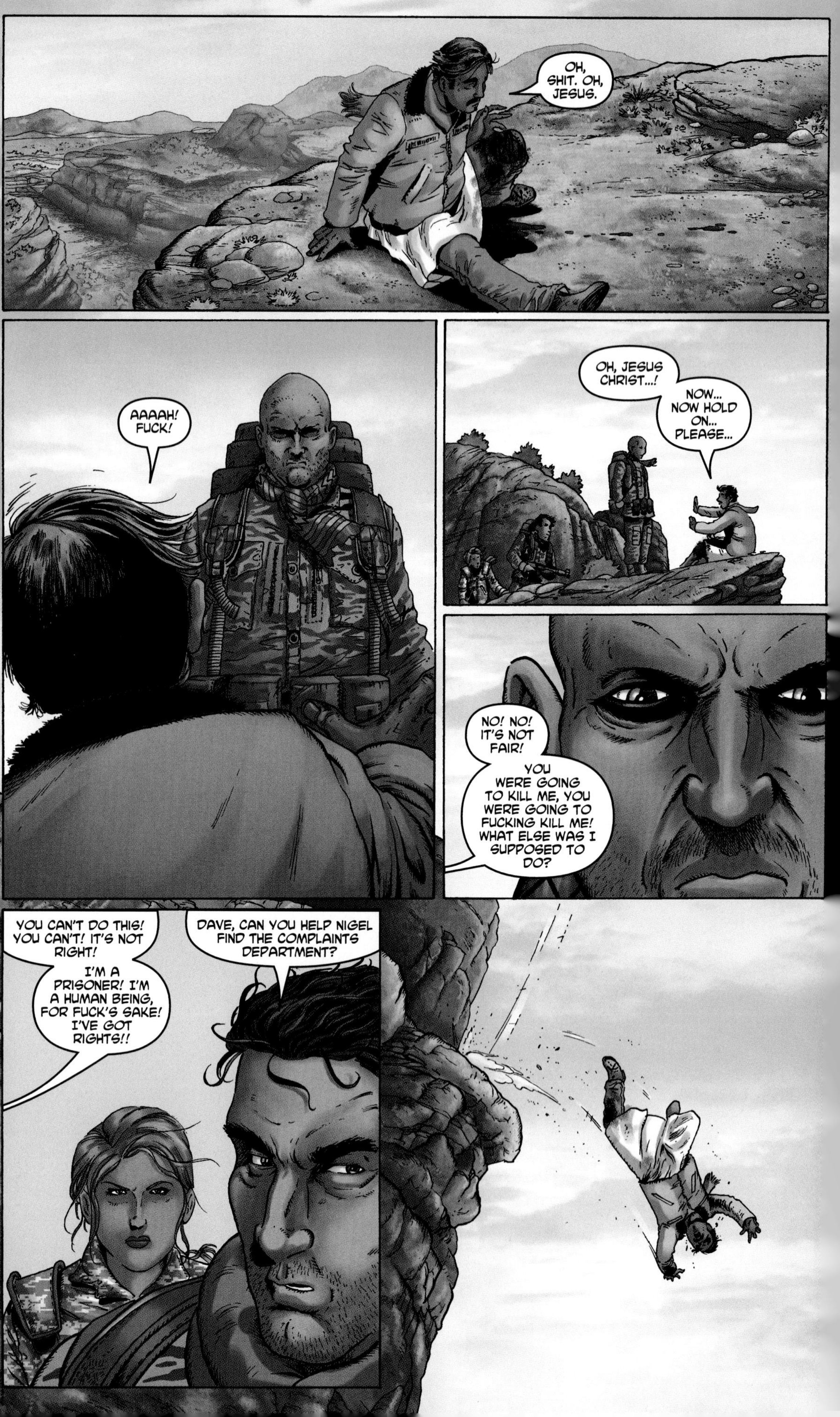
OH, SHIT. OH, JESUS.
AAAAH! FUCK!
OH, JESUS CHRIST...!
NOW... NOW HOLD ON... PLEASE...
NO! NO! IT'S NOT FAIR!
YOU WERE GOING TO KILL ME, YOU WERE GOING TO FUCKING KILL ME! WHAT ELSE WAS I SUPPOSED TO DO?
YOU CAN'T DO THIS! YOU CAN'T! IT'S NOT RIGHT!
I'M A PRISONER! I'M A HUMAN BEING, FOR FUCK'S SAKE! I'VE GOT RIGHTS!!
DAVE, CAN YOU HELP NIGEL FIND THE COMPLAINTS DEPARTMENT?

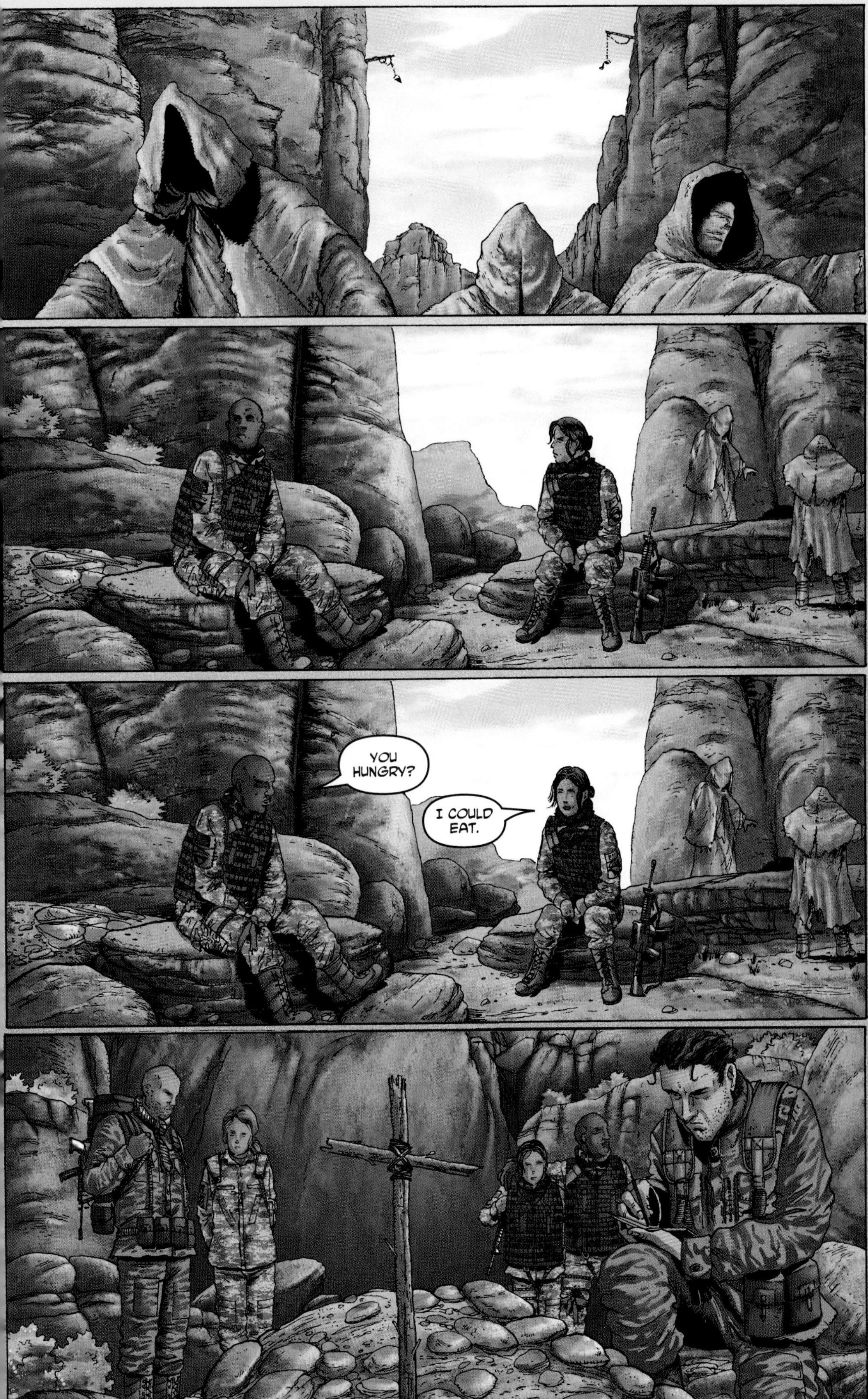
YOU HUNGRY?
I COULD EAT.

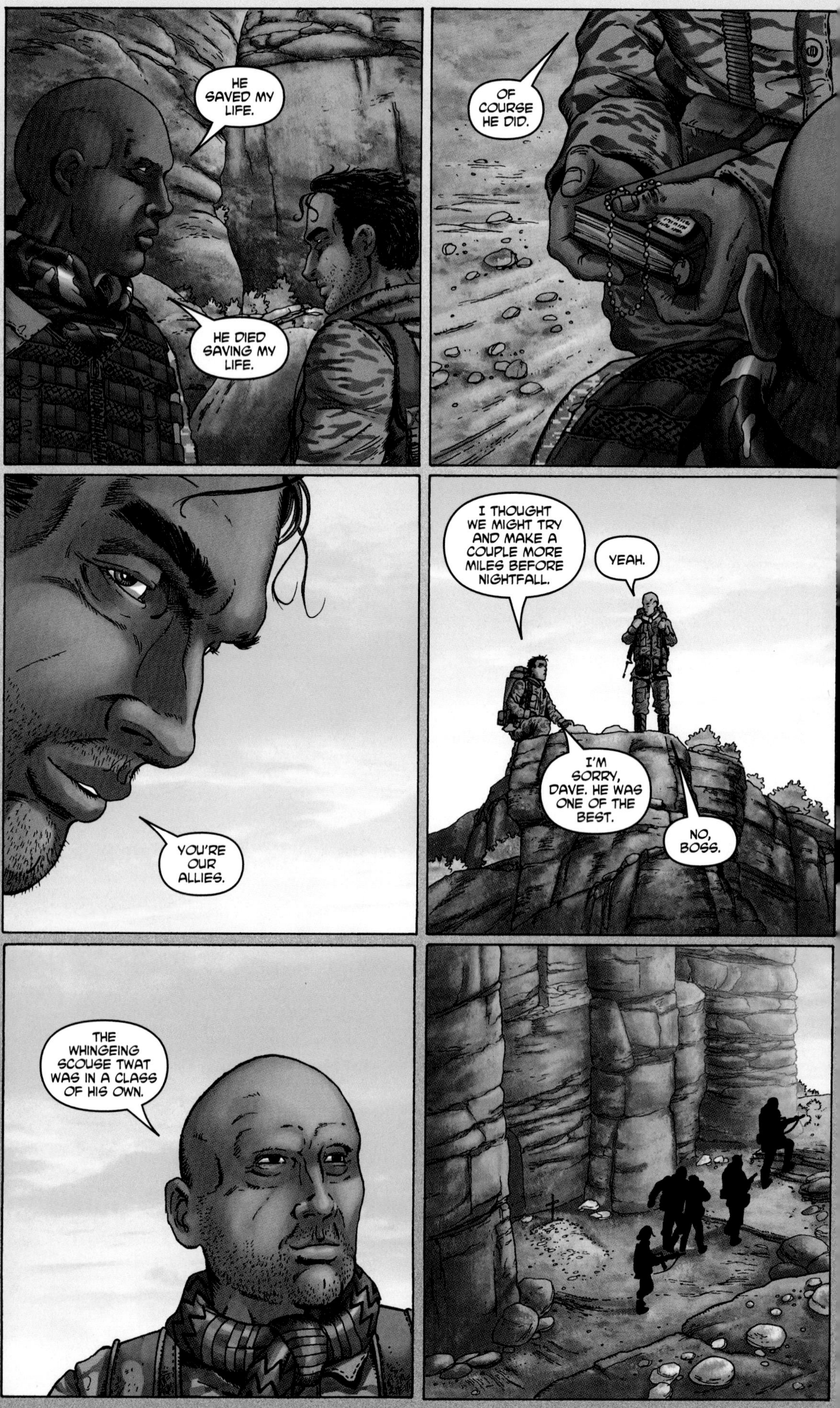

HE SAVED MY LIFE.
HE DIED SAVING MY LIFE.
OF COURSE HE DID.
YOU'RE OUR ALLIES.
I THOUGHT WE MIGHT TRY AND MAKE A COUPLE MORE MILES BEFORE NIGHTFALL.
YEAH.
I'M SORRY, DAVE. HE WAS ONE OF THE BEST.
NO, BOSS.
THE WHINGEING SCOUSE TWAT WAS IN A CLASS OF HIS OWN.

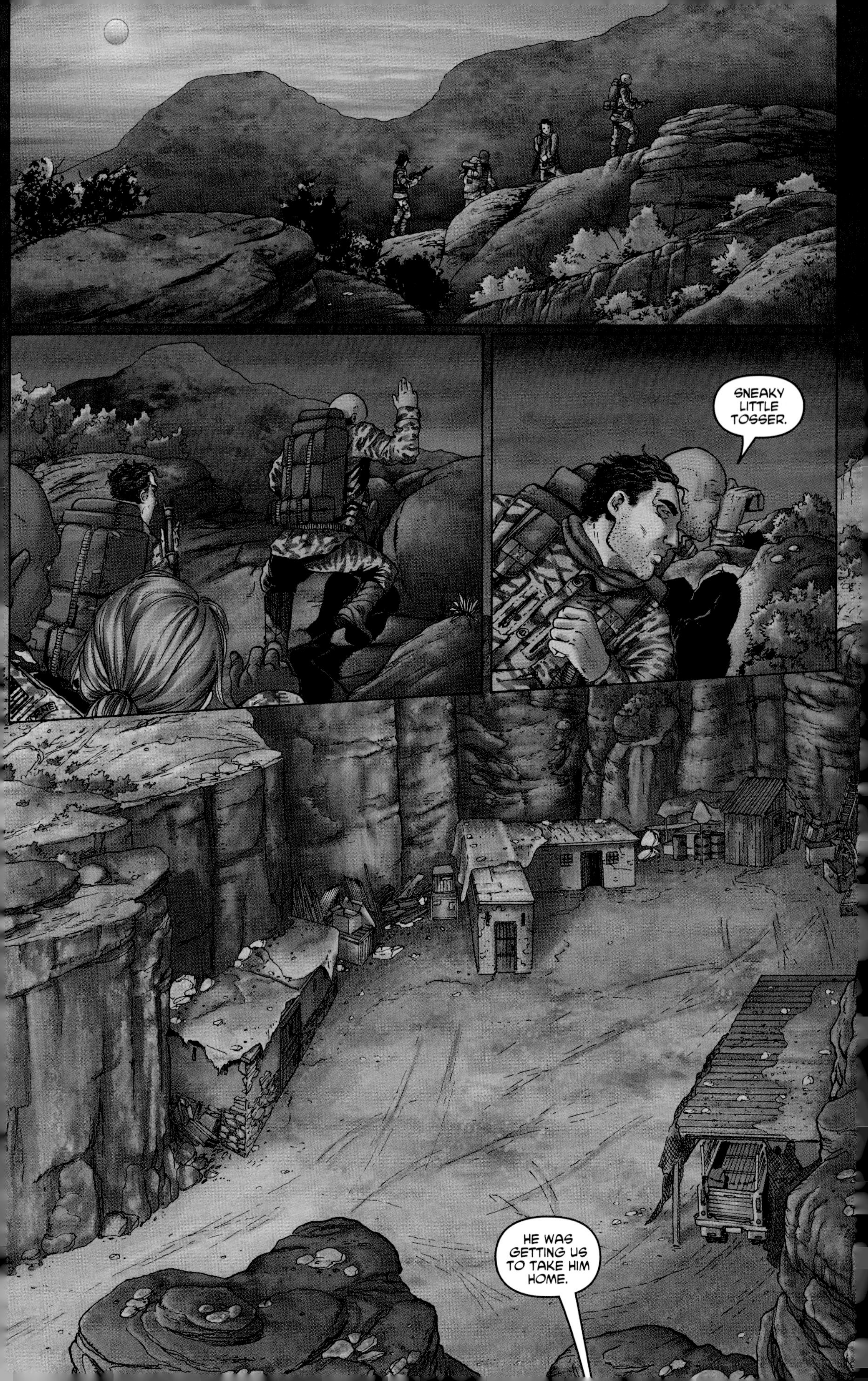
SNEAKY LITTLE TOSSER.
HE WAS GETTING US TO TAKE HIM HOME.

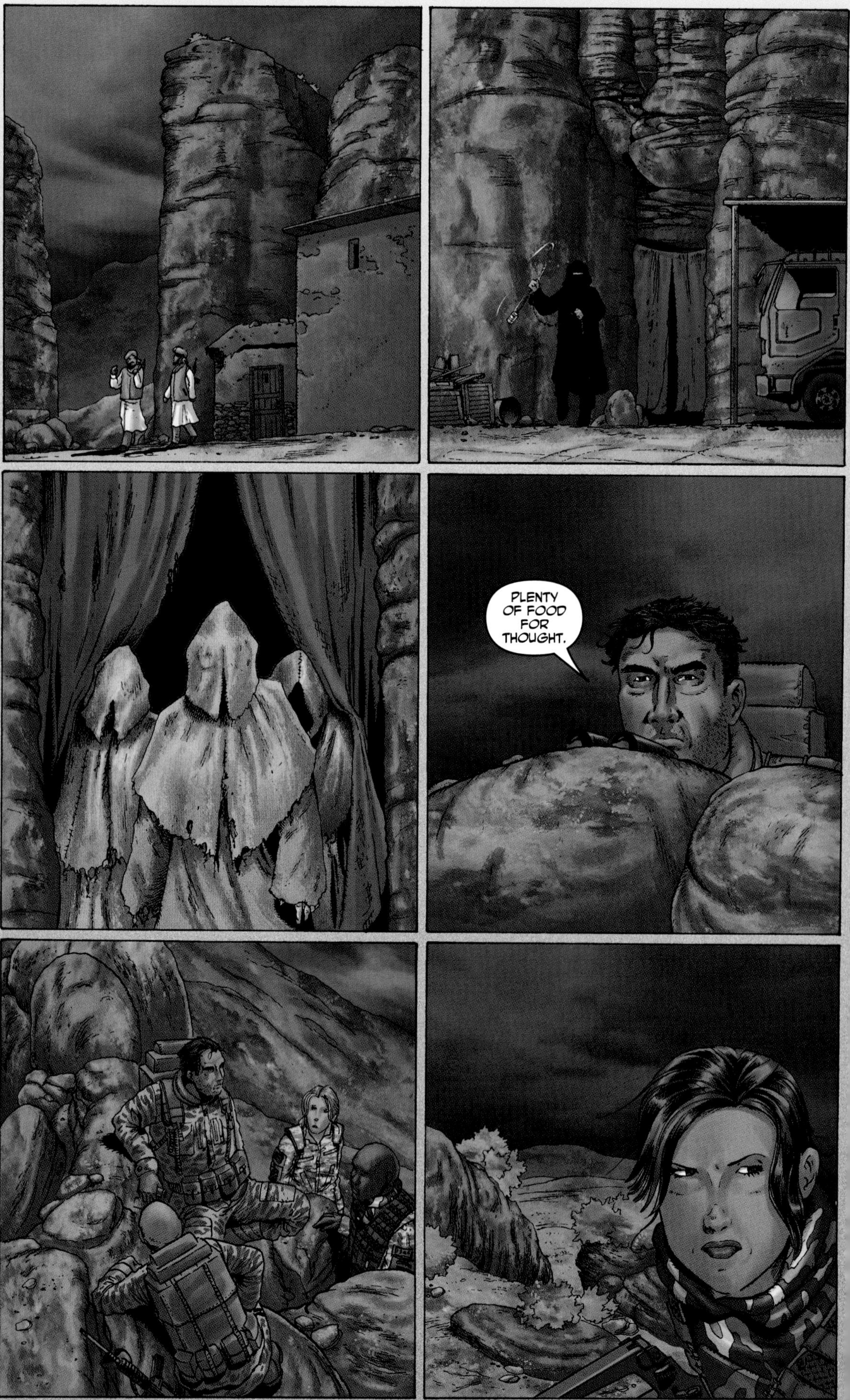
PLENTY OF FOOD FOR THOUGHT.

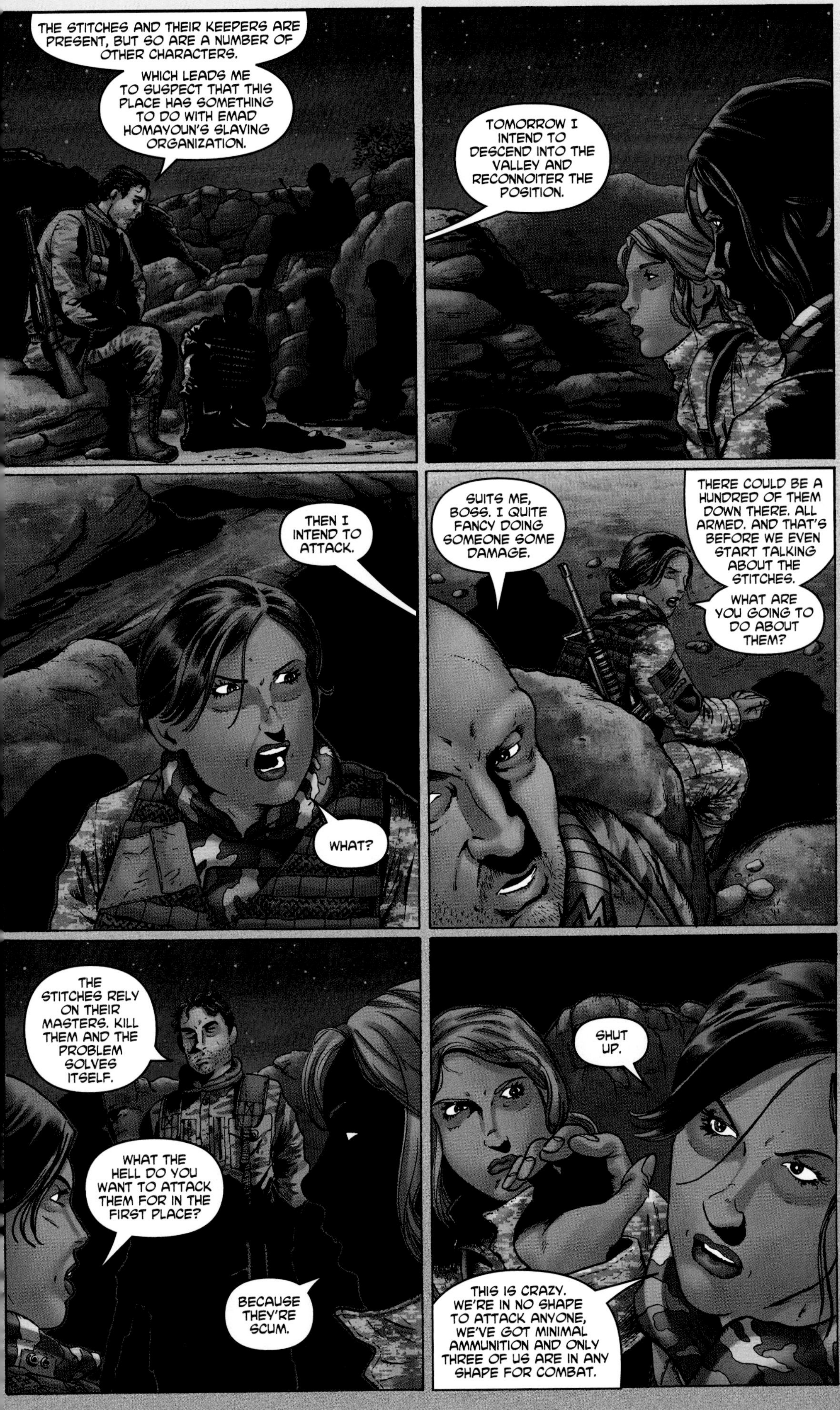
THE STITCHES AND THEIR KEEPERS ARE PRESENT, BUT SO ARE A NUMBER OF OTHER CHARACTERS.
WHICH LEADS ME TO SUSPECT THAT THIS PLACE HAS SOMETHING TO DO WITH EMAD HOMAYOUN'S SLAVING ORGANIZATION.
TOMORROW I INTEND TO DESCEND INTO THE VALLEY AND RECONNOITER THE POSITION.
THEN I INTEND TO ATTACK.
WHAT?
SUITS ME, BOSS. I QUITE FANCY DOING SOMEONE SOME DAMAGE.
THERE COULD BE A HUNDRED OF THEM DOWN THERE. ALL ARMED. AND THAT'S BEFORE WE EVEN START TALKING ABOUT THE STITCHES.
WHAT ARE YOU GOING TO DO ABOUT THEM?
THE STITCHES RELY ON THEIR MASTERS. KILL THEM AND THE PROBLEM SOLVES ITSELF.
WHAT THE HELL DO YOU WANT TO ATTACK THEM FOR IN THE FIRST PLACE?
BECAUSE THEY'RE SCUM.
SHUT UP.
THIS IS CRAZY. WE'RE IN NO SHAPE TO ATTACK ANYONE, WE'VE GOT MINIMAL AMMUNITION AND ONLY THREE OF US ARE IN ANY SHAPE FOR COMBAT.

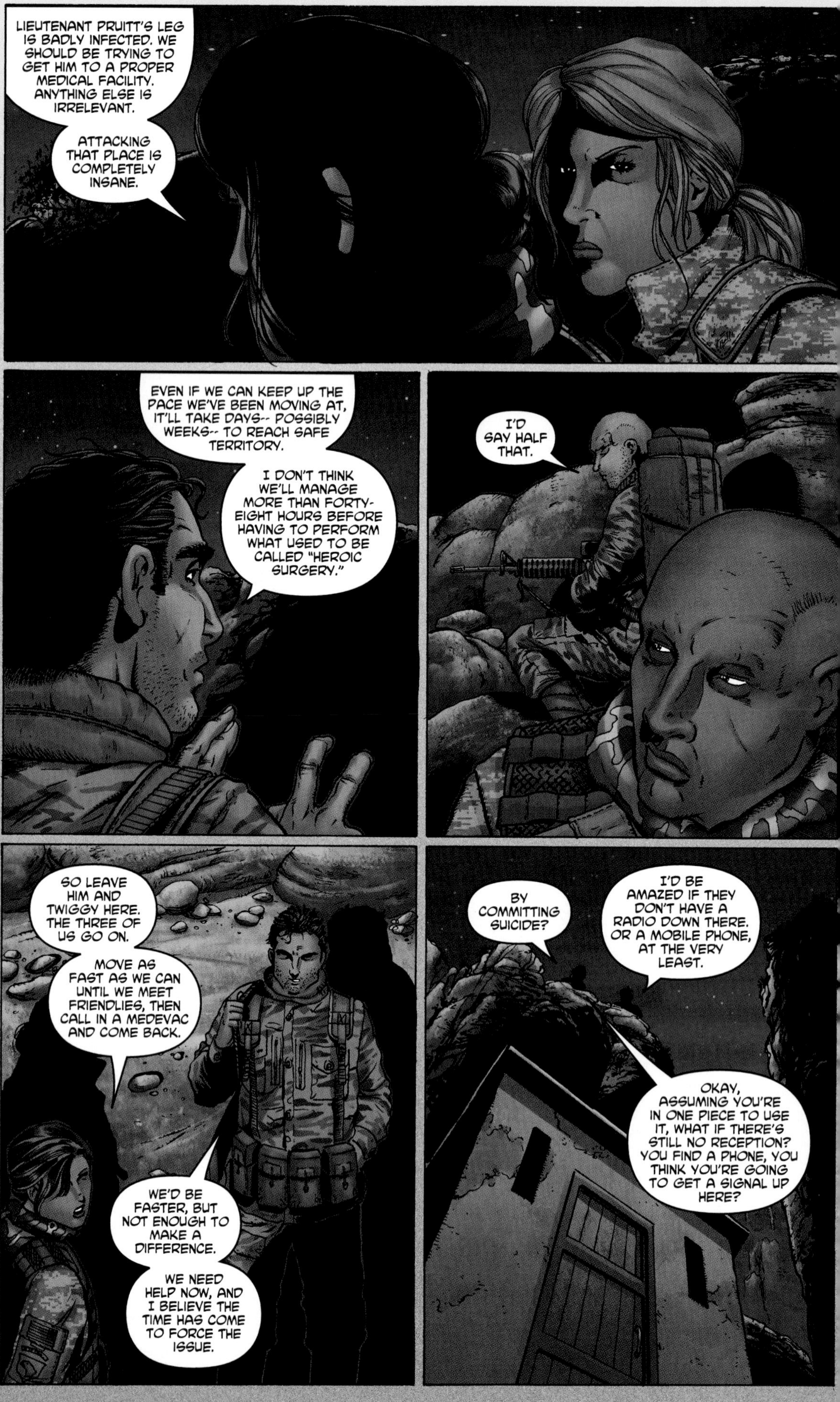
LIEUTENANT PRUITT'S LEG IS BADLY INFECTED. WE SHOULD BE TRYING TO GET HIM TO A PROPER MEDICAL FACILITY. ANYTHING ELSE IS IRRELEVANT.
ATTACKING THAT PLACE IS COMPLETELY INSANE.
EVEN IF WE CAN KEEP UP THE PACE WE'VE BEEN MOVING AT, IT'LL TAKE DAYS-- POSSIBLY WEEKS-- TO REACH SAFE TERRITORY.
I DON'T THINK WE'LL MANAGE MORE THAN FORTY-EIGHT HOURS BEFORE HAVING TO PERFORM WHAT USED TO BE CALLED "HEROIC SURGERY."
I'D SAY HALF THAT.
SO LEAVE HIM AND TWIGGY HERE. THE THREE OF US GO ON.
MOVE AS FAST AS WE CAN UNTIL WE MEET FRIENDLIES, THEN CALL IN A MEDEVAC AND COME BACK.
WE'D BE FASTER, BUT NOT ENOUGH TO MAKE A DIFFERENCE.
WE NEED HELP NOW, AND I BELIEVE THE TIME HAS COME TO FORCE THE ISSUE.
BY COMMITTING SUICIDE?
I'D BE AMAZED IF THEY DON'T HAVE A RADIO DOWN THERE. OR A MOBILE PHONE, AT THE VERY LEAST.
OKAY, ASSUMING YOU'RE IN ONE PIECE TO USE IT, WHAT IF THERE'S STILL NO RECEPTION? YOU FIND A PHONE, YOU THINK YOU'RE GOING TO GET A SIGNAL UP HERE?

WELL THEN IT'S PLAN B.

THEY HAVE TWO TRUCKS, PROBABLY WHAT THEY USE TO MOVE THE VILLAGERS OUT OF HERE. TRUCKS NEED FUEL.

FIND THEIR DUMP, IGNITE IT, AND SOMEONE'S BOUND TO NOTICE-- AERIAL RECON, EVEN SATELLITE SURVEILLANCE. OUR PROBLEM UP 'TIL NOW IS THAT WE HAVEN'T HAD THE MEANS TO MAKE A BIG ENOUGH BANG.

WHY NOT JUST STEAL A TRUCK?

EVEN IF WE GET AWAY CLEANLY, EVEN IF WE DON'T RUN INTO MORE OF THEM ON THE ROAD, WE DON'T KNOW HOW FAR IT IS TO SAFETY.

WE COULD QUITE CONCEIVABLY RUN OUT OF PETROL AND FIND OURSELVES FACING THE SAME PROBLEM THIS TIME TOMORROW.

WHAT WE HAVE TO DO IS MAKE HELP COME TO US.

AND YOU REALLY THINK YOU CAN WIPE THEM ALL OUT?

I'D CERTAINLY LIKE TO TRY.

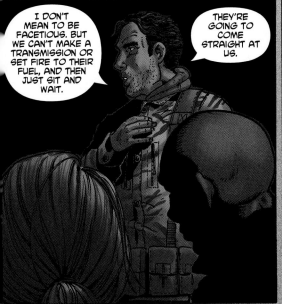

I DON'T MEAN TO BE FACETIOUS. BUT WE CAN'T MAKE A TRANSMISSION OR SET FIRE TO THEIR FUEL, AND THEN JUST SIT AND WAIT.

THEY'RE GOING TO COME STRAIGHT AT US.

BETTER TO DEAL WITH THEM AT THE BEGINNING WHILE WE STILL ENJOY THE ELEMENT OF SURPRISE.

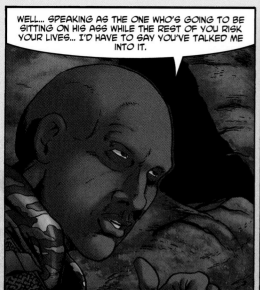

WELL... SPEAKING AS THE ONE WHO'S GOING TO BE SITTING ON HIS ASS WHILE THE REST OF YOU RISK YOUR LIVES... I'D HAVE TO SAY YOU'VE TALKED ME INTO IT.

ME TOO.

SHUT UP.

WHY DO YOU KEEP TELLING ME TO--

BECAUSE YOU'RE OUT OF YOUR DEPTH.

I'D LIKE YOU TO GIVE US COVER TOMORROW. FIND A SPOT WITH A COMMANDING VIEW OF THE POSITION, POT ANYONE WHO GIVES US TROUBLE.

WHY ME?

BECAUSE WHAT I SAW TODAY LEADS ME TO BELIEVE THAT YOU'RE A RATHER GOOD SHOT.

COUPLE OF DELTA MARKSMEN WATCHED HER ON THE RANGE BACK AT KANDAHAR.

THE WORD THEY USED WAS "PHENOMENAL."

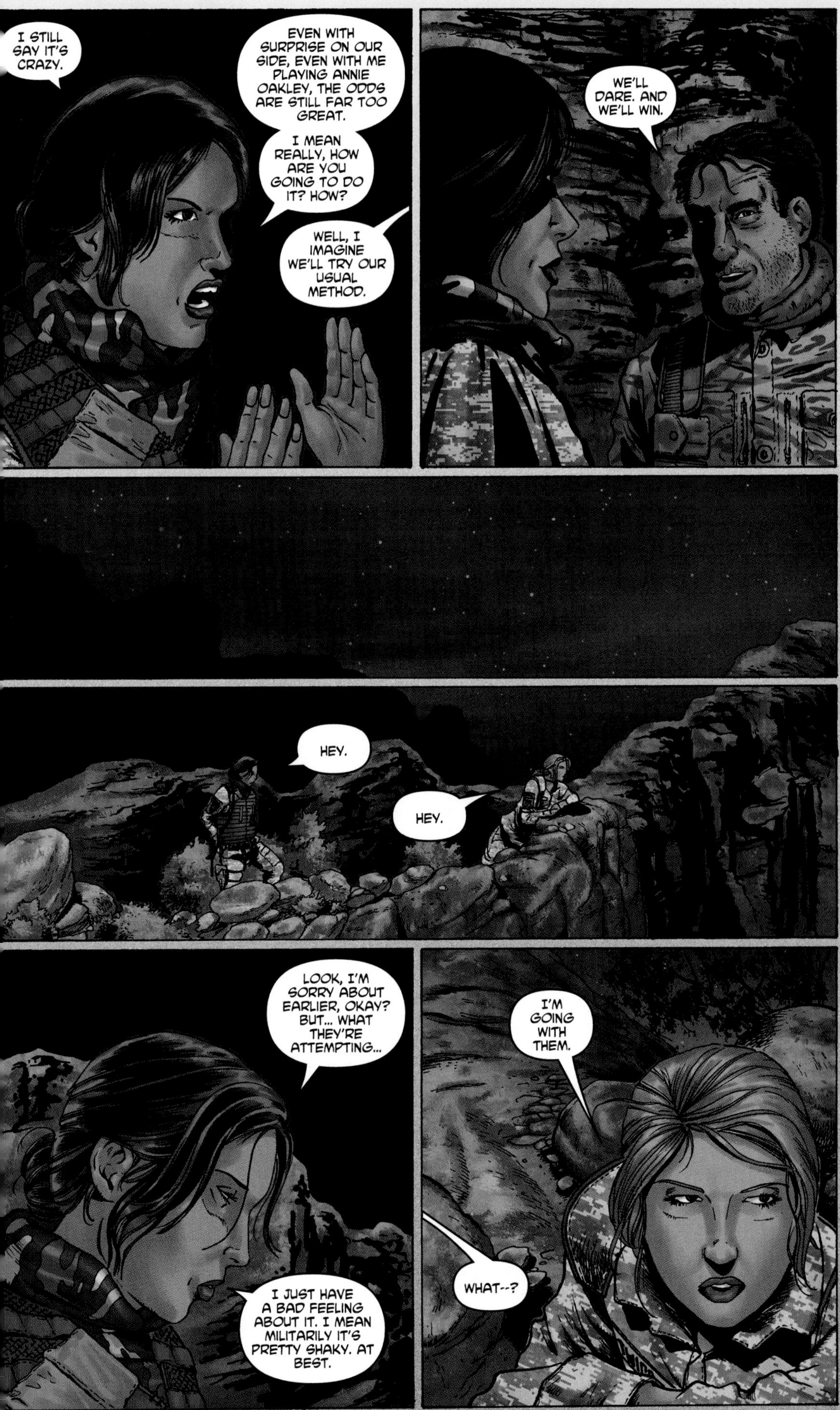
I STILL SAY IT'S CRAZY.
EVEN WITH SURPRISE ON OUR SIDE, EVEN WITH ME PLAYING ANNIE OAKLEY, THE ODDS ARE STILL FAR TOO GREAT.
I MEAN REALLY, HOW ARE YOU GOING TO DO IT? HOW?
WELL, I IMAGINE WE'LL TRY OUR USUAL METHOD.
WE'LL DARE. AND WE'LL WIN.
HEY.
HEY.
LOOK, I'M SORRY ABOUT EARLIER, OKAY? BUT... WHAT THEY'RE ATTEMPTING...
I JUST HAVE A BAD FEELING ABOUT IT. I MEAN MILITARILY IT'S PRETTY SHAKY. AT BEST.
I'M GOING WITH THEM.
WHAT--?

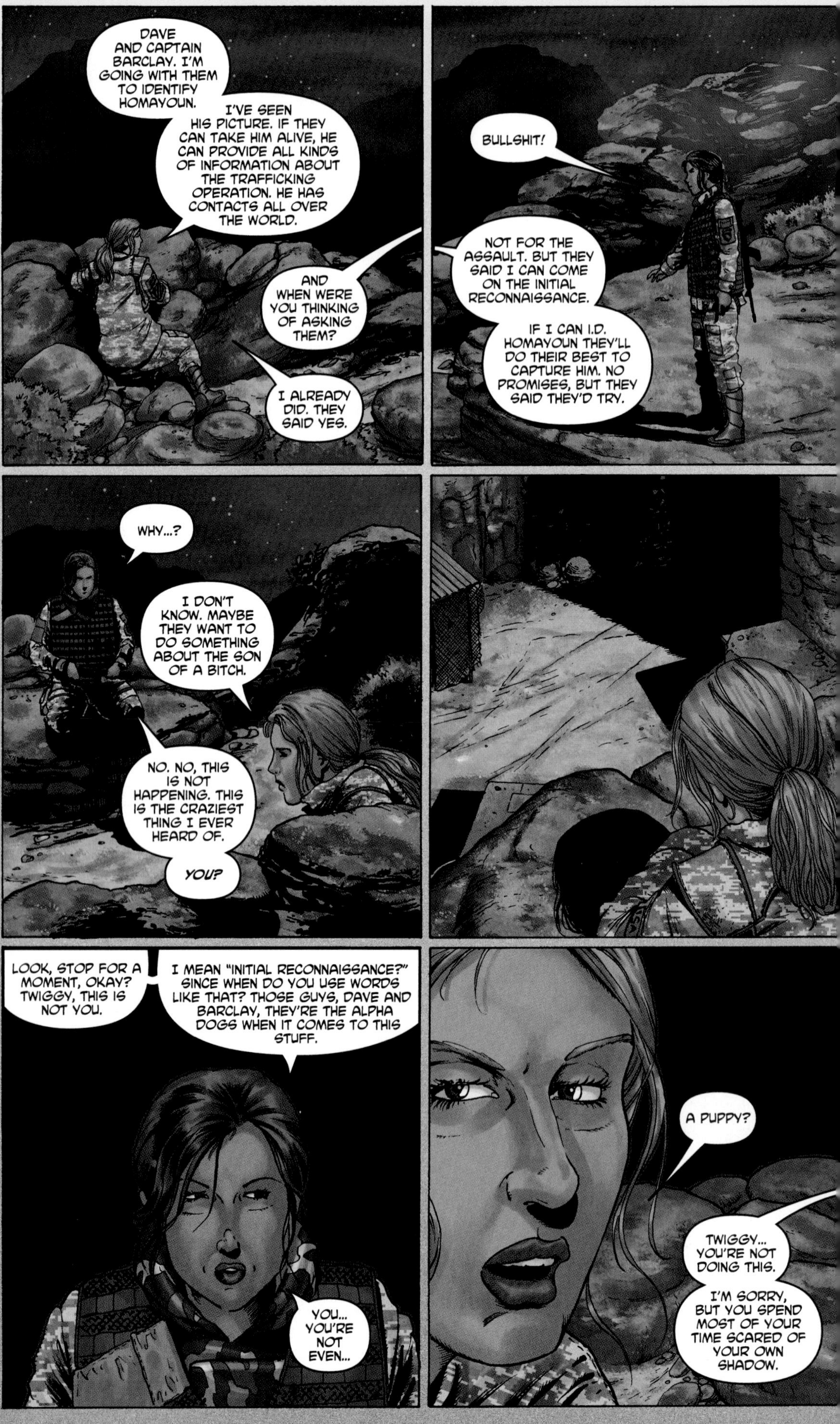

DAVE AND CAPTAIN BARCLAY. I'M GOING WITH THEM TO IDENTIFY HOMAYOUN.
I'VE SEEN HIS PICTURE. IF THEY CAN TAKE HIM ALIVE, HE CAN PROVIDE ALL KINDS OF INFORMATION ABOUT THE TRAFFICKING OPERATION. HE HAS CONTACTS ALL OVER THE WORLD.
AND WHEN WERE YOU THINKING OF ASKING THEM?
I ALREADY DID. THEY SAID YES.
BULLSHIT!
NOT FOR THE ASSAULT. BUT THEY SAID I CAN COME ON THE INITIAL RECONNAISSANCE.
IF I CAN I.D. HOMAYOUN THEY'LL DO THEIR BEST TO CAPTURE HIM. NO PROMISES, BUT THEY SAID THEY'D TRY.
WHY...?
I DON'T KNOW. MAYBE THEY WANT TO DO SOMETHING ABOUT THE SON OF A BITCH.
NO. NO, THIS IS NOT HAPPENING. THIS IS THE CRAZIEST THING I EVER HEARD OF.
YOU?
LOOK, STOP FOR A MOMENT, OKAY? TWIGGY, THIS IS NOT YOU.
I MEAN "INITIAL RECONNAISSANCE?" SINCE WHEN DO YOU USE WORDS LIKE THAT? THOSE GUYS, DAVE AND BARCLAY, THEY'RE THE ALPHA DOGS WHEN IT COMES TO THIS STUFF.
YOU... YOU'RE NOT EVEN...
A PUPPY?
TWIGGY... YOU'RE NOT DOING THIS.
I'M SORRY, BUT YOU SPEND MOST OF YOUR TIME SCARED OF YOUR OWN SHADOW.

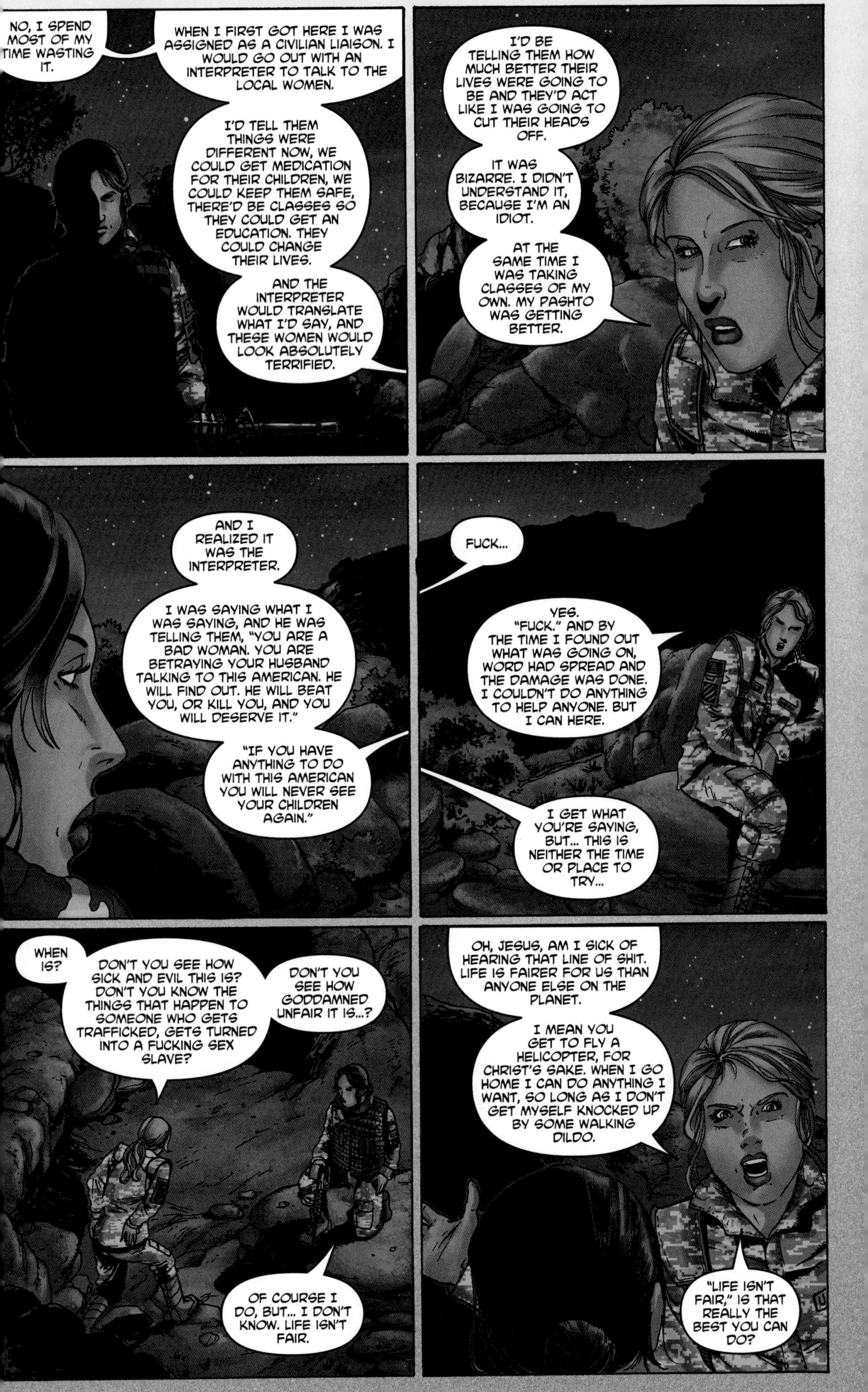
NO, I SPEND MOST OF MY TIME WASTING IT.
WHEN I FIRST GOT HERE I WAS ASSIGNED AS A CIVILIAN LIAISON. I WOULD GO OUT WITH AN INTERPRETER TO TALK TO THE LOCAL WOMEN.
I'D TELL THEM THINGS WERE DIFFERENT NOW, WE COULD GET MEDICATION FOR THEIR CHILDREN, WE COULD KEEP THEM SAFE, THERE'D BE CLASSES SO THEY COULD GET AN EDUCATION. THEY COULD CHANGE THEIR LIVES.
AND THE INTERPRETER WOULD TRANSLATE WHAT I'D SAY, AND THESE WOMEN WOULD LOOK ABSOLUTELY TERRIFIED.
I'D BE TELLING THEM HOW MUCH BETTER THEIR LIVES WERE GOING TO BE AND THEY'D ACT LIKE I WAS GOING TO CUT THEIR HEADS OFF.
IT WAS BIZARRE. I DIDN'T UNDERSTAND IT, BECAUSE I'M AN IDIOT.
AT THE SAME TIME I WAS TAKING CLASSES OF MY OWN. MY PASHTO WAS GETTING BETTER.
AND I REALIZED IT WAS THE INTERPRETER.
I WAS SAYING WHAT I WAS SAYING, AND HE WAS TELLING THEM, "YOU ARE A BAD WOMAN. YOU ARE BETRAYING YOUR HUSBAND TALKING TO THIS AMERICAN. HE WILL FIND OUT. HE WILL BEAT YOU, OR KILL YOU, AND YOU WILL DESERVE IT."
"IF YOU HAVE ANYTHING TO DO WITH THIS AMERICAN YOU WILL NEVER SEE YOUR CHILDREN AGAIN."
FUCK...
YES. "FUCK." AND BY THE TIME I FOUND OUT WHAT WAS GOING ON, WORD HAD SPREAD AND THE DAMAGE WAS DONE. I COULDN'T DO ANYTHING TO HELP ANYONE. BUT I CAN HERE.
I GET WHAT YOU'RE SAYING, BUT... THIS IS NEITHER THE TIME OR PLACE TO TRY...
WHEN IS?
DON'T YOU SEE HOW SICK AND EVIL THIS IS? DON'T YOU KNOW THE THINGS THAT HAPPEN TO SOMEONE WHO GETS TRAFFICKED, GETS TURNED INTO A FUCKING SEX SLAVE?
DON'T YOU SEE HOW GODDAMNED UNFAIR IT IS...?
OF COURSE I DO, BUT... I DON'T KNOW. LIFE ISN'T FAIR.
OH, JESUS, AM I SICK OF HEARING THAT LINE OF SHIT. LIFE IS FAIRER FOR US THAN ANYONE ELSE ON THE PLANET.
I MEAN YOU GET TO FLY A HELICOPTER, FOR CHRIST'S SAKE. WHEN I GO HOME I CAN DO ANYTHING I WANT, SO LONG AS I DON'T GET MYSELF KNOCKED UP BY SOME WALKING DILDO.
"LIFE ISN'T FAIR," IS THAT REALLY THE BEST YOU CAN DO?

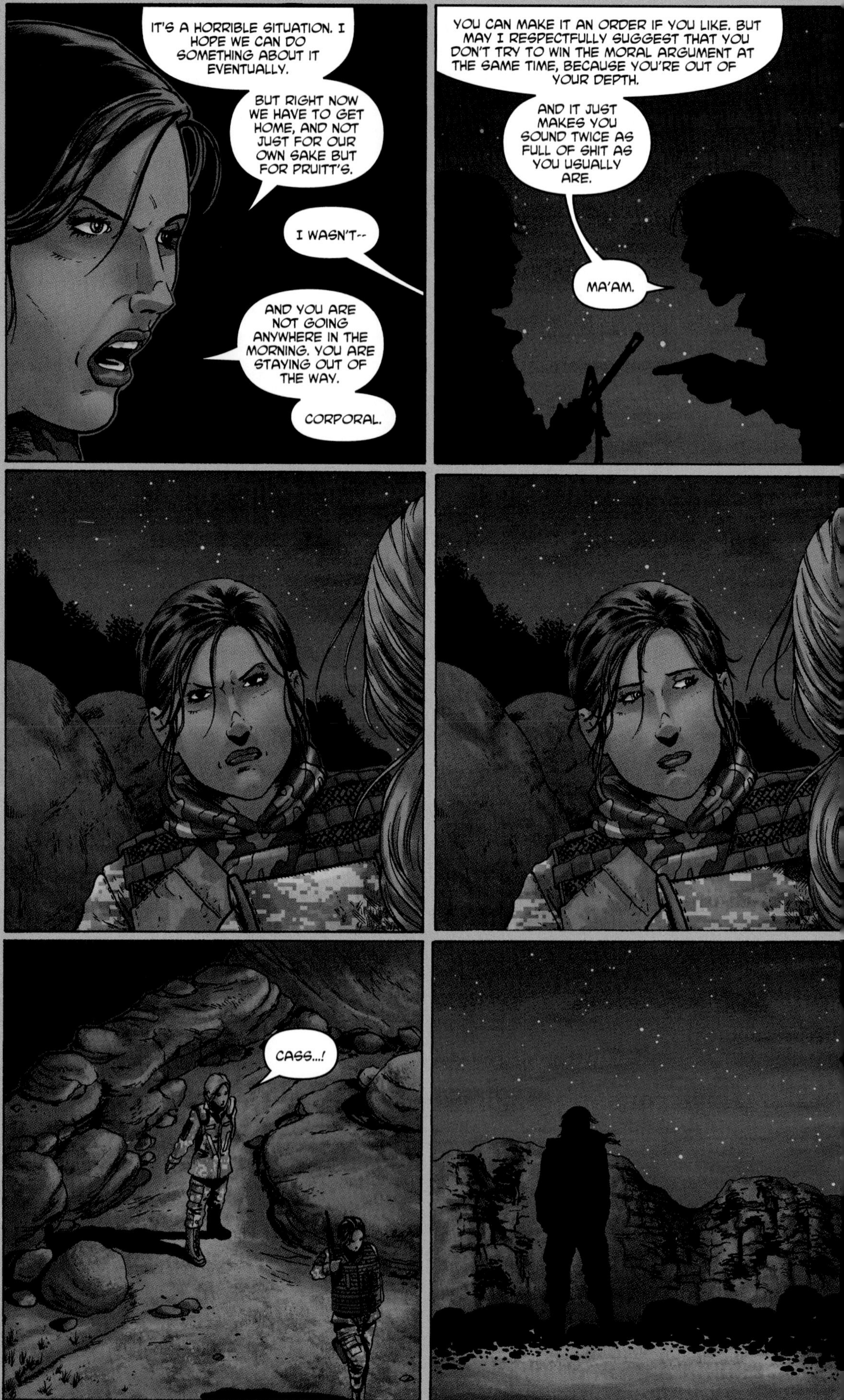
IT'S A HORRIBLE SITUATION. I HOPE WE CAN DO SOMETHING ABOUT IT EVENTUALLY.
BUT RIGHT NOW WE HAVE TO GET HOME, AND NOT JUST FOR OUR OWN SAKE BUT FOR PRUITT'S.
I WASN'T--
AND YOU ARE NOT GOING ANYWHERE IN THE MORNING. YOU ARE STAYING OUT OF THE WAY.
CORPORAL.
YOU CAN MAKE IT AN ORDER IF YOU LIKE. BUT MAY I RESPECTFULLY SUGGEST THAT YOU DON'T TRY TO WIN THE MORAL ARGUMENT AT THE SAME TIME, BECAUSE YOU'RE OUT OF YOUR DEPTH.
AND IT JUST MAKES YOU SOUND TWICE AS FULL OF SHIT AS YOU USUALLY ARE.
MA'AM.
CASS...!

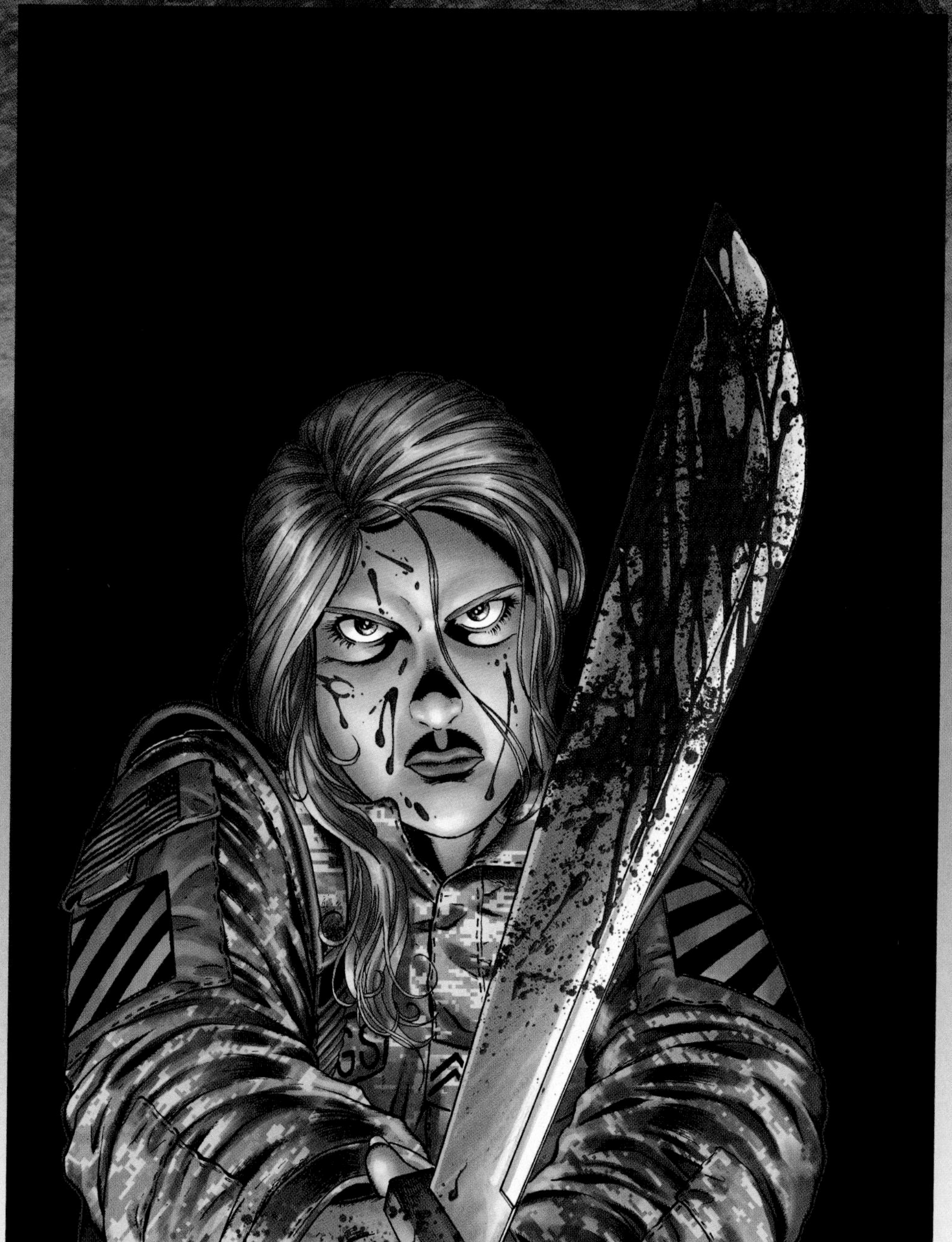

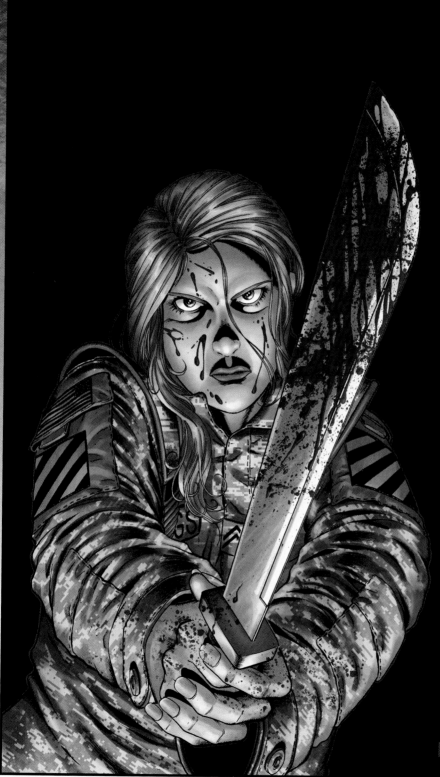

CHAPTER 6

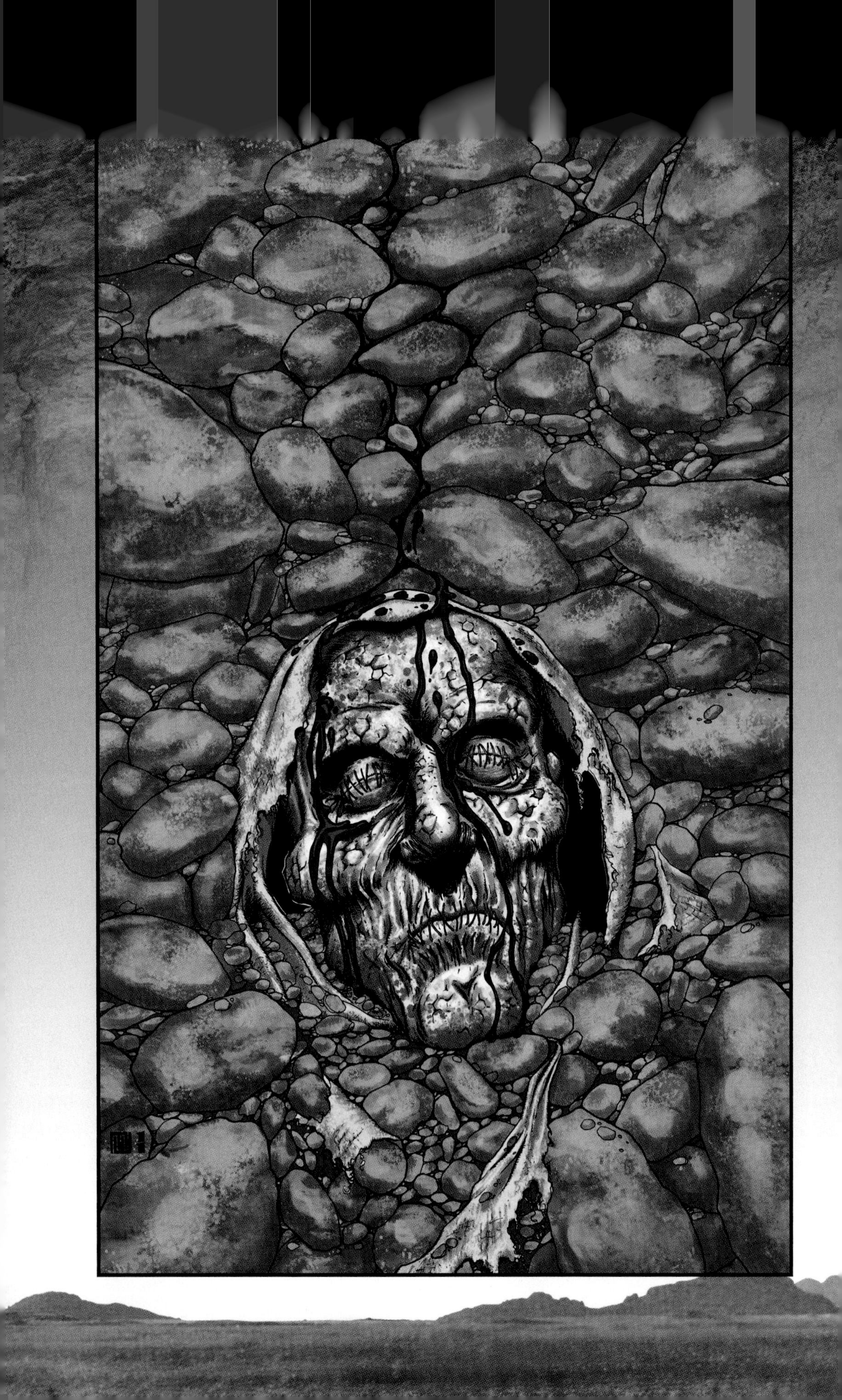

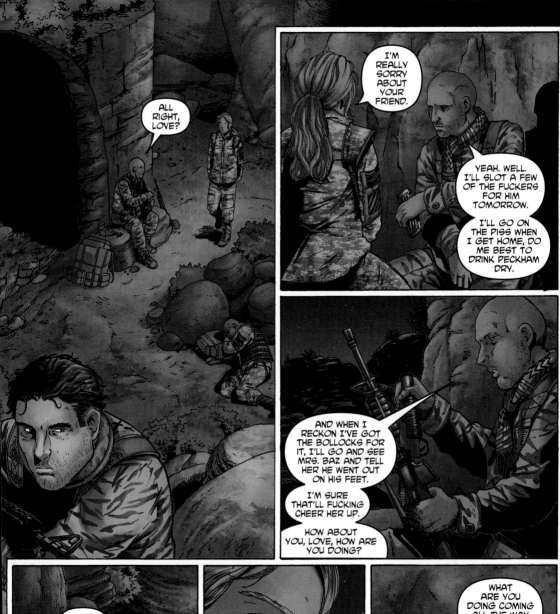

ALL RIGHT, LOVE?

I'M REALLY SORRY ABOUT YOUR FRIEND.

YEAH. WELL. I'LL SLOT A FEW OF THE FUCKERS FOR HIM TOMORROW.

I'LL GO ON THE PISS WHEN I GET HOME, DO ME BEST TO DRINK PECKHAM DRY.

AND WHEN I RECKON I'VE GOT THE BOLLOCKS FOR IT, I'LL GO AND SEE MRS. BAZ AND TELL HER HE WENT OUT ON HIS FEET.

I'M SURE THAT'LL FUCKING CHEER HER UP.

HOW ABOUT YOU, LOVE, HOW ARE YOU DOING?

I'M OKAY.

NO, I'M TERRIFIED. I ALWAYS HAVE BEEN.

ALWAYS?

ALWAYS.

WHAT?

EVERYTHING. MY MOM AND DAD. THE OTHER KIDS AT SCHOOL. THE ARMY. THE DRILL INSTRUCTORS.

LIEUTENANT PRUITT.

WHAT'S HAPPENING TO US. TOMORROW. THE NIGHT. THE DARK. EVERYTHING.

WHAT ARE YOU DOING COMING ALL THE WAY OUT HERE, THEN?

I JUST... I WANTED TO SEE SOME OF THE COUNTRY.

SO LIEUTENANT COOPER RUNS PAST ME AND SAYS, "TODAY'S THE DAY, COME ON IF YOU'RE COMING."

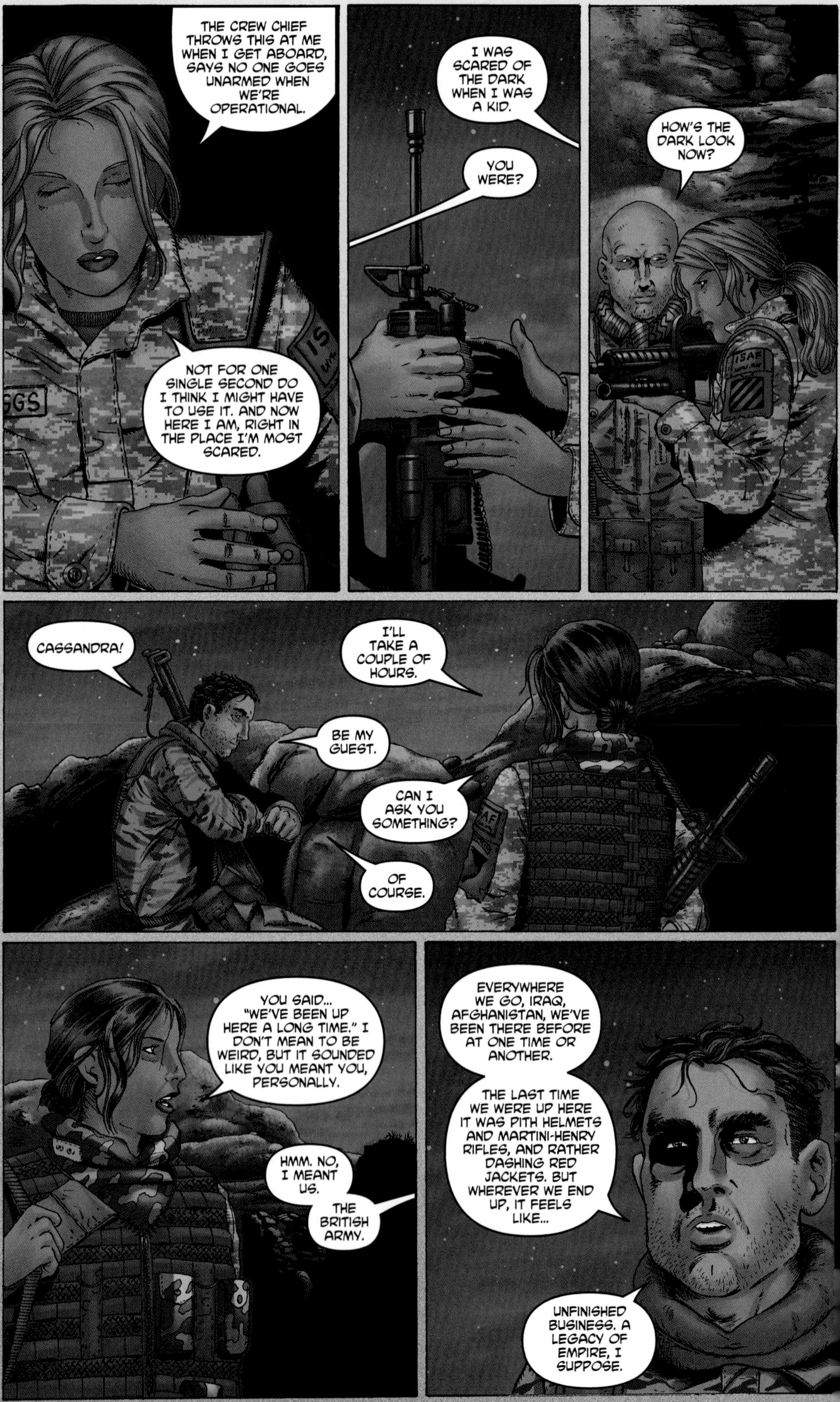

THE CREW CHIEF THROWS THIS AT ME WHEN I GET ABOARD, SAYS NO ONE GOES UNARMED WHEN WE'RE OPERATIONAL.
NOT FOR ONE SINGLE SECOND DO I THINK I MIGHT HAVE TO USE IT. AND NOW HERE I AM, RIGHT IN THE PLACE I'M MOST SCARED.
I WAS SCARED OF THE DARK WHEN I WAS A KID.
YOU WERE?
HOW'S THE DARK LOOK NOW?
CASSANDRA!
I'LL TAKE A COUPLE OF HOURS.
BE MY GUEST.
CAN I ASK YOU SOMETHING?
OF COURSE.
YOU SAID... "WE'VE BEEN UP HERE A LONG TIME." I DON'T MEAN TO BE WEIRD, BUT IT SOUNDED LIKE YOU MEANT YOU, PERSONALLY.
HMM. NO, I MEANT US.
THE BRITISH ARMY.
EVERYWHERE WE GO, IRAQ, AFGHANISTAN, WE'VE BEEN THERE BEFORE AT ONE TIME OR ANOTHER.
THE LAST TIME WE WERE UP HERE IT WAS PITH HELMETS AND MARTINI-HENRY RIFLES, AND RATHER DASHING RED JACKETS. BUT WHEREVER WE END UP, IT FEELS LIKE...
UNFINISHED BUSINESS. A LEGACY OF EMPIRE, I SUPPOSE.

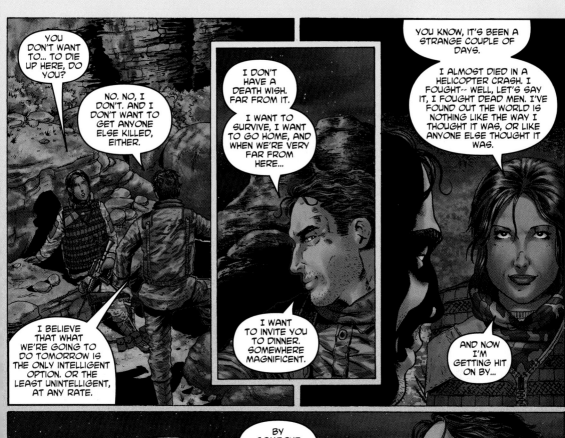

YOU DON'T WANT TO... TO DIE UP HERE, DO YOU?

NO. NO, I DON'T. AND I DON'T WANT TO GET ANYONE ELSE KILLED, EITHER.

I DON'T HAVE A DEATH WISH. FAR FROM IT.

I WANT TO SURVIVE, I WANT TO GO HOME, AND WHEN WE'RE VERY FAR FROM HERE...

YOU KNOW, IT'S BEEN A STRANGE COUPLE OF DAYS.

I ALMOST DIED IN A HELICOPTER CRASH. I FOUGHT-- WELL, LET'S SAY IT, I FOUGHT DEAD MEN. I'VE FOUND OUT THE WORLD IS NOTHING LIKE THE WAY I THOUGHT IT WAS, OR LIKE ANYONE ELSE THOUGHT IT WAS.

I BELIEVE THAT WHAT WE'RE GOING TO DO TOMORROW IS THE ONLY INTELLIGENT OPTION. OR THE LEAST UNINTELLIGENT, AT ANY RATE.

I WANT TO INVITE YOU TO DINNER. SOMEWHERE MAGNIFICENT.

AND NOW I'M GETTING HIT ON BY...

BY SOMEONE WHO'S NOT LIKE ANYONE I'VE EVER MET.

IS IT THE ACCENT?

FOR STARTERS. I'LL TELL YOU THE REST OVER DINNER.

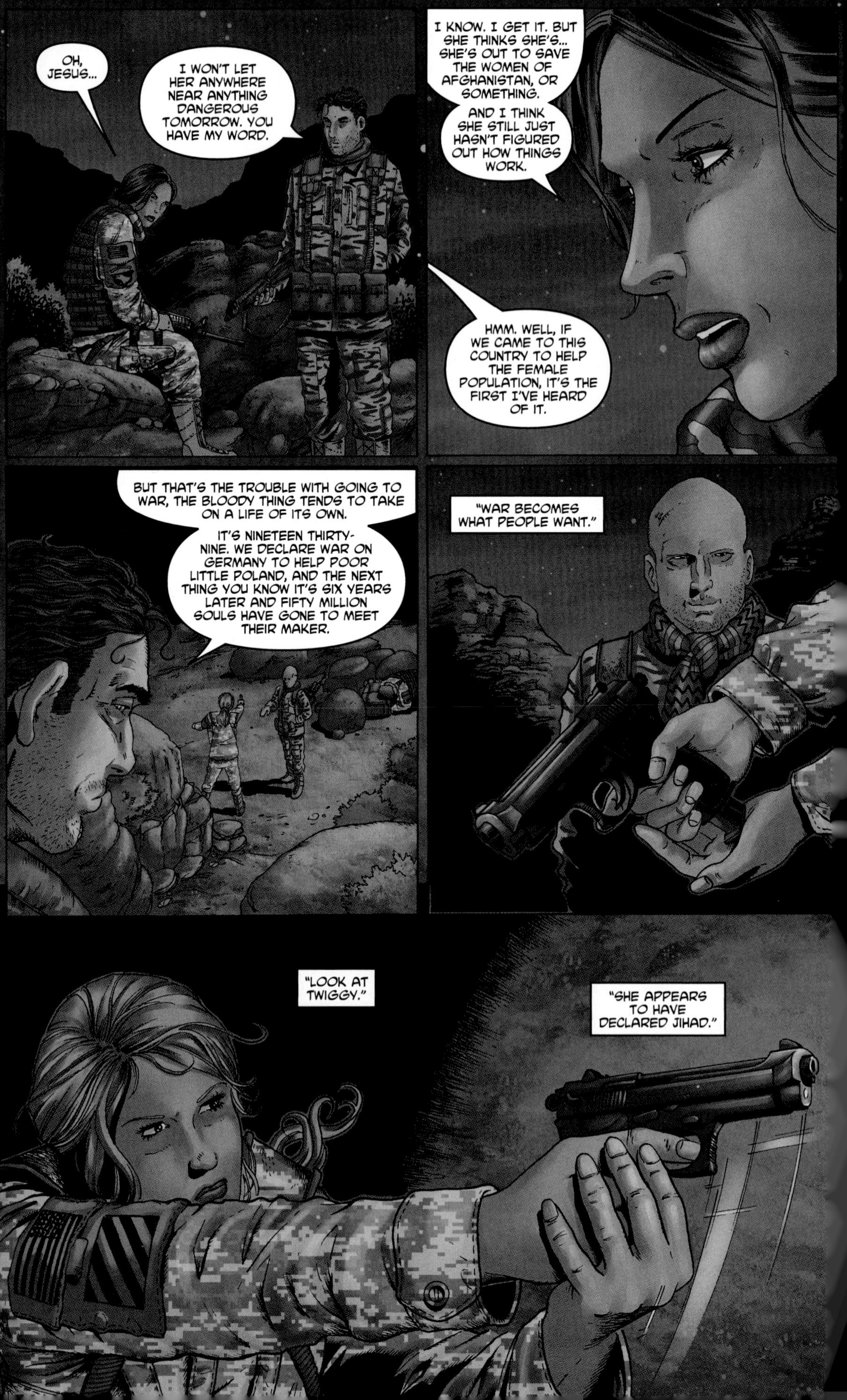
OH, JESUS...
I WON'T LET HER ANYWHERE NEAR ANYTHING DANGEROUS TOMORROW. YOU HAVE MY WORD.
I KNOW. I GET IT. BUT SHE THINKS SHE'S... SHE'S OUT TO SAVE THE WOMEN OF AFGHANISTAN, OR SOMETHING.
AND I THINK SHE STILL JUST HASN'T FIGURED OUT HOW THINGS WORK.
HMM. WELL, IF WE CAME TO THIS COUNTRY TO HELP THE FEMALE POPULATION, IT'S THE FIRST I'VE HEARD OF IT.
BUT THAT'S THE TROUBLE WITH GOING TO WAR, THE BLOODY THING TENDS TO TAKE ON A LIFE OF ITS OWN.
IT'S NINETEEN THIRTY-NINE. WE DECLARE WAR ON GERMANY TO HELP POOR LITTLE POLAND, AND THE NEXT THING YOU KNOW IT'S SIX YEARS LATER AND FIFTY MILLION SOULS HAVE GONE TO MEET THEIR MAKER.
"WAR BECOMES WHAT PEOPLE WANT."
"LOOK AT TWIGGY."
"SHE APPEARS TO HAVE DECLARED JIHAD."

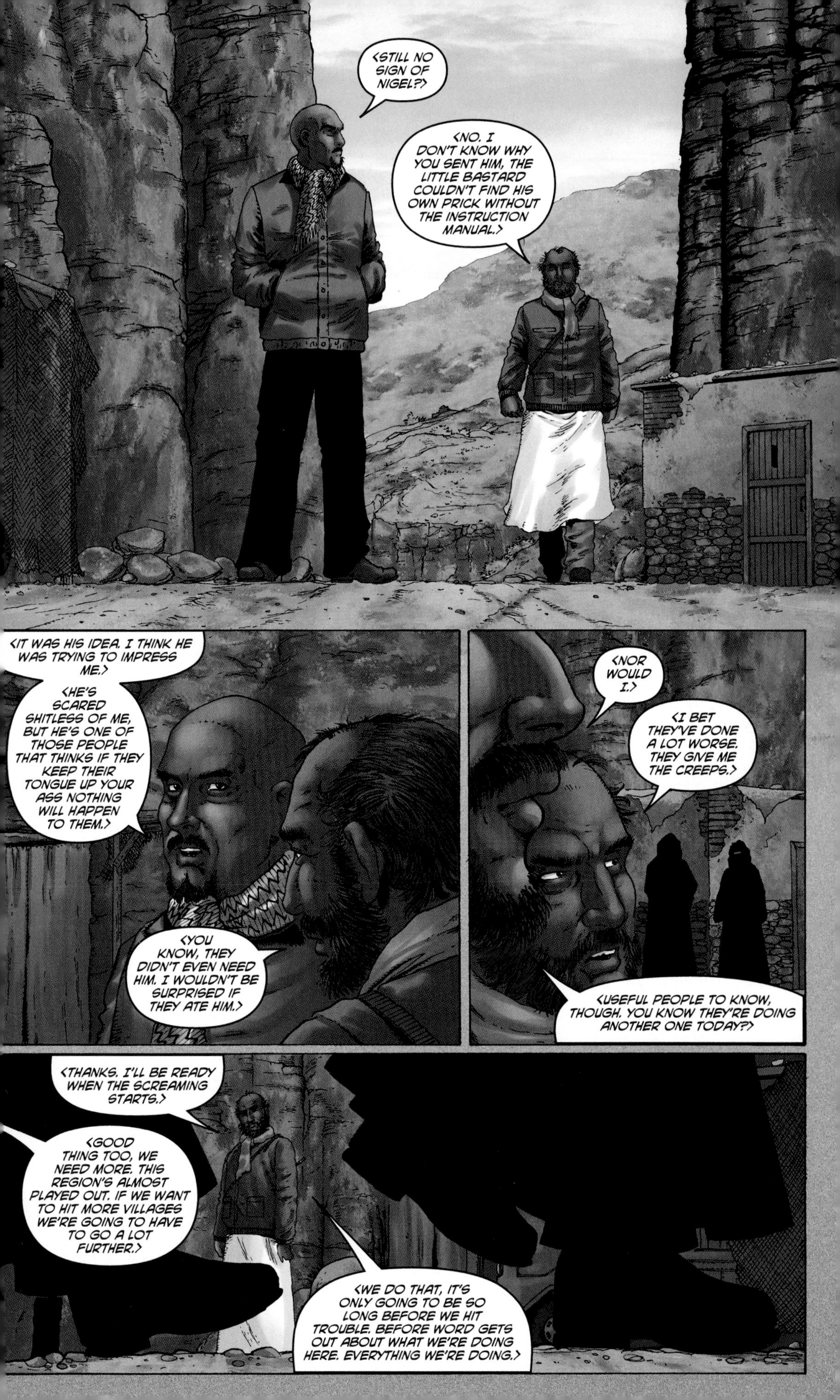
<STILL NO SIGN OF NIGEL?>
<NO. I DON'T KNOW WHY YOU SENT HIM, THE LITTLE BASTARD COULDN'T FIND HIS OWN PRICK WITHOUT THE INSTRUCTION MANUAL.>
<IT WAS HIS IDEA. I THINK HE WAS TRYING TO IMPRESS ME.>
<HE'S SCARED SHITLESS OF ME, BUT HE'S ONE OF THOSE PEOPLE THAT THINKS IF THEY KEEP THEIR TONGUE UP YOUR ASS NOTHING WILL HAPPEN TO THEM.>
<YOU KNOW, THEY DIDN'T EVEN NEED HIM. I WOULDN'T BE SURPRISED IF THEY ATE HIM.>
<NOR WOULD I.>
<I BET THEY'VE DONE A LOT WORSE. THEY GIVE ME THE CREEPS.>
<USEFUL PEOPLE TO KNOW, THOUGH. YOU KNOW THEY'RE DOING ANOTHER ONE TODAY?>
<THANKS. I'LL BE READY WHEN THE SCREAMING STARTS.>
<GOOD THING TOO, WE NEED MORE. THIS REGION'S ALMOST PLAYED OUT. IF WE WANT TO HIT MORE VILLAGES WE'RE GOING TO HAVE TO GO A LOT FURTHER.>
<WE DO THAT, IT'S ONLY GOING TO BE SO LONG BEFORE WE HIT TROUBLE. BEFORE WORD GETS OUT ABOUT WHAT WE'RE DOING HERE. EVERYTHING WE'RE DOING.>

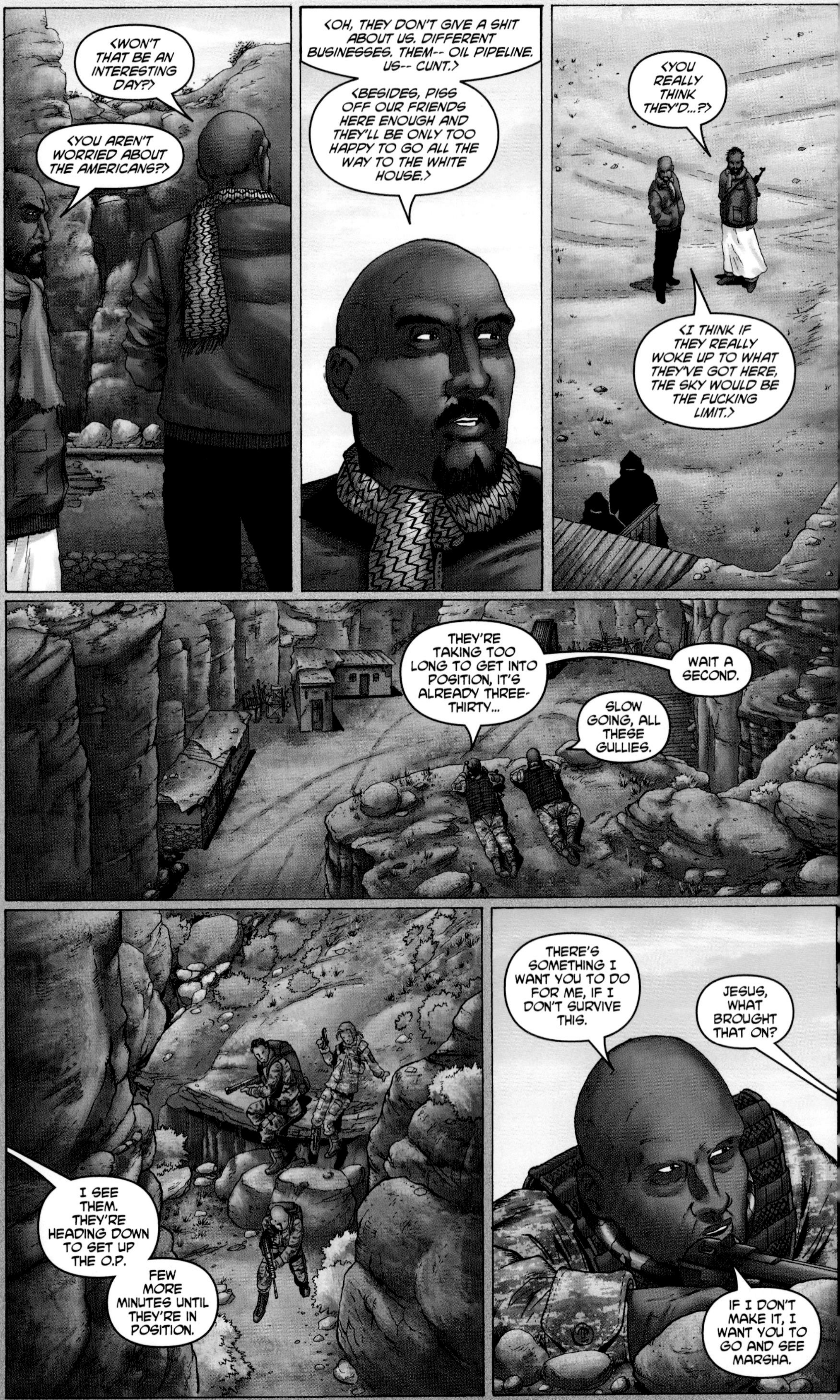

<WON'T THAT BE AN INTERESTING DAY?>
<YOU AREN'T WORRIED ABOUT THE AMERICANS?>
<OH, THEY DON'T GIVE A SHIT ABOUT US. DIFFERENT BUSINESSES. THEM-- OIL PIPELINE. US-- CUNT.>
<BESIDES, PISS OFF OUR FRIENDS HERE ENOUGH AND THEY'LL BE ONLY TOO HAPPY TO GO ALL THE WAY TO THE WHITE HOUSE.>
<YOU REALLY THINK THEY'D...?>
<I THINK IF THEY REALLY WOKE UP TO WHAT THEY'VE GOT HERE, THE SKY WOULD BE THE FUCKING LIMIT.>
THEY'RE TAKING TOO LONG TO GET INTO POSITION, IT'S ALREADY THREE-THIRTY...
WAIT A SECOND.
SLOW GOING, ALL THESE GULLIES.
I SEE THEM. THEY'RE HEADING DOWN TO SET UP THE O.P.
FEW MORE MINUTES UNTIL THEY'RE IN POSITION.
THERE'S SOMETHING I WANT YOU TO DO FOR ME, IF I DON'T SURVIVE THIS.
JESUS, WHAT BROUGHT THAT ON?
IF I DON'T MAKE IT, I WANT YOU TO GO AND SEE MARSHA.

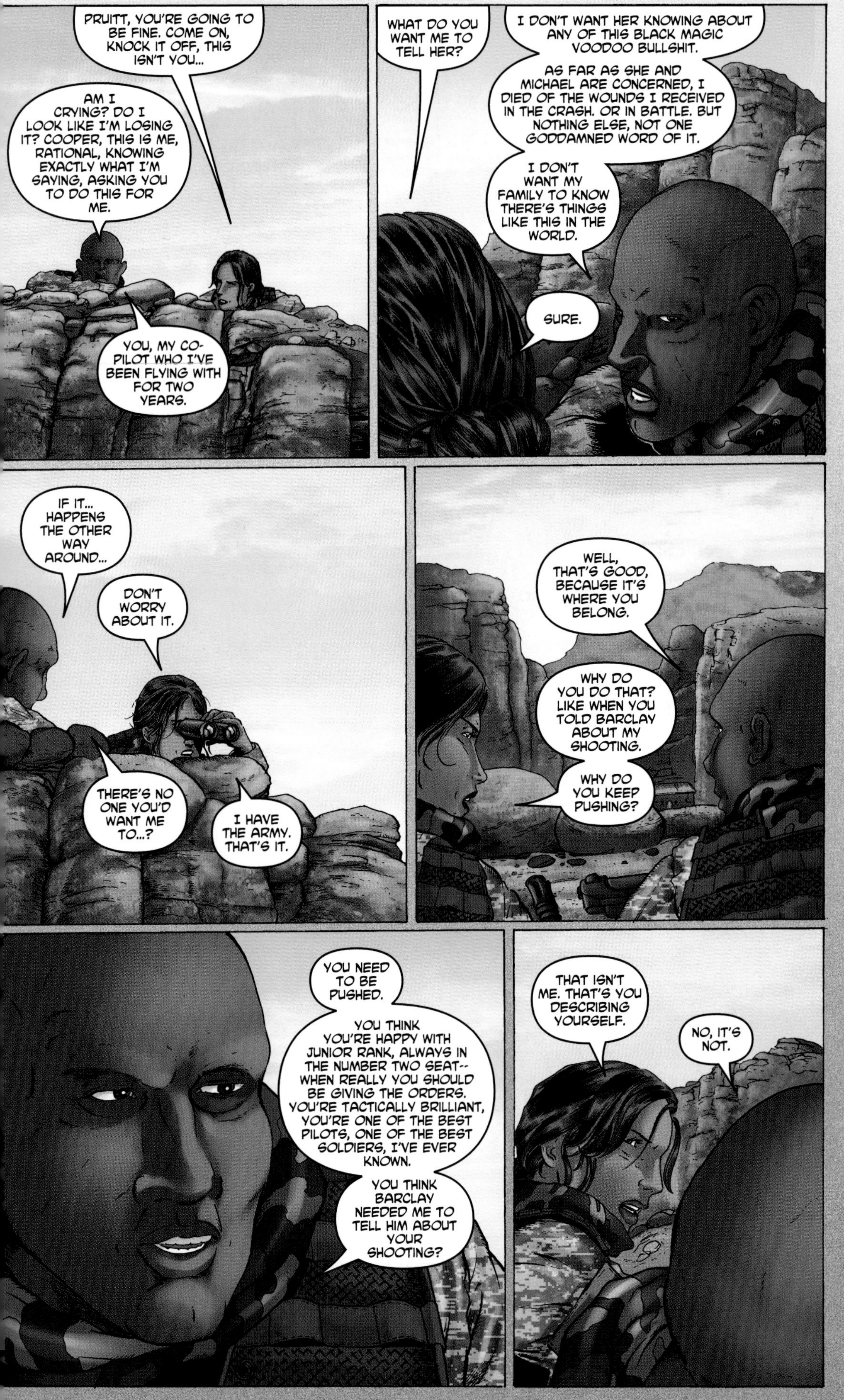
PRUITT, YOU'RE GOING TO BE FINE. COME ON, KNOCK IT OFF, THIS ISN'T YOU...
AM I CRYING? DO I LOOK LIKE I'M LOSING IT? COOPER, THIS IS ME, RATIONAL, KNOWING EXACTLY WHAT I'M SAYING, ASKING YOU TO DO THIS FOR ME.
YOU, MY CO-PILOT WHO I'VE BEEN FLYING WITH FOR TWO YEARS.
WHAT DO YOU WANT ME TO TELL HER?
I DON'T WANT HER KNOWING ABOUT ANY OF THIS BLACK MAGIC VOODOO BULLSHIT.
AS FAR AS SHE AND MICHAEL ARE CONCERNED, I DIED OF THE WOUNDS I RECEIVED IN THE CRASH. OR IN BATTLE. BUT NOTHING ELSE, NOT ONE GODDAMNED WORD OF IT.
I DON'T WANT MY FAMILY TO KNOW THERE'S THINGS LIKE THIS IN THE WORLD.
SURE.
IF IT... HAPPENS THE OTHER WAY AROUND...
DON'T WORRY ABOUT IT.
THERE'S NO ONE YOU'D WANT ME TO...?
I HAVE THE ARMY. THAT'S IT.
WELL, THAT'S GOOD, BECAUSE IT'S WHERE YOU BELONG.
WHY DO YOU DO THAT? LIKE WHEN YOU TOLD BARCLAY ABOUT MY SHOOTING.
WHY DO YOU KEEP PUSHING?
YOU NEED TO BE PUSHED.
YOU THINK YOU'RE HAPPY WITH JUNIOR RANK, ALWAYS IN THE NUMBER TWO SEAT-- WHEN REALLY YOU SHOULD BE GIVING THE ORDERS. YOU'RE TACTICALLY BRILLIANT, YOU'RE ONE OF THE BEST PILOTS, ONE OF THE BEST SOLDIERS, I'VE EVER KNOWN.
YOU THINK BARCLAY NEEDED ME TO TELL HIM ABOUT YOUR SHOOTING?
THAT ISN'T ME. THAT'S YOU DESCRIBING YOURSELF.
NO, IT'S NOT.

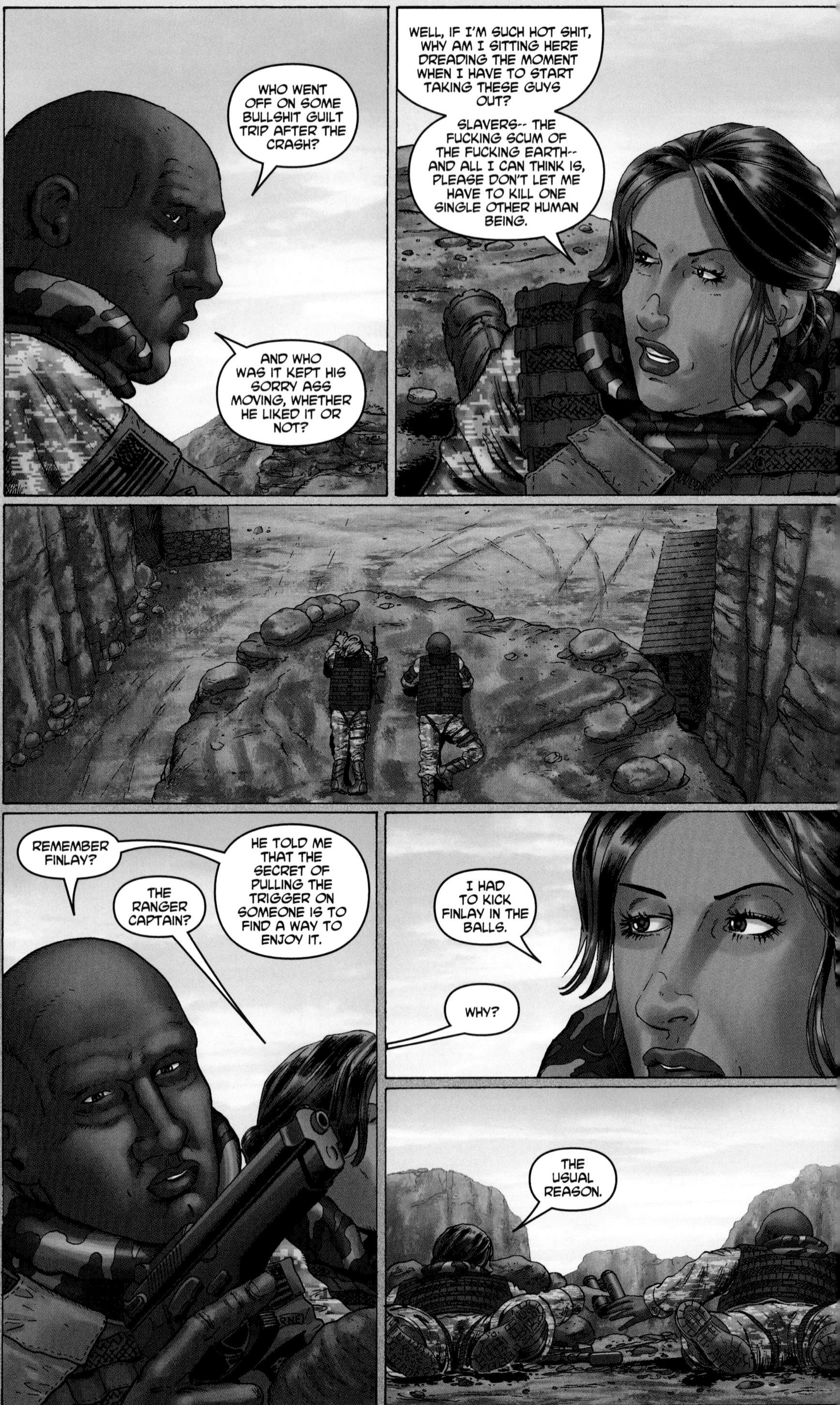
WHO WENT OFF ON SOME BULLSHIT GUILT TRIP AFTER THE CRASH?
AND WHO WAS IT KEPT HIS SORRY ASS MOVING, WHETHER HE LIKED IT OR NOT?
WELL, IF I'M SUCH HOT SHIT, WHY AM I SITTING HERE DREADING THE MOMENT WHEN I HAVE TO START TAKING THESE GUYS OUT?
SLAVERS-- THE FUCKING SCUM OF THE FUCKING EARTH-- AND ALL I CAN THINK IS, PLEASE DON'T LET ME HAVE TO KILL ONE SINGLE OTHER HUMAN BEING.
REMEMBER FINLAY?
THE RANGER CAPTAIN?
HE TOLD ME THAT THE SECRET OF PULLING THE TRIGGER ON SOMEONE IS TO FIND A WAY TO ENJOY IT.
I HAD TO KICK FINLAY IN THE BALLS.
WHY?
THE USUAL REASON.

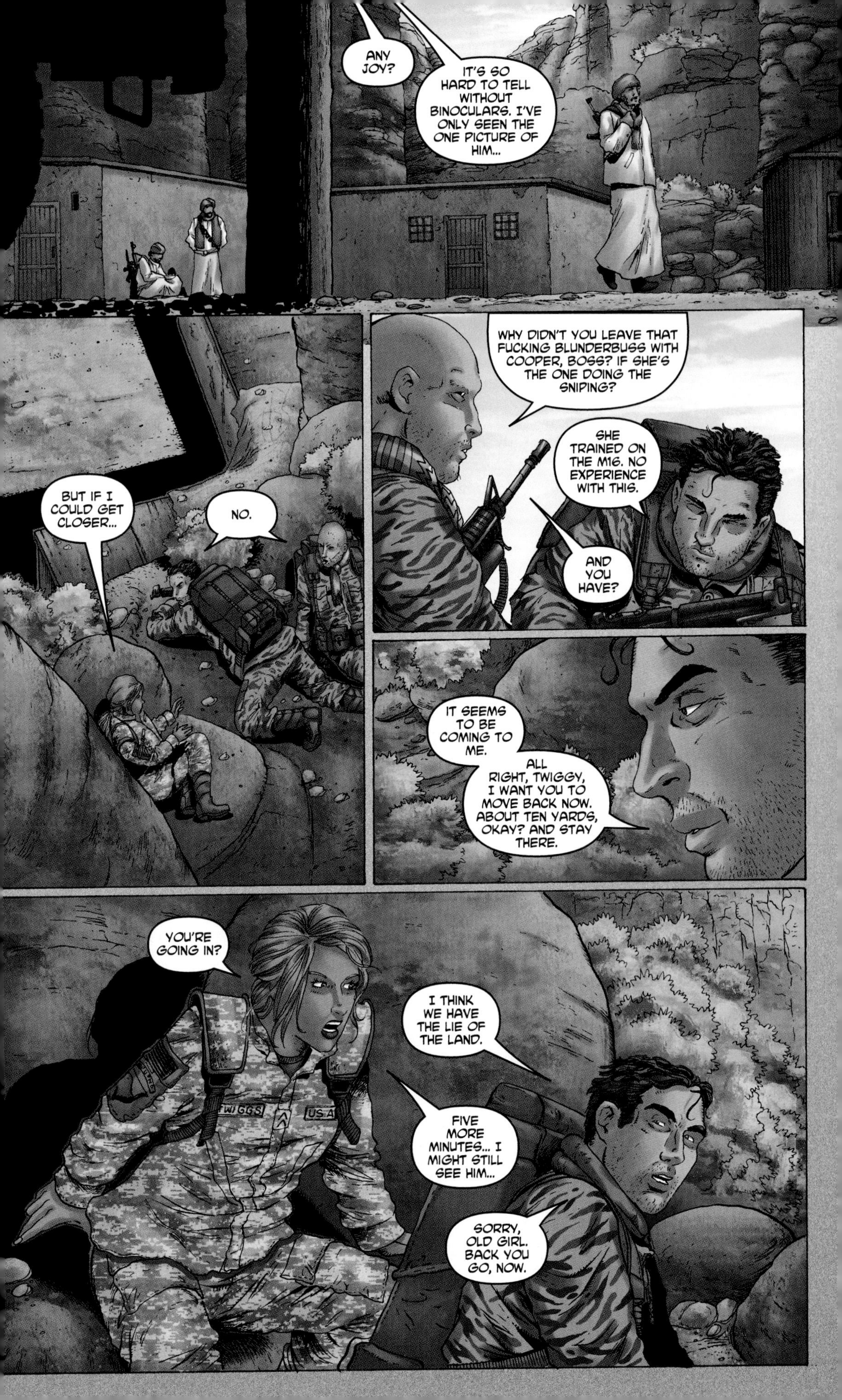
ANY JOY?
IT'S SO HARD TO TELL WITHOUT BINOCULARS. I'VE ONLY SEEN THE ONE PICTURE OF HIM...
BUT IF I COULD GET CLOSER...
NO.
WHY DIDN'T YOU LEAVE THAT FUCKING BLUNDERBUSS WITH COOPER, BOSS? IF SHE'S THE ONE DOING THE SNIPING?
SHE TRAINED ON THE M16. NO EXPERIENCE WITH THIS.
AND YOU HAVE?
IT SEEMS TO BE COMING TO ME.
ALL RIGHT, TWIGGY, I WANT YOU TO MOVE BACK NOW. ABOUT TEN YARDS, OKAY? AND STAY THERE.
YOU'RE GOING IN?
I THINK WE HAVE THE LIE OF THE LAND.
FIVE MORE MINUTES... I MIGHT STILL SEE HIM...
SORRY, OLD GIRL. BACK YOU GO, NOW.
TWIGGS
U.S.A

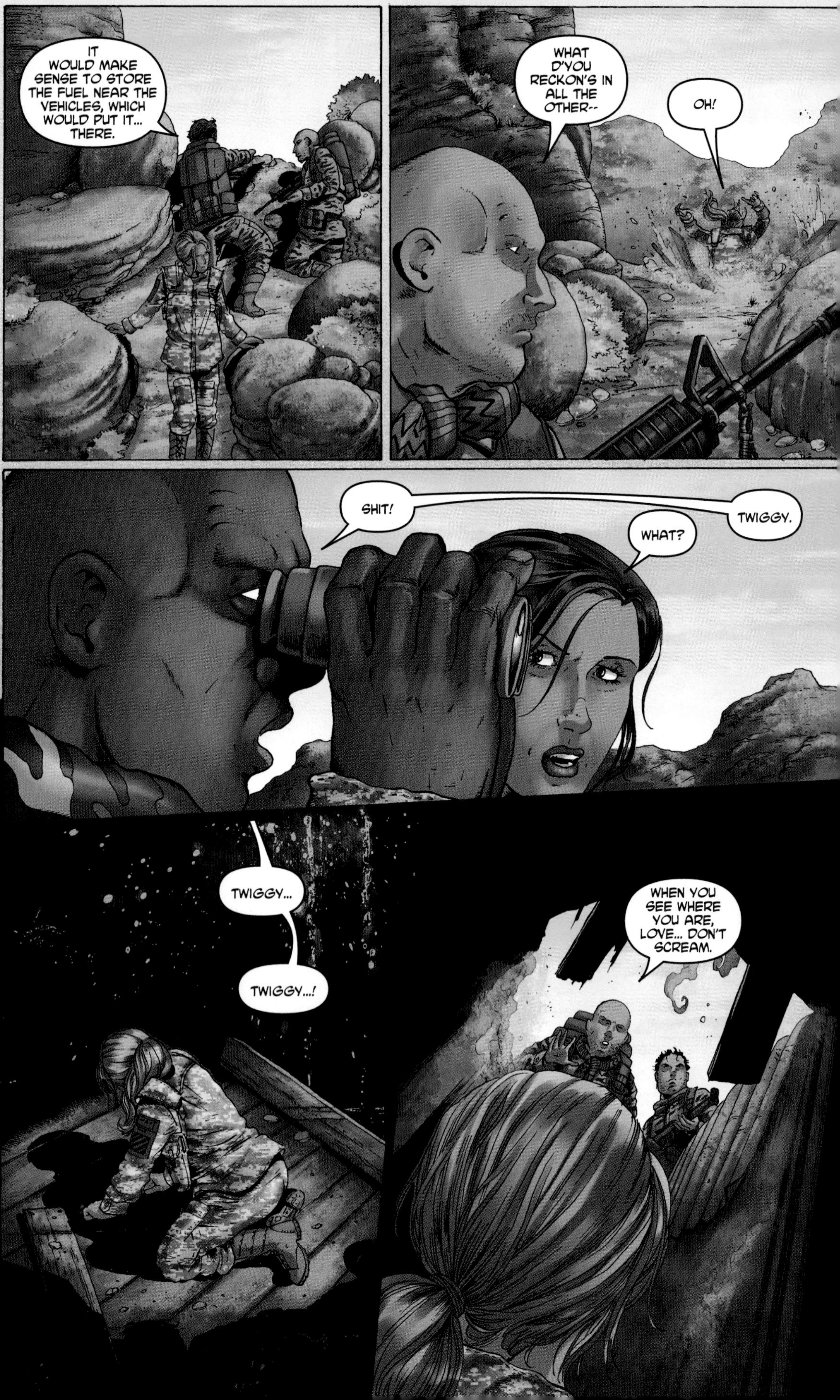
IT WOULD MAKE SENSE TO STORE THE FUEL NEAR THE VEHICLES, WHICH WOULD PUT IT... THERE.
WHAT D'YOU RECKON'S IN ALL THE OTHER--
OH!
SHIT!
TWIGGY.
WHAT?
TWIGGY...
TWIGGY...!
WHEN YOU SEE WHERE YOU ARE, LOVE... DON'T SCREAM.

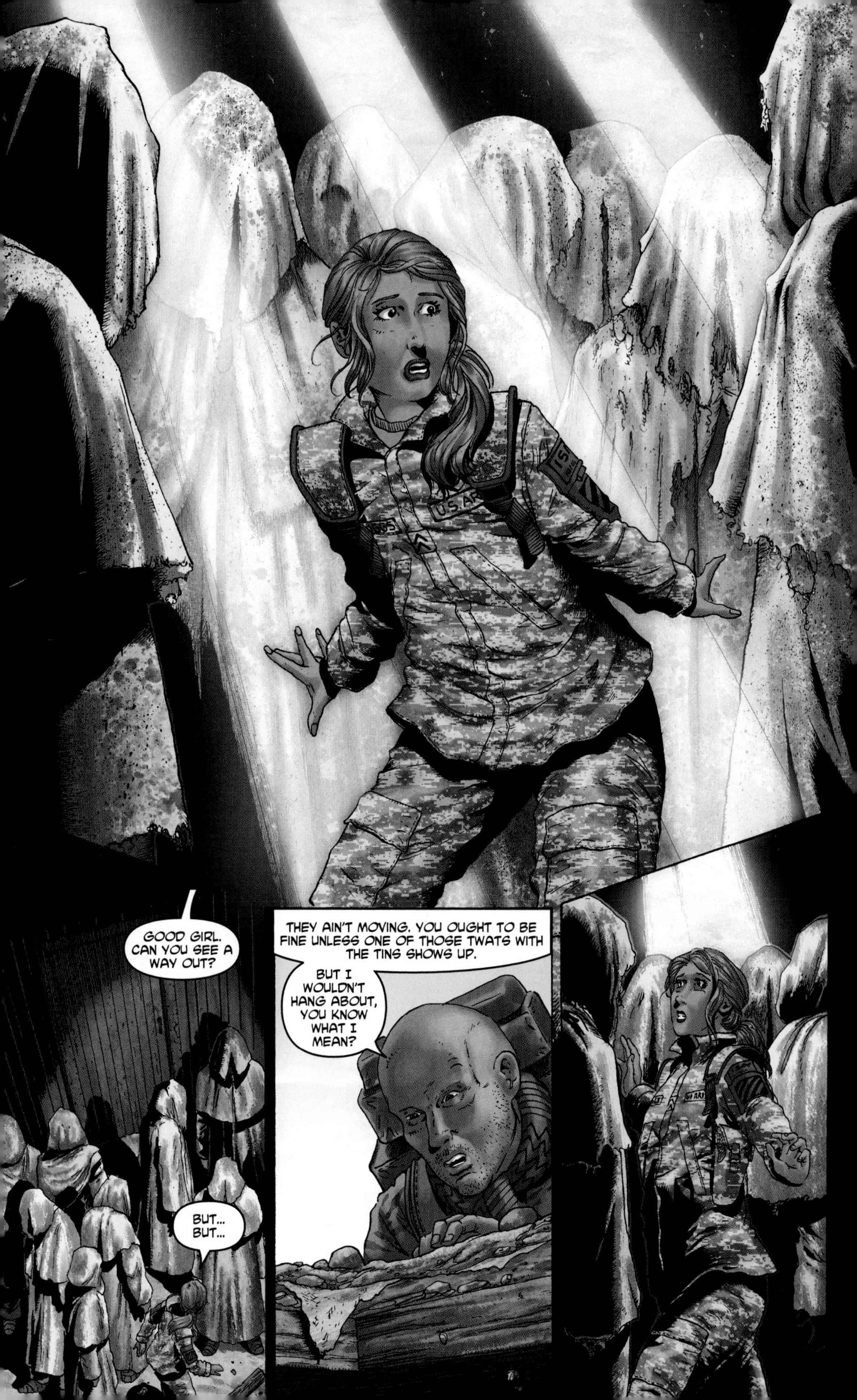
GOOD GIRL. CAN YOU SEE A WAY OUT?
BUT... BUT...
THEY AIN'T MOVING. YOU OUGHT TO BE FINE UNLESS ONE OF THOSE TWATS WITH THE TINS SHOWS UP.
BUT I WOULDN'T HANG ABOUT, YOU KNOW WHAT I MEAN?

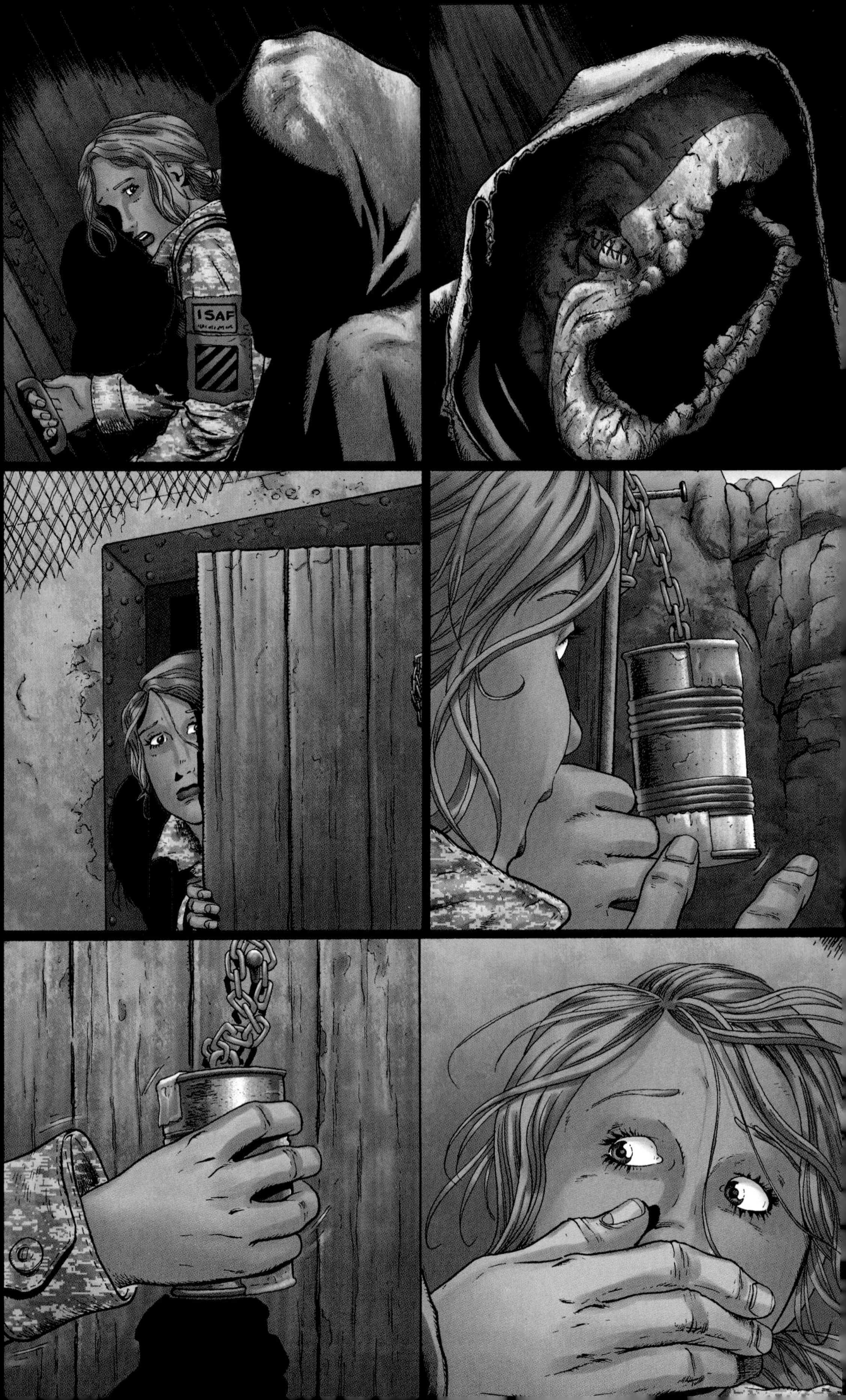
ISAF

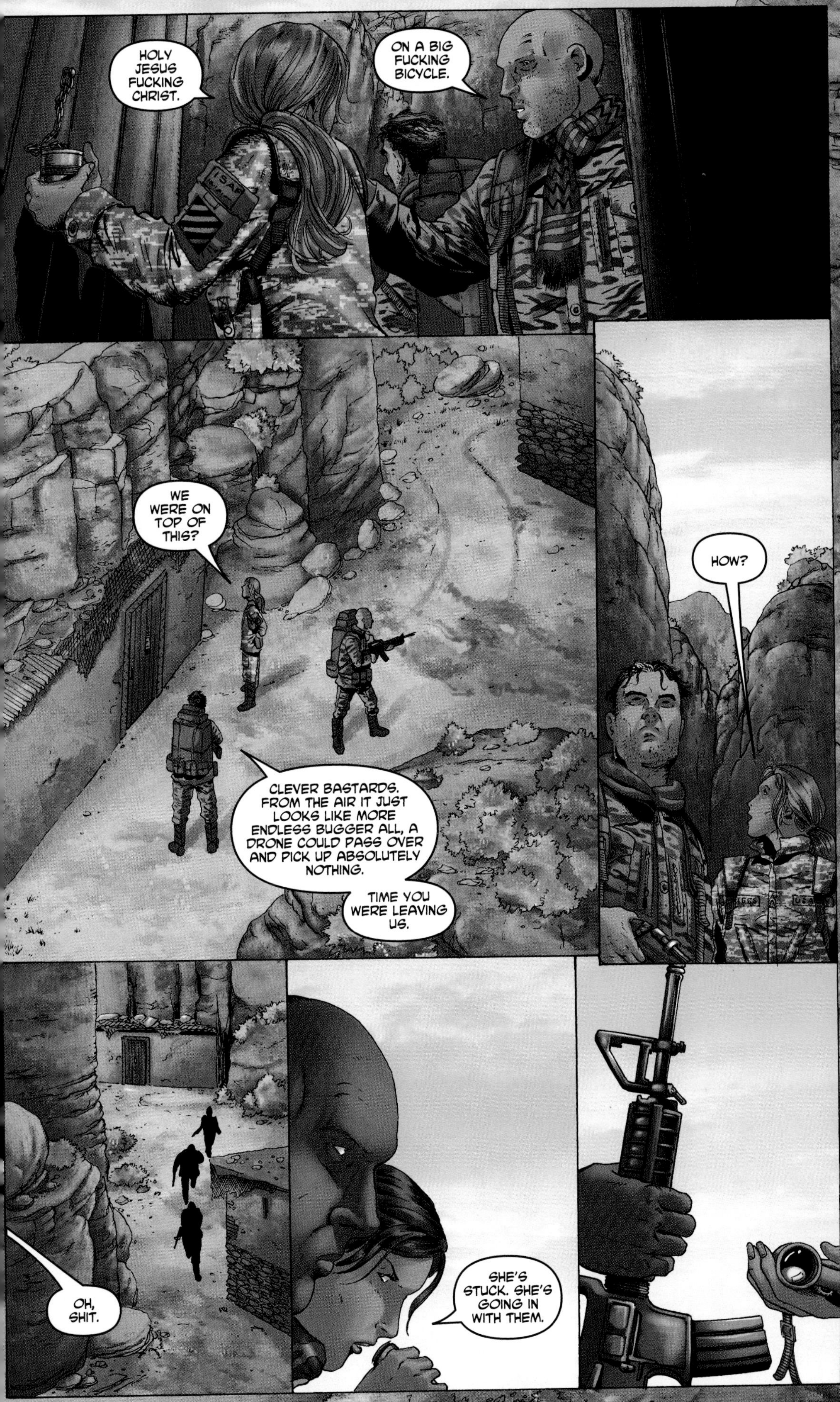
HOLY JESUS FUCKING CHRIST.
ON A BIG FUCKING BICYCLE.
WE WERE ON TOP OF THIS?
CLEVER BASTARDS. FROM THE AIR IT JUST LOOKS LIKE MORE ENDLESS BUGGER ALL, A DRONE COULD PASS OVER AND PICK UP ABSOLUTELY NOTHING.
TIME YOU WERE LEAVING US.
HOW?
OH, SHIT.
SHE'S STUCK. SHE'S GOING IN WITH THEM.

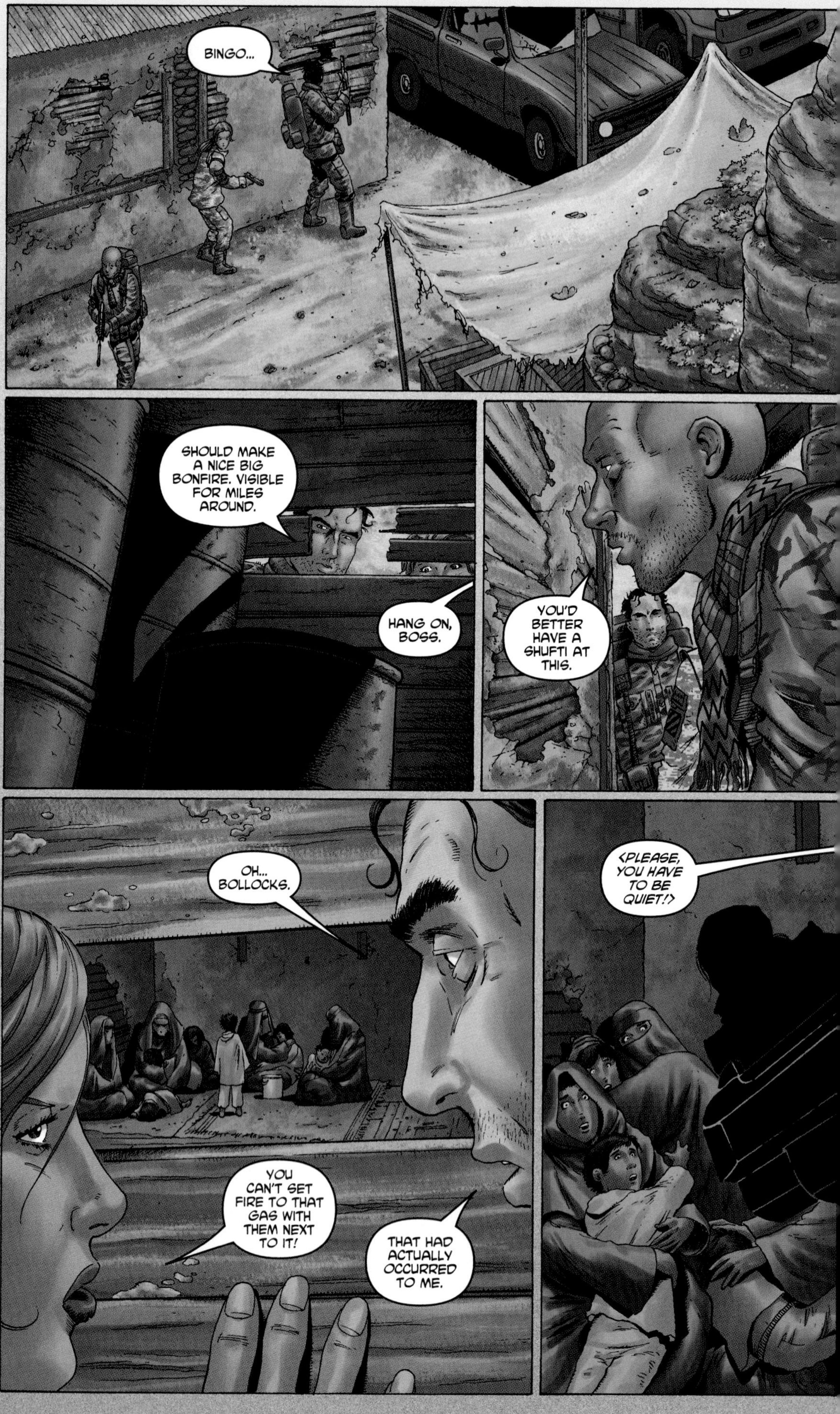
BINGO...
SHOULD MAKE A NICE BIG BONFIRE. VISIBLE FOR MILES AROUND.
HANG ON, BOSS.
YOU'D BETTER HAVE A SHUFTI AT THIS.
OH... BOLLOCKS.
YOU CAN'T SET FIRE TO THAT GAS WITH THEM NEXT TO IT!
THAT HAD ACTUALLY OCCURRED TO ME.
<PLEASE, YOU HAVE TO BE QUIET!>

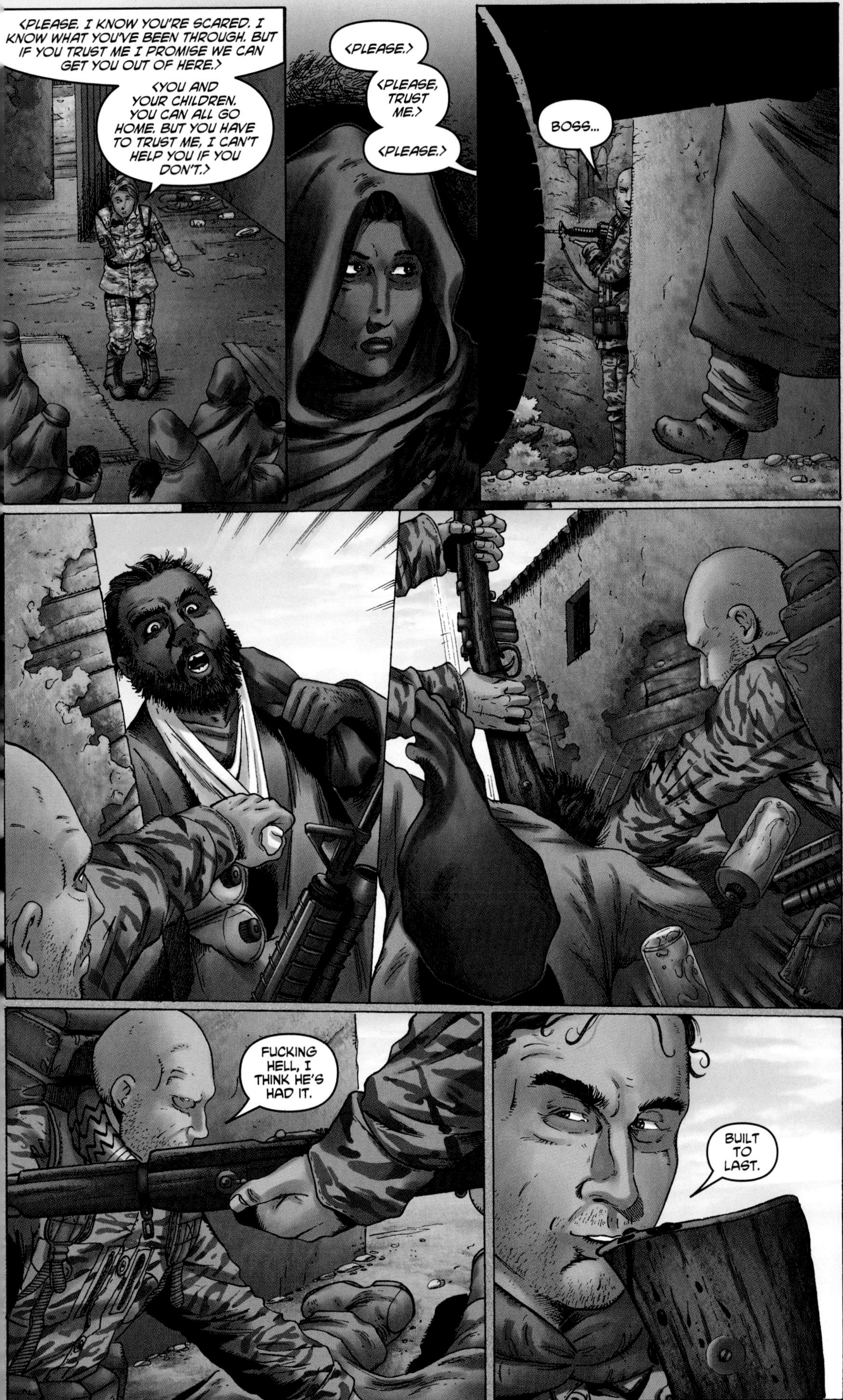
<PLEASE. I KNOW YOU'RE SCARED. I KNOW WHAT YOU'VE BEEN THROUGH. BUT IF YOU TRUST ME I PROMISE WE CAN GET YOU OUT OF HERE.>
<YOU AND YOUR CHILDREN. YOU CAN ALL GO HOME. BUT YOU HAVE TO TRUST ME, I CAN'T HELP YOU IF YOU DON'T.>
<PLEASE.>
<PLEASE, TRUST ME.>
<PLEASE.>
BOSS...
FUCKING HELL, I THINK HE'S HAD IT.
BUILT TO LAST.

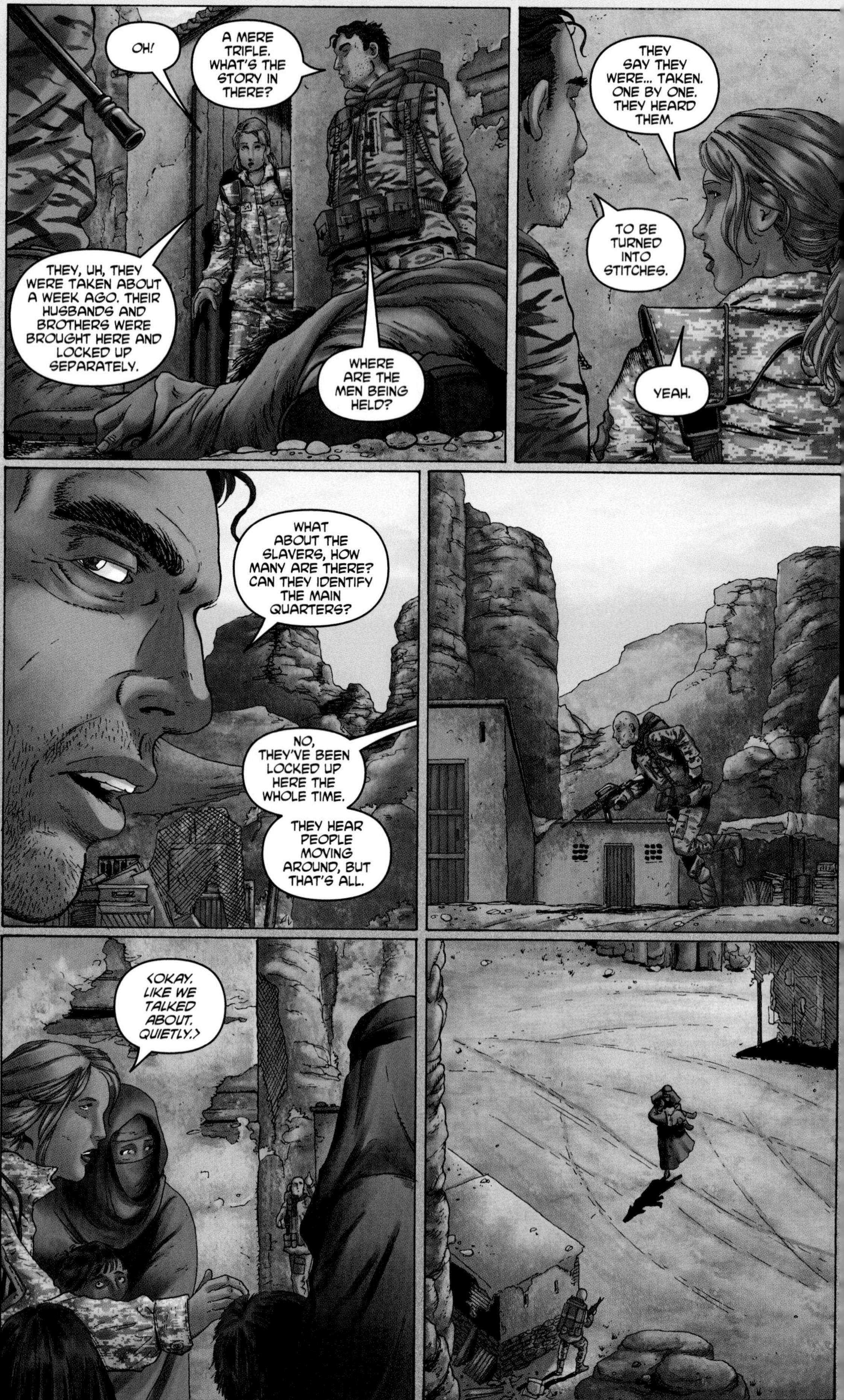

OH!
A MERE TRIFLE. WHAT'S THE STORY IN THERE?
THEY, UH, THEY WERE TAKEN ABOUT A WEEK AGO. THEIR HUSBANDS AND BROTHERS WERE BROUGHT HERE AND LOCKED UP SEPARATELY.
WHERE ARE THE MEN BEING HELD?
THEY SAY THEY WERE... TAKEN. ONE BY ONE. THEY HEARD THEM.
TO BE TURNED INTO STITCHES.
YEAH.
WHAT ABOUT THE SLAVERS, HOW MANY ARE THERE? CAN THEY IDENTIFY THE MAIN QUARTERS?
NO, THEY'VE BEEN LOCKED UP HERE THE WHOLE TIME.
THEY HEAR PEOPLE MOVING AROUND, BUT THAT'S ALL.
<OKAY. LIKE WE TALKED ABOUT. QUIETLY.>

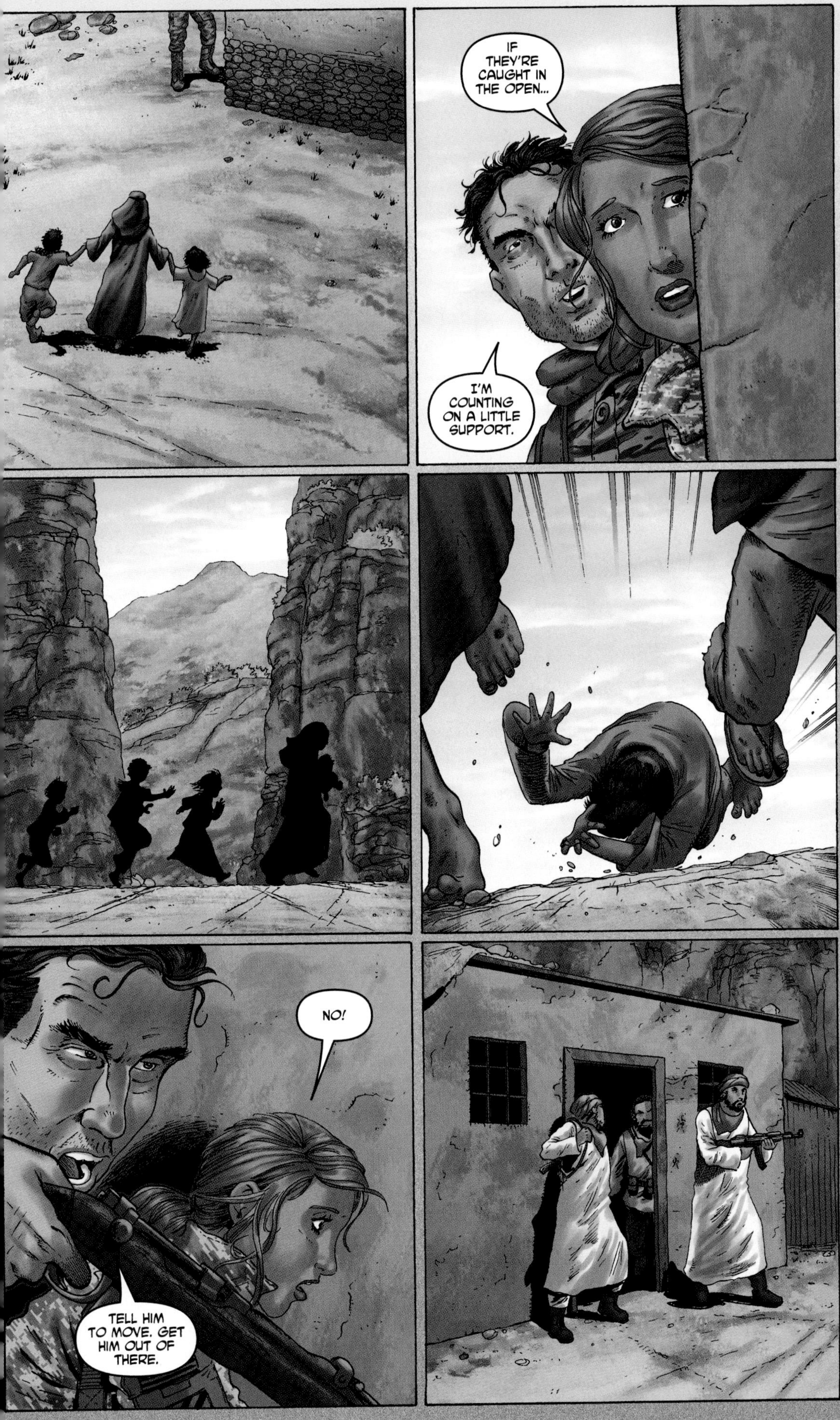
IF THEY'RE CAUGHT IN THE OPEN...
I'M COUNTING ON A LITTLE SUPPORT.
NO!
TELL HIM TO MOVE. GET HIM OUT OF THERE.

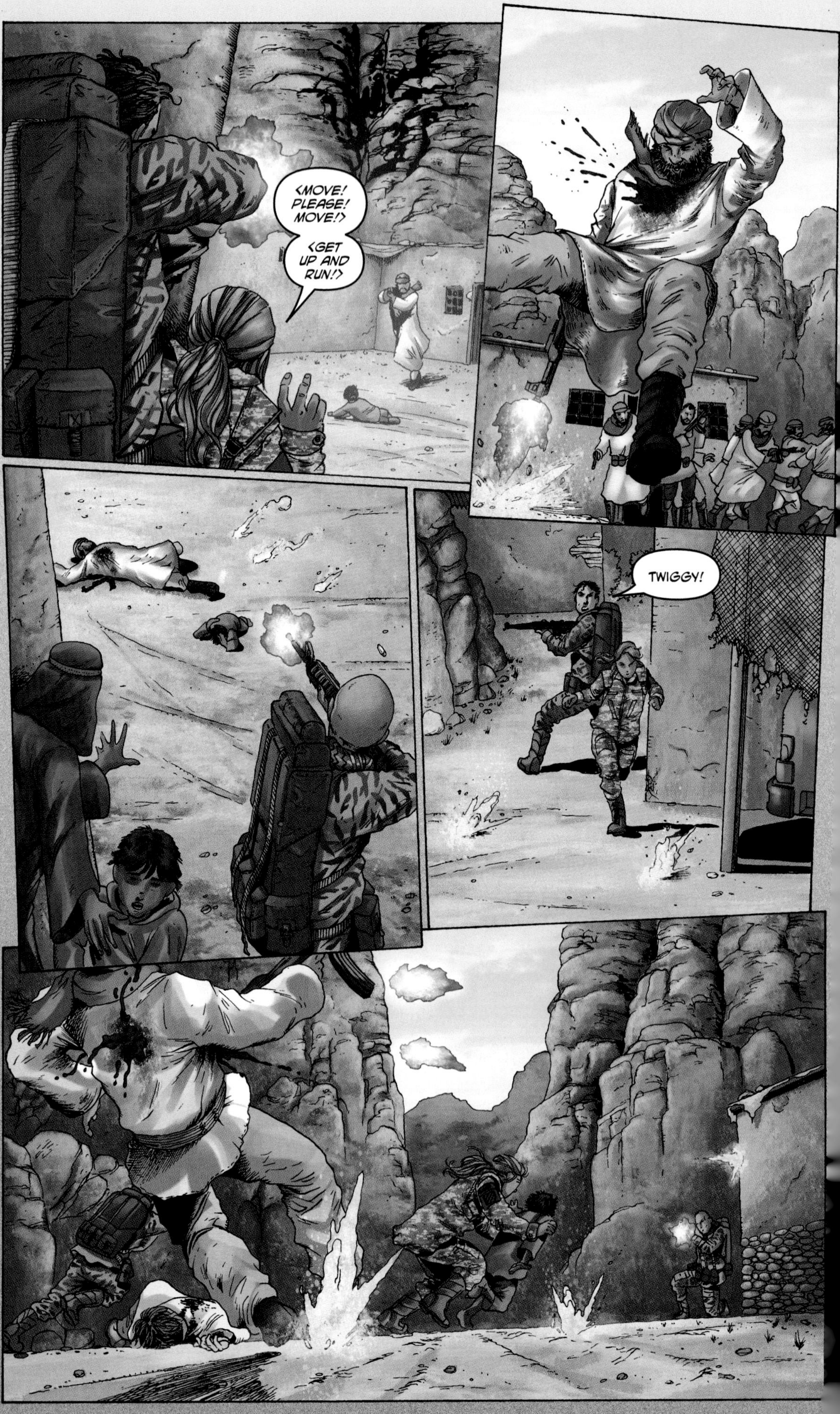

<MOVE! PLEASE! MOVE!>
<GET UP AND RUN!>
TWIGGY!

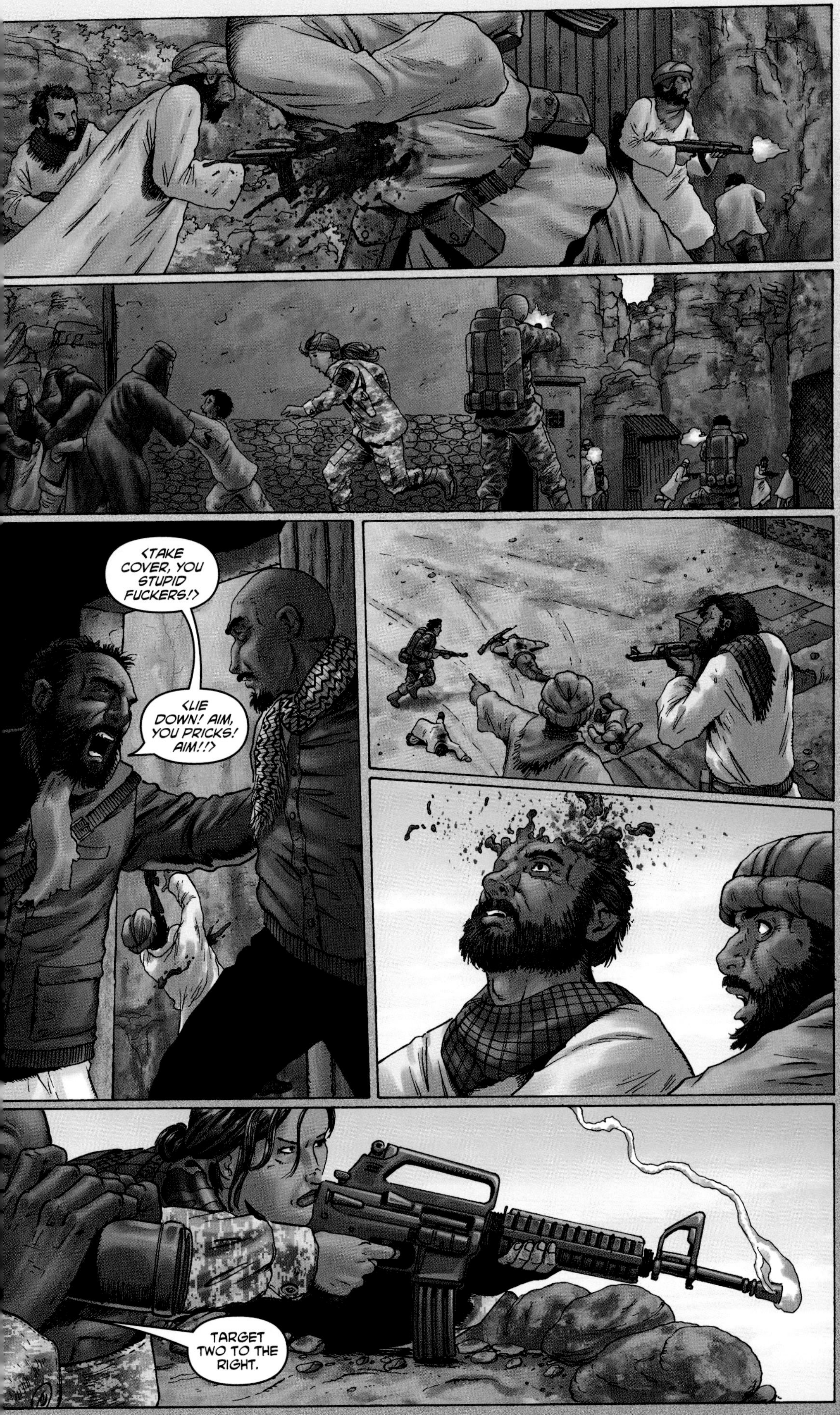

<TAKE COVER, YOU STUPID FUCKERS!>
<LIE DOWN! AIM, YOU PRICKS! AIM!!>
TARGET TWO TO THE RIGHT.

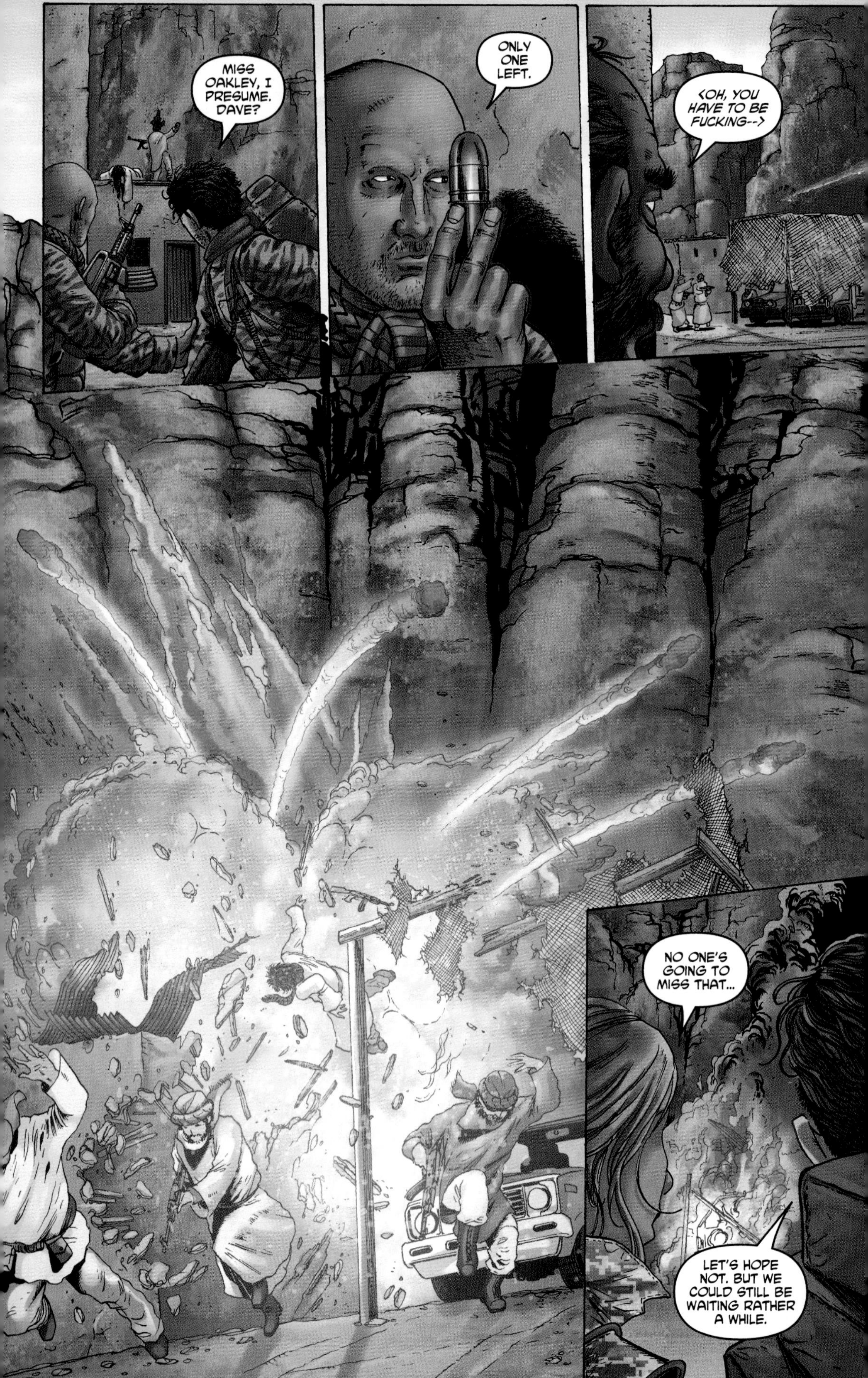
MISS OAKLEY, I PRESUME. DAVE?
ONLY ONE LEFT.
<OH, YOU HAVE TO BE FUCKING-->
NO ONE'S GOING TO MISS THAT...
LET'S HOPE NOT. BUT WE COULD STILL BE WAITING RATHER A WHILE.

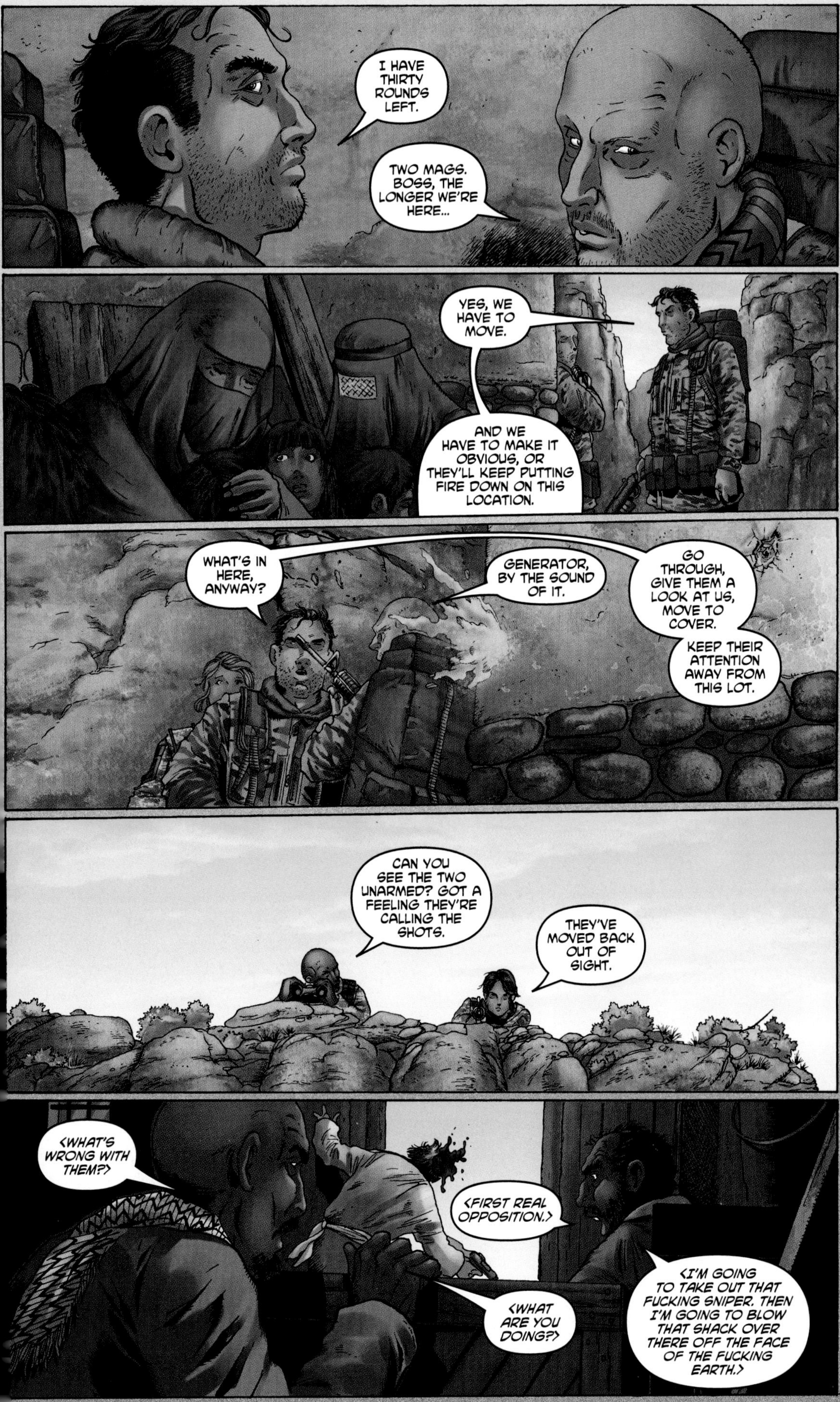
I HAVE THIRTY ROUNDS LEFT.
TWO MAGS. BOSS, THE LONGER WE'RE HERE...
YES, WE HAVE TO MOVE.
AND WE HAVE TO MAKE IT OBVIOUS, OR THEY'LL KEEP PUTTING FIRE DOWN ON THIS LOCATION.
WHAT'S IN HERE, ANYWAY?
GENERATOR, BY THE SOUND OF IT.
GO THROUGH, GIVE THEM A LOOK AT US, MOVE TO COVER.
KEEP THEIR ATTENTION AWAY FROM THIS LOT.
CAN YOU SEE THE TWO UNARMED? GOT A FEELING THEY'RE CALLING THE SHOTS.
THEY'VE MOVED BACK OUT OF SIGHT.
<WHAT'S WRONG WITH THEM?>
<FIRST REAL OPPOSITION.>
<I'M GOING TO TAKE OUT THAT FUCKING SNIPER. THEN I'M GOING TO BLOW THAT SHACK OVER THERE OFF THE FACE OF THE FUCKING EARTH.>
<WHAT ARE YOU DOING?>

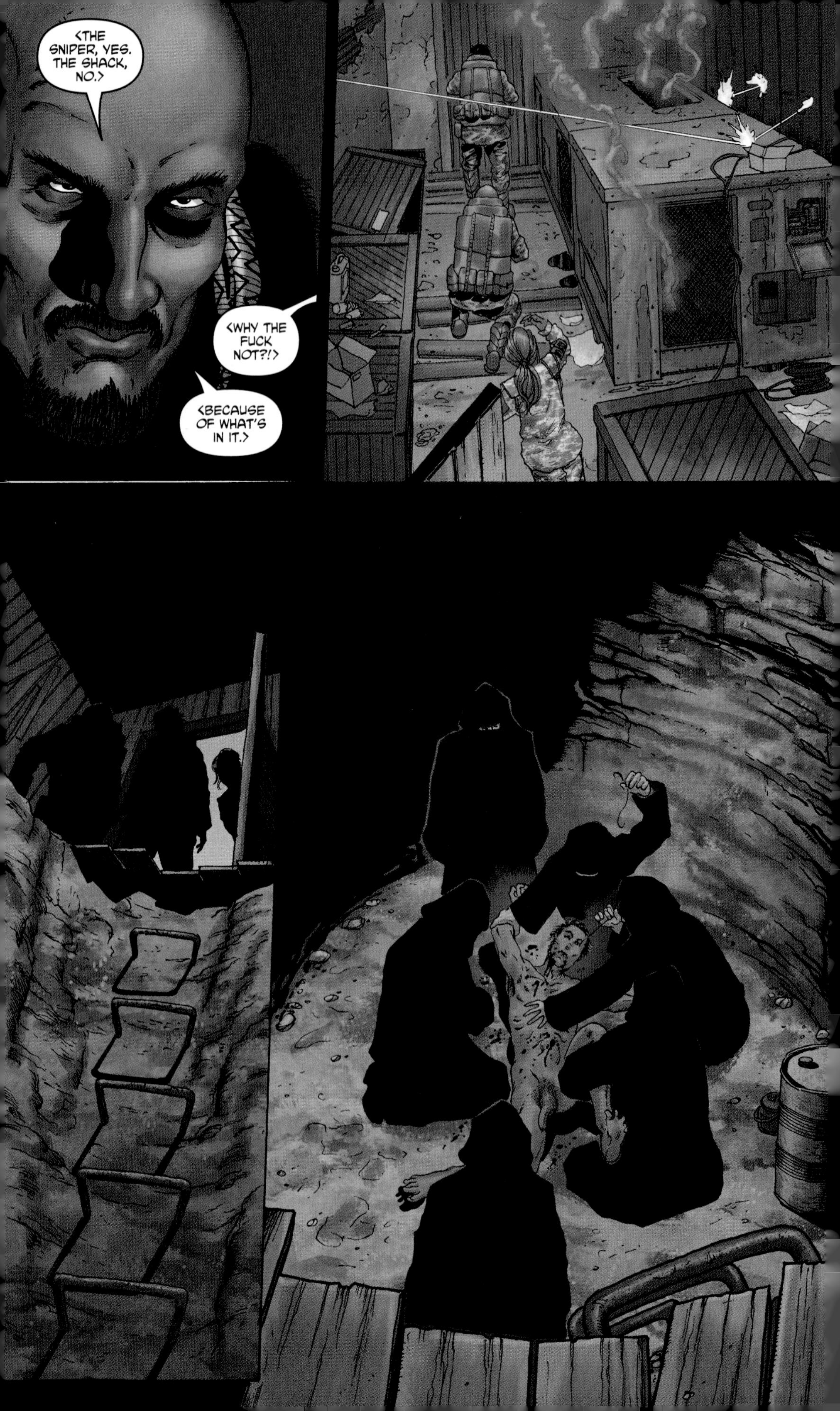
<THE SNIPER, YES. THE SHACK, NO.>
<WHY THE FUCK NOT?!>
<BECAUSE OF WHAT'S IN IT.>

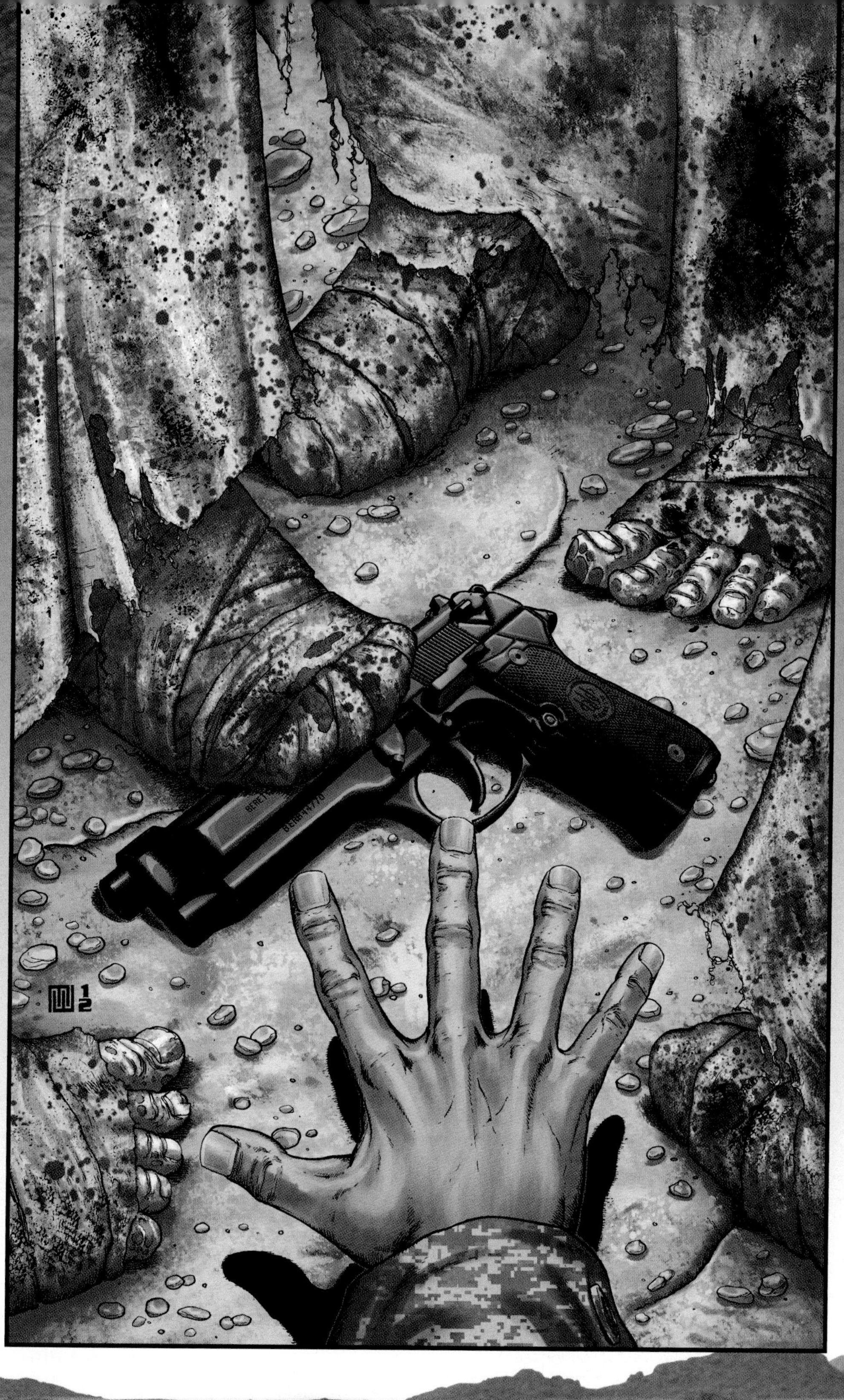

CHAPTER 7

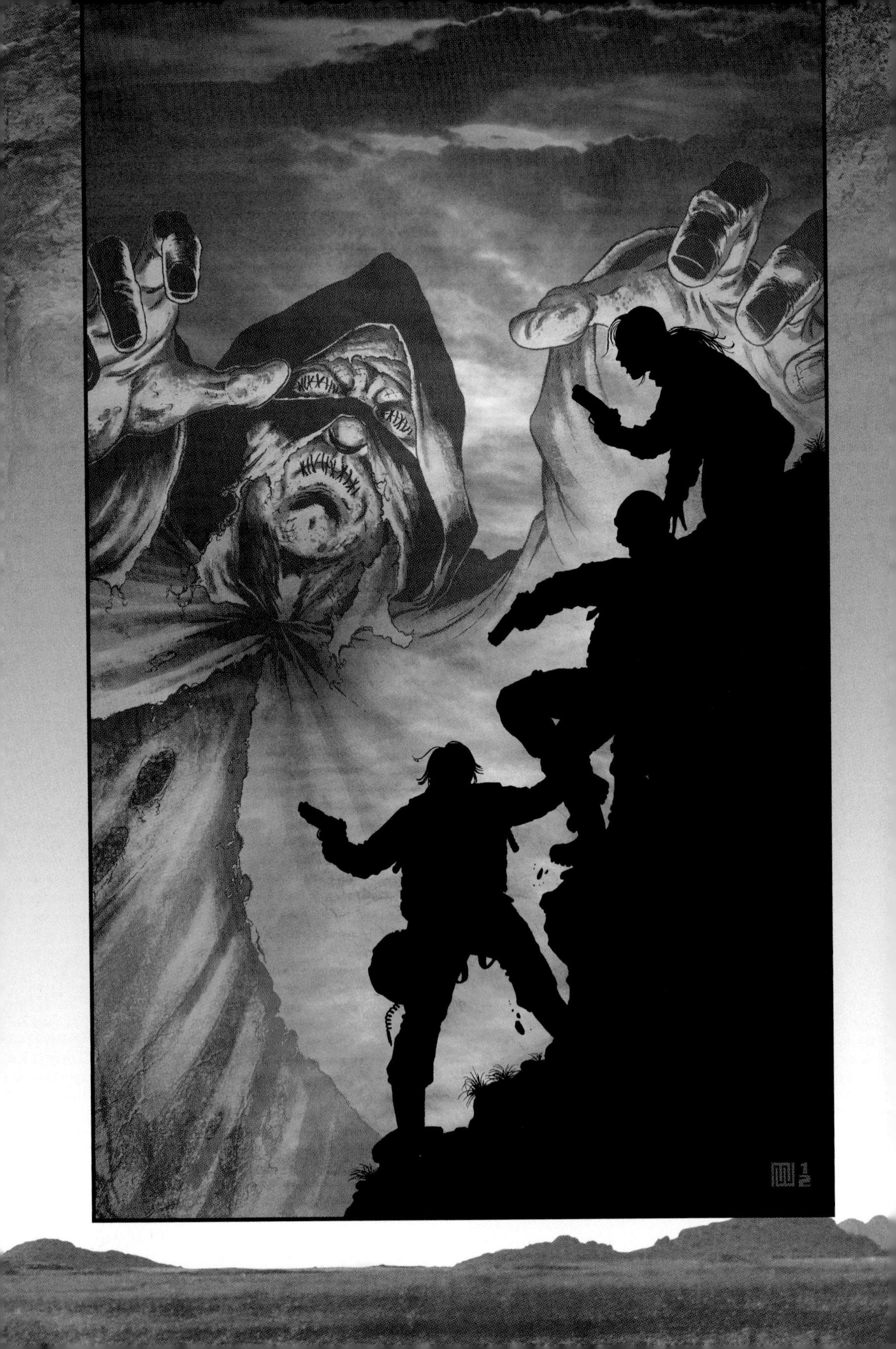

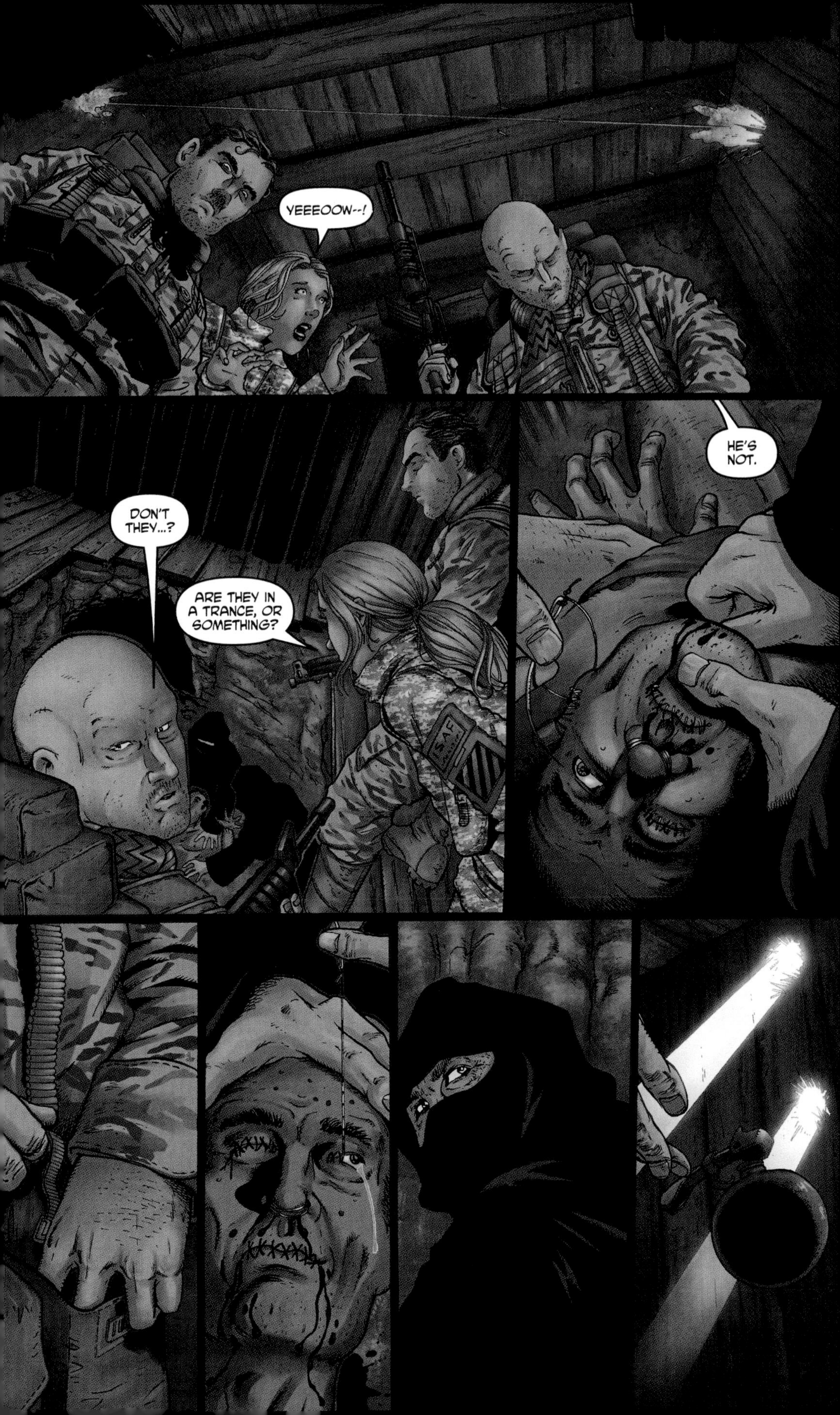
YEEEOOW--!
DON'T THEY...?
ARE THEY IN A TRANCE, OR SOMETHING?
HE'S NOT.

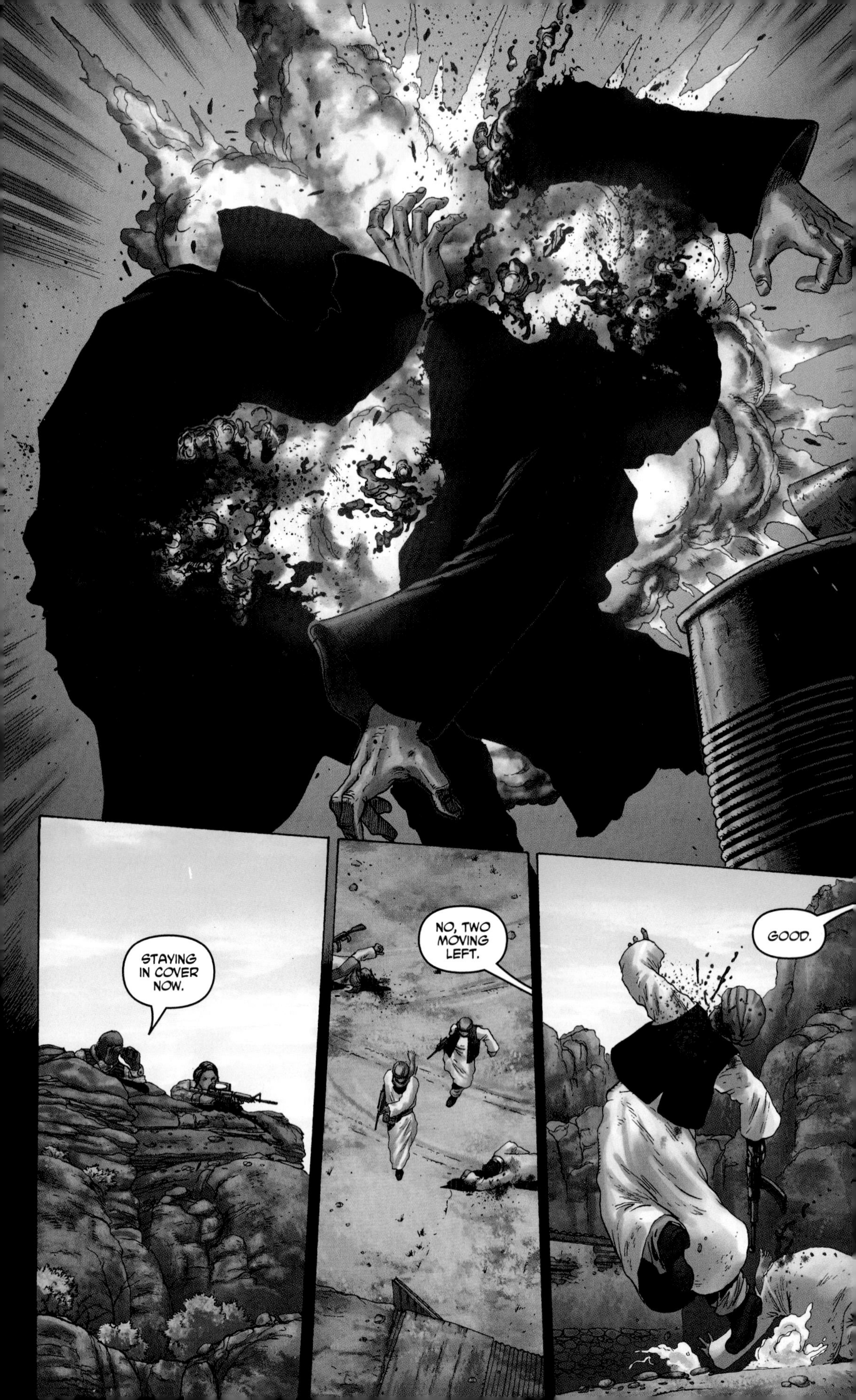
STAYING IN COVER NOW.
NO, TWO MOVING LEFT.
GOOD.

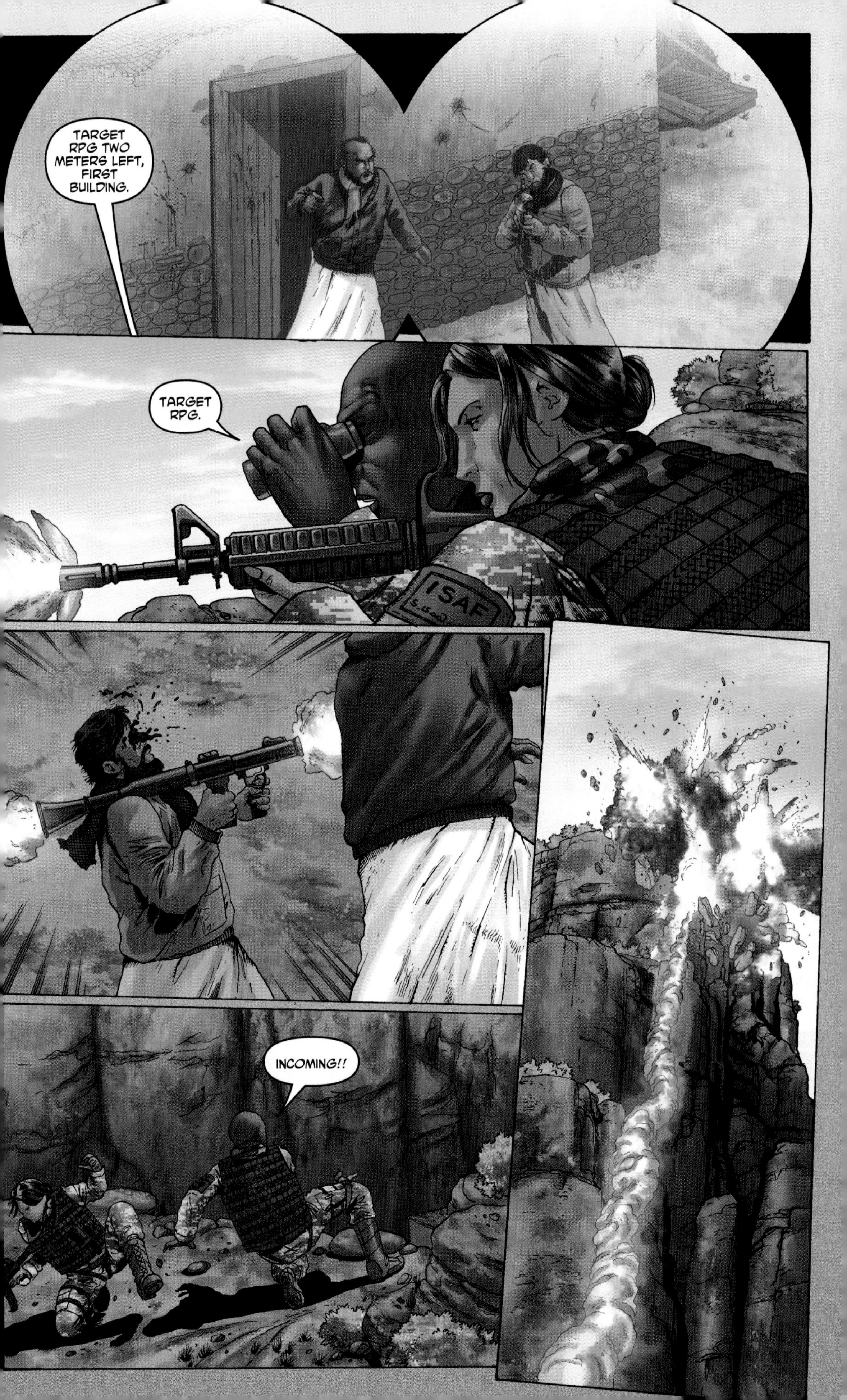
TARGET RPG TWO METERS LEFT, FIRST BUILDING.
TARGET RPG.
ISAF
INCOMING!!

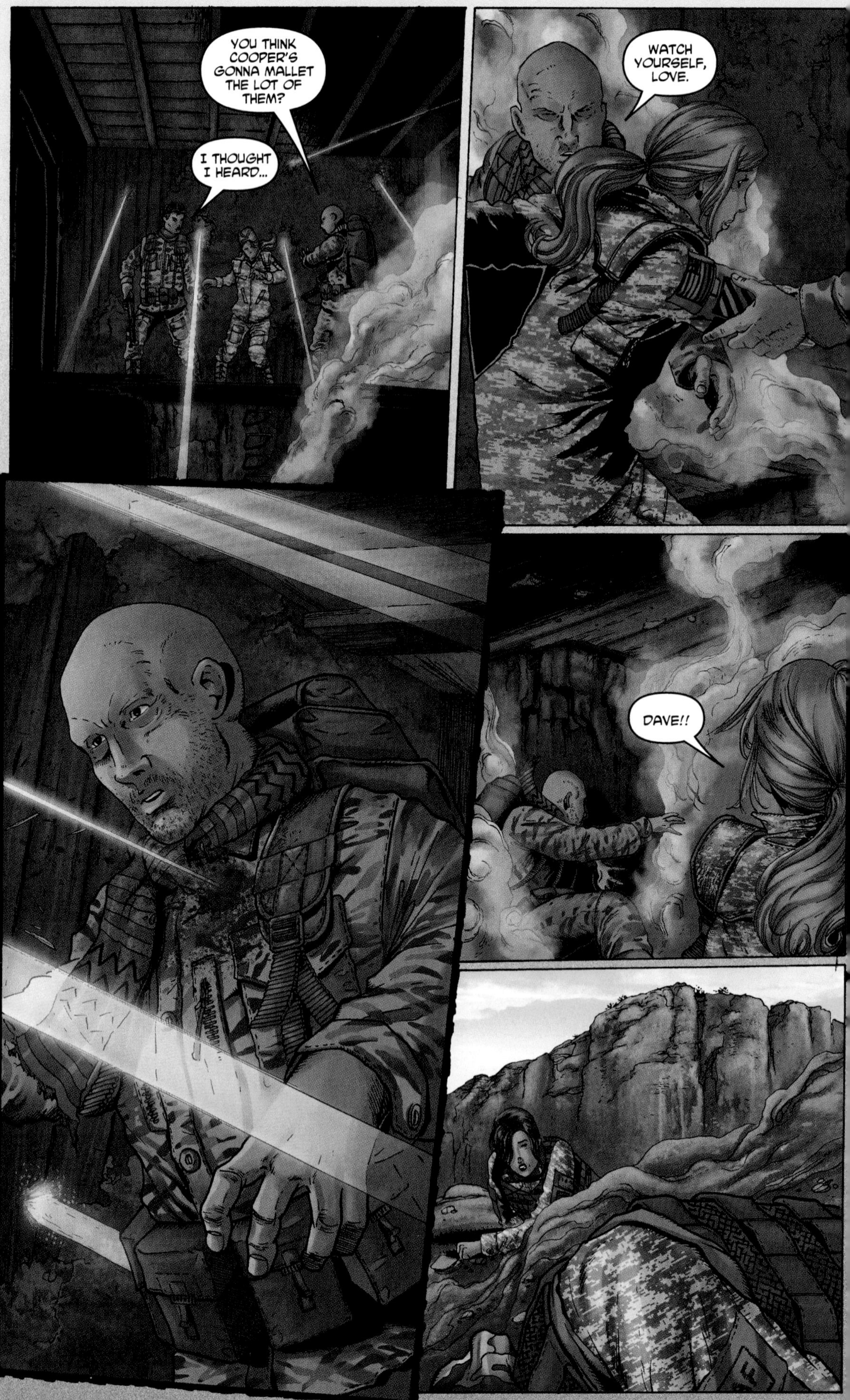
YOU THINK COOPER'S GONNA MALLET THE LOT OF THEM?
I THOUGHT I HEARD...
WATCH YOURSELF, LOVE.
DAVE!!

MMMOOOHH...
DON'T MOVE HIM! YOU CAN'T MOVE HIM!
GOT TO MOVE HIM. THEY COME IN HERE NOW, WE HAVEN'T AN EARTHLY.
NO...!
IT'S ALL RIGHT, LOVE.
MISSED ALL THE GOOD BITS.
GET MOVING. I'LL BE RIGHT BEHIND YOU.

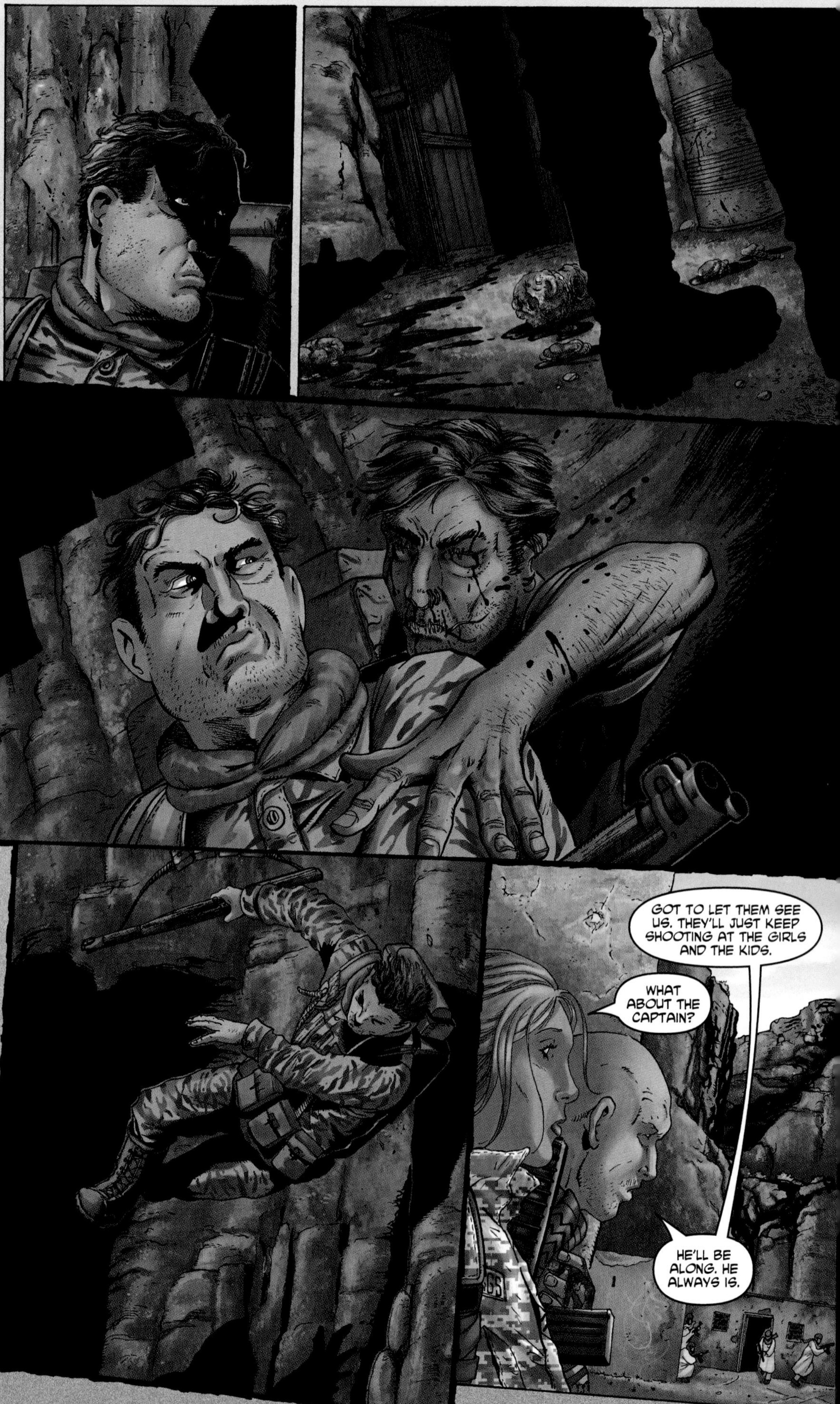
GOT TO LET THEM SEE US. THEY'LL JUST KEEP SHOOTING AT THE GIRLS AND THE KIDS.
WHAT ABOUT THE CAPTAIN?
HE'LL BE ALONG. HE ALWAYS IS.

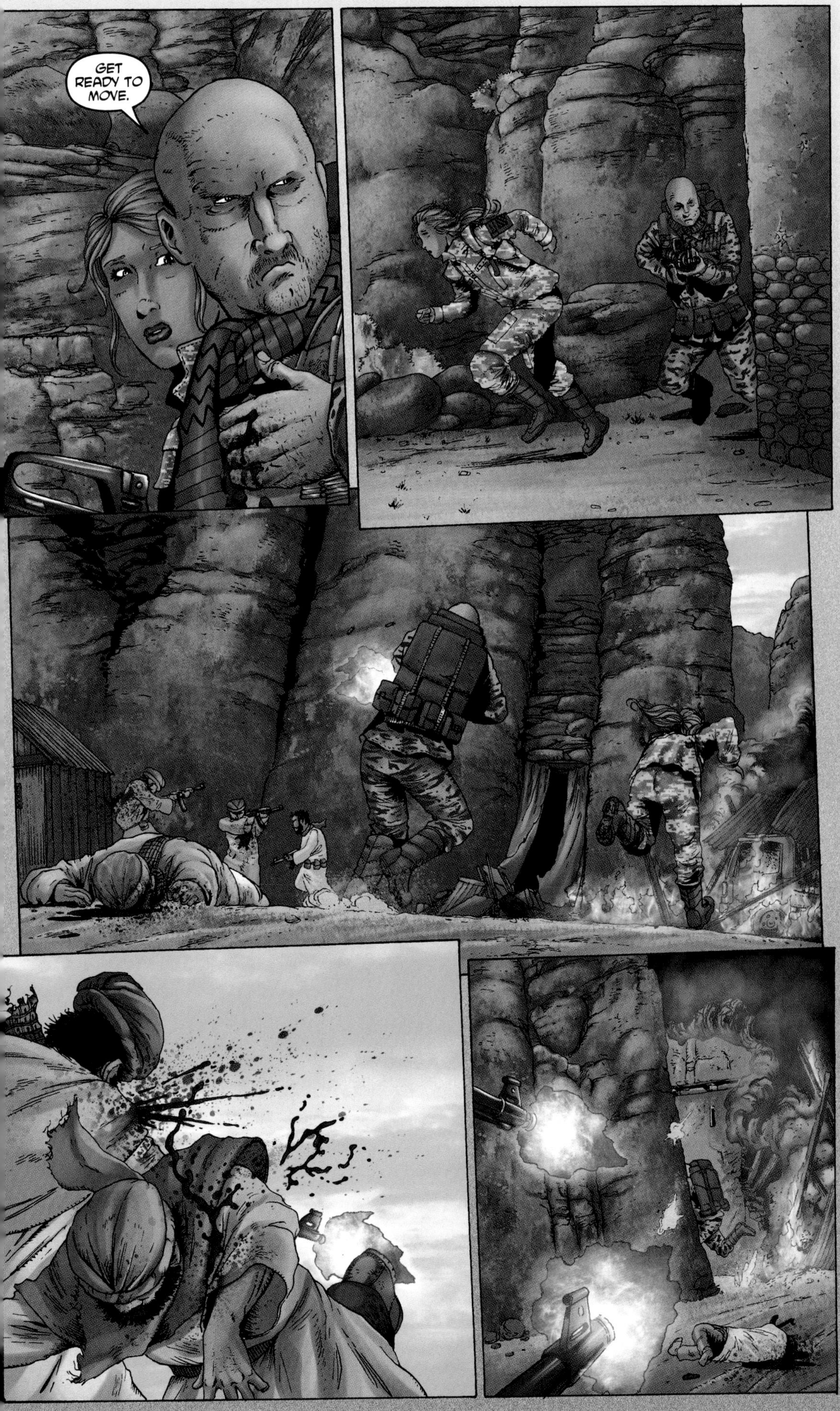
GET READY TO MOVE.

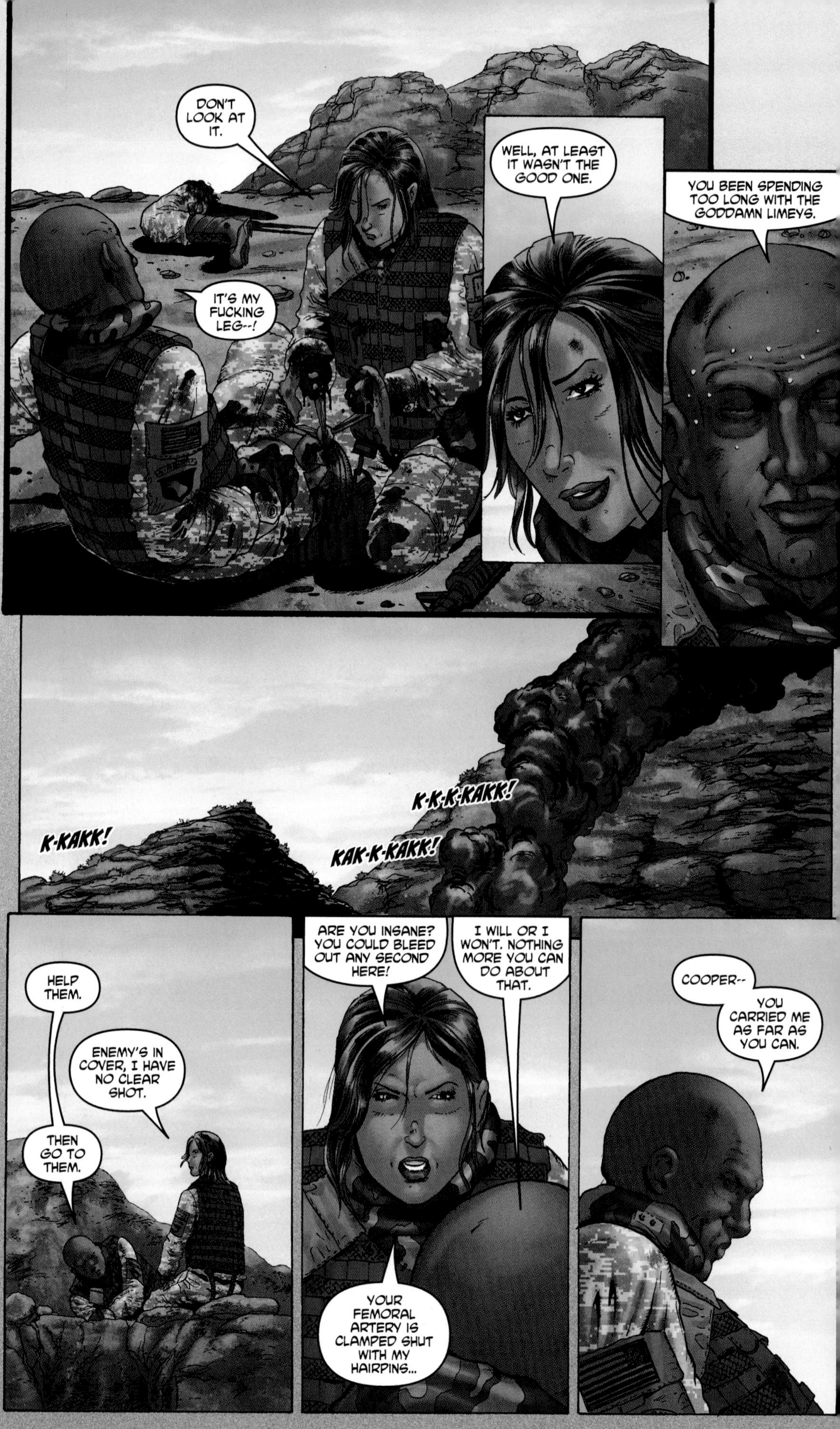

DON'T LOOK AT IT.
IT'S MY FUCKING LEG--!
WELL, AT LEAST IT WASN'T THE GOOD ONE.
YOU BEEN SPENDING TOO LONG WITH THE GODDAMN LIMEYS.
K-KAKK!
K-K-K-KAKK!
KAK-K-KAKK!
HELP THEM.
ENEMY'S IN COVER, I HAVE NO CLEAR SHOT.
THEN GO TO THEM.
ARE YOU INSANE? YOU COULD BLEED OUT ANY SECOND HERE!
YOUR FEMORAL ARTERY IS CLAMPED SHUT WITH MY HAIRPINS...
I WILL OR I WON'T. NOTHING MORE YOU CAN DO ABOUT THAT.
COOPER--
YOU CARRIED ME AS FAR AS YOU CAN.

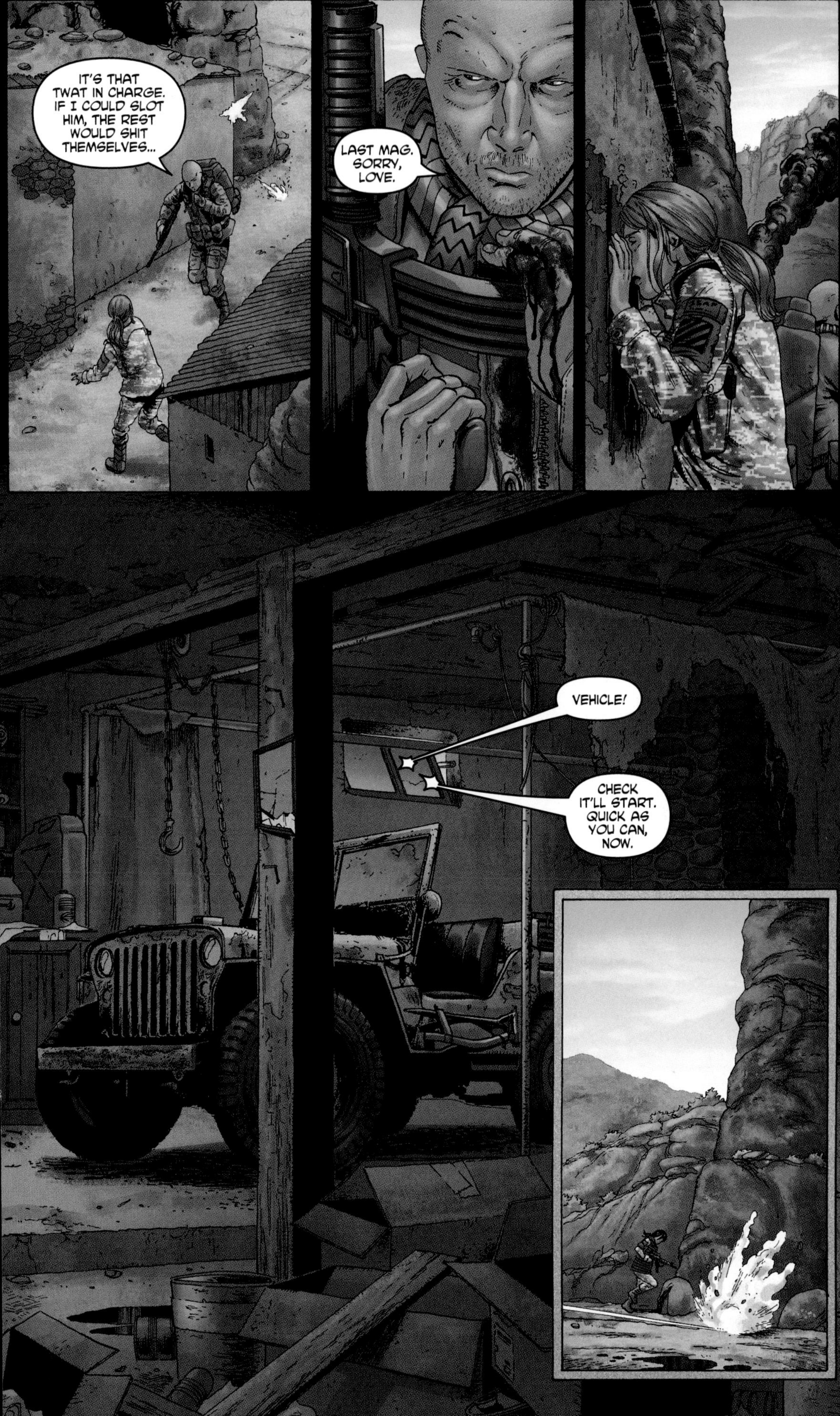
IT'S THAT TWAT IN CHARGE. IF I COULD SLOT HIM, THE REST WOULD SHIT THEMSELVES...
LAST MAG. SORRY, LOVE.
VEHICLE!
CHECK IT'LL START. QUICK AS YOU CAN, NOW.

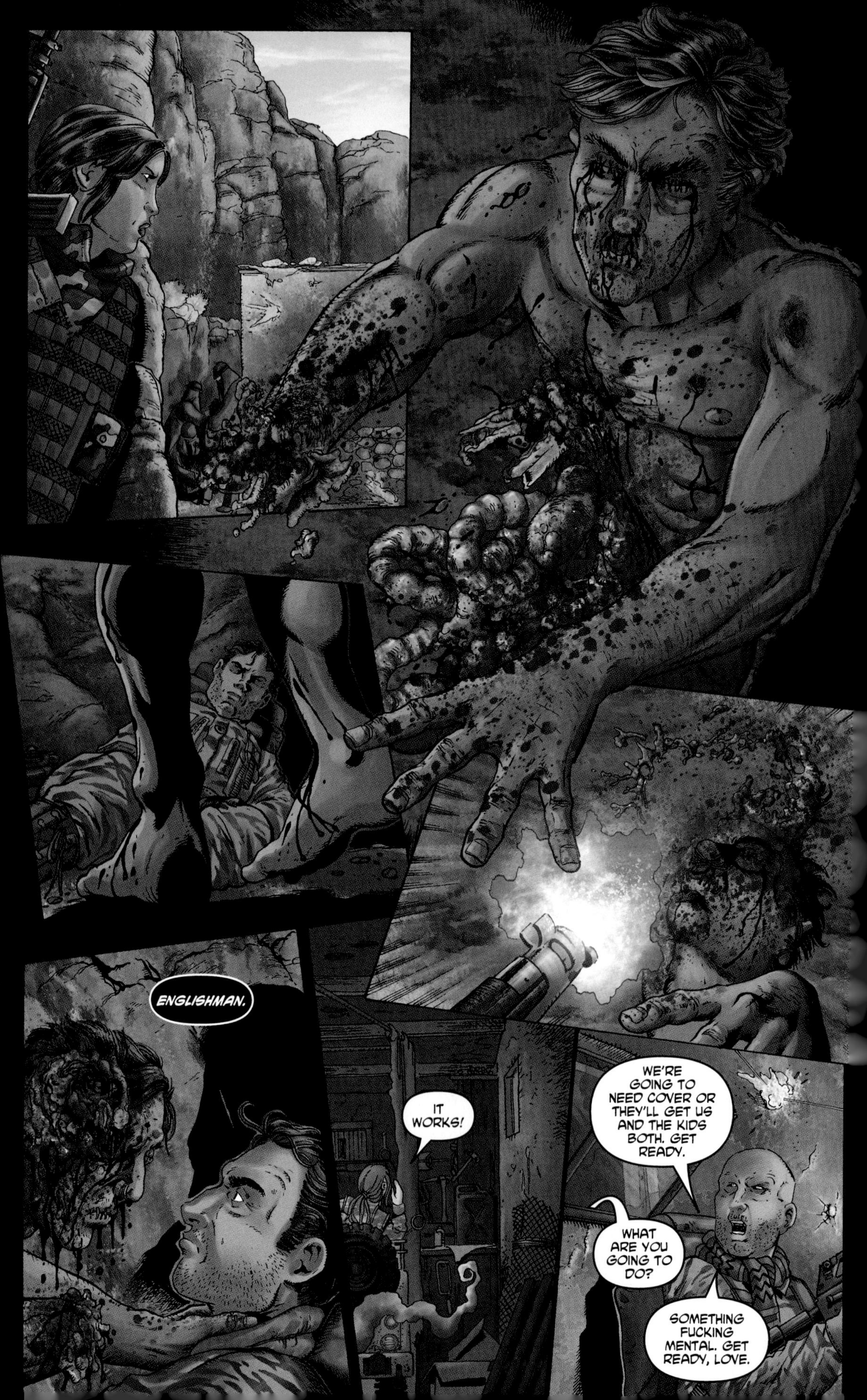
ENGLISHMAN.
IT WORKS!
WE'RE GOING TO NEED COVER OR THEY'LL GET US AND THE KIDS BOTH. GET READY.
WHAT ARE YOU GOING TO DO?
SOMETHING FUCKING MENTAL. GET READY, LOVE.

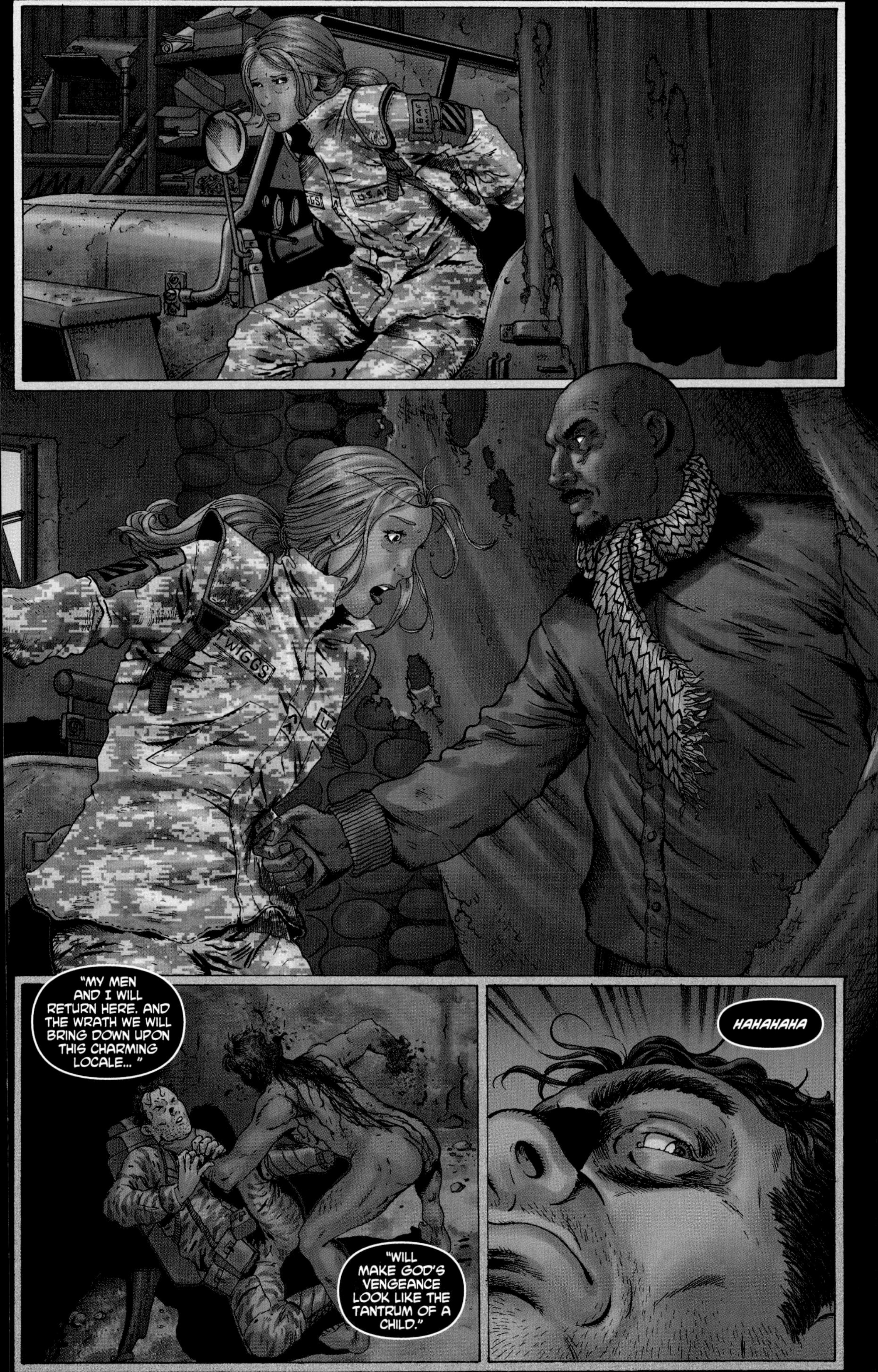
TWIGGS
"MY MEN AND I WILL RETURN HERE. AND THE WRATH WE WILL BRING DOWN UPON THIS CHARMING LOCALE..."
"WILL MAKE GOD'S VENGEANCE LOOK LIKE THE TANTRUM OF A CHILD."
HAHAHAHA

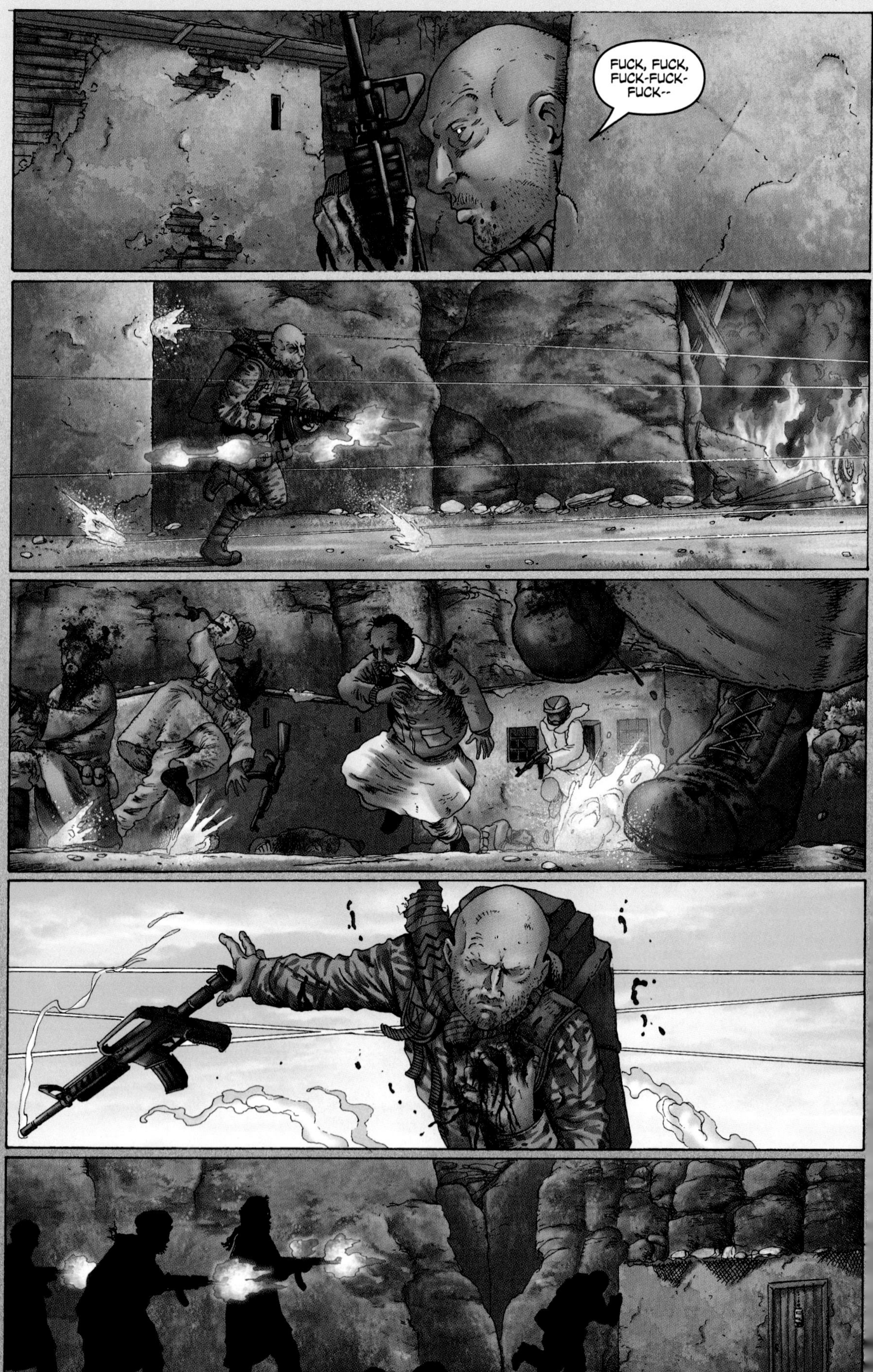
FUCK, FUCK, FUCK-FUCK-FUCK--

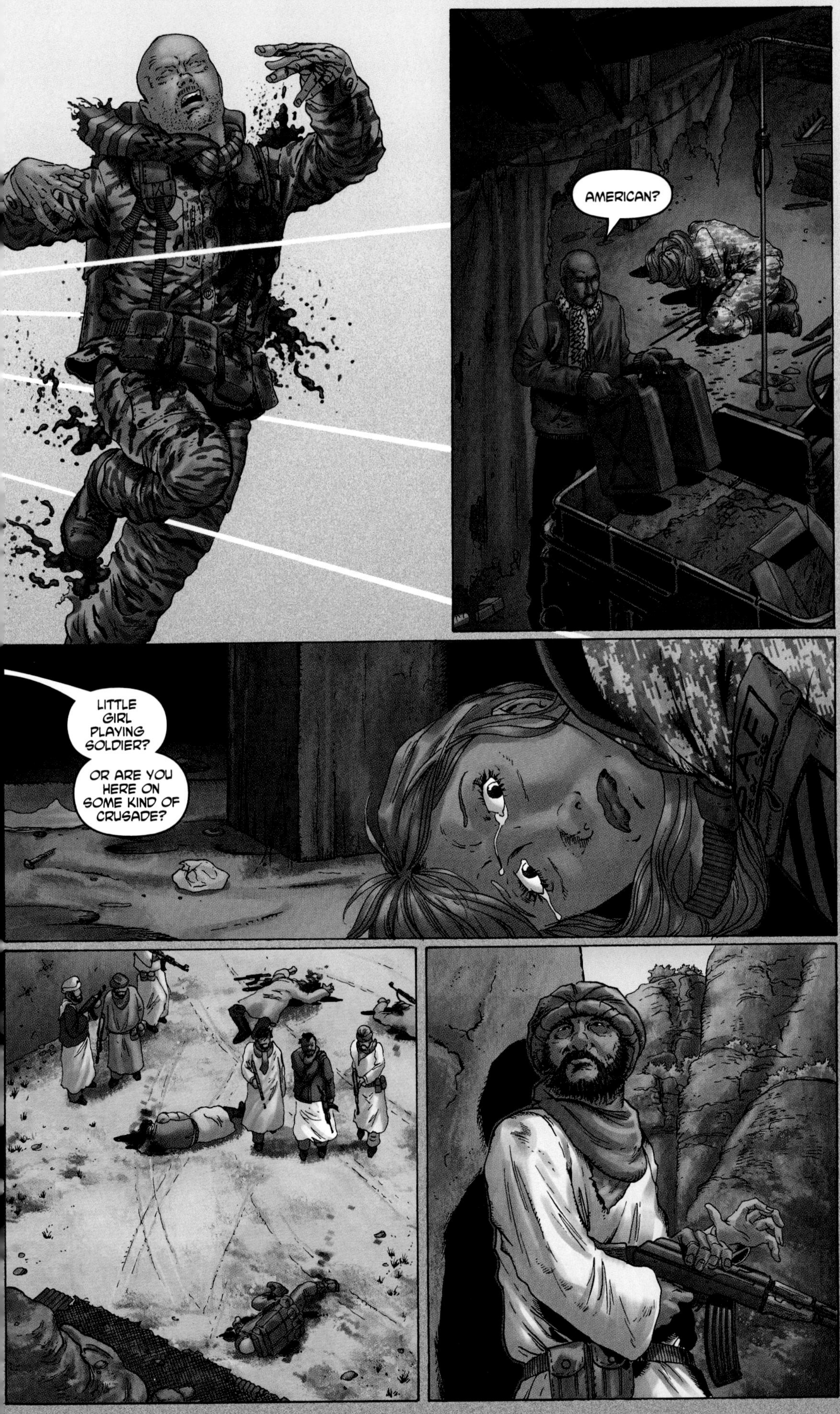
AMERICAN?
LITTLE GIRL PLAYING SOLDIER?
OR ARE YOU HERE ON SOME KIND OF CRUSADE?

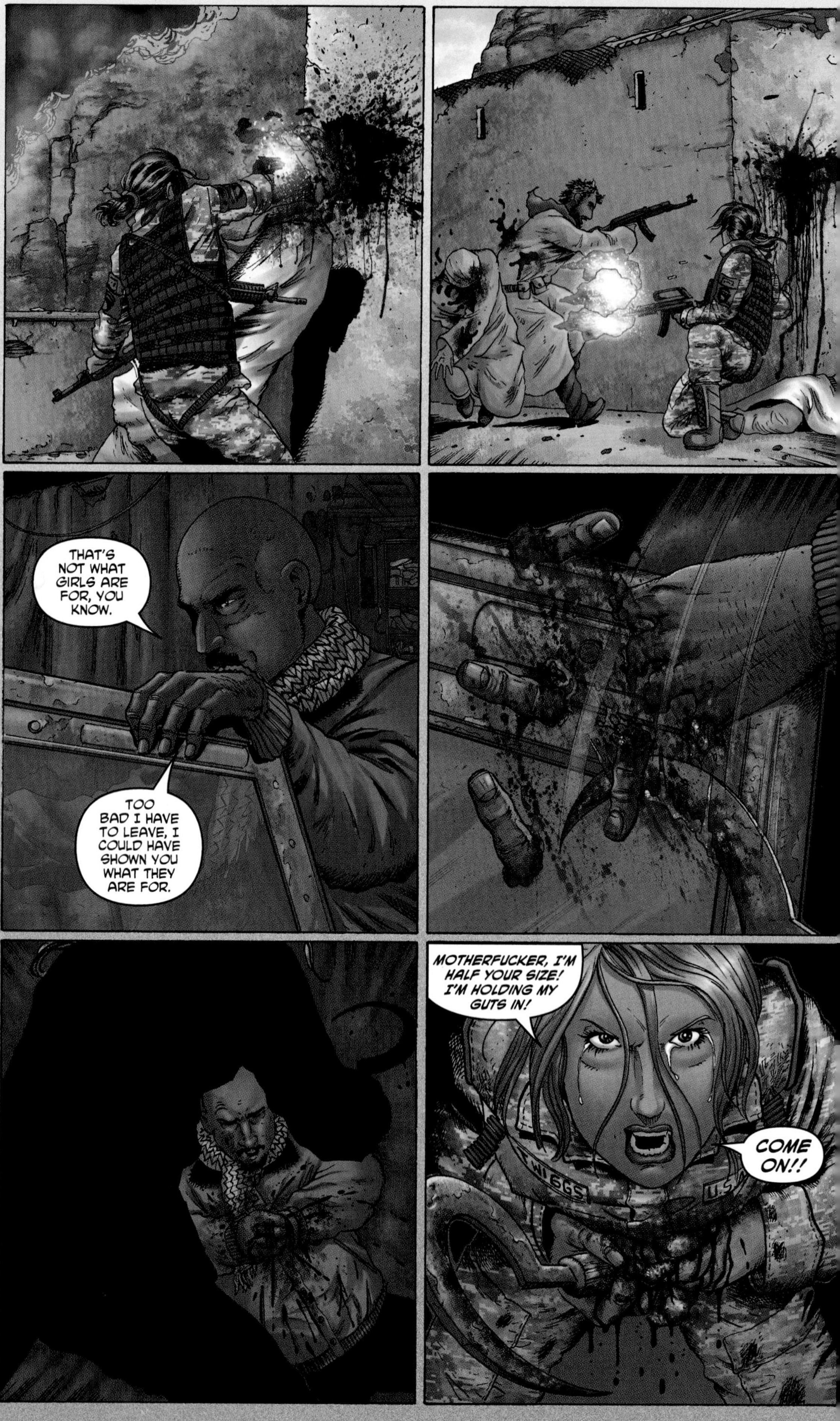
THAT'S NOT WHAT GIRLS ARE FOR, YOU KNOW.
TOO BAD I HAVE TO LEAVE, I COULD HAVE SHOWN YOU WHAT THEY ARE FOR.
MOTHERFUCKER, I'M HALF YOUR SIZE! I'M HOLDING MY GUTS IN!
COME ON!!

...TNNK...TNNK...

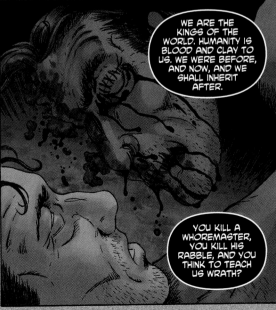

WE ARE THE KINGS OF THE WORLD. HUMANITY IS BLOOD AND CLAY TO US. WE WERE BEFORE, AND NOW, AND WE SHALL INHERIT AFTER.

YOU KILL A WHOREMASTER, YOU KILL HIS RABBLE, AND YOU THINK TO TEACH US WRATH?

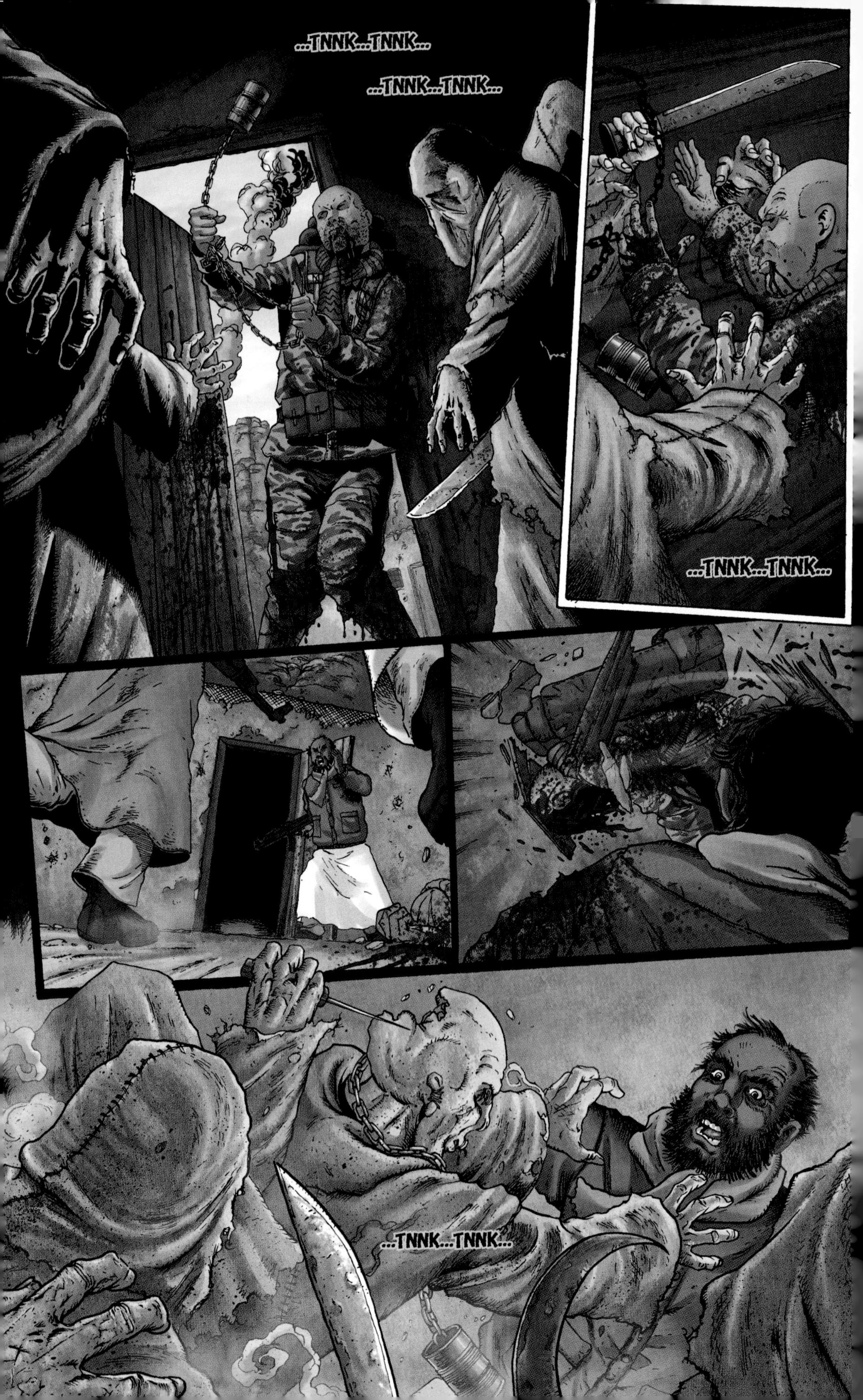
...TNNK...TNNK...
...TNNK...TNNK...
...TNNK...TNNK...
...TNNK...TNNK...

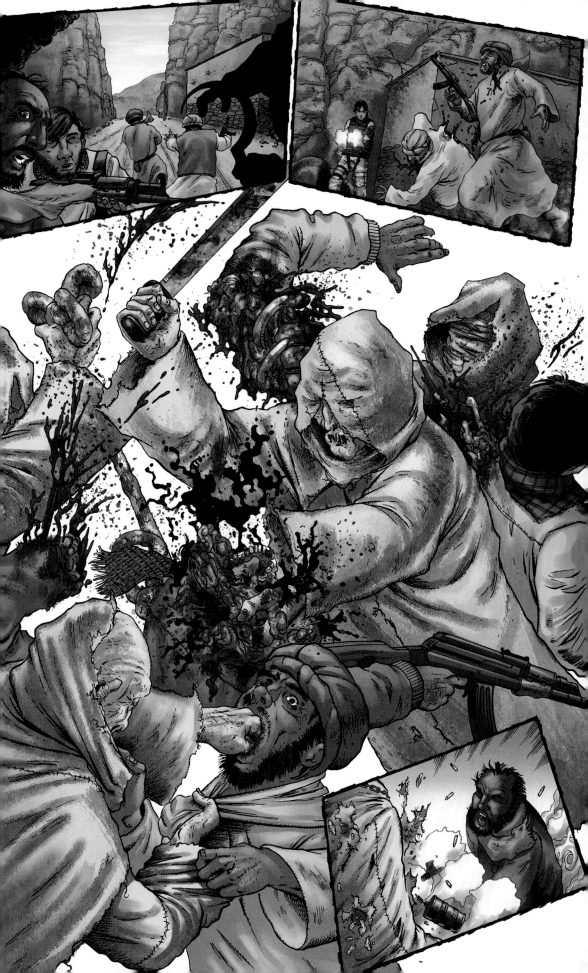

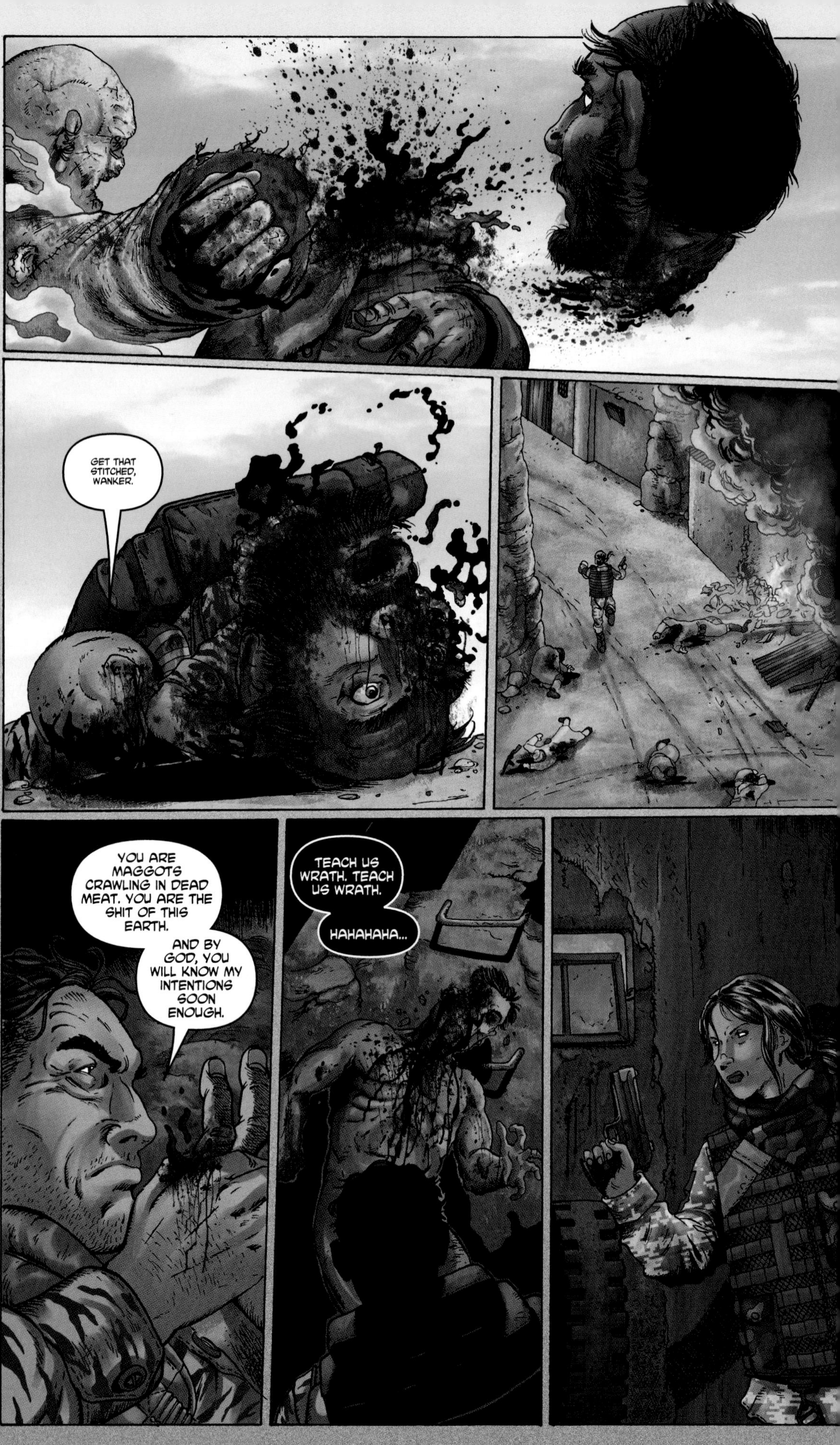
GET THAT STITCHED, WANKER.
YOU ARE MAGGOTS CRAWLING IN DEAD MEAT. YOU ARE THE SHIT OF THIS EARTH.
AND BY GOD, YOU WILL KNOW MY INTENTIONS SOON ENOUGH.
TEACH US WRATH. TEACH US WRATH.
HAHAHAHA...

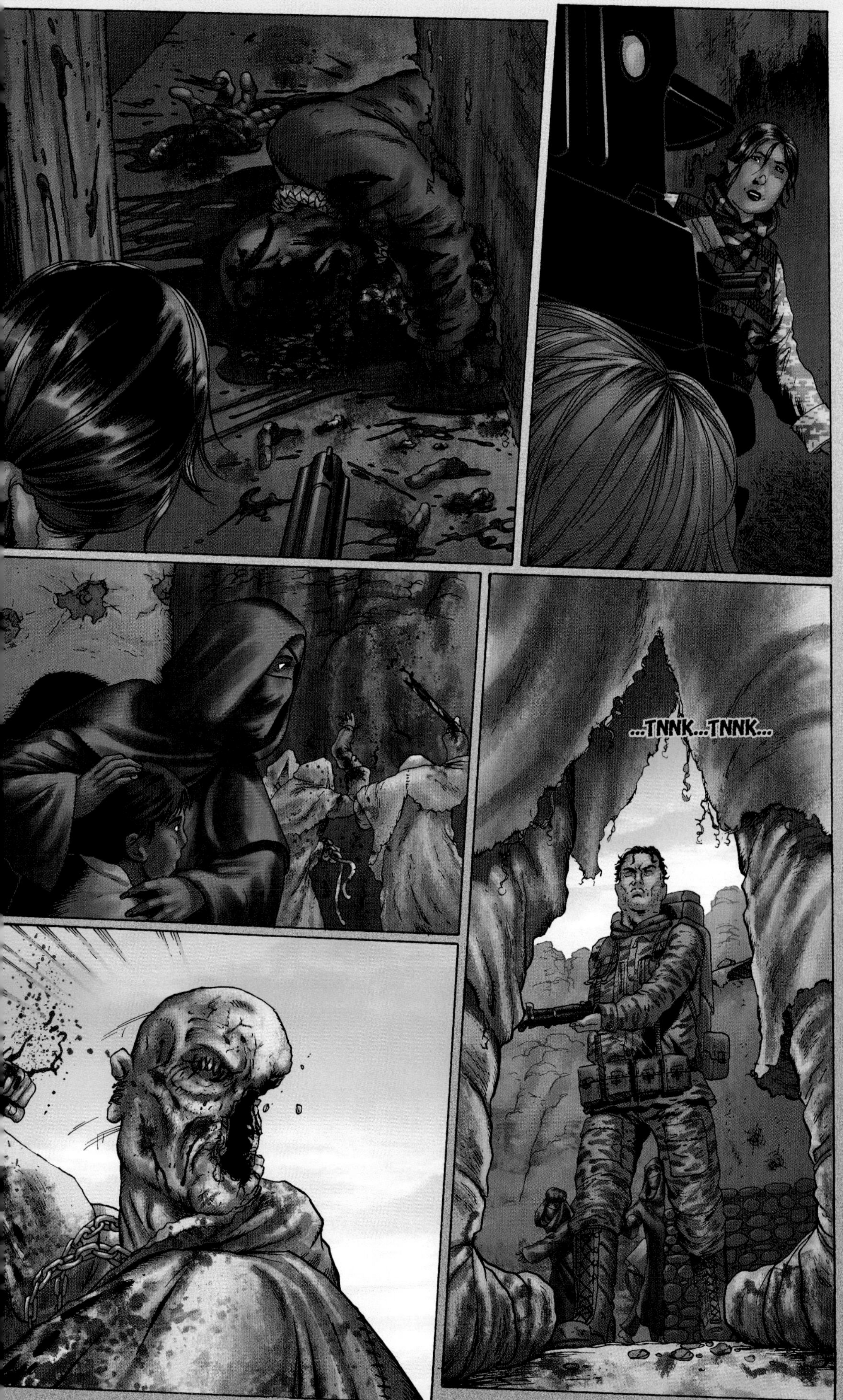
...TNNK...TNNK...

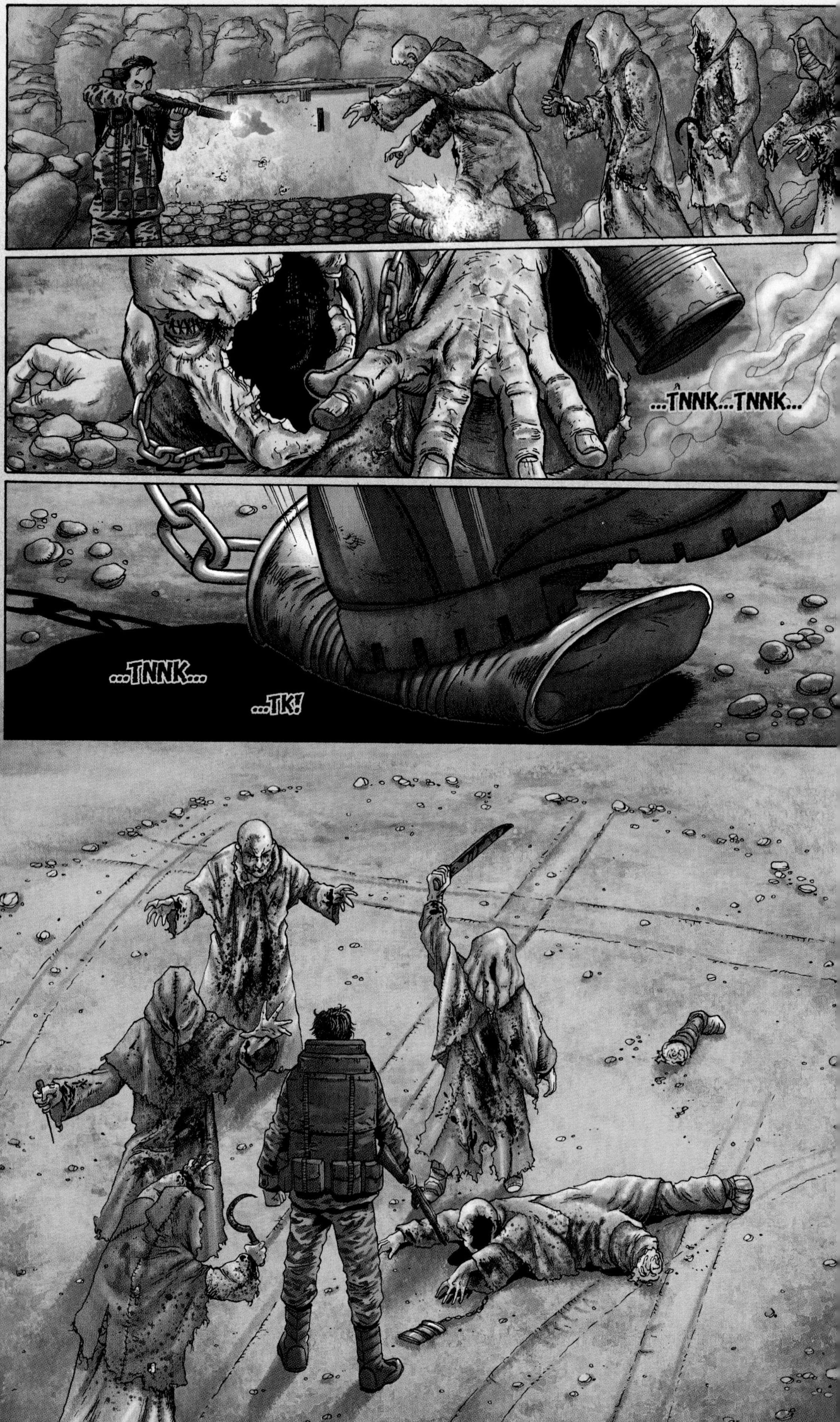
...TNNK...TNNK...
...TNNK...
...TK!

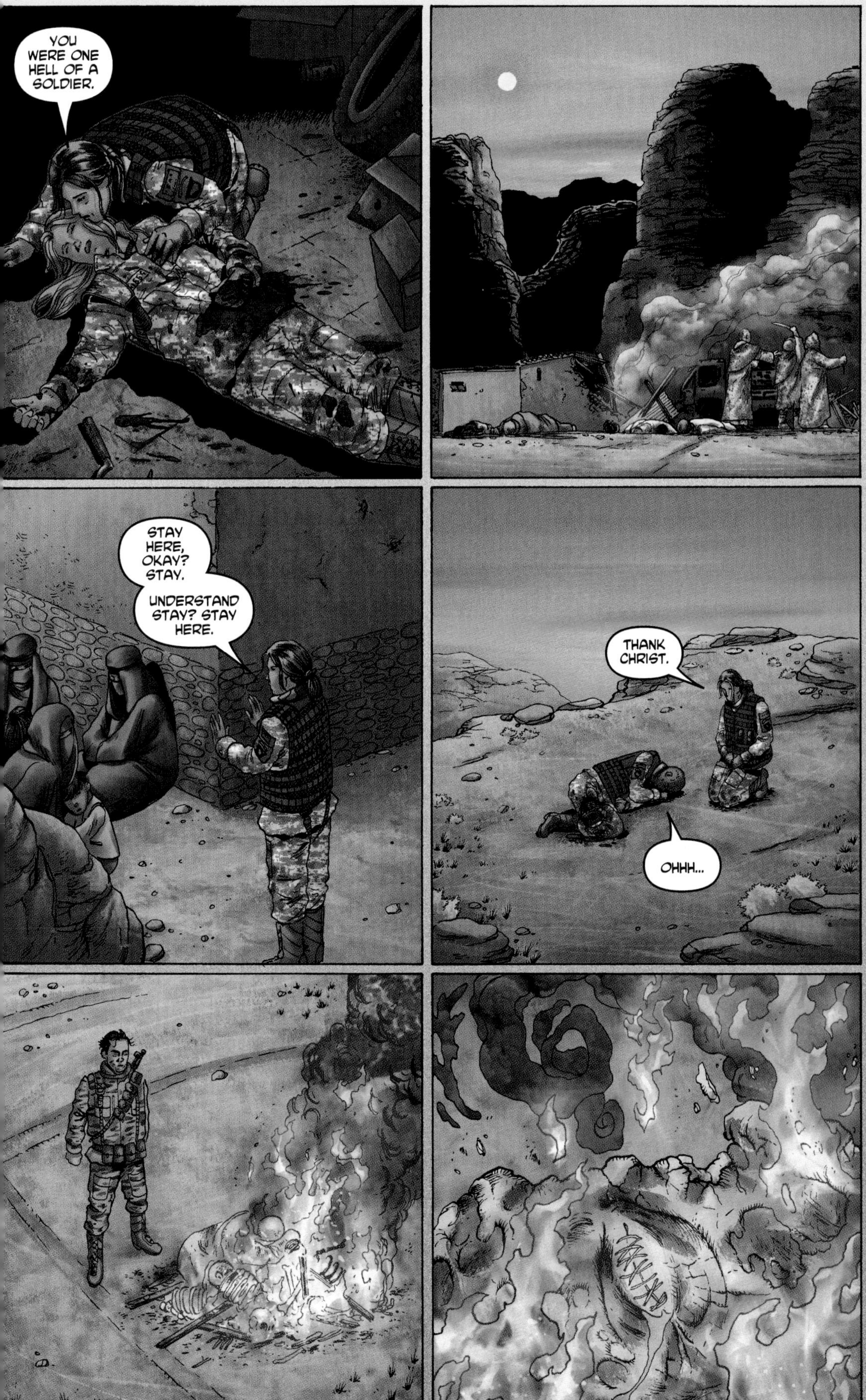
YOU WERE ONE HELL OF A SOLDIER.
STAY HERE, OKAY? STAY.
UNDERSTAND STAY? STAY HERE.
THANK CHRIST.
OHHH...

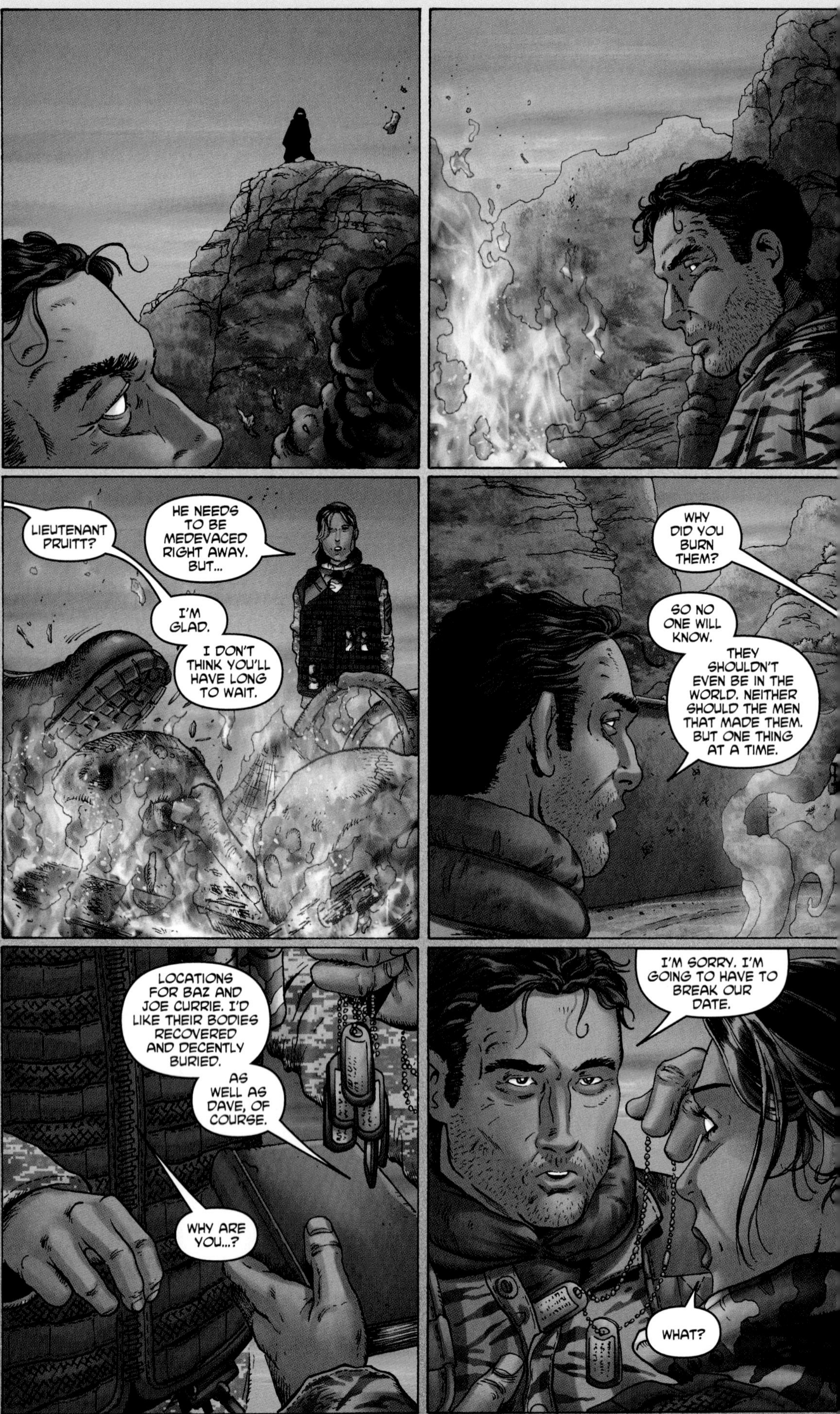

LIEUTENANT PRUITT?
HE NEEDS TO BE MEDEVACED RIGHT AWAY. BUT...
I'M GLAD.
I DON'T THINK YOU'LL HAVE LONG TO WAIT.
WHY DID YOU BURN THEM?
SO NO ONE WILL KNOW.
THEY SHOULDN'T EVEN BE IN THE WORLD. NEITHER SHOULD THE MEN THAT MADE THEM. BUT ONE THING AT A TIME.
LOCATIONS FOR BAZ AND JOE CURRIE. I'D LIKE THEIR BODIES RECOVERED AND DECENTLY BURIED.
AS WELL AS DAVE, OF COURSE.
WHY ARE YOU...?
I'M SORRY. I'M GOING TO HAVE TO BREAK OUR DATE.
WHAT?

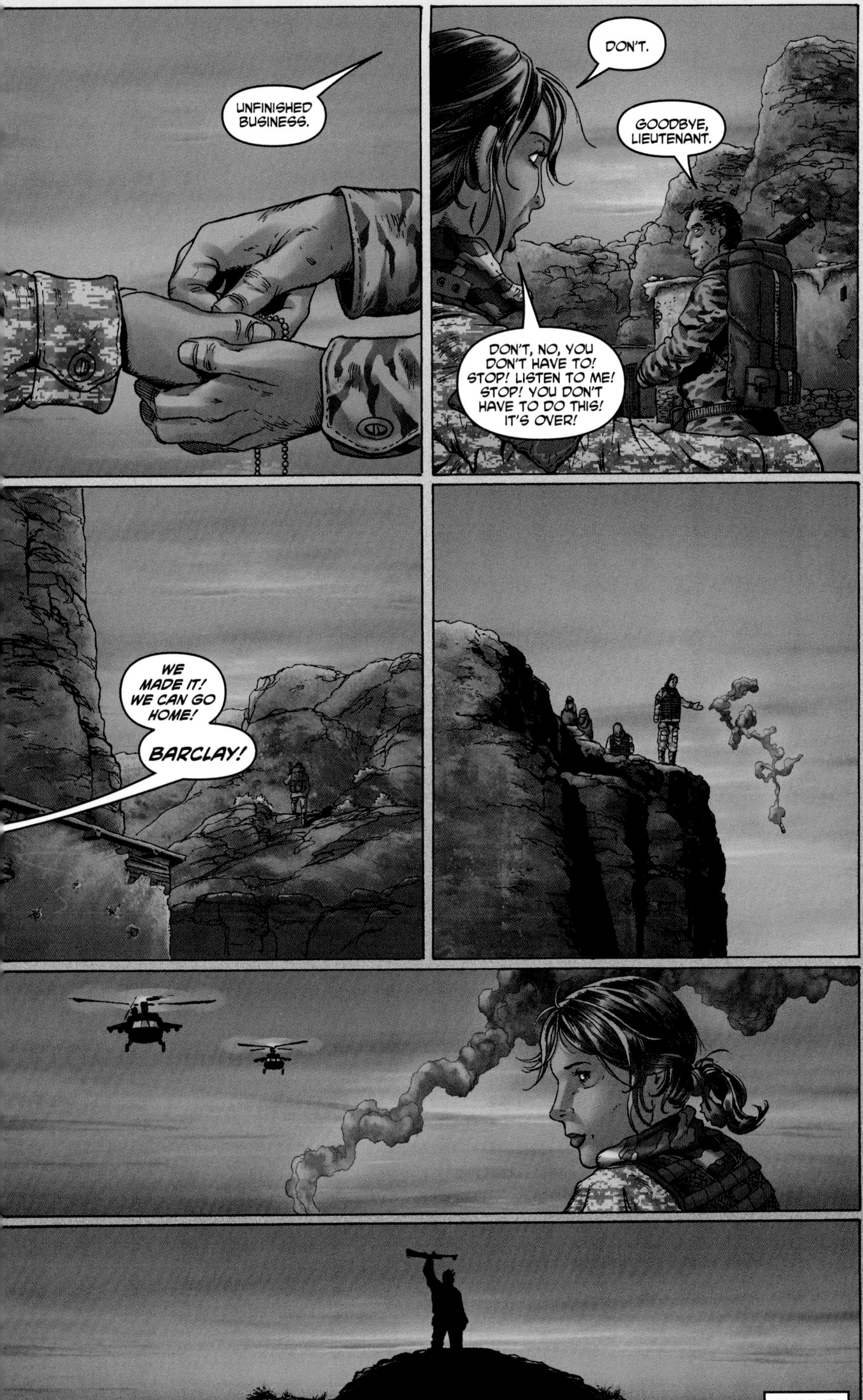

UNFINISHED BUSINESS.
DON'T.
GOODBYE, LIEUTENANT.
DON'T, NO, YOU DON'T HAVE TO! STOP! LISTEN TO ME! STOP! YOU DON'T HAVE TO DO THIS! IT'S OVER!
WE MADE IT! WE CAN GO HOME!
BARCLAY!
THE END

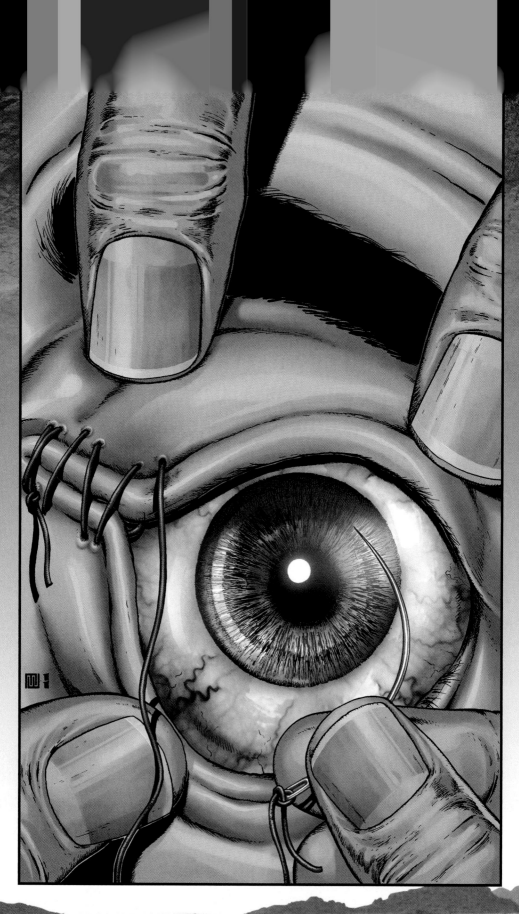

GORE COVER GALLERY

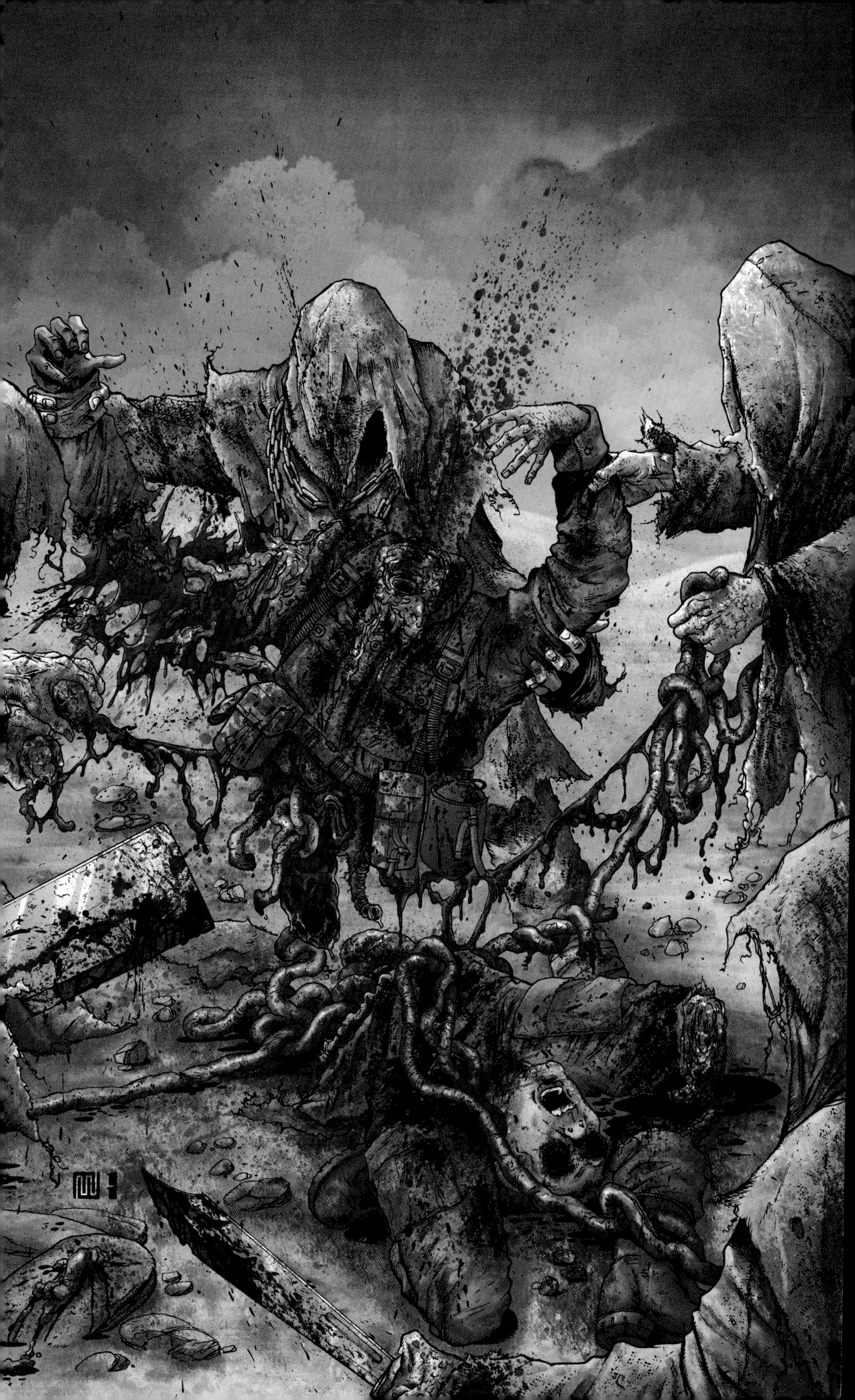

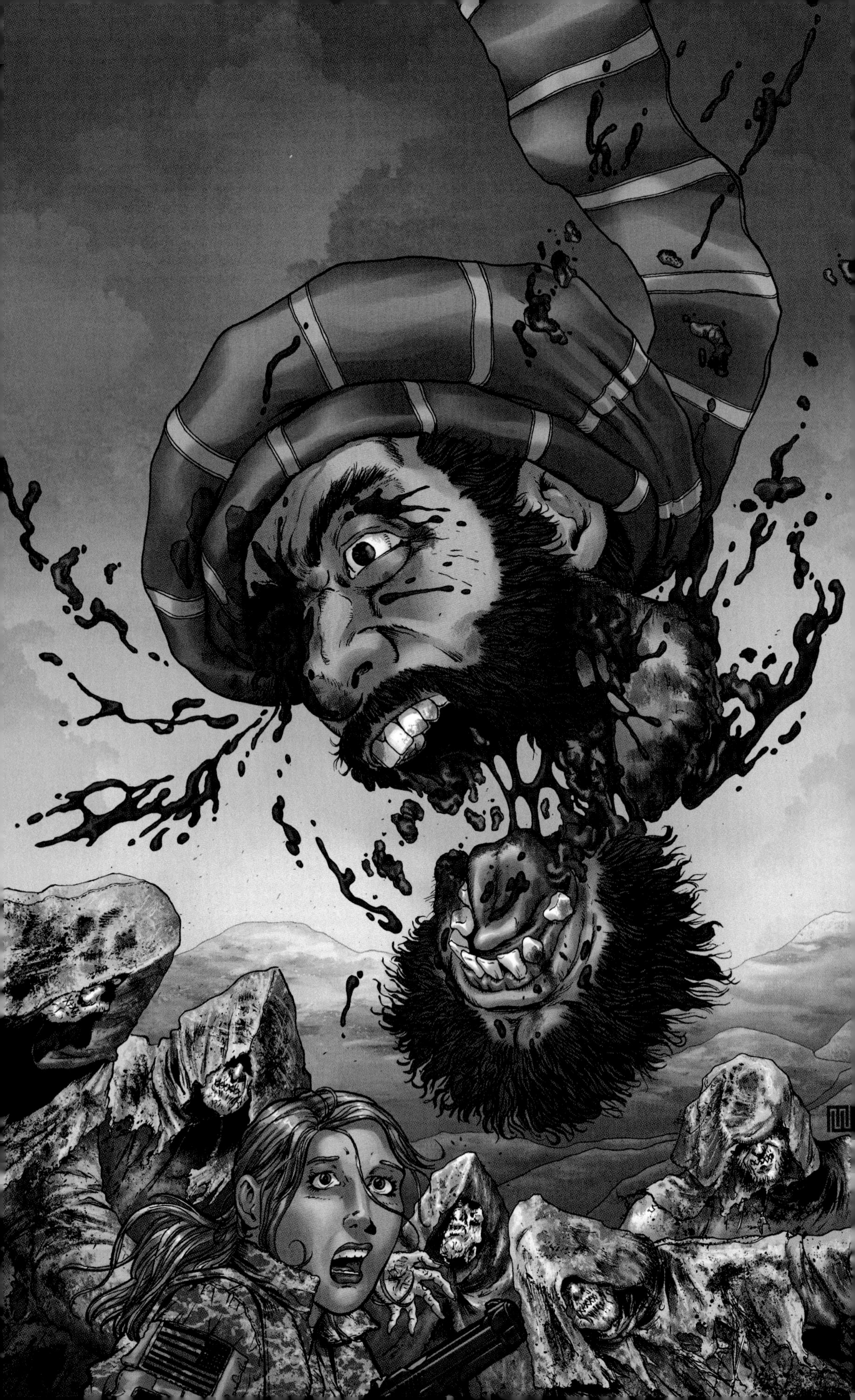

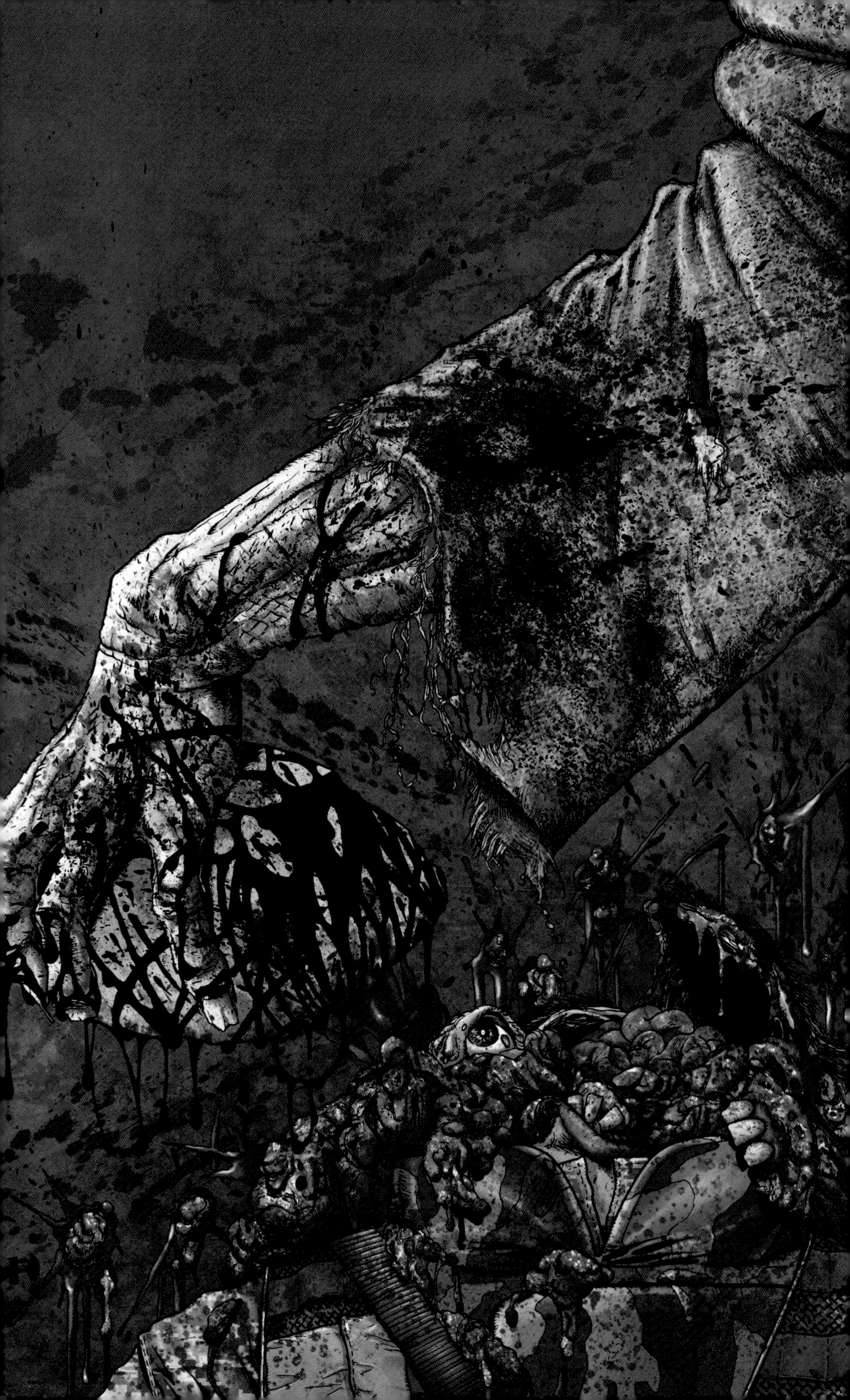

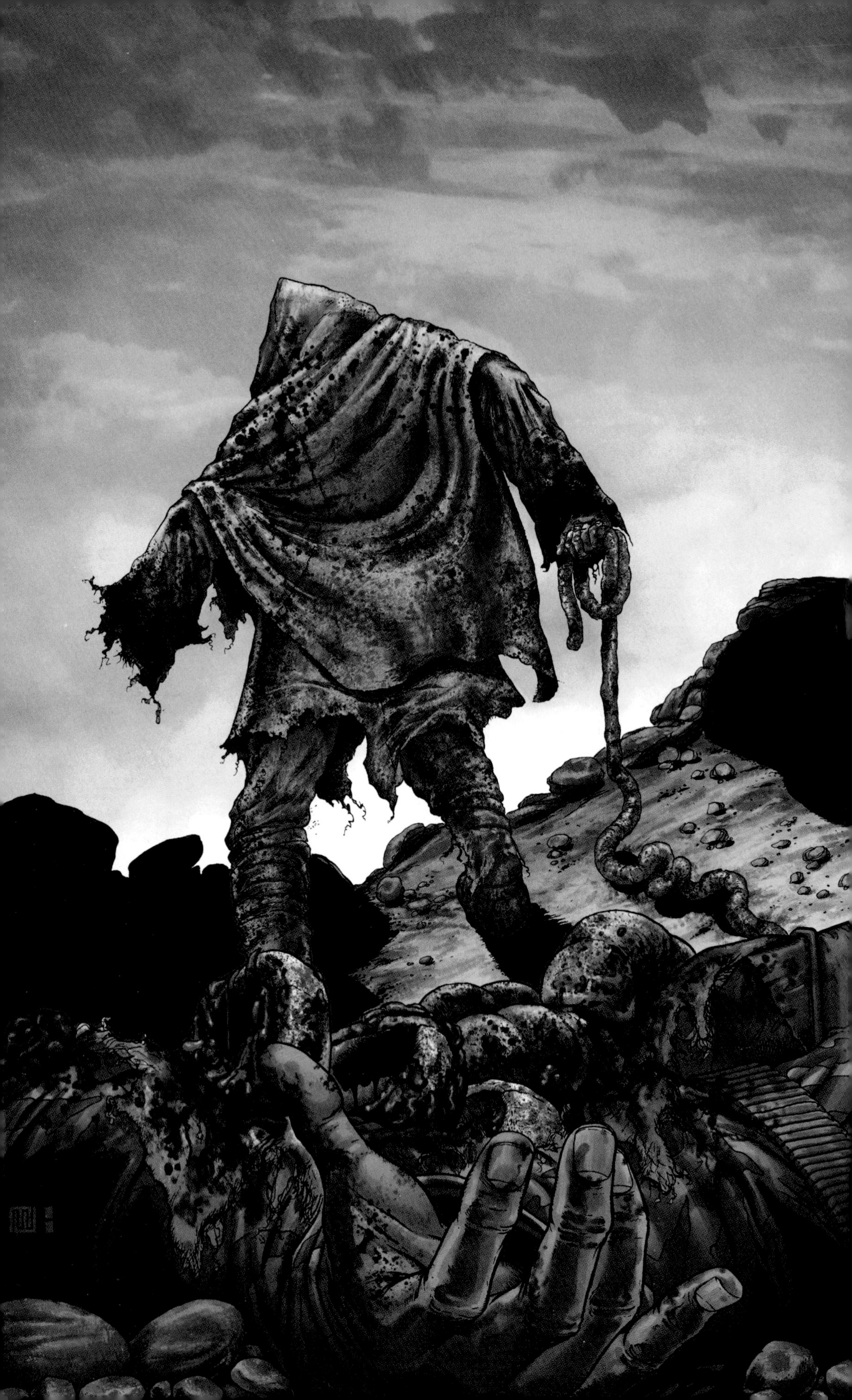